"This book celebrates and extends T. F. Torrance's significant and formative engagement with Patristic and Orthodox thought. It is a ground-breaking and exemplary achievement of ecumenical scholarship which models an exciting new development in Orthodox theology, the close, critical and charitable appraisal of modern Western theologians by Orthodox scholars."

—**KHALED ANATOLIOS**
University of Notre Dame

"This volume is the first of its kind in that it brings together a rich variety of scholarly resources discussing and analysing TFT's relationship with both Eastern and Oriental Orthodoxy. The intention throughout is to develop Torrance's legacy by exploring in new depths the profoundly important conversation he opened up with these traditions. TFT considered the agreements that resulted from his remarkable engagement with Orthodoxy to be his most significant legacy. Consequently, this volume is essential reading for scholars of Torrance's thought and will be of major interest to students of Orthodox theology and ecumenism."

—**ALAN TORRANCE**
University of St. Andrews

"The appearance of this book marks what one hopes will be a new chapter in contemporary theological and ecumenical conversation, in which the legacy of the great Greek Fathers and the treasures of modern Orthodox theology are enlivened and joined with the evangelical message of Torrance in his recasting of theology after Barth. Torrance's offerings are here deepened, if possible, by a more thorough confrontation with patristic theology. A new path is being charted for ecclesial theology in the service of Christ and his Gospel."

—**GEORGE HUNSINGER**
Princeton Theological Seminary

"Tom Torrance must have been one of the very few Protestant theologians in his day who was keen to engage with Orthodox theology. This volume celebrates that engagement in a series of essays by mostly young Orthodox scholars and a few Protestant scholars who continue his engagement with Orthodox theology on various themes central to Torrance's theology. It is a fitting tribute to a remarkable man."

—**ANDREW LOUTH**
University of Durham

"TF Torrance was one of the most important Christian theologians and ecumenists of the twentieth century. The depth of his understanding of Orthodox theology was unique among theologians of his generation. The contributors of this volume extend his legacy by amplifying Torrance's insights on the contribution that the Orthodox tradition can offer to the ecumenical discussion, but also challenging Orthodox theologians to self-criticism in light of Torrance's engagement with Orthodox theology. Even more valuable is the window that allows us to see Torrance as mentor, friend and pastor, and which reveals his deep passion and commitment to Christian unity. In our paradoxical situation of globalization that has led to increased fragmentation, and at a time when the fervent ecumenical hope for Christian unity has long since past, the appearance of this book is both timely and urgent."

—**ARISTOTLE PAPANIKOLAOU**
Fordham University

"This splendid volume, focusing on Thomas' Torrance's long engagement with the culture and thought of Orthodoxy, celebrates the witness of one of the greatest Protestant friends of the Eastern Church, who came to that ecumenical position from the basis of a deep study of the Fathers, as well as engagement with some of the work of the 20th century's leading Orthodox thinkers. Torrance was a rare combination of great churchman (Moderator of the Church of Scotland), historical theologian, intellectual powerhouse, and realistically grounded ecumenist. His deeply informed dialogue with Orthodoxy makes his work one of the highpoints of 20th century Ecumenical movement: a legacy from which much can still be learned. This superb collection of essays and reminiscences by leading-edge scholars patiently investigates aspects of Torrance's multi-faceted labors. It covers his correspondence with Florovsky, his relation with Staniloae, his careful and rich patristic work, and his assessment of British Orthodoxy in his own day. This is a book that, as George Hunsinger says in his elegant Foreword, is truly a 'landmark volume.' The editors, Prof. Todd Speidell and Fr. Matthew Baker of righteous memory, have put us all in their debt."

—**JOHN A. MCGUCKIN**
Columbia Univversityw

"This is a rich and revelatory volume, not only illuminating Torrance's perennially fruitful engagement with patristic and modern Orthodox theology but also perpetuating his robust but generous vision of Christian ecumenism. Scholars and students from East and West alike will find this an immensely stimulating read."

—**MARCUS PLESTED**
Marquette University

T. F. Torrance and Eastern Orthodoxy

T. F. Torrance and Eastern Orthodoxy:

Theology in Reconciliation

EDITED BY

Matthew Baker and Todd Speidell

T. F. TORRANCE AND EASTERN ORTHODOXY
Theology in Reconciliation

Wipf & Stock
An Imprint of Wipf and Stock Publishers
199 W. 8th Ave., Suite 3
Eugene, OR 97401

www.wipfandstock.com

ISBN 13: 978-1-4982-0813-0

Manufactured in the U.S.A.

The icon of St. Athanasius the Great on the front cover is by the hand of Julia Bridget Hayes (www.ikonographics.net)

To His All-Holiness Patriarch Bartholomew
Archbishop of Constantinople and New Rome
Ecumenical Patriarch

in thanksgiving and prayers
for his labors on behalf of Orthodoxy
and the unity of the Christian *oikoumene*

εἰς πολλὰ ἔτη, Πάτερ καὶ Δέσποτα

In loving memory of Rev. Father Matthew Baker

(April 5, 1977–March 1, 2015)[1]

1   All royalties from book sales will go to Matthew's widow, Katherine, and six
children, Isaac, Elias, George, Eleftheria, Cyril, and Matthew Jr.

The Contributors

Rev. Protopresbyter George Dragas, Ph.D., Professor of Patristics, Holy Cross Greek Orthodox School of Theology

Rev. Economos Brendan Pelphrey, Ph.D., Presiding Priest, St. Sophia Greek Orthodox Church (San Antonio, Texas)

Jason R. Radcliff, Ph.D., Adjunct Prof. of Patristics, The George Mercer, Jr. Memorial School of Theology; Humanities Teacher, The Stony Brook School

Dr. Vladimir Cvetković, Honorary Research Fellow, Institute for Philosophy and Social Theory, University of Belgrade

Mark Mourachian, Ph.D., Asst. Prof. of Greek and Latin, Chair, Dept. of Humanities and Science, St. Charles Borromeo Seminary

Donald Fairbairn, Ph.D., Robert E. Cooley Professor of Early Christianity, Gordon-Conwell Theological Seminary

Dr. Alexis Torrance, Assistant Professor of Theology, University of Notre Dame

Nikolaos Asproulis, M.Th., Ph.D.c., Hellenic Open University; Academic Associate of Volos Academy for Theological Studies

Stoyan Tanev, Ph.D. in Physics and Ph.D. in Theology, Associate Professor, Department of Technology and Innovation, University of Southern Denmark, Odense, Denmark; Adjunct Professor, Faculty of Theology, Sofia University "St Kliment Ohridski," Sofia, Bulgaria

Dn. Dr. Alexei V. Nesteruk, Senior Research Lecturer, University of Portsmouth, Great Britain; and Visiting Professor, St Andrew's Biblical and Theological Institute, Moscow, Russia

John Taylor Carr, M.T.S., Classical Languages Instructor, New England Classical Academy

Emmanuel Gergis, M.A., M.Litt., Ph.D.c., University of Aberdeen, Lecturer in Patristics and Systematic Theology, St. Cyril Orthodox Christian Society; General Editor, The Alexandria School Journal

Contents

Foreword

Thomas F. Torrance (1913–2007) was perhaps the greatest English-language theologian of his generation. I like to think there were at least three T. F. Torrances all rolled up into one: the distinguished Reformed dogmatic theologian, the apologetic proponent of dialogue between theology and science, and (least well known) the historian of doctrine who wrote on almost every major figure from the fourth through the twentieth century. He was also a pastor and teacher, an ecumenical dialogue partner, one of Karl Barth's very best students (whom Barth at one point hoped would become his successor), the editor of the English translation of Barth's *Church Dogmatics,* not to mention of Calvin's New Testament commentaries, and the editor and founder of a major theological journal, *The Scottish Journal of Theology,* which still exists.

Among Torrance's various theological and ecumenical commitments, his profound interest in Eastern Orthodoxy — not only in the legacy of the Greek church fathers, but also in face-to-face encounter with Eastern Orthodox theologians — cannot be overlooked. Indeed, these latter aspects of his work may prove crucial to interpreting his entire legacy for present-day theology. I will never forget my surprise when he told me that his favorite theologian was not Karl Barth but Athanasius. An icon of the great Alexandrian forms the frontispiece of what is perhaps Torrance's best and most accessible work, *The Trinitarian Faith* (T&T Clark, 1988), which is studded with Greek patristic citations.

Torrance drove the lessons he learned from Barth in the direction of Eastern Orthodox theology in order to enrich his own Reformed tradition. In this he parallelled, to some degree, that other great interpreter of Barth, Hans Urs von Balthasar, who raided Barth in order to re-shape his own Roman Catholic theology. Today Barth's legacy is hotly contested by scholars who divide over taking him in a "catholic" or a "modernist" direction. Barth at least was clear that he intended his massive output as a theology for the Church, to be judged and received by the Church, for the sake of more faithful mission and preaching.

Absolutely central to Barth's vision of theology were the conciliar statements of Nicaea and Chalcedon, along with the trinitarian

Christology of the Greek Fathers, which he knew and defended. Like the Roman Catholic reception of Barth by Balthasar and his heirs today, the contemporary Orthodox reception of Torrance's construal of Barth and his legacy, as represented so splendidly in this volume, is testimony to the ecumenical character of Torrance's theology and its immense promise for the future.

Eastern Orthodox theology today has enormous contributions to make to the broader ecumenical conversation in the areas of Christology, ecclesiology, liturgy, theology of baptism and Eucharist, and soteriology. It also has much to learn in the process. The success of such contributions will depend in part on the ability of Orthodox theologians to make themselves heard by exercising not only faithful commitment to their own tradition, but also on a necessary spirit of self-critique and sympathetic willingness to hear and to embrace all that is orthodox in the offerings of their Western Christian interlocutors.

All these virtues are demonstrated most remarkably in the present landmark volume devoted to T. F. Torrance and Eastern Orthodoxy. The appearance of this book marks what one hopes will be a new chapter in contemporary theological and ecumenical conversation, in which the legacy of the great Greek Fathers and the treasures of modern Orthodox theology are enlivened and joined with the evangelical message of Torrance in his recasting of theology after Barth. Torrance's offerings are here deepened, if possible, by a more thorough confrontation with patristic theology. A new path is being charted for ecclesial theology in the service of Christ and his Gospel.

George Hunsinger
Hazel Thompson McCord Professor of Systematic Theology
Princeton Theological Seminary

Preface

The year 2013 marked the one-hundredth anniversary of the birth of T. F. Torrance (1913–2007). *Participatio: The Journal of the Thomas F. Torrance Theological Fellowship* published its first volume in 2009. In its 2013 volume for Torrance's centenary, the editors chose a theme very close to Torrance's heart: the dialogue between Reformed Christianity and Eastern Orthodoxy. The volume attracted an international representation of Orthodox contributors and led to this present book. The title, *T. F. Torrance and Eastern Orthodoxy: Theology in Reconciliation*, recalls Torrance's 1975 collection of patristic and ecumenical studies, *Theology in Reconciliation: Essays Towards Evangelical and Catholic Unity in East and West* (Wipf and Stock, 1996).

Since Torrance's death, an increasing secondary body of literature is emerging from young scholars. Jason Robert Radcliff's recent work *Thomas F. Torrance and the Church Fathers: A Reformed, Evangelical, and Ecumenical Reconstruction of the Patristic Tradition* (Eugene, OR: Pickwick, 2014), could be read as a companion volume to this present book. Wipf and Stock Publishers deserve credit for their role in continuing and furthering Torrance's significance and legacy by publishing new books about T. F. Torrance, republishing many of his original volumes, and making available many of his previously uncollected significant essays in their new Thomas F. Torrance Collected Studies (*Gospel, Church, and Ministry*, Vol. 1, ed. Jock Stein, 2012).

The editors express their gratitude to Jim Tedrick, Managing Editor of Wipf and Stock Publishers, for his interest in publishing this new book on T. F. Torrance and Orthodoxy. Members of *Participatio*'s editorial staff: Jason Radcliff, Jock Stein, and Russell Vincent Warren have given generously of their time to revisit a recent journal issue and convert it into a substantially new book. Fr. Matthew Baker especially deserves credit for his tireless efforts not only on behalf of this volume but also for playing a key role in forwarding Torrance's ecumenical legacy.

Todd H. Speidell
Editor, *Participatio:*
The Journal of the Thomas F. Torrance Theological Fellowship

Introduction
T. F. Torrance and Eastern Orthodoxy

The sincere and growing interest in Eastern Orthodoxy on the part of many Western Christians, Protestant and Roman Catholic, is presently beyond doubt. Yet when T. F. Torrance (1913–2007) began his work, this was not entirely so. With such figures as Yves Congar, Michael Ramsey, and Jean Daniélou, Torrance belonged to a relatively small category of Western European churchmen of his time engaged not only with the ancient Greek Fathers, but likewise with contemporary Orthodox theologians. In this sense, he anticipated important conversations of today, in which the Greek patristic theme of deification and the contributions of Orthodox theologians attract widespread interest in the Western theological world. Although its fruits began to be shown only in later decades, the roots of Torrance's interest in the Orthodox East were prepared long before. One wonders about the possible impact of his visits to Athens, Istanbul, and the Middle East in 1936 as a recipient of the Blackie scholarship for classical studies, during which time he attempted even to master modern Greek. His doctoral research on the Apostolic Fathers, while reflecting a radically Protestant viewpoint unacceptable to the Orthodox which Torrance himself would later leave behind, foreshadowed the patristic interests of his later mature work.

By his own account, Torrance's dialogue with living Orthodoxy began within the Faith and Order movement, through interactions with theologians like Georges Florovsky and Chrysostom Constantinides in various commissions and study groups through the 1950s and early 60s. His friendship with Methodios Fouyas, Metropolitan of Axum (Ethiopia) and later Archbishop of the Greek Orthodox Church in Great Britain, was a crucial context for exchange and collaboration beginning in the late 1960s, particularly as regards interest in the Alexandrian Fathers. Torrance was closely involved with Fouyas' "Foundation for Hellenism in Great Britain" and with various journals founded by Fouyas under the aegis of the Greek Orthodox Patriarchate of Alexandria: *Ekklesiastikos Pharos, Abba Salama,* and *Ekklesia kai Theologia.* Through Fouyas, who had built close cooperative relations with the ("miaphysite") Ethiopian

Church, Torrance's thinking on Alexandrian Christology had some influence on the official dialogue between non-Chalcedonian and Chalcedonian Orthodox Churches. Torrance's friendships with Nikos Nissiotis (a former student of Barth) and the Greek-American theologian Angelos Philippou are also worthy of note.

Another forum of exchange was teaching. Torrance had important relationships of mentoring and exchange with several students of Greek Orthodox background at New College, Edinburgh. Among these were George Dragas and Constantine Dratsellas. Dragas went on to be closely involved with Torrance in the international Orthodox-Reformed dialogue, co-drafting with him the agreed statement on the Trinity. Dragas recounts how, following the completion of Constantine Dratsellas' first doctorate in Athens, the prominent Greek theologian Panagiotes Trembelas told Dratsellas he must study with "the two best theologians in the West": Joseph Ratzinger at Regensburg, and T. F. Torrance at Edinburgh. Dratsellas wrote a Ph.D. thesis on the soteriology of St. Cyril of Alexandria under Torrance's direction. Torrance's Christian charity and fatherly devotion toward his students were demonstrated when he took a week out of his work to fly to Athens in order to spend several days praying at the bedside of Dratsellas, who was dying a premature death from a brain tumor.

Torrance was also responsible for introducing to the English-speaking world the best-known Orthodox theologian on the ecumenical stage today: John Zizioulas (1931–), currently titular metropolitan of Pergamum. Zizioulas taught as Torrance's assistant in dogmatics at Edinburgh in the years 1970–1973 before moving on to Glasgow. A tacit debate between two theologians, of great importance and still being carried on by others, runs as a sub-current through their respective writings on the Trinity, person and nature, and the Cappadocian Fathers.

The 1970s saw Torrance's dialogue with Orthodoxy move to wider scale. In 1973, he was named "honorary protopresbyter" of the Greek Orthodox Patriarchate of Alexandria, an unprecedented gesture, which understandably caused consternation among some Orthodox. When serving as Moderator of the Church of Scotland in 1976–1977, he took the unusual step of making his first foreign visits as Moderator, not to other Reformed communities, but to the ancient Orthodox patriarchates of the East. At this time, he made a request to Ecumenical Patriarch Demetrios of Constantinople to open an official international Reformed-Orthodox Dialogue. Torrance's contributions to this dialogue, especially regarding the doctrine of the Holy Trinity, still call for a deeper consideration and assessment. Also of great significance for the Orthodox was Torrance's work on patristic hermeneutics, collected in his 1995 volume, *Divine Meaning*. The present volume constitutes nothing less than an international symposium on Torrance's theology. The authors originate from the Orthodox Churches of Bulgaria, Greece, Russia, and Serbia, and from the archdioceses of the Patriarchate of Constantinople in Great Britain and in the United States. Also contributing are one theologian from the non-Chalcedonian Coptic Orthodox Church of Alexandria (Emmanuel Gergis), another from the Melkite Greek Catholic Church (Mark Mourachian), and two from Protestant traditions (Jason Radcliff and Donald Fairbairn).

The first section provides three historical perspectives on Torrance and his relations with Orthodoxy. In a lively interview, George Dragas recalls his close collaboration with Torrance in various scholarly and ecumenical activities, and gives his own Orthodox appraisal of Torrance's Trinitarian theology. This is followed by a memoir by Brendan Pelphrey, a student of Torrance in the early 70s and now an Orthodox priest, on the impact Torrance made in leading him to Orthodoxy. Lastly, Jason Radcliff, author of the recent *T. F. Torrance and the Church Fathers* (Pickwick, 2014), draws from previously unresearched archives to provide an historical overview and introduction to the theology of the official Orthodox-Reformed dialogue directed by Torrance, posing insights as regards the theological shortcomings and enduring contributions of that dialogue.

The essays in the central portion of this book combine historical and constructive interests. Careful sympathetic and critical attention is given to Torrance's readings of church fathers, as in Vladimir Cvetkovic's essay on Torrance as an interpreter of St. Athanasius. The essays pursue Torrance's insights further in relation to areas and figures of the patristic tradition he engaged only suggestively or not at all, as in Cvetkovic's discussion of St. Maximus, Donald Fairbairn on justification in St. Cyril of Alexandria, Mark Mourachian on theological realism in Torrance and St. Ephrem the Syrian, and Alexis Torrance's study placing T. F. Torrance's theology of baptism in dialogue with the 5th century desert ascetic St. Mark the Monk.

The palette here is not simply patrological, but "neopatristic." As is appropriate both to Orthodox theology and to Torrance, historical patristics and contemporary systematics, as well as natural sciences, converse. Nikolaos Asproulis' essay examines Torrance and Zizioulas' divergent appraisals of the Cappadocian Fathers, uncovering the debate between the two theologians and its import for theological method. Affinities between Torrance and the Romanian theologian and confessor Dumitru Staniloae (1903-1993) on the theme of the rationality and cosmology are explored by Taylor Carr. The pieces by Stoyan Tanev and Alexei Nesteruk, both physicists with theological training, extend Torrance's inquiries into the inter-relations of theology and the natural sciences with a deeper engagement of the later Byzantine patristic tradition up to St. Gregory Palamas as well as more recent thinking in physics, addressing themes of energy, space, cosmology, and the anthropic principle. Emmanuel Gergis' study highlights Torrance's contributions to the understanding of the Alexandrian Christology professed by the Coptic Orthodox Church, drawing comparisons with more recent Coptic theologians and pointing the way towards fuller doctrinal agreement between Chalcedonian and non-Chalcedonian churches.

The symposium concludes with several valuable primary sources relating to Torrance's relations with Orthodoxy. Torrance's correspondence with Georges Florovsky is reproduced, with introduction and annotation by Matthew Baker discussing the historical context and theological significance of their exchanges. Finally, two little-known pieces by Torrance, "The Orthodox Church in Great Britain" and "The Relevance of Orthodoxy," are reprinted to close the volume.

Recently, there are signs of a new genre of studies by English-speaking Orthodox scholars, engaging major Western Christian theologians. The first-fruits of this new genre were George Demacopoulos and Aristotle Papanikolaou's edited volume *Orthodox Readings of Augustine* (St. Vladimir's Seminary Press, 2008), and Marcus Plested's monograph *Orthodox Readings of Aquinas* (Oxford University Press, 2012). The present book solidifies and expands this genre, as the first publication of predominantly Orthodox scholars engaging with a modern Western systematic theologian. Not insignificantly, the common ground here remains the legacy of the church fathers, as a living source for theology today.

This book also revisits a historic theological exchange that up to this point remains still very little known, especially outside of Great Britain. The discussions between Anglicans and Orthodox in England from the 1920s onward are familiar to many and the subject of several scholarly studies. Yet for all the importance of those exchanges, it might be argued that a far more *dogmatically* weighty conversation was being conducted from a center north of the border. That conversation deserves to be at least as well known as the Anglican-Orthodox exchanges that once so informed the perception of Orthodoxy in the English-speaking world.

The official bilateral Orthodox-Reformed dialogue inaugurated by Torrance is formally concluded, with little hope of revival. The "Agreed Statement on the Holy Trinity" produced by this dialogue has received neither official acceptance by the holy synods of the autocephalous Orthodox Churches nor wide reception by Orthodox theologians. Conversely, Torrance's vision was perhaps always too catholic, and Reformed identity too contested, to allow his theology to be considered as representative of all Christian bodies claiming that name. This is all the more relevant today, when the Barth-influenced return to Nicaea Torrance favored has given way to a watery theological liberalism in many communities with roots in the Reformed tradition.

Yet the conversation initiated by Torrance continues elsewhere. New generations are discovering his work. Alexei Nesteruk's recent translation of Torrance's classic *Space, Time and Incarnation* (Oxford, 1969) into Russian promises only wider Orthodox engagement. Torrance's re-orientation of Protestant theology after Barth towards the classical patristic tradition is now making its mark among some evangelicals. It is to be hoped that this will lead some to follow Torrance, and go beyond him, into a deeper discovery of the evangelical theology of the Fathers and their Orthodox tradition.

As readers will quickly discover, not all that Torrance held is acceptable to the Orthodox.[1] The disagreements are real, and they are not trifling. But the affinities also are significant. Orthodox theologians have

---

1   One point of disagreement not treated in this book would be the theology of holy orders. See Thomas F. Torrance, "The Ministry of Women: An Argument for the Ordination of Women," *Touchstone Magazine,* Fall 1992, and the reply by Patrick Henry Reardon, "Women Priests: History and Theology – A Response to Thomas Torrance," *Touchstone Magazine,* Winter 1993. The exchange concludes in "On the Ordination of Women: A Correspondence Between Thomas F. Torrance and Patrick Henry Reardon," *Touchstone Magazine,* Spring 1993. Accessible online at www.touchstonemag.com/docs/navigation_docs/archives.php. See also Thomas F. Torrance, *Royal Priesthood: A Theology of Ordained Ministry* (revised edition: A&C Black, 1993). Torrance's positive but still fundamentally "presbyterian" understanding of episcopate, while reflecting a view strangely not too far from the common Latin

much to gain from Torrance on multiple fronts: his forceful and lucid presentation of Athanasian-Cyrilline Christology, especially regarding the high priestly work of Christ; his creative development of early patristic hermeneutics, and rigorous treatment of theological epistemology, in response to modern challenges; his patristic-inspired forays into theology-science dialogue. One hopes, likewise, it will be evident from this volume that those who have learned their theology from Torrance still have more to learn from Orthodoxy — not least, from a more extensive and less jaundiced consideration of later Byzantine patristic tradition, with its ascetic and liturgical dimensions, which Torrance surveyed preciously little. The theological dialogue begun by this great Scotsman and his Orthodox friends ought to continue, and move to a deeper level. This modest offering is an opening in that direction.

Matthew Baker
January 18, 2015
Feast of Sts. Athanasius and Cyril of Alexandria

---

understanding of episcopacy from the medieval period up to Vatican II, would likewise be judged inadequate in the eyes of Orthodoxy.

Part I

Historical Background
and Memoirs

Chapter 1

Interview with Protopresbyter George Dion. Dragas regarding T. F. Torrance

Matthew Baker [hereafter MB]: *Father George, I've been blessed to have known you for a number of years now, during which time we have enjoyed many conversations together about a common interest: your beloved friend and teacher, Thomas Torrance. Please tell our readers a little about yourself, where you're from, and when and how you came to know Professor Thomas Torrance.*

GDD: Matthew, thank you for facilitating this interview, which is very important for me, because Professor Torrance, of blessed memory, has been much more than a friend and teacher to me. He was a mentor, a guide, a supporter, a caring father, a key person in my life and career, whose memory is always alive in my heart and mind and to whom I owe a great deal for what I am today. If I write my memoirs or biography, as students and friends have been urging me to do, T. F. Torrance will be shown to be my great companion and benefactor in many pivotal circumstances and events. I will restrain myself in answering this interview in a detailed fashion, as I would have liked, and stick to your questions, answering them succinctly and focusing on Torrance himself and his extraordinary person and work, rather than on what he means to me personally.

As regards myself, I was born and raised in Athens, Greece, where I received my first education in science, and developed my theological interests and aspirations. At a crucial moment in my life I went to Scotland, basically to learn English, which I had found impossible to learn in Greece. But thanks to a scholarship I received, through the support of an unexpected (really, God-sent) philhellene friend, Principal Norman Porteous, Professor of Old Testament, Hebrew and Semitic languages, I ended up not only learning English, but also earning a theology degree from Edinburgh University. It was there at this university that I first heard of and met with Professor Torrance, and it was Principal Porteous who urged me to become acquainted with him. Torrance was one of my professors, to whom I was greatly attracted from the beginning, and who embraced me and became my supporter, mentor and guide for many years long after. There were at that time, in the 1960s, a very noticeable number of international students from all over the world that attended his lectures, many of whom had come to do research under him.

MB: *As a young theology student in a foreign country, what were your first impressions of Torrance? How did he conduct himself – in personal interactions, in the classroom? What kinds of things did you learn from him then?*

GDD: Having spent a year in the philosophy department, learning English and studying philosophy, I passed the Hellenicum (Higher Greek) and the Hebraicum (Higher Hebrew) and acquired the Attestation of Academic Fitness (the Scottish equivalent to the English GCE – a prerequisite for enrolling in the University) by sitting Higher exams (in Greek and Science), I entered the first year of Theology – thanks to my first benefactor, Professor Porteous, who guided me in my first year in Scotland. Professor Torrance taught Christian Dogmatics in the second year, but his name, along with that of Karl Barth, resounded in the corridors of New College and in the Student's Residence annexed to it, especially at meals. It was precisely this constant talk of "TFT," – as students called him – that made me venture a secret entry into one of his introductory lectures. This was the first time I saw him and heard him speak. Having entered the classroom on the second floor, I was surprised to see a Greek Archimandrite sitting among the students. I approached him, asked for a blessing and introduced myself to him.

He was Fr. Cornelius from the Brotherhood of the Holy Sepulcher in the Orthodox Patriarchate of Jerusalem (now Geron Metropolitan Cornelius of Petra). He told me that Torrance was a brilliant professor and that he had been sent there just to follow his lectures. I learned from him that there was also another Greek student, an assistant to Professor Panagiotes Trempelas of Dogmatics in the School of Theology of the University of Athens, Constantine Dratsellas, who had also been sent there to do a doctorate under Torrance's guidance on St. Cyril of Alexandria's Soteriology.[1] Torrance lectured on Christology and Soteriology. He spoke freely, but he also passed out lengthy lectures in typed form. I still have them all and treasure them as a great heirloom, although most of them have now been published: my fellow-student and friend Robert Walker, a nephew of Torrance, has recently edited them in two impressive volumes on the Incarnation and the Atonement.[2]

I was captivated by that first lecture to the extent that I ran to his office afterwards to introduce myself to him and to seek his permission to attend his classes, although I was at this time only a first year student. This was my first full encounter with him, which I cherish as a momentous event because he gave me the starting point to my studies. He let me into his office expressed his happiness that I was a Greek and then, showing me an icon of St. Athanasius,[3] which was placed in the center of his room, he told me that this was "the theologian" that I should make my primary mentor. The emphasis on St. Athanasius had already emerged in the lecture that I had attended. I clearly remember his statement, that if we wish to become theologians we must read and absorb three great books: Athanasius' *De Incarnatione*, Anselm's *Cur Deus Homo* and Kierkegaard's *Philosophical*

1 I established a life friendship with both Archimandrite Cornelius Rodousakes and Constantine Dratsellas. Shortly afterwards I typed Dratsellas' Ph.D. thesis, with my two little Greek and English typewriters, as I was eager to learn what a Ph.D. thesis was all about. It was entitled *Questions of the Soteriological Teaching of the Greek Fathers with special reference to St. Cyril of Alexandria* and was published in the Journal Θεολογία (Athens 1969).

2 *The Incarnation: The Person and Life of Christ*, edited by Robert T. Walker (Paternoster Press and IVP, 2008), and *Atonement: The Person and Work of Christ*, edited by Robert T. Walker (Paternoster and IVP Academic, 2009).

3 This icon was an original, painted by a well-known Greek iconographer, Rallis Kopsidis. It had been given as a gift to Torrance by another Greek theologian, Angelos Philippou (or Philips), whom Torrance praised to me as the most brilliant of the Greeks, due to his extraordinary Oxford DPhil thesis on "The nature of evil according to Gregory of Nyssa". I had the privilege later to read his thesis and to meet him in America.

Fragments. These books, he said, bring us face to face with the basis of Christian Dogmatics, the event of the Incarnation, the fact that God has become man. Without this basis we could not really understand Christian doctrine.

With regard to Torrance's interaction in class, I would say that it was overpowering. He taught with tremendous conviction and profound erudition. He sounded like a prophet who communicated the word of God that was coming down from heaven into the class. Sometimes I felt that his lectures were like attending a Liturgy. It was word, imbued with sacramental quality. It was like a full river that moved constantly and consistently. But at the same time there was gentleness to it all, which came out in his answers to all sorts of questions raised by keen, confused, or even disagreeable students. On the whole, students' reactions to him were positive, but there were also some negative or lukewarm. I consider myself one of his luckiest undergraduates, because on numerous occasions he invited me to have lunch with him at a small Chinese restaurant behind New College, where we discussed the theological questions that I constantly raised. He had no other free time to address my questions and chose this option because he did not want to disappoint me. He also invited me to accompany him to several important debates and special lectures in the University and on one occasion he enrolled me in the Edinburgh University philosophical society, in the David Hume Tower, and encouraged me to participate in the open debates that were conducted there involving students and professors. There were, of course, other students who enjoyed the same kindness, but I always thought that I did better, because of my keenness to raise questions and clarify the profound points of his teaching.

MB: *If I recall correctly, your first publication was a translation into Greek of one of Torrance's articles. Which article was that and where was it published? How did this all come about?*

GDD: The article I translated into Greek was "The Implications of *Oikonomia* for Knowledge and Speech of God in Early Christian Theology," which was originally published in Hamburg-Bergstedt, Germany (1967) in a volume dedicated to Oscar Cullmann on his 65th Birthday.[4] My translation into Greek was published in the Journal of the Patriarchate of

---

4   See *Auszug aus Oikonomia: Heilsgeschichte als Thema der Theologie,* edited by Felix Christ (published by Herbert Reich Evang. Verlag GMBH, Hamburg-Bergstedt, Germany 1967), 223–238.

Alexandria *Ekklesiastikos Pharos*, which was reactivated at that time by Archbishop Methodios (Fouyas) of Aksum.[5] As to how this came about, I recall that I was given an offprint of this article by Iain Torrance, TFT's son, and I was so fascinated in reading it that I translated it into Greek with the intention to publish it. The opportunity for publishing it arose in Edinburgh when I met with Archbishop Methodios for the first time. He had come to Edinburgh with Patriarch Nikolaos VI of Alexandria and Archbishop Athenagoras (Kokkinakis) of Thyateira and Great Britain to receive honorary Doctorates at the University – an event prompted by Torrance. The article was reprinted in a revised form much later (1995) in Torrance's volume on patristic hermeneutics entitled *Divine Meaning* – a volume which Tom very lovingly dedicated to my wife Ina and me. What fascinated me about this article was the constructive theological and epistemological character of Tom's reading of patristic hermeneutics. I should add that hermeneutics is one of Torrance's special contributions – an amazing contribution that fully flourishes in his books *Divine Meaning* and *Theological Science*.

MB: *After finishing your BD at Edinburgh, you did a Masters at Princeton Theological Seminary. Torrance was at that point a visiting scholar in Princeton, and Georges Florovsky was also teaching there. If memory serves me right, you had the unique benefit of having them both as readers for your Masters thesis. How did all this work out? What was your topic? And what was the relationship like between Torrance and Florovsky?*

GDD: At my graduation in 1970, Torrance gave me a letter, written to him by the external examiner Eric Mascall of King's College London, which placed me at the top of the finalists in Dogmatics and suggested that I should be encouraged to pursue further studies. As a result of this, Torrance called me and suggested to me that I consider going to Princeton to work with Florovsky on Athanasius. He also suggested that I concentrate on the disputed authorship of Athanasius' two treatises *Against Apollinaris*. In his view, these two treatises were genuine Athanasian works, but had been characterized as pseudepigrapha because they were an obvious obstacle to a 19th century scholarly casuistry that saw a latent Apollinarianism in Athanasius' Christology – a point that had been and still is adopted in the general manuals of *Dogmengeschichte*.

5 See *Ekklesiastikos Pharos*, vol. 51 (1969–70), 32–48, 186–200.

Torrance praised Florovsky as the only theologian who would make him think twice if he disagreed with what he proposed or wrote, and advised me that it would be an excellent opportunity for me to get into the great Athanasius, whose theological legacy he considered fundamental in his efforts for theological reconstruction, having Florovsky as my guide.

In September 1970 I met Florovsky at Princeton University for the first time, and he accepted me as a postgraduate student working on Athanasius' anti-Apollinarian treatises. He praised Torrance as a leading theologian to whom Orthodox theologians ought to listen very carefully and said that he was delighted that I had been his student. Being at this time a visiting professor at Princeton Theological Seminary, where I had been enrolled for a Th.M. degree, Florovsky could be, and accepted to be, my supervisor. By divine providence, it happened that Torrance too was visiting professor at Princeton Theological Seminary in the following year and he too acted as my advisor. My thesis, reviewing and evaluating the debate between supporters and opponents on the paternity of the two "Athanasian" anti-Apollinarian treatises and defending the former, was accepted unanimously by Florovsky and Torrance, both of whom encouraged me to work further on it and produce a Ph.D. thesis. I followed their advice two years later, having published a summary of my Princeton Th.M. thesis in Archbishop Methodios of Aksum's journal *Abba Salama*.[6]

MB: *You taught patristics from 1974 to 1995 at the University of Durham. You also wrote your Ph.D. dissertation on Athanasius* Contra Apollinarem *there. Did Torrance have anything to do with your going to Durham? What was his involvement with your dissertation? I know he wrote the introduction when it was published in 1985.*

GDD: After Princeton I went to Greece for a short interim, and in the Fall of 1973 I returned to Edinburgh to continue my research on Athanasius' two treatises *Contra Apollinarem* under the direction of Torrance. I had hardly finished my first Ph.D. year when at the prompting of Professor Tom I applied for a Lectureship in Patristics in Durham University.

6 See "St. Athanasius' two treatises *Contra Apollinarem*: second thoughts on the research of the critics," *Abba Salama*, 6 (1974), 84–96. This essay has been reprinted in my collection of Athanasian essays, entitled: *Saint Athanasius of Alexandria: Original Research and New Perspectives* (Orthodox Research Institute, Rollinsford NH, 2005), 133–150.

My referees were Torrance, Florovsky and Archbishop Methodios Fouyas. In September 1974 I started teaching at Durham and a year later transferred my Ph.D. registration from Edinburgh to Durham, where I continued my research on my own. This new development was decisive for my future career and although I recognize the grace of God in all this, I have no doubt that Torrance was God's primary agent. It was Torrance that introduced me to Athanasius and supported me in Edinburgh. It was he again that sent me to Princeton and introduced me to Florovsky who sealed my commitment to Athanasius and the Fathers of the Church. It was Torrance who also introduced me to Archbishop Methodios Fouyas in 1970, who later came from Ethiopia to baptize my two sons in Durham and a little later ordained me to the priesthood in 1980 when he became Archbishop of Thyateira and Great Britain and made me a close collaborator in his ecclesiastical and academic pursuits. Finally, it was Torrance who suggested to me the topic of my Ph.D. thesis and fully appreciated and recognized the tremendous labor that I put into it – including pioneering literary research using computers – and its significance for Patristic studies, calling it an epoch-making work, whereas others who came to know it tried to suppress it or passed over it in silence because it signaled a radical revision of the set views on Athanasius' Christology in the standard manuals of the early history of dogma (Grillmeier, Kelly, etc.).

MB: *Did you continue to see Torrance frequently while you were teaching in England?*

GDD: Yes, we met often and exchanged letters frequently. In 1973–74, when I started my doctorate in Edinburgh, I was his research assistant. Then, in '74, through his insistence, I applied to Durham and with his support I was elected lecturer in Patristics at Durham University. He was delighted, as this was close to Edinburgh. All through the 1970s, I visited him on many occasions as I gave lectures to different societies in Scotland. Every time I crossed the border I visited him. In 1976, I published an essay devoted to him, on the significance of his being made Moderator of the Church of Scotland, at the request of Archbishop Methodios of Aksum.[7] In 1978 I was present with my wife at the Guildhall

7 "The Significance for the Church of Professor T. F. Torrance's Election as General Moderator of the Assembly of the Church of Scotland," *Ekklesiastikos Pharos,* 58 (1976), 214–226.

in London, when he received the prestigious *Templeton Foundation Prize for Progress in Religion*. Again in 1978, he introduced me to the Brussels based *Académie Internationale des Sciences Religieuses*, of which he was the president. As a matter of fact, I was invited for three successive years to address the themes of the year for this assembly, and as a result I was voted in as life-member and then elected to serve as vice-president during the years 1981–1984. Also, in the late 1980s and early 1990s, I served as priest in Glasgow while teaching in Durham, and my wife and I would visit him on several occasions on our way back to England. Every new essay or book he published, I was among the first to receive a copy. He supported me twice to become a professor of Church History in Scotland – in Aberdeen and in Edinburgh – and he nearly succeeded, except for the fact that his opponents got in the way. And of course, we also met many times in the context of the official Orthodox-Reformed Theological dialogue in the 1980s and early 1990s. At a gathering of family, friends, colleagues and former students at Carberry Tower for his 80th birthday in 1993, I toasted him with a paper, which was also published in Archbishop Methodios' journal *Ekklesia kai Theologia*.[8]

MB: *Who were some of the other important theological figures connected with Torrance during this period?*

GD: Some of the important figures associated with him during the period of our interactions were John Zizioulas, Roland Walls, and James Torrance, his assistants, John McIntyre and his other colleagues in the Faculty of Theology in Edinburgh, Alasdair Heron, Donald McKinnon, Eric Mascall and many important professors in Europe and America, especially those connected with the World Alliance of Reformed Churches and the Brussels-based International Academies of Philosophical and Religious Sciences. His Orthodox connections included Methodios Fouyas, Chrysostom Constantinides, Constantine Dratsellas, Nikos Nissiotis, Angelos Philippou, among others. I am aware that there were a great number of theologians who corresponded with him, but what is most impressive in this connection is his prompt response to each of them. I remember him telling me that he responded to all his incoming mail on the day it arrived, before going to bed, and

---

8 "Professor T. F. Torrance on his 80th Birthday," *Ekklesia kai Theologia* 12 (1993), 566–76.

this certainly applied to me, as well. He used a unique typewriter, because it had mixed Greek and English letters –n=η, e=ε, p=ρ, etc.!

MB: *Methodios Fouyas was the Archbishop who ordained you to the priesthood in 1980. It seems to me that his relationship with Torrance was one that ran rather deep. What kinds of scholarly and ecumenical activities did they engage in together?*

GD: Fouyas did his doctorate in the 1960s in Manchester, before becoming a bishop in the Patriarchate of Alexandria. Fouyas' *Doktorvater*, Arnold Ehrhardt, was a friend of Torrance. When I first met Fouyas in Edinburgh on the occasion of his receiving the doctorate in 1970, he told me that he had exchanged extensive correspondence with Torrance and that my name was frequently mentioned in his letters to him. Tom and Methodios collaborated through the 1970s and 1980s and in various academic and publishing ventures, including Fouyas' journals, *Ekklesiastikos Pharos* and *Abba Salama, Texts and Studies and Church and Theology*. I was also involved in several of these.

In 1973, Tom visited Addis Ababa for the "Year of St. Athanasius" (d. 373) celebrations with Methodios, who was at this time Archbishop of Aksum. Tom delivered lectures there, which were later published in one of Fouyas' journals, and I believe he subsequently visited Alexandria at this point as well. On this occasion he was given the honorary title of Protopresbyter of the Patriarchate of Alexandria, and a pectoral cross, which is a sign of the office of protopresbyter. This unprecedented and unusual event caused some controversy among the Orthodox at the time. It was officially explained, however, that this honor was an *ad hoc* event, and did not in any sense establish a precedent. It was, rather, a spontaneous act of honoring a person who had made such incredible contributions to the understanding of the legacy of the Church of Alexandria, and especially of St. Athanasius the Great, bishop of Alexandria, as well as to the rapprochement of Reformed Christians to Orthodoxy.

When Tom was elected Moderator in 1977, it was through Fouyas' mediation that Tom was able to visit the Patriarchate of Alexandria and other Orthodox Churches – an unprecedented event; he was the first Reformed Moderator to visit in his term of office Orthodox Churches along with sister Churches of the Reformed tradition. Further close and extensive collaboration took place in the 1980s, after Methodios became

Archbishop in England. This was also the period of the Official Orthodox-Reformed dialogue.

It was also Tom who arranged for Methodios to give the opening sermon to the General Assembly of the Church of Scotland in May 1981, which was later published as a pamphlet and was distributed to all the parishes in Scotland. Accompanying Fouyas as his chaplain, I distinctly remember how Fouyas, the Orthodox Archbishop in Britain, charmingly asked the Moderators of the General Assembly, who entertained him to tea in the Moderator's official Edinburgh residence, why they used the term "Assembly" instead of "Synod," since that is what it was, and the latter was the ancient term? And why not say "Bishops" or "Archbishops" since that is what Moderators of Presbyteries and of local Presbyterian Churches were? "Of course, Tom Torrance," he said, "would really like to be Patriarch of Alexandria, and that we cannot give him; but we would recognize him as Patriarch of Scotland!" "My dear Methodios, you are too kind to me," Tom replied afterward.

MB: *Torrance was elected Moderator of the Church of Scotland in 1976. It was shortly after that he also made the first motions to open up an international theological dialogue between Reformed and Orthodox Christians. You participated together with Torrance in the 1980s and early 1990s in numerous meetings of this dialogue. Please tell us something about all this.*

GDD: As Torrance explains in his introduction to the first volume of the official dialogue papers, the roots lay in the Faith and Order movement in the 1950s – he particularly mentions here his dialogue with Florovsky and Constantinides in that context. Then, there developed in the early 1970s in different countries various local discussions between Orthodox and Reformed. But the specifically international dialogue grew more directly out of Tom's friendship with Fouyas and his connections with the Patriarchate of Alexandria.

In 1977, Torrance paid official visits as Moderator of the Church of Scotland to Ecumenical Patriarch Demetrios in Constantinople, and then, accompanied by Fouyas, to Archbishop Seraphim of the Church of Greece, Archbishop Makarios of the Church of Cyprus, Patriarch Nikolaos VI of Alexandria and Patriarch Benediktos of Jerusalem, indicating his interest in the Orthodox Churches and proposing rapprochement of Orthodox and Reformed through theological dialogue. When in Constantinople he submitted to the Ecumenical Patriarch an official proposal from the Geneva-based World Alliance of the Reformed Churches (WARC) for joint theological dialogue between Reformed and Orthodox. The official response of the Patriarch was positive and suggested that a delegation of Reformed Theologians from the WARC visits the Fanar in order to discuss the matter further and specify procedures. Thus, in 1978 a Reformed delegation headed by the President James I. McCord of WARC and including Torrance visited the Patriarch and the appropriate Committee of the Patriarchate headed by Metropolitan Chrysostom (Constantinides) of Myra and they agreed to hold initial Consultations to explore the prospect of holding an official theological dialogue (three of these were actually held in 1979, 1981 and 1983). On this occasion President McCord also submitted two Memoranda for the proposed Dialogue, which explained the Reformed position and suggested that the dialogue should begin with the doctrine of the Trinity. TFT was behind these Memoranda and there is a story to tell which to me marks a sort of "new phase" in my relation to him.

Earlier in that same year we were at a meeting of the *Academie des Sciences Religieuses*. During an interlude he approached me and said to me, "George, I need your opinion about something. Can we meet privately for half an hour or so?" "Yes, of course," I said. We met in my room, and he presented to me a Memorandum – actually the second Memorandum, which McCord later presented to Patriarch Demetrios. "Read it," he said, "and tell me what you think. Be frank and critical." I read it. It was detailed, and in the heart of it there was a specific proposal that the theological dialogue should start with the doctrine of the Trinity according to the Nicene theology of Athanasius and Cyril and not that of the Cappadocian Fathers. He justified this by pointing out certain serious problems that Orthodox theology had developed over the years by over-reliance on the Cappadocians to the neglect of the Alexandrians and more or less suggested that the dialogue with the Reformed theologians would supply the answers to the problems of the Orthodox!

After I read it, Tom asked: "Well, what do you think, do you agree?" I said: "I don't." He said: "Why? Tell me." I replied: "Professor Tom, this will not fly. Let me go through it and explain why." He listened to me for a half an hour without saying a word, while I went sentence by sentence through his memorandum. Among other things, I said: "No Orthodox would approve of this opposition between the Alexandrians and the Cappadocians – we do not see the Fathers this way. Likewise, when you first go to approach an Orthodox Patriarch to ask him for a dialogue, you should not come with criticisms about his Orthodox theologians and their theological tradition. Rather, you should first present your credentials as Christians and state that in faithful obedience to the will of Christ you approach the Orthodox with a wish to be reconciled. You need first to explain to them who you are, what you believe and practice as Reformed Christians, that you have ordained clergy and sacraments, synods and so forth, and what all these mean to you." I also suggested that he give the patriarch a copy of the Reformed Prayer Book as a gift. He was baffled, and asked: "Which Prayer Book? Every Reformed Church has its own." "All of them that your delegates represent(!)," I said. Then after being silent for a moment, he replied: "George, can I ask you a favor? Can you write a memorandum as if you were the Reformed, requesting a dialogue with the Orthodox?" On his insistence I did so and sent it to him a little later. He revised it and used it for his memorandum to the Ecumenical Patriarch. After he returned from his visit to the Phanar in July 1979, he wrote me a letter and thanked me for my help with the memorandum. He said that he presented both memoranda, the one that I wrote and the one that he wrote and I did not agree with! And, he added, Patriarch Demetrios was delighted with both! Patriarch Demetrios was a gentle, benign man, to whom Torrance later dedicated an edited book of essays, *The Incarnation,* commemorating the 1700th anniversary of the 2nd Ecumenical Council in 1981, in which I also had an essay. In practice, these essays were yet another way of emphasizing the First Ecumenical Council (Nicaea 325) over the Second (Constantinople 381).

Two more initial exploratory consultations for the international Orthodox-Reformed Dialogue took place at the WARC headquarters in Geneva in 1981 and at the Patriarchal Center in Chambésy in 1983, where papers were offered dealing with the Trinity and with authority in the Church. TFT was a contributor and chief player. It was only after this point that the process started to invite all the autocephalous Orthodox Churches to send delegates for an official bi-lateral dialogue between the Orthodox Church and the World Alliance of Reformed Churches (WARC). The Professor of Canon Law at Aristotle University in Thessalonica, was president of the dialogue on the Orthodox side; Lukas Vischer, the new President of the WARC, who succeeded President McCord of Princeton, was on the Reformed side. The first official theological consultations took place in Leuenberg in 1988, then in Minsk in 1990. The papers from these meetings and the two memoranda presented by the Reformed to the Ecumenical Patriarch can be found in the two published volumes of the dialogue papers, which Tom edited.[9]

MB: *The International Orthodox-Reformed Dialogue produced an Agreed Statement on the Holy Trinity in 1991. Regarding the former statement, which I believe you had a hand in drafting together with Torrance, I have been asked why it is the Orthodox today seem to take no notice of it, or else have forgotten it. Could you enlighten our readers on the status of this document, its particular nature and scope?*

GDD: With the agreement of the plenary, the Statement on the Trinity was drafted by Tom and myself during the year 1989, revised at a meeting of the dialogue in Geneva in 1991 and was finally ratified and made public in 1992.

Tom and I had been appointed to prepare a draft to be considered by the joint Commission at its next meeting. The process of writing up this document was an interesting one. We had hardly come back from the first Consultation in Switzerland when, two or three weeks later, I received a full draft from Tom. "George, I have done my piece, and I need your reaction!" I phoned him, and said that I need a little time, given my many other academic responsibilities, and also regularly travelling every week to Glasgow from Durham to take care of the church services and other pastoral needs there. He phoned me several times expressing his eagerness to get my reaction and collaboration in order to produce the agreed statement draft in good time. He was quite determined to get things done quickly – a typical characteristic of "Torrancian" behavior!

My concern was that his draft of the statement was much too Reformed and "Torrancian." There was terminology there which, while claiming to be patristic and Athanasian, was in fact full of neologisms, which would be unfamiliar to the Orthodox. Thus, to avoid the confrontation which was inevitable, I produced my own full draft, explaining that this presented a more Orthodox approach and should be considered along with his Reformed draft! It hardly passed a week when I received a new draft from Tom, which had married the two. Tom attempted to assure me that my concerns had now all been taken care of, and we could now have a meeting to go over it together and then send the document to the members of the joint commission, so that it could be

9 Thomas F. Torrance, ed., *Theological Dialogue Between Orthodox and Reformed Churches*, 2 vols. (Edinburgh: Scottish Academic Press, 1985, 1993).

used at the next meeting. He suggested that we meet at his home the following Monday; after my morning services in Glasgow, I could spend the night at his place and we could do the work early in the morning before I returned to Durham.

I really did not fully agree with his new, combined statement. It was still dominated by his original draft, and mine was just watered down at crucial points. My main problem was his insistence of putting his "Athanasian-Cyrillian axis" (his term) against the "Orthodox Cappadocian deviation" (his term also). So I prepared my strategy very carefully for our meeting. We met at his home in Edinburgh. He was up early; he had prepared breakfast, and he said that everything was ready (two clear copies placed on a table!) for our discussion. He probably sensed that I wasn't keen on the meeting! I will never forget the moment when he looked at me and said: "I'm all ears, George." "Professor Tom," I said, "I appreciate very much your prompt responses and the hard work that you have put into this document. I understand your position very clearly, having been your student for several years. Nevertheless, I have serious questions and doubts about its structure. It is still dominated by your Reformed understanding of the Fathers – a point that we have discussed before. But the main problem I have with this new document is the terminology. Although this is in accord with your perspective of doing theology in reconstruction, which is a very fine ecumenical prospect for rapprochement, some of the key terms you use are not found in the patristic theology of the Orthodox and stand in contradiction to what they hold to be the case."

I was not sure how best to explain this, other than by translating the draft into Greek for him to see in order to show precisely the difficulty of translating his problematic terms, and how unacceptable some of this terminology was to the Orthodox. To give an example: it would be most odd to speak of "hypostatic essence," or "personal essence," or "essential hypostasis" in Greek – the language in which the Fathers to whom Torrance appealed allegedly wrote: hypostatike ousia, prosopike ousia, ousiodis hypostasis? These phrases are strange, and do not appear in the Fathers. This is just but one example. Other problematic examples could be produced from some of his language regarding "the divine monarchy" and "the doctrine of perichoresis." These neologisms are unheard of in any Orthodox patristic or theological manual. And this was more than a merely terminological problem. The real problem, it seemed to me, was a certain tendency almost to cancel out the distinction between essence and hypostasis, which is basic to Orthodox patristic theology. Tom's indefatigable energy produced another revised common draft, which was presented to the next meeting in Minsk. I was unable to attend that meeting, but apparently a further revision was requested by the Orthodox! We did this together, and at another joint meeting of us two with the two co-chairmen in Geneva a final Statement was produced. This was approved by the full Commission at Kapel (near Zürich) in 1992 and was included in the second volume of proceedings that Tom published in 1993.

As regards this official Agreed Statement on the Trinity several things should be known. It was a general and balanced agreement on initial points, which was not accepted as if it clarified all problems or questions. The critical question of the *filioque* was never actually discussed in the dialogue: in fact it was strategically left for later – and that was on my advice to Tom, because I said, "If you start with the *filioque* we will never get anywhere." Further, it must also be understood, that in the Orthodox Church, it is not enough that all the autocephalous churches send official delegates to a dialogue and sign on to an agreed statement. This is still an initial step, although a significant one. For such a statement to be considered authoritative by the Orthodox requires official acceptance by the holy synods of all the Orthodox autocephalous churches, which constitute one conciliar Orthodox Catholic Church. On a final note, I would add that the commentary on the *Agreed Statement*, which Tom published in the second volume of dialogue papers as well as in his book *Trinitarian Perspectives*, although it is entitled "A Common Reflection on the Agreed Statement," was pretty much all a work of Tom but was respectfully received by the full Commission. So, it was all a significant exchange, and a starting point, which still calls for further work and discussion.

MB: *Could you summarize then, if possible, your view of some of the criticisms that Orthodox theologians might perhaps legitimately raise against Torrance's Trinitarian theology?*

GDD: Torrance emphasized the monarchy of the whole Trinity *against* the unique monarchy of the Father. This emphasis was supported by his employment of his doctrine of *perichoresis* (or co-inherence) of the three persons with reference to the origin of the persons themselves, *against* the explicit patristic doctrine of the Father being the "source" or "cause" of the persons of the Son and the Spirit. Both of these emphases are based on Torrance's premise that what God is in his revelation, that also he is "antecedently and eternally in himself," a premise that Torrance shared with Barth, Rahner, and with many Western theologians more generally, namely that the Trinity as revealed in the economy is wholly identical with the essential Trinity in eternity.

From the Orthodox point of view, this simple *tout court* identification is not acceptable or adequate, because God does not reveal his essence, or *what* He is, in his economic activity, but rather reveals Himself as the Trinity of the Father, the Son and the Holy Spirit, through his energies. For the Orthodox, all the Fathers, Alexandrians and Cappadocians, and not only the Greek-speaking, but also the early Latin Fathers (Hilary, Ambrose, etc.), state that we do not know *what* God is (his essence – *ousia*), but *that* he is (his existence – *to einai*). Tom in fact accepts this statement when he says that theological statements "are not descriptive, but indicative." What he does not, however, go on to say, is that this "indicative" is based on God's acts (energies – *energeiai*) towards us in creation and salvation (in the economy), which, while they are not separated, cannot be simply *identified* with God's eternal essence. Actually, this distinction is found precisely in St. Athanasius, as well as all the Greek Fathers after him. It was also acknowledged even by some of the medieval doctors in the West.

Torrance suspected a hint of Origenist subordinationism in the Cappadocians and especially in St. Basil. However, "cause" (*aition, aitia*) in St. Basil and later Fathers does *not* mean that the Son and the Spirit are somehow less than, or subordinate to the Father. In my view, however, the Basil against whom Torrance reacted was the Basil of Zizioulas – he was reacting against the position which Zizioulas claimed to derive from Basil. Zizioulas not only defended, quite rightly, the monarchy of the Father in the generation of the Son and the procession of the Spirit, but also went further – rather unwarrantedly – and claimed that the person (*hypostasis*) of the Father is the cause of the common divine *ousia*. In a way, he subordinated the divine ousia to the *hypostasis* of the Father. Torrance opposed this and pointed out, also rightly, that in the Nicene terms which Athanasius defended, the Son is from the essence of the Father (*ek tes ousias tou Patros*) and one in essence (*homoousion*) with the Father, which means that there is and can be no division between the cause and the effect in God which the monarchy of the Father suggests. But Torrance, too, went further than this, and claimed – also rather unwarrantedly – that Athanasius did not see the Father as the cause of the Son because the *homoousion* implies that there can be no subordination as suggested by the scheme of cause and effect. What he meant was the opposite to Zizioulas, namely, that the *hypostasis* is subordinated to the *ousia*. I remember my objecting to Tom's statement that the Godhead (the term he prefers for translating *ousia*) is a "person," a concept that emerges in a sentence in the *Agreed Statement on the Trinity*.

The difference between Torrance and Zizioulas here can be understood in terms of the alleged difference of the two "Nicene" Creeds, which is spelt out in the Western manuals of *Dogmengeschichte*: The Creed of Constantinople 381 changed the phrase "*ek tes ousias tou Patros*" of the Creed of Nicaea 325 to say simply "*ek tou Patros*," which is how we recite the Creed today. Tom, for very specific reasons, favored a return to the earlier formula; Zizioulas, contrariwise, saw the later formula as a great advance upon the earlier, and invested it with his own perception. But in my view, there is no contradiction between these two formulae, and both Torrance and Zizioulas read too much later modern debate into the phraseology of these two formulae - as if they imply the priority of the person/s over the Godhead or the Godhead over the person/s. Nowhere does Athanasius deny the unique monarchy of the Father within the Trinity, or attribute the monarchy to a *perichoresis* of the three persons, as Torrance seems to claim. But, by the same token, nowhere does Basil say that the person or hypostasis of the Father is the cause of his own *essence*, which implies the absolute monarchy of the Father in the Divine Trinity, as Zizioulas seems to claim. To my mind, there is a false dialectic at work here in this debate. And it is also, on both sides, because both play Fathers against Fathers – something that St. John of Damascus precisely warned against in his *De Fide Orthodoxa* – but also say too much about the relation of ousia to *hypostasis* in the patristic doctrine of the Trinity, which is unwarranted in the teachings of the Fathers. In others words they say more about the Trinity *ad intra* than is warranted by the patristic tradition, Torrance because of his emphasis on ontological unity and Zizioulas because of his emphasis of the ontology of person.

Dear Matthew, as you and I know, there has been in recent years a great deal of academic discussion on Torrance's and Zizioulas' expositions of the doctrine of the Trinity. I am convinced that we need another interview, in order to go into further details on this much-debated issue. One point I want to stress is this: that both theologians have contributed greatly to the revival in modern theological discussions between Eastern and Western theological traditions of the significance of the doctrine of the Trinity and of the early Fathers of the Church. As to the way forward, I would repeat what Torrance's main concern has been throughout his theological teaching and writing: that we need to cut behind the divisions that have been solidified in the divided Eastern and Western Traditions. To do this, in my view, means to rediscover the *consensus patrum*, by following the call of Father Florovsky, Torrance's greatly respected friend, and Zizioulas' respected mentor, to return to the sources, the Fathers, and produce a "neo-patristic synthesis."

MB: *Is there anything more that you'd like to add regarding this good and brilliant man in Christ, your teacher and friend Professor Tom – his personality, piety, life and mind? Or, if you like, what are your last impressions of him?*

GDD: Iain Torrance once said to me something that answers this last question perfectly: "People like my father are unique and appear extremely rarely in the history of the Church." The dedication, the vision, the faith, the generosity, the piety, the brilliance – there is hardly any virtue that graces a human being that was not remarkably evident in Professor Tom. I was blessed with exceptional teachers and mentors, but this one seems to be always with me. When I left Britain for America in 1995, Professor Tom gave me his blessing, so to speak, but not without expressing his regret that he would be "losing" me. I assured him that this would never happen. My mother, who just reposed in the Lord this year, had also expressed a similar sentiment when I left Greece, to which I always responded that the bodily separation had made the spiritual intimacy immensely greater. Just as with her and with my father, so with Tom: physical separation and even death seem to be a secondary incident, which does not affect my feelings and my continued joy for having had them as dear mentors and companions in my life. In the Orthodox tradition, we remember the departed by singing "Eternal memory" – *Aionia e mneme.* Such is Professor Tom's memory for me.

Chapter 2

God and Rationality: A Reminiscence

Brendan Pelphrey

Professor T. F. Torrance – even now I cannot bring myself to call him "Tom," as did his friends, or "TFT," as do theologians – was one of the most important influences on my life, and a significant reason why my wife and I eventually became Orthodox Christians. I think of him often, especially when I am teaching. Sometimes my wife reminds me, now that my hair has gone white, to go into a meeting with the bearing of Professor Torrance.

I was, however, neither his best nor his favorite student. That category was left, I always thought, for those who were getting their second PhD, the first one being in a field like particle physics or mathematics, or perhaps theology. Some of my fellow students had already studied his work, and had come from different parts of the world to hear him lecture. But when I met Professor Torrance I had never heard of him or, for that matter, of the Orthodox Church or the church fathers whose works he taught.

In the Fall of 1971 I arrived at Edinburgh with my wife and six-week-old son. Why we came was untypical, certainly not something we had long planned or expected. I had just been discharged from the US Army after two years' service as a medic during the Vietnam War. What to do now? I conferred with my former philosophy professor, Oets ("O.K.") Bouwsma, an elderly Christian man who had been a friend of Ludwig Wittgenstein. I had been drafted out of his philosophy classes in graduate school at the University of Texas, and deeply respected him. Originally at the University of Nebraska, during his career Professor Bouwsma seemingly lectured from time to time everywhere: at Harvard, Yale, Princeton, Berkeley, Oxford, and Cambridge. As an emeritus professor at the University of Texas, he let his Christian faith show and impressed me most with his guided reading of *The Brothers Karamazov*. When I was being sent off to Vietnam he mailed me a postcard from Berkeley which read, "remember Herzenstube."

It was a reference to the *Brothers*: Dr. Herzenstube – whose name means "Heart-room" or, "Room in the Heart" – understood Mitya's innocence, as opposed to those who tried to view Mitya in terms of the godless science of Freud or Dr. Claude Bernard. (Bernard, an early pathologist in France, thought that all human behavior could be understood in terms of neurological activity.) Dr. Bouwsma's reference was also to the fact that I had left the study of medicine – specifically psychiatry – to come back to his classes in philosophy.

I wanted to leave the country, I said. Where should I continue to study philosophy? Oxford? Cambridge? Prof. Bouwsma thought for a while and shook his head. These days, he said, he would not recommend studying philosophy anywhere. Maybe theology? And then he brightened up. "Edinburgh! That's where you should go." And so we did.

In retrospect, I realize that Dr. Bouwsma knew exactly where he was sending me. A life-long, pious member of the Christian Reformed Church, he knew about the work of T. F. Torrance. Perhaps more to the point, he also realized that I was struggling with issues of faith, not simply philosophy. His answer was to point me towards the study of the church fathers.

Now at Edinburgh, I was still leery of too much "Christian" theology. I tried to play it safe by enrolling at the same time in the Old College, the University of Edinburgh, as well as at New College. My plan was to study comparative religions, concentrating in Divinity Studies at New College and taking courses in Hinduism and comparative religion at the Old College. As it happened, however, if one wanted to study comparative religion at that time it was required to study Christian theology as well, which in those years meant Dogmatic Theology. That is how I wound up in lectures by Professor Torrance, Chair of the Department of Christian Dogmatics. Thankfully, he did not spend his time exclusively with graduate students, but threw himself directly into lectures to the incoming freshmen.

Those first lectures were an extraordinary experience. In my youthful exuberance, I used to run the two miles or so from New College, down the Mound and past Princes Street, to our flat in Leith, to tell my wife about what Professor Torrance taught that day. He was turning my thinking upside-down, I would say – borrowing a phrase which we heard often in his lectures. He outlined concepts of the Trinity, the Incarnation, Salvation, Resurrection – and physics – in ways I had never heard.

Soon, I dropped my courses on Indian religion and, when it was possible, set aside the courses in Divinity Studies. Previously I had not thought about Dogmatics and certainly not about Karl Barth, but now I was one of Torrance's faithful students. I took careful notes, which I still have. And I read everything I could find, wading into Barth, Calvin, the church fathers and even, in self-defense, all the works of Luther, since I was one of the few students at Edinburgh with a Lutheran background. (In the classroom, Professor Torrance would occasionally poke fun at my Lutheranism in gentle ways, pointing out for example that Calvin was a careful theologian, while Luther was a pastor who simply reacted to events around him. Sometimes, the Professor referred to me as "Extra-Calvinisticum," in a teasing reference to the Lutheran's position on the omnipresence of the risen Christ.)

Today it seems strange to say that Professor Torrance's lectures were stimulating, because in fact much of what he said must have gone right over our heads, especially since a large number of the students were just out of secondary school. Never one to use a two-syllable word where a four-syllable word would do, he also emulated German syntax in his lectures and on paper. Anyone who has poured over his essays and books knows his penchant for a single sentence which could take up most of an entire page, perhaps with a bit of Greek, Latin, German, Hebrew, or French thrown in, along with the requisite quotations from Athanasius, Einstein, or Niels Bohr. I remember once trying to locate the verb in a very, very long sentence. *Following at last a careful search as in the German along a complicated argument the theology of God of which it was trying to explain at last on the next page I, at the very end, the verb found.* But once you worked it out, Torrance was shining a light onto some mystery that earlier had not made sense, and now seemed perfectly clear. His favourite exercise, I think, was to bring topics into relationship which before seemed mutually exclusive – most famously the studies of modern physics and theology. Because I was a bit older than many of the students, and already had a degree in philosophy as well as several years' study of science and medicine, it often fell to me to "translate" what we had just heard to the younger students in the class. This was a salubrious task, because it forced me to try to condense and understand the lectures, and to remember them by repeating them.

Nevertheless, it must be said, I did not impress the Professor very favourably in the beginning. Early on, I asked for an appointment to complain about my grade on an essay, the subject of which (I shall always remember) was "The Christian Apprehension of God." It was marked "60," in red, and I was chagrined. The Professor kindly agreed to see me, immediately raising an eyebrow at my "hippie" flared jeans and Carnaby-street tie. I asked him what was so terribly wrong with my essay, that it earned only a D-. Here I was, cowed by coming back to university after so long an absence in the Army, and I was nearly failing already.

He took the paper from me, re-read it quickly, and marked out the "60." Very deliberately, he re-marked it "65," underlined the new number, placed a full stop (period) after it, and then wrote a large B inside a circle. "My dear boy," he said, looking over his famous half-lens reading glasses, "why are you disappointed? That 65 is a B. Didn't you know?"

Years later, he would write a scathing letter to an authority figure in my Lutheran Church in America, who had been under the impression that I was imbibing Calvinism in some obscure college in Scotland. After pointing out, in the most gracious way possible, the apparent ignorance of the Lutheran gentleman regarding both universities and theological matters, Professor Torrance went on to say in his letter that the standards in our American theological colleges were abysmally low. I was doing A-level work, he said, while in America, even theological students at Princeton were producing what he would regard as C-level work at New College. After that I was not bothered any more by Lutheran theologians, and I have kept my copy of that letter to this day.

In preparing for this reflection, I located a keepsake from Edinburgh: a little green New College booklet which lists the professors and students at New College for the year 1975–1976, my last year there. Professor Torrance appears first in the list. It was a nod, without doubt, to the fact that he was respected all over the world, and had brought together at New College some of the best minds in theology at the time.

I felt that all the professors at New College were exemplary, but for that brief period the lectures offered in Dogmatics could not be equalled anywhere. Students came from English universities, from Tübingen, from America, from Africa, India, and Taiwan to hear Professor Torrance, assisted by Fr. Roland Walls from the Community of the Transfiguration, Fr. Noel O'Donoghue from Ireland, Prof. John Zizioulas (now, Metropolitan John of Pergamon) from Greece, and Dr. Gian Tellini from Italy. It was an unforgettable time.

Professor Torrance's lectures were precise, challenging, delightful, and always very professorial. At that time in Scotland it was not the norm for students to ask questions or to interrupt a lecturer, especially a senior professor. There would be time for questions at the end of the hour, although it was often difficult to pose sensible questions because of the volume of information we were receiving. But I remember an American student (it *would* be an American!) who once kept interrupting Professor Torrance's lecture with "I think this" and "I think that." Finally, our professor's patience wore thin. Looking sternly over his reading glasses, he interrupted the interruption. "Mister Brown," he said in exasperated but very measured tones, "I do not *care* what you think!" The class was shocked into silence and the lecture continued without further interruption. But of course he did care. A highlight of any semester were the hours devoted to what he called *quaestiones disputatae*. A proposition would be given to us, and the debate would begin. Sometimes he brought in other professors for these lively discussions: Professor Zizioulas, or his close friend and friendly rival, Fr. Roland Walls. Sitting like a panel at the table in front of the room, they would challenge one another, and us, with problems. Students took turns taking notes at these and at the Dogmatics seminars, and I still have some of my type-written notes, corrected in Prof. Torrance's own hand, which were to be distributed to the participants.

I especially remember one: Did Jesus heal the sick through his divine nature, or in his human nature? When it was his turn, Prof. Zizioulas banged his hand on the table. "What is human?" he thundered. After a long silence – we were afraid to say anything at all, I think – a lively discussion followed. Students and panel eventually agreed that true humanity is divine, and that the divine nature had emptied itself without change, into humanity – and that Prof. Torrance's presentations on the hypostatic union as understood by St. Athanasius were, indeed, the truth.

Professor Torrance's friendship with the well-known hermit and contemplative, Fr. Roland Walls, was legendary. Yet the contrast between the two men could not have been greater. Torrance was always the Professor: dignified in his bearing, impeccably dressed in tweed jacket and tie, reading over his carefully-prepared notes in class, interrupting himself only to write on the blackboard – often in Hebrew, Greek, or German.

Fr. Roland was quite the opposite: holes in his sleeves, rumpled and looking much like a street-sleeper, apt to close his eyes and pray during a lecture as to tell us stories about some saint, or read from Henri Nouwen or Julian of Norwich or even from the teachings of the Buddha. Famously,

Fr. Roland had once been turned away from a church where he was supposed to deliver the sermon, by the doorkeeper who thought he was a bum. But, as has been observed by those who knew them both, the two men were not only friends but were in many ways remarkably alike in personality.

Both men were deeply prayerful in their own ways. Neither could abide what Fr. Roland called "nonsense" in the study of theology. They read the same things and enjoyed conversation about anything, theological or not, although neither would have made any distinction between "secular" and "sacred." And it was Prof. Torrance's genius to invite Fr. Roland to lecture in Dogmatics at New College – something for which Roland insisted he was not prepared, his studies at Cambridge having been in New Testament. As faculty members they loved to argue with each other, but often explained the same things to their classes at the same time, though in entirely different ways.

Prof. Torrance would lecture about the hypostatic union, citing all sorts of references from the 2nd century to the present, throwing in quotations from the Old Testament, from Athanasius' *Contra Arianos*, from Barth, Bohr, and various theories of particle physics. Fr. Roland would chide us the next day about allowing too much theological "nonsense" to get in the way of our practice of prayer, in which we would meet the Incarnate God. They were speaking about the same thing.

Ultimately Fr. Roland would become my mentor and spiritual guide for many years, until his death in 2010. At New College, however, I kept one foot in each camp: the "dogmatics circle" around Prof. Torrance, and the "prayer-circle" around Fr. Roland. As a student, both in the years preparing for the BD Honours and then for the PhD, I would listen to Prof. Torrance on some subject – let's say, Gregory of Nyssa on the divine Darkness – and then take a bus to see Fr. Roland at his skete in Roslin, to work out how St. Gregory could make a difference in practical life.

It is not that Prof. Torrance did not pray, however, far from it. We always began classes with prayer, and his piety and, if I may say, his mysticism would show through even when he was attempting to be professorial. He would read to us from the works of John Calvin and John Chrysostom, mixing them up a bit; or from Calvin and John of the Cross; and ask us to identify who wrote what. We always got them nearly all wrong, and he would smile and say, "You see, Calvin was a mystic, not a Calvinist."

Once, I became the subject of some debate between these two mentors, Prof. Torrance and Fr. Roland, who were generally perceived as polar opposites by the student body and who frequently tussled over the fate of us students in faculty meetings. It seems they had a difference of opinion over my program. Later, Fr. Roland took me aside and said, "I told Tom that you were a breath of fresh air. I think he feels you have opened the window too far."

I still do not know with certainty what that meant, but it had to do I think with loyalty, or not, to the study of Dogmatic Theology. Unlike the fellows who had previously worked on nuclear bombs but who were now at New College to argue about the relationship of science to theology, I did not remain entirely in the Dogmatics department under Professor Torrance's direction. In the first year I had gotten interested in the Christian ethics of Dietrich Bonhoeffer and Helmut Thielicke, having encountered them in the Department of Christian Ethics and Practical Theology.

Prof. Torrance, on the other hand, seemed very cool about the entire Department. To be blunt, he did not support the idea that there *is* such a thing as "Christian Ethics." Eventually, however, he encouraged me to complete the first Joint-Honors degree to be offered at New College, combining Dogmatics with Practical Theology and Ethics. Always one to think in terms of relationships rather than analysis (which he characterized as "tearing things apart"), I think he secretly liked the idea of exploring ethics through the lens of dogmatic theology. And then there were the stories we heard from him about his personal life. He told of growing up in China, the son of missionary parents. I particularly enjoyed the tale about his father wanting to buy a horse to pull a cart, somewhere in western China. Not getting his tones quite right, his father asked for a "maa" (horse), and his Chinese servant kept looking at him incredulously. Finally the Chinese man said, "But you are already married!" Rev. Torrance had been saying that he needed an "ahmaa" (old woman) to pull his cart. Capping this story, the professor told us that he sometimes still dreamed in Mandarin. Now, many years later and having spent ten years in China myself, I have the same experience and wish he could have lived long enough for us to discuss it once more.

After I finished my studies in Scotland, my wife and I were privileged to meet Professor Torrance again in other places. He graciously came to my parents' home in Austin, Texas, when he was giving a visiting lecture in Austin at the Presbyterian Theological Seminary. We sat on stools at my mother's purple bar and he told anecdotes about his life. One of these had to do with the time Fr. Roland shut himself up in his hut at the Community of the Transfiguration.

At the Community in Roslin, Scotland, there was a common-house in the front of the property, and a little fence that separated it from the back part of the property where the individual huts, and the chapel-hut, were. Although there were no locks on any doors, everyone respected silence and a closed door. But one day, Fr. Roland had shut himself up in his hut for so long that the brothers became worried. Silence, yes, but too much solitude was too much.

There was no telephone at the Community, so I do not know how, but eventually someone telephoned Professor Torrance to ask if he could get Roland to come out of his hut. The Professor drove there immediately, he said, and knocked loudly on the door. Silence. He knocked again. Silence. Finally he shouted, "Roland, this is Tom. You come out this minute!" The door opened, and Fr. Roland chided him: "You don't have to shout, you know!" These and many other stories kept my parents entertained until well into the night.

During our years in Hong Kong, Professor Torrance appeared again when he was there to give guest lectures for one of his former students, a Chinese national who was then a professor at one of the local theological seminaries. It felt strange to meet my former Scottish professor at a Chinese café in Hong Kong, and later I talked with my friend, the Dean of the Anglican Cathedral, about it. At one point I complained that, as a professor of theology at the Lutheran Seminary, I did not have anywhere near the *gravitas* of my famous former professor, the translator of Barth's works and an *aficionado* both of the ancient Eastern fathers and of modern science. He told me not to worry. "Your job," he said, "is not to be a Professor Torrance, but to interpret him to people who wouldn't understand him otherwise."

What did he teach that was so hard to grasp? Lamentably, perhaps too many things, since after his death the New College faculty seemed no longer capable of presenting studies of his calibre. (The faculty gradually abandoned Dogmatics altogether and slid into what was called "divinity studies," which I regarded as a sort of amalgam of contemporary theological perspectives and political correctness.) But essentially, Professor Torrance was shedding light, as I see it, on three things:

First, all knowledge – and particularly science itself – is grounded in exploring and grasping what *is*, rather than in what we *think*. It requires the "self-disclosure" of what is (Being) to the investigator; it is not merely logical constructs and it is certainly not thinking about thinking. That being true, theological knowledge is therefore grounded in the Being and Acts of God, God's self-disclosure, and not in logic or emotion or even faith (Torrance constantly referred to "ontology," what is, rather than "psychology," what we think or feel).

Second, true knowledge is gained through reconciliation and relationships, not through analysis and the logical breaking-apart of things. Therefore, knowledge of God involves an experiential relationship with God, not merely thinking about God (or rather, what we *think* of as "god"). It involves drawing near to Reality and humbling ourselves before it. Ultimately, theological knowledge means our human existence coming into reconciliation with God's Being, begun from God's side through the Incarnation, obedience, and Resurrection of Christ, and answered in our own lives. (He frequently cited Barth's dictum about God's Yes! to our No.)

Finally, theology is truly the queen of the sciences. It carries us beyond ordinary logic into the *ana*-logic, or higher Logic, of God. To obtain knowledge in any form of science requires a measure of self-emptying: recognizing that our concepts are only hypotheses that may or may not dimly reflect reality. When the object of inquisition is the Divine Being, Who is above our ability to think or grasp, we must empty ourselves through repentance and wait for the self-revelation of God to us.

Then, when God reveals Himself to us, we are ourselves transformed. Putting this all together, we have something very practical. Let God reveal Himself to you, as is promised in the book of Hebrews. (Professor Torrance never tired of quoting the passage, "For whoever would draw near to God must believe that he exists and that he rewards those who seek him.") Empty yourself in obedience to God, and wait for Him. God cannot be fully *understood* (that is the apophatic side of theology) but God has revealed Himself: that God is a mystery of the Trinity, that He has emptied Himself into humanity, that death has been overcome.

And God *can* be experienced, through and in the sacramental life of the Church. Let the power of the resurrection of Christ draw you into a relationship with God, and therefore with all humanity and with yourself. Above all, partake of the Eucharist, which is at the center of the Christian life and which shapes us into the image of Christ.

These dimensions of his lectures were all carefully drawn from the writings of the church fathers, especially the Cappadocians. He never tired of speaking about Athanasius, Basil, and the Gregories – Gregory of Nyssa and Gregory the Theologian (to whom he mistakenly referred as "Gregory Nazianzen," as textbooks did universally at the time). This insistence upon the careful theology of the Nicene and Post-Nicene Fathers, with some reference to those who went before them, led me and perhaps other students directly to the Orthodox Church. It kept us from succumbing to the whims of contemporary theologies that kept being promulgated in the decades that followed.

On a visit to America, in an encounter with students at a prestigious Lutheran seminary during those years, I asked the young men (at that time there were not any women) what they were studying most. They answered, "Modern theology." Foolishly, I replied, "Since the Reformation?" They were startled. "No, since the 1960s," they said. Then they asked me what we were studying. "Ancient theology," I said. "Before the Reformation?" they asked. "No," I said, thinking of Torrance: "Before the fifth century!"

Finally, there were music and the arts. I know that most of us may not think immediately of music when we think of Dogmatic Theology, but Professor Torrance did. He constantly appealed to Mozart, as opposed to Bach and Beethoven. The reason was that Mozart, the Professor said, was inspired by angelic hymns and soared into the heavens, "above logic" and certainly above symmetry. Mozart was unpredictable. In the face of Mozart, Bach's measured and perfectly symmetrical chords seemed tedious. So, he said, we should be careful that our theology would be more like Mozart and less like Bach.

We also had to think about painting and sculpture. Torrance compared painters like Reubens, Rembrandt, or even Renoir with Suerrat, Picasso, Mondigliani, and Pollock. What is happening in pointillism and later, in abstract and expressionist painting? he asked rhetorically. The disintegration of culture, he would answer with a smile, before we had the opportunity to make our remarks; the tearing apart of thought, as opposed to laying bare Reality, by attempting to understand it on its own terms.

Performance art was also coming into vogue, so one day he discussed a recent performance. The "artist" had smashed a grand piano with a sledge-hammer. This, our professor thought, demonstrated beyond doubt that western society had fallen completely apart. No longer able to synthesize and to see relationships, which are the real nature of thought itself, we had fallen into analyzing everything to pieces until we could only smash things.

The Professor's impassioned speech about the disintegration of form in art was given more than once, but it was always gripping. It required a lengthy detour into discussions about the nature of language, the Socratic dialogues, Realism, and Nominalism. What is art, indeed, if it is not looking deeply at something and framing it, so that it can be seen in a new way – not destroying it? What is theology, if it is not listening to God rather than analyzing our own ideas about God and smashing this "God" to pieces?

Not many years after finishing at New College, my wife and I were recruited to be missionaries in Hong Kong. I was to teach Systematic Theology at the Lutheran Theological Seminary, which had students from all church backgrounds from many parts of the world. Shortly after arriving, I was asked to draw up an entire Systematics curriculum. This posed an insurmountable problem for me, however, in light of Torrance's teaching. Is there such a thing as "Systematic Theology"?

Both Professor Torrance and Fr. Roland taught that true theological thought is not "systematic," because God is not "systematic." Systematic Theology, Prof. Torrance said, was a scholastic left-over from the Middle Ages, unthinkingly embraced by modern theologians who were attempting to reason their way to God. But God is above-logic, unpredictable except in hindsight, not to be confined by careful propositions. Of course I always wanted to ask the Professor why, if that were so, both Barth and Torrance managed to write so much careful "systematic" theology – enough to choke Jonah's fish. But I didn't ask that. Instead, I turned instinctively to the church fathers, as our Professor taught us. Thus it happened that on my first official day at the Lutheran Seminary, in my first assignment, I found I was not really Lutheran at all. I drafted a series of courses and syllabi which my Professor would have approved, I think, as "Dogmatic Theology" – the historic teaching of the Church. We were going to read the church *fathers*, whose works happily had been translated long ago into Chinese by Presbyterian missionaries, just around the time of the Torrance's service in China. We would explore the theology of the Cappadocians, rather than reasoning our way through the usual maze of special and general revelation, anthropology, the fall, justification and the like, with an addendum that may or may not mention the Holy Trinity. We would begin with the mystery of the Trinity and go from there.

The outline of courses I would eventually teach was not really mine, therefore, but stemmed from Torrance's lectures, as well as from a letter from Fr. Roland. Roland had written, "Teach them the *mysteries* of the faith – the Trinity, Creation, the Incarnation, the Sacraments, the Apocalypse. And give them plenty of Bible to hang it on." Similarly, Prof. Torrance had given the students an essay in our first week, which stated plainly that (in opposition to most theology then going around) Dogmatics begins in Christ, not in ourselves, in the mystery of God, not in some construct about general and special revelation.

In the end, this was both an Orthodox proposition, much like the outline of chapters in *The Orthodox Way* by Metropolitan Kallistos (Ware), and also, I think, the real direction of all those lectures by Professor Torrance. We were exploring mysteries beyond our comprehension, but not beyond the experience of the Church. We were inquiring into the Mind of God, which had been revealed, inasmuch as we could bear it, by the Incarnate Logos.

Today, I often remember Professor Torrance when I am in a classroom, when I am counselling someone (I suggested one of his books, *God and Rationality*, to a young Jewish woman just yesterday) or at the Divine Liturgy. He was always a gentleman and always a scholar, but he wore a crumpled wool hat to school because he was unabashedly Scottish. He tried to look stern, but could not really bring himself to do it; his smile was winning. He pointed us to Scripture and to the Tradition of the Church – which, at least for me, meant the historic One, Holy, Catholic and Apostolic Church, the Church of Orthodoxy – and away from ourselves, into the awesome mysteries of God, the Church, and the Sacraments. I picture Professor Torrance standing behind his wooden lectern, smiling after making an especially remarkable point. I imagine his voice: "There . . . we considered the doctrine of Christ from its aspect of mystery, from its source in the eternal decision of God, and from the aspect of those who in the church are drawn by the Spirit into communion with Christ, and participate in the mystery hid from the ages, but now revealed and set forth in the Gospel of the Incarnate Saviour. There we considered the doctrine of Christ *sub specie aeternitatis*, in the light of His divine glory, in terms of His relation in Being and Person to the life of the Father, Son, and Holy Spirit in the eternal communion of the Trinity... We try to do this by penetrating into its inner logic – not by arguing logico-deductively from fixed premises, but by seeking to lay bare the precision embedded in the intrinsic of the subject-matter."[1]

1   From "The Hypostatic Union," a summary of lectures handed out to the students on mimeographed legal-size sheets, in about 1972.

In closing I wanted to cite an especially favourite Bible verse of Prof. Torrance's that would begin our day in his classroom. Both T. F. and J. B. Torrance liked to quote from the Letter to the Hebrews, and it seems nearly impossible to single out one passage over another. Perhaps this will do, as in my mind I can hear him reading aloud: "Therefore, brethren, since we have confidence to enter the sanctuary by the blood of Jesus, by the new and living way which he opened for us through the curtain, that is, through his flesh, and since we have a great priest over the house of God, let us draw near with a true heart, in the assurance of faith, with our hearts sprinkled clean from an evil conscience and our bodies washed with pure water . . ." (Hebrews 10:19–22).

Memory eternal, Professor Torrance!

Chapter 3

T. F. Torrance and Reformed-Orthodox Dialogue

Jason Radcliff

Introduction

The relationship between T. F. Torrance and Eastern Orthodoxy is well-documented in this important volume. However, the interaction between Torrance and the Orthodox tradition goes far deeper than a shared commitment to the church fathers or mutual appreciation of one another's theological tradition (both of which have been explored in detail in this book). The Reformed and Orthodox churches interacted in significant ecumenical conversation during the last two decades of the 20th century; a dialogue spearheaded by Torrance.

The Reformed-Orthodox Dialogue, as it is called, took place during the 1980s and 1990s, although more informal dialogue had been going on prior between Orthodox and Reformed. The basic skeleton of the Dialogue consisted of papers and subsequent discussion. Following the Dialogue, Torrance collected and published the papers as *Theological Dialogue Between Orthodox and Reformed Churches Volume I*[1] and *Theological Dialogue Between Orthodox and Reformed Churches Volume II*.[2] Torrance also preserved copies of much of the correspondence surrounding the Dialogue as well as copies of the Official Minutes which contain notes on many of the discussion points raised after the delivery of the papers; these are preserved in the *Thomas F. Torrance Manuscript Collection* in the Princeton Theological Seminary Library Archives in Princeton, New Jersey. These correspondence and minutes help one to

---

1 Thomas F. Torrance, *Theological Dialogue Between Orthodox & Reformed Churches Volume I* (Edinburgh: Scottish Academic Press, 1985).

2 Thomas F. Torrance, *Theological Dialogue Between Orthodox & Reformed Churches Volume II* (Edinburgh: Scottish Academic Press, 1993).

"read in between the lines" and gain a fuller picture of what happened at the Reformed-Orthodox Dialogue.

This essay presents an overview and examination of some key theological themes pertaining to the Reformed-Orthodox Dialogue as well as offering something of a "behind the scenes" look at the Dialogue on the basis of the related correspondence and Minutes. This chapter argues that in the Dialogue the Reformed and Orthodox both shared a commitment to the Greek Fathers as well as to a Christological and Trinitarian approach which has much to offer to current conversations in systematic and historical theology.[3] This essay suggests that certain elements of the Dialogue should perhaps be left with Torrance and the 1980s as Reformed, evangelicals, and Orthodox continue any kind of ecumenical dialogue today. Yet the approach of Torrance and the Reformed-Orthodox Dialogue is an excellent example and some points of application are offered in conclusion with the hope of impetus for further ecumenical discussion between Orthodox and Reformed.

Reformed-Orthodox Dialogue: A brief introduction and overview

Informal ecumenical dialogue between the Reformed and Orthodox traditions occurred in the years preceding the official Reformed-Orthodox Dialogue[4] but the formal Dialogue in which Torrance was involved

---

3   See Jason R. Radcliff, *Thomas F. Torrance and the Church Fathers: A Reformed, Evangelical, and Ecumenical Reconstruction of the Patristic Tradition* (Eugene: Pickwick, 2014) for an overview and examination of Torrance and the church fathers. Torrance's unique approach to the Fathers was more than a simple reading; rather Torrance reconstructed the Fathers in light of the evangelical and Christocentric theology of the Reformation. For Torrance this looks like a synthetic combination of Irenaeus, Athanasius, Cyril, Calvin, Barth, Mackintosh, etc. and a reconstruction of their theology around the Nicene doctrine of the ὁμοούσιον τῷ Πατρί (*of one Being with the Father*).

4   See the two helpful *Memoranda,* one in each volume of *Theological Dialogue Between Orthodox and Reformed Churches* for outlines of the history surrounding the Dialogue and also for the historical precedent. Protestants and Orthodox had really been in dialogue in some form since shortly after the Reformation. On this see George Mastrantonis, *Augsburg and Constantinople: The Correspondance between the Tübingen Theologians and Patriarch Jeremiah II of Constantinople on the Augsburg Confession* (Brookline: Holy Cross Orthodox Press, 1982) for correspondence between Lutheran and Orthodox theologians in the 16th century. See in particular pages 3–20 for the history of their dialogue and correspondence.

happened between the Reformed (headed by the World Alliance of Reformed Churches) and the Orthodox (headed by the Greek Orthodox Patriarchate) in 1981, 1983, 1988, and 1990. Prior to the official Dialogue, the Reformed and Orthodox had been engaged in dialogue for some time. Correspondence, in this case a letter written by the Orthodox to the World Alliance of Reformed Churches, highlights previous dialogue, which had been transpiring since the mid-twentieth century: In North America, the World Alliance of Reformed Churches and the Standing Conference of Canonical Orthodox Bishops in the Americas had been in theological dialogue since 1968; in Eastern Europe and Russia, the World Alliance of Reformed Churches had been in Dialogue with churches connected to the Moscow Patriarchate since 1972; in Romania, the Reformed Church in Romania had been in dialogue with the Orthodox Church since 1964.[5]

According to Torrance, the motivation for the dialogue arose out of "deep theological rapport" between Torrance and Methodios Fouyas, who was the (Greek) Orthodox Archbishop of Thyateira and Great Britain at the time of the Dialogue[6] and a close friend with Torrance.[7] Notably, in many of Torrance's footnotes in his other books, Methodios appears often

---

5 See the letter in The Thomas F. Torrance Manuscript Collection. Special Collections, Princeton Seminary, Box 170.

6 There were other "major players" in the Dialogue as well e.g. George Dragas (now Professor of Patrology at Holy Cross Greek Orthodox School of Theology), a former student of Torrance and coauthor of *The Agreed Statement on the Holy Trinity* (see below for further discussion on this important document which is in many ways the "fruit" of the Dialogue), James McCord (who was the President of Princeton and President of the World Alliance of Reformed Churches at the time), and the role of Georges Florovsky (a Russian Orthodox theologian active at St. Sergius in Paris, St. Vladimir's in New York, as well as Princeton University and Harvard University) in the years leading up to the Dialogue cannot be overstated: in one of Torrance's early books he insists upon the ecumenical relevance of the occurrence that at a recent ecumenical dialogue when he discovered "Calvin's language on the lips of Professor Florovsky..." See Thomas F. Torrance, *Conflict and Agreement in the Church: Volume 1: Order & Disorder* (London: Lutterworth, 1959), 227. The present volume contains important correspondence between Torrance and Florovsky as well as critical commentary by Matthew Baker.

7 Fouyas gave Torrance the office of "honorary protopresbyter" of the Patriarchate of Alexandria. See The Thomas F. Torrance Manuscript Collection for some interesting memorabilia relating to this. Box 214 contains various pectoral crosses only given to ordained Orthodox priests and Box 202 contains a picture of Torrance wearing one of these Orthodox pectoral crosses, surrounded by what seem to be Orthodox bishops and Priests.

in support of Torrance's ideas.[8] The "theological rapport" between Fouyas and Torrance was over the Greek patristic theology as encapsulated especially in Athanasius of Alexandria and Cyril of Alexandria.[9] Whilst the Reformed proposed the Dialogue, the Orthodox responded with great enthusiasm, stating in a letter to Torrance: "We greet you in love and we received you with great honour. You represent in the most official way the large and well-respected world of the Reformed Churches. You came here with the sacred and concrete purpose to make the official proposal for the opening of the Theological Dialogue with Orthodoxy."[10]

The Reformed-Orthodox Dialogue attempted to investigate the common roots between the Reformed and Orthodox traditions on the basis of the Greek patristic theology in which both traditions are rooted and, as such, the patristic doctrines of Trinity and Christology steered the Dialogue. According to the Minutes from the meeting where the Reformed officially proposed the Dialogue, in his introductory greeting to the Orthodox Patriarchate during their official proposal for dialogue, James McCord "stressed how the Reformed feel themselves historically very close to the Orthodox in a common concern for the truth of the Apostolic Faith and for the unity of the Church in that same faith."[11] The Minutes also record that Torrance notes he established his opinion while Moderator of the General Assembly of the Church of Scotland that any Orthodox and Reformed theological dialogue should begin on the doctrine of the Trinity and move forward from there.[12] So, the Reformed

8   See Thomas F. Torrance, *The Christian Doctrine of God* (Edinburgh: T&T Clark, 1995), 80.

9   Torrance, *Theological Dialogue Between Orthodox & Reformed Churches Volume I*, x. Throughout many of his books Torrance calls for a return to "the Athanasius-Cyril axis of classical theology" as a way forward for theological unity, cutting behind divisions and distinctions which have haunted theology for centuries. See Thomas F. Torrance, *Theology in Reconciliation: Essays Towards Evangelical and Catholic Unity in East and West,* Reprint (Eugene: Wipf & Stock, 1996), 14.

10   See this letter in The Thomas F. Torrance Manuscript Collection. Special Collections, Princeton Theological Seminary Library. Box 170.

11   See the Minutes from the visit of the delegation from the World Alliance of Reformed Churches to the ecumenical patriarchate in Istanbul, July 26–30, 1979 in The Thomas F. Torrance Manuscript Collection. Special Collections, Princeton Theological Seminary Library. Box 170.

12   See the Minutes from the visit of the delegation from the World Alliance of Reformed Churches to the ecumenical patriarchate in Istanbul, July 26–30, 1979 in The Thomas F. Torrance Manuscript Collection. Special Collections, Princeton Theological Seminary Library. Box 170.

and Orthodox, spearheaded by Reformed Torrance and Orthodox Methodios, began the Reformed-Orthodox Dialogue on the basis of their common fount: the Apostolic Faith as preserved by the Greek Fathers and encapsulated in their Trinitarian and Christocentric theology.

Torrance and the inherent ecumenicity of the Reformed tradition

For Torrance, however, the impetus for the Dialogue went much deeper than "theological rapport" and shared commitments to the Trinitarian theology of the Greek Fathers. Torrance believed strongly that the Reformed tradition in which he was a part was inherently ecumenical and, as such, very much rooted in the Greek Fathers. In an attempt to categorize the Reformed tradition on the "timeline" of church developments, Torrance even argues for a similarity between Orthodox autocephalous churches[13] and the autonomous nature of the Reformed churches,[14] which according to the Official Minutes the Orthodox found very interesting indeed.[15]

As such, part of the basis for the Dialogue came from Torrance's understanding of the Reformed tradition as inherently "catholic." In Torrance's *Memorandum* published in *Theological Dialogue Between Orthodox and Reformed Churches Volume I,* Torrance stresses how the Reformed tradition never sought to be a "new" church but rather sees itself as a prophetic movement of reform within the catholic church.[16]

13 From αὐτοκεφαλία, self-heading.

14 Torrance, *Theological Dialogue Between Orthodox & Reformed Churches Volume I,* 10.

15 The Thomas F. Torrance Manuscript Collection. Special Collections, Princeton Theological Seminary Library. Box 170.

16 See also the Minutes from the visit of the delegation from the World Alliance of Reformed Churches to the ecumenical patriarchate in Istanbul, July 26–30, 1979 in Thomas F. Torrance Manuscript Collection. Special Collections, Princeton Theological Seminary Library. Box 170. Torrance says elsewhere: "The Reformation was not a movement to refound the Church, or to found a new Church; for the whole reforming movement would undoubtedly have continued within the Roman Church had it not been for the bigoted and arrogant recalcitrance of its hierarchy, which insisted in binding the movement of the Word and Spirit by the traditions of men and making it of none effect, and when that failed, in throwing it out altogether, just as the early Christians were thrown out of the synagogues and followed with maledictions and anathemas." See Torrance, *Conflict and Agreement in the Church: Volume 1,* 77.

Torrance states, "the Reformed Church is the Church reformed according to the Word of God so as to restore to it the face of the ancient Catholic and Apostolic Church."[17] At the very outset of his first *Memorandum* which he delivered at the opening of the first session of the dialogue, Torrance further articulates that the Reformed tradition "does not set out to be a new or another Church but to be a movement of reform within the One Holy Catholic and Apostolic Church of Jesus Christ . . . "[18] Torrance understands himself as a part of the Western tradition inheriting the great catholic/ecumenical tradition of the Greek Fathers and their theology. For Torrance, therefore, it is not and should not be unusual for Reformed to look to their rootedness in the Greek patristic tradition. Torrance explains that the Reformed Churches have always been guided by "classical Greek theology," the "great Alexandrian and Cappadocian theologians," the Augustinian doctrine of grace, and the Trinitarian theology of the Greek Fathers.[19]

Torrance sees the Reformed tradition rooted in the foundation of the Apostolic and Catholic Faith. According to Torrance, both the Orthodox and Reformed should embrace their own pietistic distinctiveness as developed within their respective "cultural and historical milieu,"[20] whilst simultaneously seeking to return to the theological core in which they are both rooted. For Torrance, the Reformed tradition, while being unique from Orthodoxy in many ways, is rooted in the very same catholicity.[21] Torrance felt that it was on this common basis that the two traditions could hope for rapprochement and theological agreement.

More deeply, Torrance sees a shared commitment to the substance of the theology of the Greek Fathers, making the Reformed and Orthodox traditions both ecumenical and catholic. He argues that the Reformed

---

17   Torrance, *Conflict and Agreement in the Church: Volume I*, 76.

18   Torrance, *Theological Dialogue Between Orthodox & Reformed Churches Volume I*, 3.

19   Ibid., 4. He sees the Reformer John Calvin particularly indebted to Gregory Nazianzen. See this point articulated also in Torrance, *Trinitarian Perspectives* (London: T&T Clark, 1994), 21–40.

20   Ibid., 5.10.

21   According to the Official Minutes, the Orthodox wondered how the Reformed could hold to any doctrine (the question of authority). The Reformed pointed to the Reformed emphasis on synodical and conciliar consensus. See the Minutes in The Thomas F. Torrance Manuscript Collection. Special Collections, Princeton Theological Seminary Library. Box 170.

tradition adheres to the Apostolic Faith[22] and practice[23] and contends for a way forward in ecumenicity with a focus on the truly catholic and Apostolic Deposit of Faith and *kerygma*.[24] For Torrance this means ecumenical dialogue rooted in the Greek patristic doctrines of Trinity and therein Christology.

Torrance and the Greek patristic rootedness of the Reformed churches

Important for Torrance in the Dialogue was his conviction that the Reformed church is absolutely rooted in the Greek patristic tradition. The fount of this Greek patristic rootedness can be found in what he calls the "Athanasius-Cyril axis of classical theology"[25] and in Athanasius of Alexandria whom Torrance calls "the foundation of classical theology."[26] In Torrance's *Memorandum on Orthodox and Reformed Relations* Torrance argues for the "patristic character" of Reformed theology, something which the Orthodox questioned in subsequent discussion.[27]

Torrance sees the Protestant tradition as inherently patristic. In this he follows the Protestant Reformers' understanding of their movement. Martin Luther, for example, considered the Fathers to be important "conversation partners" when doing theology.[28] Torrance is even more

22   Thomas F. Torrance, *Theological Dialogue Between Orthodox & Reformed Churches Volume I*, 6. Torrance states: "While the Reformed Churches in the sixteenth and seventeenth centuries produced catechetical and confessional formulations for the guidance of their life, teaching and proclamation of the Gospel, these were and are held only as 'secondary standards' subordinate to the Apostolic Faith as mediated through the New Testament, and to the Catholic doctrine as defined by the Apostles' and Nicene-Constantinopolitan Creeds."

23   Ibid., 8-10.

24   Ibid., 91. Torrance states: "The *kerygma* refers not merely to proclamation about Christ but to the Reality proclaimed, Jesus Christ who is personally, actively and savingly at work through the *kerygma*." See more generally pp. 91–107.

25   Thomas F. Torrance, *Theology in Reconciliation* Reprint (Eugene: Wipf & Stock, 1996), 9.

26   See Torrance's essay "Athanasius: A Study in the Foundation of Classical Theology" in *Theology in Reconciliation*, 215–256.

27   See the Official Minutes in The Thomas F. Torrance Manuscript Collection. Special Collections, Princeton Theological Seminary Library. Box 170.

28   Manfred Schulze, "Martin Luther and the Church Fathers," in *The Reception of the Church Fathers in the West: From the Carolingians to the Maurists*, ed. Irena Backus (Leiden: Brill, 2001), 613.

so in line with the Reformed theologian John Calvin in his conception of the Reformation's rootedness in the Greek patristic tradition. Calvin saw the Reformers as in line with tradition and antiquity; for Calvin, it was the Roman Catholics that had departed.[29] Calvin consistently turned to Greek Fathers such as John Chrysostom and Cyril of Alexandra both of whom he sees as exemplary theologians.[30] In addition, Calvin had great respect for the Cappadocian Fathers, especially Gregory Nazianzen[31] whom he referred to in regards to his own doctrine of the Trinity.[32] Calvin also deeply respected Hilary of Poitiers[33] and he referred to Irenaeus of Lyons throughout his writings.[34]

Furthermore, Torrance sees himself standing squarely within the classical and ecumenical Scottish tradition of theology, very much in line with ancient patristic Christianity. According to Torrance, contra the "hyper-Calvinist" stream prevalent in Scottish theology, a classical and patristic stream also exists which can be traced back to the ancient church.[35] Torrance sees both Robert Boyd[36] and John Forbes of Corse[37] as indebted to the Greek Fathers and John McLeod Campbell's emphasis upon the personal nature of the atonement as inherently patristic and evangelical.[38]

29   Anthony N. S. Lane, *John Calvin: Student of the Church Fathers* (London: T&T Clark, 1999), 33.

30   Irena Backus, *Historical Method and Confessional Identity in the Era of the Reformation (1378–1615)* (Leiden: Brill, 2003), 693.

31   Johannes van Oort, "John Calvin and the Church Fathers," in *The Reception of the Church Fathers in the West*, 691.

32   Calvin, *Institutes*, I.13.17 citing Gregory Nazianzen *Sermon on Sacred Baptism*.

33   Oort, "John Calvin and the Church Fathers," in *The Reception of the Church Fathers in the West*, 688.

34   Ibid., 685–686.

35   See Thomas F. Torrance, *Scottish Theology: From John Knox to John McLeod Cambell* (Edinburgh: T&T Clark, 1996), 66–74.

36   Ibid., 66–74. See also some correspondence between Torrance and George Dragas on this subject: The Thomas F. Torrance Manuscript Collection. Special Collections, Princeton Theological Seminary Library. Box 104.

37   Ibid., 80.

38   Ibid., 287–315.

The patristic and theological approach of Torrance to the Dialogue

In the Reformed-Orthodox Dialogue, Torrance urges for a focus upon Athanasius and Cyril, especially their emphasis on the Nicene doctrine of ὁμοούσιον contra the Cappadocian-Byzantine trajectory.[39] Torrance contends that the best method for discussion and the best approach for agreement is on the basis of Athanasian-Cyrilline theology[40] and the common roots of Alexandrian and Cappadocian theology, as well as the Conciliar Statements which these important church fathers informed.[41] Torrance recalls that in the discussions following the papers presented, everyone "kept returning to the need for a dynamic understanding of the living Triune God in the inseparability of his Being and Act."[42] Via this focus, Torrance believed the Reformed and Orthodox traditions would be able to return to their common fount and "cut behind" the theological dualism which problematically informed later developments in the Byzantine East and Augustinian West.[43] Torrance argues this will bring about theological agreement and ecumenical rapprochement between Chalcedonians and non-Chalcedonians, Orthodox and Reformed, and Roman Catholics and Evangelicals.[44] Torrance argues that both the Reformed and Orthodox need to return to their core fulcrum of the Athanasius-Cyril axis of classical theology.

Shared commitment: Christological and Trinitarian approach

In the Reformed-Orthodox Dialogue, Reformed and Orthodox agreed upon a commitment to a Trinitarian and Christocentric approach

39 Torrance, *Theological Dialogue Between Orthodox & Reformed Churches Volume II*, 5.

40 According to the Official Minutes, in the discussion, Emilianos wonders: "Is not Torrance in danger of over-absolutizing Athanasius in relation to the Cappadocians?" See The Thomas F. Torrance Manuscript Collection. Special Collections, Princeton Theological Seminary Library. Box 170.

41 Torrance, *Theological Dialogue Between Orthodox & Reformed Churches Volume I*, 11.

42 Ibid., xxiii.

43 Ibid., 11.

44 Ibid., 10–11.

to theology. In his writing related to the Dialogue Torrance argues that they must remain focused upon the Nicene ὁμοούσιον inasmuch as it is the "king-pin" of the Nicene-Constantinopolitan Creed, which Torrance believes expresses the core evangelical belief that in Jesus Christ humanity is confronted with the very self-giving and self-revealing of God as he is in himself.[45] Torrance proposes a return to the Athanasian-Cyrilline axis of theology; a commitment to which the Orthodox agreed.[46]

At the Dialogue the Reformed and Orthodox embraced the Cappadocian formula of "μία οὐσια, τρεῖς ὑπόστασεις" (one Being, three Persons).[47] However, throughout Torrance encouraged them to utilize the phrase in what he saw as a more Athanasian sense with an insistence on the unity of Persons or in his words the "perfect equality of the Father, Son and Holy Spirit, in each of whom the Godhead is complete," rather than an emphasis on the threeness of the Persons.[48] Throughout Torrance's other texts on the doctrine of the Trinity (such as *The Trinitarian Faith*[49] and *The Christian Doctrine of God*[50]) Torrance is concerned by what he sees as the Cappadocian and Byzantine division of God's οὐσια and ὑπόστασεις and God's οὐσια and ἐνέργια (energy), which he sees in nascence in the Cappadocians, only emerging in full force in the later Byzantine tradition, Gregory Palamas in particular.[51] According to Torrance, the Dialogue should therefore focus upon Athanasius' conception of the procession of the Holy Spirit from the οὐσία of the Father inasmuch as it cuts behind divisions between East and West[52] in

45   Thomas F. Torrance, *The Incarnation: Ecumenical Studies in the Nicene-Constantinopolitan Creed A.D. 381* (Edinburgh: Handsel Press, 1981), xi–xv. The Orthodox indeed agreed that this is a lynchpin. See pp.1–15 of the same book.

46   Torrance, *Theological Dialogue Between Orthodox & Reformed Churches Volume II*, 3–13.

47   Torrance, *Theological Dialogue Between Orthodox & Reformed Churches Volume I*, 79 where he refers to Athanasius, Gregory Nazianzen, Cyril of Alexandria, and John of Damascus.

48   Torrance, *Theological Dialogue Between Orthodox & Reformed Churches Volume I*, 87. Indeed, the "coinherent Trinitarian relations" (see p. 6–7) or "being in internal relations" (see p. 20).

49   Thomas F. Torrance, *The Trinitarian Faith* (Edinburgh: T&T Clark, 1988).

50   Thomas F. Torrance, *The Christian Doctrine of God* (Edinburgh: T&T Clark, 1996).

51   See e.g. Torrance, *The Trinitarian Faith*, 38–39.

52   Torrance, *Theological Dialogue Between Orthodox & Reformed Churches Volume I*, xi.

its important emphasis upon the dynamic unity of the three Persons of the Godhead rather than the unity or the Trinity only.[53]

According to Torrance, the Reformed and Orthodox concluded at the Dialogue that they agreed "on the content of the doctrine [of the Trinity]."[54] In many ways the "fruit" of the Dialogue was their *Agreed Statement on the Holy Trinity*[55] which they produced to highlight this agreement. Torrance and his former student George Dragas, drafted this important text.[56] After examining and reflecting upon key texts such as Athanasius' *Ad Serapionem*, Basil's *On the Holy Spirit*, Gregory Nazianzen's *Theological Orations*, Calvin's *Institutes* and Karl Barth's *Church Dogmatics*,[57] as well as the papers presented at the dialogues, the Reformed and Orthodox produced *The Agreed Statement on the Holy Trinity*. The key points of the *Agreed Statement* are: (1) The centrality of God's revelation of himself as Trinity; (2) the distinctiveness of the three Trinitarian hypostases; (3) the view that the order of hypostases in the Trinity begins with the Father who has monarchia; (4) yet the Godhead is undivided and One; (6) the perichoretic mutual indwelling of all members of the Trinity; (7) the affirmation of the formula "μία οὐσια, τρεῖς ὑπόστασεις" and; (8) the assertion that the doctrine of the Trinity is true and actual and indeed the core of the Apostolic and Catholic Faith.[58] This hugely important document represents a major achievement in

53   Thomas F. Torrance, *Trinitarian Perspectives: Toward Doctrinal Agreement* (Edinburgh T&T Clark, 1994), 13–20, especially 18–20.

54   Torrance, *Theological Dialogue Between Orthodox & Reformed Churches Volume II*, xxi.

55   Torrance, *Theological Dialogue Between Orthodox & Reformed Churches Volume I*, 219–226; Torrance, *Trinitarian Perspectives*, 115–122.

56   The Thomas F. Torrance Manuscript Collection in Princeton contains some fascinating correspondence between Torrance and Dragas as they worked to complete the *Agreed Statement*.

57   Torrance, *Theological Dialogue Between Orthodox & Reformed Churches Volume I*, xxvii.

58   See further discussion on this in Jason R. Radcliff, "T. F. Torrance in light of Stephen Holmes' Critique of contemporary Trinitarian Thought," *Evangelical Quarterly* 86.1: 21–38 and Jason R Radcliff, "T. F. Torrance and the Patristic Consensus on the Doctrine of the Trinity" in *The Doctrine of the Trinity Reconsidered: Essays in Response to Stephen R. Holmes,* ed. T. A. Noble and J. S. Sexton (Milton Keynes: Paternoster, 2015), 68-81. See also Jason Radcliff, "Thomas F. Torrance's Conception of the *Consensus Patrum* on the Doctrine of Pneumatology" in *Studia Patristica LXIX*, ed. Markus Vincent and Allen Brent (Leuven: Peeters, 2013), 417–433 for more on Torrance on the Pneumatology of *The Agreed Statement*.

ecumenical theology inasmuch as it presents a doctrine of the Trinity which preserves both Greek and Latin commitments to the Trinity of Persons (Greek) and unity of Being (Latin) in God the Holy Trinity.[59]

Divergence: Which Fathers?

On the basis of the Trinitarian and Christocentric conversation and in light of their shared commitment to the Greek Fathers the Reformed and Orthodox came also to realize their differences in theology which, in large part, stemmed from differences in appropriation of the Fathers. In short, the Reformed distinctive was a Word-based (Christocentric) approach whereas the Orthodox distinctive was a Church-based (synthetic) approach. The Reformed, accordingly, had "favorites" which they emphasized whereas the Orthodox attempted to emphasize the whole tradition as a synthetic whole.

For Torrance, the Cappadocians and later Byzantines departed from what he saw as the Athanasius-Cyrilline Christocentric approach to theology. The task of the Reformed-Orthodox dialogue, as Torrance saw it, was to return to the common evangelical foundation. Torrance sees the Cappadocian development as a move away from the axis of Athanasius and Cyril.[60] Questions arose throughout the Dialogue concerning whether God interacts with the world primarily by means of his uncreated energies (the Orthodox view) or in Christ (the Reformed view).[61] Torrance argues that perhaps the essence/energies distinction was taken too seriously because of Vladimir Lossky's interpretation of Gregory Palamas. Torrance considers that stressing the theology of Palamas (or, at least, Lossky's reading of it) is unhelpful because of Palamas' Neo-Platonic dualism, something which Torrance calls a sort of "eastern Augustinianism."[62]

---

59   See Torrance, *Trinitarian Perspectives* for both *The Agreed Statement* itself as well as some of Torrance's reflections upon its significance.

60   Torrance, *Theological Dialogue Between Orthodox & Reformed Churches Volume II*, 13–21.

61   See e.g. the account in the Official Minutes regarding the discussion following Emilianos' paper. The Thomas F. Torrance Manuscript Collection. Special Collections, Princeton Theological Seminary Library. Box 170.

62   The Thomas F. Torrance Manuscript Collection. Special Collections, Princeton Theological Seminary Library. Box 170. Torrance's issue with the essence/energies distinction is that it ultimately makes God unknowable as he is in himself. Torrance

The Official Minutes from the John Knox International Reformed Centre Geneva 15–18 February 1981 highlight much discussion regarding authority for the Reformed and Orthodox traditions. In the discussion the Reformed emphasize an ongoing consensus of *doctrine* whereas the Orthodox emphasize an ongoing consensus of *figures*.

The Reformed approach reveals a commitment to a Word-based and Christocentric appropriation of the Greek Fathers and a turn to their consensus of doctrine. The Minutes record heated discussion following Emilanos' paper (which emphasized God's interaction with the world through his energies). In critique of the essence/energies distinction, Torrance states: "here we must be aware of the apostolic nature of the church, and the obedience of the Church to the truth of the Apostles. That is why the Fathers were not infrequently criticized and corrected by the Councils. We have to note the magisterial authority of the Councils vis-à-vis the Fathers."[63] Accordingly, throughout the Minutes Torrance consistently insists upon a return to the Christocentric theology of Athanasius.

In contrast, the Orthodox approach to the Fathers in the Dialogue highlights a more synthetic "church-based" theology. In response to Torrance's critiques by means of a utilization of the theology of Athanasius in the paper's thrust, Chrysostomos (of the Orthodox) states: "of course the Fathers could be cited in this direction but one must attempt to grasp the totality of the consensus patrum"[64] and Emilianos states: "Is not Torrance in danger of over-absolutizing Athanasius in relation to the Cappadocians?"[65] Rather than pitting one Father against another, the Orthodox consistently suggest a more synthetic approach whereby theology is done by means of the whole church tradition. Along these lines the Orthodox mention the importance of the "line of continuity"

sees this basic dualism asserted in Gregory of Nyssa, John of Damascus, Thomas Aquinas, Peter Lombard, and Gregory Palamas, et al.

63   See the Minutes from the John Knox International Reformed Centre Geneva 15–18 Feb. 1981 contained in The Thomas F. Torrance Manuscript Collection. Special Collections, Princeton Theological Seminary Library. Box 170.

64   See the Minutes from the John Knox International Reformed Centre Geneva 15–18 Feb. 1981 contained in The Thomas F. Torrance Manuscript Collection. Special Collections, Princeton Theological Seminary Library. Box 170.

65   Ibid.

for the *Consensus Patrum*. Chrysostomos states: "There is a magisterial element in the weight of tradition."[66]

Reformed: Cappadocians or really Zizioulas?

When the Reformed-Orthodox Dialogue is read afresh and explored in the 21st century, it becomes clear that "there is more than meets the eye." Some key theological points under consideration at the Dialogue suggest certain activity going on "behind the scenes." As such, perhaps some of these points should be reconsidered today.

Led by Torrance the Cappadocian Fathers (especially Basil the Great) come under certain critique by the Reformed at the Dialogue. Torrance consistently urges for a return to the "Athanasius-Cyril axis" and bifurcates this from the Cappadocians. Torrance contends that the Cappadocians departed from a more Athanasian and dynamic conception of the doctrine of the Trinity. The Cappadocians are often pitted against Athanasius and Cyril by Torrance, on the doctrine of the Trinity in particular.[67] By contrast, current theological and patrological scholarship tends towards viewing the Cappadocians and Athanasius and indeed more broadly the Greek and Latin Fathers as complementary to one another if not basically identical on the doctrine of the Trinity.[68]

It is notable, however, that Torrance's critique of the Cappadocians was not prevalent in his earlier writings.[69] Indeed, this critique really only becomes a major part of Torrance's theology in the 1980s and during the Reformed-Orthodox Dialogue, arising in the publications surrounding the Dialogue as well as in *Trinitarian Faith*.[70] Torrance's critique makes far more sense if one is aware of a deeper debate going on between

---

66   Ibid.

67   For Torrance the Cappadocians, especially Basil, divide God's Being from God's Persons in a way that Athanasius and Cyril and their conception of God's Being as dynamically Trinitarian do not.

68   See e.g. some recent books in this trajectory: Lewis Ayres, *Nicaea and Its Legacy* (Oxford: Oxford University Press, 2006) and Stephen R. Holmes, *The Holy Trinity: Understanding God's Life* (Milton Keynes: Paternoster, 2012).

69   For example, in *Theology in Reconstruction* and *Theology in Reconciliation*.

70   Notably, Torrance considered this book to be directly relevant to the Reformed-Orthodox Dialogue. See Torrance's comments on this in a letter written to Demetrius I, the Ecumenical Patriarch dated 1988 contained in The Thomas F. Torrance Manuscript Collection. Special Collections, Princeton Theological Seminary Library. Box 172.

Torrance and John Zizioulas, his former colleague at New College, Edinburgh.[71] Zizioulas' emphasis upon the Cappadocians and their encapsulation of "social Trinitarianism" which focuses upon the threeness of God's Persons has been critiqued by recent scholarship as being more "Zizioulian" and existential than Cappadocian and patristic.[72] Torrance's published critiques in the Dialogue and elsewhere, while not mentioning Zizioulas, are clearly critiques of Zizioulas' reading of the Cappadocians and thus are probably more about the 1980s than the 380s.[73] Torrance's openness in the Dialogue (and in others of his published books) to many elements in the Cappadocians would suggest that he does not dismiss the Cappadocians entirely; rather Torrance is concerned by certain emphases in their theology which were being focused upon[74] during his own time by Zizioulas.

Therefore in light of recent scholarship and building off the ground laid by the Dialogue, perhaps Reformed and Orthodox today ought to reconsider some of Torrance's bifurcations. Perhaps Athanasius, Cyril, and the Cappadocians (and more broadly East and West, Greek and Latin) offer more complementary theological approaches, particularly

---

71   The connection goes even deeper: In a Draft Letter from Torrance to the center of the Ecumenical Patriarchate in Phanar (a term from the Greek φανάριον, which is the name of the neighborhood where the Patriarchate is located and used as shorthand for the Patriarchate), Istanbul dated March 17th, 1988 Torrance states ". . . it was I who brought John Zizioulas to Edinburgh and thus introduced him to our Church and theological life in Great Britain, and have supported him in every way I could . . . " George Dragas even went so far as to call Torrance Zizioulas' "greatest benefactor" (for this see a letter from George Dragas written to Torrance dated March 22nd, 1988 contained in The Thomas F. Torrance Manuscript Collection. Special Collections, Princeton Theological Seminary Library. Box 170).

72   See e.g. Holmes, *Holy Trinity*, 12–16; 145–146. See also Radcliff, "Thomas F. Torrance's Conception of the *Consensus Patrum* on the Doctrine of Pneumatology," 431–432. Torrance himself accuses Zizioulas of an "existentialising interpretation of the Greek Fathers." For this quote see a Draft Letter from Torrance to the center of the Ecumenical Patriarchate in Phanar, Istanbul dated March 17th, 1988 in The Thomas F. Torrance Manuscript Collection. Special Collections, Princeton Theological Seminary Library. Box 170.

73   See Radcliff, "T. F. Torrance in light of Stephen Holmes's Critique of contemporary Trinitarian Thought," 32–33 and Radcliff, "T. F. Torrance and the Patristic Consensus on the Doctrine of the Trinity" for more on this point.

74   Perhaps "over-absolutized" would be an even better term, to use the language of Emilianos.

on the doctrine of the Trinity, than was once thought. Perhaps they could actually be considered to be in line with one another.[75]

Reformed: Palamas or really Lossky?

The Reformed, again led by Torrance, heavily critique Gregory Palamas and the essence/energies distinction so central to Orthodox theology. Palamas is critiqued for holding to a theological dualism which divides God's Acts from God's Being.[76] Torrance understands this to undermine the basic theological point, preserved by the Nicene *homoousion*, that what God is to us he really is in himself.

Torrance sees in Gregory Palamas an unhappy distinction between God's essence and energies.[77] In the Dialogue Torrance depicts Athanasius and Palamas as intrinsically opposed to one another in basic theology on this point.[78] Perhaps an untitled manuscript Torrance preserved in his personal collection influenced Torrance's reading of Gregory Palamas.[79] In this manuscript, the author argues that Palamas replaced the Athanasian emphasis on salvation via Christ's vicarious humanity with salvation by means of God's uncreated energies. Related to this reading of Palamas, Dorothea Wendebourg argues that Gregory Palamas essentially undid Trinitarian theology by conceiving of three tiers in God: οὐσία, ὑποσάστεις, and ἐνέργεια, thereby making God unknowable

75   However, the current trend of Ayers, Holmes, etc., is perhaps too overly synthetic and flattens out real distinctions between the Greek and Latin patristic traditions. A via media between Torrance and the new trajectory is perhaps more correct: there are real distinctions between Greek and Latin patristic theology but these differences are complementary rather than contradictory.

76   See e.g. the Thomas F. Torrance Manuscript Collection. Special Collections, Princeton Theological Seminary Library. Box 170. Torrance believes the essence/ energies distinction makes God unknowable in himself.

77   See Torrance, *The Trinitarian Faith*, 38–39, especially footnote 69 on p. 38. See also *Theology in Reconciliation*, 252.

78   Torrance, *Theological Dialogue Between Orthodox & Reformed Churches Volume I*, 11. The Orthodox suggest that Torrance over-absolutizes Athanasius against the Cappadocians. See the Minutes in The Thomas F. Torrance Manuscript Collection. Special Collections, Princeton Theological Seminary Library. Box 170.

79   See The Thomas F. Torrance Manuscript Collection. Special Collections, Princeton Theological Seminary Library. Box 198. However, the importance of the presence of this paper in Torrance's collection should not be overemphasized; judging from the great mass of correspondence, receipts, and handwritten notes in the Manuscript Collection, Torrance seemed to save almost everything!

in himself.[80] Views along these lines seem to have been the accepted scholarly consensus by at least non-Orthodox theological scholarship during Torrance's time. Given this account of Gregory Palamas' essence/ energies distinction, of course Torrance would have problems with the ostensible dualism.

Notably, the Official Minutes, however, bring to light some very interesting discussion which indicates that perhaps Torrance's problem was rather more with Vladimir Lossky (and his reading of Palamas in particular) than Gregory Palamas himself. In a discussion in 1983, Torrance suggests that the essence/energies distinction, as understood during his own time, seemed to be more "Losskian" than Palamite.[81] Regrettably, Torrance did not engage Palamas directly in his published texts but only the Palamas of Lossky. However, the discussion at the Dialogue indicates Torrance did not take issue with Palamas so much as with Lossky's reading of Palamas.[82]

Reformed and Orthodox could perhaps revisit the role of Gregory Palamas in the *Consensus Patrum* as they engage one another in ecumenical dialogue today. Palamas is absolutely central to the Orthodox in theological thinking[83] and his essence/energies distinction arguably has much from which Reformed can learn. For example, according to the Orthodox theologian John Meyendorff, for Palamas, God interacts with the world personally.[84] Notably, in his defense of the essence/ energies distinction, Palamas counters natural theology in ways much akin to Torrance.[85] Palamas' insistence on knowledge of God and

80   See Dorothea Wendebourg, "From the Cappadocian Fathers to Gregory Palamas: The Defeat of Trinitarian Theology," *Studia Patristica* 17.1 (1982): 194–9. Wendebourg's critique is substantially similar.

81   See The Thomas F. Torrance Manuscript Collection. Special Collections, Princeton Theological Seminary Library. Box 170. Torrance says that Lossky "injected ideas from Boehme and Eckhart into Palamas."

82   Matthew Baker also argues for this point. See Matthew Baker, "The Place of St. Irenaeus of Lyons in Historical and Dogmatic Theology According to Thomas F. Torrance," *Participatio: The Journal of the Thomas F. Torrance Theological Fellowship*, Volume II: 42.

83   See the essay entitled "Gregory Palamas and the Tradition of the Fathers" in Georges Florovsky, *Bible, Church, Tradition: An Eastern Orthodox View*, Collected Works of Georges Florovsky: V. 1 (Belmont: Nordland, 1972)

84   See John Meyendorff, *Introduction A l'étude de Grégoire Palamas* (Paris: Patristica Sorbonensia, 1959). See especially pp. 195–256 and 279–310.

85   Gregory Palamas, *Defense of those who practice Hesychasm*, II.3.68. See Jean Meyendorff, *Grégoire Palamas: Défense des Saints hésychastes: Introducion, texte*

union with God through God's energies could be read as an attempt to objectively root knowledge of God as well as salvation. Throughout his writings Palamas asserts God's personal presence in his energies[86] as well as the Christocentric[87] and enhypostatic nature of the energies.[88] This is arguably another way of emphasizing the important Reformed insistence upon the "divine initiative" in salvation and revelation, to use the beautiful language of Torrance's beloved teacher H. R. Mackintosh in his splendid little book.[89]

Orthodox: Augustine or really "Augustinianism"?

In the Dialogue Torrance accuses Augustine of neoplatonic dualism.[90] More broadly, many Orthodox theologians tend to be strongly allergic to Augustine.[91] These Orthodox theologians hold Augustine responsible for "most of what went wrong with the west in the middle ages . . . "[92] Indeed, Augustine and Augustinianism were not discussed in

critique, traduction et notes (Louvain: Spicilegium Sacrum Lovaniense, 1959) for the critical edition of this text and Gregory Palamas, The Triads, trans. Gendle and ed. Meyendorff, for the English translation of a selection from Meyendorff's critical edition. See also Gregory Palamas, The One Hundred and Fifty Chapters, 26–29. See Robert E. Sinkewicz, Saint Gregory Palamas: The One Hundred and Fifty Chapters (Toronto: The Pontifical Institute of Mediaeval Studies, 1988).

86   Gregory Palamas, Defense of those who practice Hesychasm, III.2.7 and The One Hundred and Fifty Chapters, 109ff.

87   See e.g. Gregory Palamas, Defense of those who practice Hesychasm, III.1.35.

88   See e.g. Gregory Palamas, Defense of those who practice Hesychasm, II.3.8. See also III.1.9.

89   See H. R. Mackintosh, The Divine Initiative (London: Student Christian Movement, 1921).

90   See e.g. Torrance's comments in Minutes from the Orthodox Reformed Consultation, Orthodox Centre of the Ecumenical Patriarchate, Chambesy, Geneva, 6–11, March 1983 in The Thomas F. Torrance Manuscript Collection. Special Collections, Princeton Theological Seminary Library, Box 170.

91   See e.g. John Romanides, The Ancestral Sin (Ridgewood: Zephyr, 2008); Franks, Romans, Feudalism, and Doctrine (Brookline: Holy Cross Orthodox Press, 1981); Christos Yannaras, Elements of Faith: An Introduction to Orthodox Theology, trans. K. Schram (Edinburgh: T&T Clark, 1991); Orthodox and the West (Brookline: Holy Cross Orthodox Press, 2006).

92   See Aristotle Papanikolaou and George E. Demacopoulos, "Augustine and the Orthodox: 'The West' in the East," in Orthodox Readings of Augustine, ed. Aristotlte Papanikolaou and George E. Demacopoulos (Crestwood: St Vladimir's Seminary Press, 2008), 33.

great detail in the Dialogue; after all, they were turning to the classical theology of Athanasius and Cyril. Nonetheless, Augustinian theology is generally used negatively in the Dialogue.[93]

However, current scholarship on Augustine now tends to avoid viewing Augustine in light of neoplatonism and in contrast with Greek patristic theology.[94] Indeed, theological scholarship is tending towards seeing Augustine and the Cappadocians and, indeed, more broadly the Greek Fathers and the Latin Fathers to be in line with one another theologically, particularly on the doctrine of the Trinity (the doctrine on which they have most often been pitted against one another).[95]

It is key to note that in the Dialogue Torrance was mainly critical of "Augustinian thought" rather than Augustine himself.[96] Elsewhere in the Torrance corpus Torrance critiques Augustinian thought for dividing God from his Word and critiques the Latin tradition for emphasizing the juridical aspect of the atonement dividing God from Christ.[97] Notably, Torrance critiques Roman Catholicism and Federal Calvinism for doing something similar.[98] On the other hand, Torrance actually sees Augustine as essentially Greek in his doctrine of the Trinity.[99] Herein, Torrance was

---

93   See e.g. the Minutes in The Thomas F. Torrance Manuscript Collection. Special Collections, Princeton Theological Seminary Library. Box 170. Palamas and the essence/energies distinction is delineated as "eastern Augustinianism." This was not a compliment!

94   Holmes, *Holy Trinity,* especially 144–146. See e.g. Ayres, *Nicaea and Its Legacy* and *Augustine and the Trinity* (Cambridge: Cambridge University Press, 2010); Khaled Anatolios, *Retrieving Nicaea: The Development and Meaning of Trinitarian Doctrine* (Grand Rapids: Baker, 2011); John M. Rist, *Augustine: Ancient Thought Baptized* (New York: Cambridge University Press, 1994); Michel René Barnes, "Rereading Augustine's Theology of the Trinity" in *The Trinity: An Interdisciplinary Symposium on the Trinity,* ed. Stephen T. Davis, Daniel Kendall and Gerald O'Collins (Oxford: Oxford University Press, 1999); *Orthodox Readings of Augustine* ed. by Aristotle Papanikalou and George E. Demacopoulos (Crestwood: St. Vladimir's Seminary Press, 2008).

95   See T. A. Noble, *Holy Trinity: Holy People* (Eugene: Pickwick, 2013), 215–217.

96   See, e.g., Thomas F. Torrance, *Gospel, Church, and Ministry,* ed. Jock Stein (Eugene: Pickwick 2011), 209 and Torrance, *Theological Dialogue Between Orthodox & Reformed Churches Volume I,* 12.

97   See e.g. "Karl Barth and the Latin Heresy," *Scottish Journal of Theology* 39, no. 4 (January 1, 1986), 470–479.

98   See e.g. *Theology in Reconciliation,* 9–10 and Torrance's Introduction to *The School of Faith: The Catechisms of the Reformed Church* (London: James Clarke, 1959), xvi–xxi.

99   See Torrance, *Trinitarian Perspectives,* 22.

ahead of his time considering the prevalence of the so called "de Régnon thesis."[100] Today as East and West engage in dialogue on the doctrine of the Trinity, as Tom Noble states, "Torrance's Trinitarian theology holds out the best hope of combining the concerns for divine Unity with the concerns of the social Trinitarians."[101]

Perhaps, then, Augustine should not be swept away with critiques of Augustinianism. Both East and West, indeed Orthodox, Protestant, and Catholic are turning to Augustine as a Father to be revered from whom much can be learned. Perhaps as Reformed and Orthodox engage in Dialogue today Augustine might be reconsidered as a Father of great merit and one who adds much to further theological conversation. Whereas both the Reformed (at least Torrance) and the Orthodox were apprehensive about Augustinian thought in the Dialogue, Reformed and Orthodox today might turn towards utilization of Augustine and Augustinian theology in ecumenical dialogue.

Orthodox: Synthetic or really neo-palamite?

Throughout the Dialogue, the Orthodox argue for a synthetic reading of the tradition. As highlighted above, Torrance and the Reformed are accused of emphasizing "select theologians" over others. This critique is surely valid and Torrance is open about his emphasis upon the "Athanasius-Cyril axis of classical theology"[102] and Athanasius, "the foundation of classical theology."[103] Indeed, Torrance probably could have been more synthetic in his reading of theological history.

Yet, are the Orthodox equally as selective in their reading of theological history? Throughout the Dialogue, they insist upon reading Athanasius and Cyril through the lens of the Cappadocians and, even more so, through the lens of Gregory Palamas. This is generally consistent with the Orthodox approach to reading the Fathers.[104]

---

100 On the sharp distinction between Greek (Cappadocian) Triadology, which focuses on the threeness of the Persons in God, and of Latin (Augustinian) Triadology, which focuses on the oneness of the Being of God, see Théodore de Régnon, *Études de théologie positive sur la Sainte Trinité* (Paris: Retaux, 1898).

101 Noble, *Holy Trinity: Holy People*, 215 fn. 41.

102 Torrance, *Theology in Reconciliation*, 14.

103 Torrance, *Theology in Reconstruction*, 215–266.

104 See e.g. Florovsky's essay: "Gregory Palamas and the Tradition of the Fathers" in his book *Bible, Church, Tradition*. See also *Augustine and Orthodoxy* for a collection

It is probably not unfair to suggest that every reader of the Fathers has a lens through which they view them, typically consisting of a small handful of select theologians.[105] This is not to approve of subjective readings of the theological tradition but simply to say everyone has their favorites. Here, perhaps the Reformed-Dialogue highlights how all traditions could learn to read the Fathers more synthetically whilst also accepting that it is okay to have favorites.

Conclusion

Torrance and the Reformed-Orthodox Dialogue have much from which the contemporary theological conversation can learn. The irenic and gracious approach of both the Reformed and Orthodox is notable as well as their commitment to the Trinitarian theology of the Greek Fathers. However, as noted above, differences do exist and these should not be dismissed.

A major point that must be considered is: how representative is Torrance of the Reformed tradition in his return to the Greek Fathers? As explored above, Torrance is in line with the Reformers, especially John Calvin, in his emphasis upon the Trinitarian theology of the Greek Fathers. However, it is true that despite this historical precedent, commitment to the Greek Fathers is all too uncommon amongst Protestants.[106] Yet, despite Torrance's unfortunate uniqueness compared to contemporary Protestantism, he is consistent with the Reformers. As such, his example is one to be upheld as a helpful "pointer" towards Protestantism's roots and the perspective of the early Protestants who saw themselves as preserving the face of the ancient church in response to the medieval Roman Catholic tradition which had in large part departed.

Torrance and the Reformed-Orthodox Dialogue are seriously underutilized in the current scholarly conversation on the doctrine of the Trinity. As highlighted above, the current trend is to see East and

of essays by Orthodox theologians. Generally, Augustine is critiqued most often for not holding to the essence/energies distinction of Gregory Palamas.

105   See Jason R. Radcliff, "T. F. Torrance and the *Consensus Patrum*: A Reformed, Evangelical, and Ecumenical Reconstruction of the Church Fathers," PhD Thesis, the University of Edinburgh, 2013, 9–88 for discussion of the selective reading of Protestants, Roman Catholics, and Eastern Orthodox.

106   See further K. J. Stewart, "Evangelicalism and Patristic Christianity: 1517 to the Present," *Evangelical Quarterly* 80 (2008).

West as complementary to one another on the doctrine of the Trinity. As explored above, the Reformed-Orthodox Dialogue proceeded on the basis of their reading of the Greek patristic doctrine of the Trinity, which is in many ways a dynamic combination of the doctrine of the Trinity in the East (emphasis on God's Persons) and West (emphasis on God's Being), as traditionally bifurcated by the "de Régnon thesis." As such, Torrance, the Reformed-Orthodox Dialogue, and, in particular, *The Agreed Statement on the Holy Trinity* should be much more widely utilized in this conversation.[107] The Reformed-Orthodox Dialogue has already said much of what is being said by the contemporary conversation and *The Agreed Statement on the Holy Trinity* offers an accessible and brief document capturing many of the basic points current theological scholarship is making. In the contemporary discussion, Torrance and the Reformed-Orthodox Dialogue have much to offer and should therefore play a driving role.

In the final analysis, Torrance and the Reformed-Orthodox Dialogue bequeath to contemporary ecumenical dialogue and theological thought seeking to be truly catholic an approach that is centralized upon the Trinitarian and Christocentric theology of the Greek Fathers. This positively tethered approach offers a basis that has already proven fruitful and will no doubt continue to serve future generations of ecumenical theology, should they wisely turn to Torrance and the Reformed-Orthodox Dialogue.

---

107   See e.g. two recent books with ecumenical slants: Holmes, *The Holy Trinity* and Edward Siecienski, *The Filioque: History of a Doctrinal Controversy* (Oxford: Oxford University Press, 2010). Both books are about the patristic doctrine of the Trinity and contain chapters on the 20th century; neither discusses Torrance.

Part II

Essays Patristic and Constructive

Chapter 4

T. F. Torrance as Interpreter of St. Athanasius

Vladimir Cvetković

Every student of Maximus the Confessor, especially if interested in the saint's doctrines of the Logos and *logoi* or of the Mystery of Christ, would be delighted to read Thomas F. Torrance's account of Athanasius of Alexandria. This is due in no small part to the fact that these doctrines, which are considered by the current Maximian scholarship as lonely meteorites in the sky of patristic thought, seem to appear already in the works of Athanasius. Andrew Louth, a former student of Torrance, has described Maximus as an heir of the Alexandrian Christological tradition of Athanasius and Cyril,[1] the tradition to which T. F. Torrance refers as the "Athanasius-Cyril axis" of Greek patristic theology.[2] Maximus was clearly indebted to the Alexandrians in their understanding of the Incarnation as the Son of God assuming a human nature and living a human life. However, this strand of Byzantine theology, dominant from the sixth

---

1 Andrew Louth, *Maximus the Confessor* (London: Routledge, 1996), 27.

2 Thomas F. Torrance, *Theology in Reconciliation* (Grand Rapids: Eerdmans, 1975), 9.

century onward, did not always fully exploit ideas developed by Athanasius in his earliest works *Contra Gentes* and *De Incarnatione Verbi*. For Torrance these works were crucial:[3]

> For they broke new ground and put forward a new scientific method in showing how a conjunctive and synthetic mode of thought could penetrate into the intrinsic subject-matter of theology with positive results: in disclosing the organic way in which creation and redemption are to be understood from a point of central reference (or *skopos*) in the Incarnation of the Word or Son of God, and in developing an intelligible structure of understanding reaching back to a creative centre in God, which throws an integrating light upon all theological relations and connections.[4]

These two major contributions of Athanasius may be easily transposed to ideas found three centuries later in Maximus. First, for both Athanasius and Maximus the Incarnation is a point of central reference for understanding creation and deification. Second, the development of an intelligible structure of understanding is dependent upon the creative center in God, evident in Athanasius' intrinsic rationality of the created order and in Maximus' hierarchy of *logoi* of creation and their link with the Logos. The third point of convergence between Athanasius and Maximus derives from the application of the aforementioned rational capacities to the interpretation of Holy Scripture. According to Torrance, and similar to Maximus' view, Athanasius holds that the relationship between the Logos of God and the *logoi* of the Scripture is discerned through engagement in rational exegesis, which is in conformity with "the speaking and acting of God upon us in Jesus Christ."[5]

The aim of the present essay is not to prove the impact of Athanasius on Maximus, but rather, in line with Torrance's intention, to elucidate the role of Athanasius in developing an overall theology of

3 According to the testimonies of Torrance's former student George D. Dragas, Torrance considered Athanasius' *De Incarnatione* one of the three most important books for his theology students to read. The other two books were Anselm's *Cur Deus Homo* and Kierkegaard's *Philosophical Fragments*.

4 Thomas F. Torrance, "Athanasius: Foundations of Classical Theology," in *Theology in Reconciliation*, 256. Also reprinted in Thomas F. Torrance, *Divine Meaning: Studies in Patristic Hermeneutics* (Edinburgh: T&T Clark, 1995), 219.

5 Thomas F. Torrance, "The Hermeneutics of Athanasius," in *Divine Meaning: Studies in Patristic Hermeneutics*, 234.

reconciliation. Yet the reference to Maximus is pertinent for at least two reasons. First, it seems that Maximus' theology, more than the theology of any other later Greek or Latin author, embodies the Alexandrine Christological tradition of Athanasius and Cyril, which was so crucial for Torrance. Second, the recent developments of Maximian scholarship prove the reconciling capacity of his theology, not only in the ecumenical context, but also in the broader context of the whole creation. Thus, it is in accordance with Maximus' major claim that the incarnation of the Logos is to be found in threefold form (in the creation, in the Scripture, and in the Person of Jesus Christ)[6] that we intend to explore Torrance's interpretation of the thought of Athanasius.

The Peculiarity of Torrance's Reception of Athanasius

Before pursuing further, it would be pertinent to shed some light on the context in which Torrance employs the theology of Athanasius. The reception of Athanasius in modern scholarship is far from being unanimous. The tendencies to lionize Athanasius so evident in the nineteenth century theological reception of the Alexandrine bishop, found especially in the works of Johann Adam Möhler and John Henry Newman,[7] were replaced by images of Athanasius as a manipulative politician,[8] or even a rogue,[9] in the twentieth century.[10] The reception of Athanasius' Christology, a central subject for Torrance, is mostly seen from the perspective of later developments. According to these views the significance of the humanity of Christ especially was undervalued. Two important Christological accounts, Aloys Grillmeier's in *Christ in Christian Tradition* and Richard Hanson's in *The Search for the Christian Doctrine of God*,[11] follow the twentieth century trend of the vilification

---

6   *Amb.* 7, 91:1084CD; *Amb.* 33, 1285C-1288A.

7   J. A. Möhler, *Athanasius der Grosse* (Mainz: Kupferberg, 1827); J. H. Newman, *Arians of the Fourth Century* (London: Rivington, 1833).

8   Eduard Schwartz, *Gesammelte Schriften 3: Zur Geschichte des Athanasius* (Berlin: de Gruyter, 1959).

9   R. Klein, *Constantius II. und die christliche Kirche* (Darmstadt: Wissenschaftliche Buchgesellschaft, 1977).

10   Joseph T. Lienhard, "The 'Arian' Controversy: Some Categories Reconsidered," *Theological Studies* 48 (1987): 416n3.

11   Aloys Grillmeier, *Christ in Christian Tradition* (New York: Sheed & Ward, 1975), 308–29; Richard P. C. Hanson, *The Search for the Christian Doctrine of God:*

of Athanasius. They debunk Athanasius' Christology with the same accusation that he underestimated Christ's human agency. In his analysis of Athanasius on the human soul in Christ, Grillmeier argues for the deficiency of Athanasius' view of Christ's humanity, in that the Logos was deprived of Christ's inner experiences such as anguish and ignorance.[12] And though Hanson admits that Athanasius in his *Tomos ad Antiochenos* 7 and *Ep. ad Epictetum* teaches that Christ possesses a human soul, he mostly relies on Grillmeier's portrayal of Athanasius' Christology based on the saint's refusal to acknowledge human mind and soul in Jesus.[13] Hanson concludes that one does not have to go as far as Harnack, who argued that Athanasius' Christology erases every feature of the historical Jesus of Nazareth;[14] instead he portrays the Logos as taking on himself "ignorant flesh" in order to accomplish redemption, just as an astronaut puts on a space-suit to operate in outer space where there is no air[15]

Torrance's approach to Athanasius is completely different from those of Grillmeier and Hanson. This is due especially to his vision of the Alexandrine bishop as a severe opponent of every cosmological and epistemological dualism in the doctrine of Christ. For Torrance, a return to the obsolete categories of *Logos-sarx* versus *Logos-anthropos* Christologies, or "body" versus "flesh," would not serve to express the proper Christological position while combating Gnosticism and docetism, but would only lead one to lapse back into dualism.[16] Torrance provides convincing evidences that the interpretation of the Athanasian notions of human soul and mind or the "ignorance of the flesh" offered by Grillmeier and Hanson are erroneous, as Charles S. Twombly has also demonstrated.[17] Although in Torrance's view the claim that Christ lacked a rational soul and mind is so excessively distorted that it needs no refutation, he nevertheless touches on this issue in order to prove that the Christ of Athanasius is not deprived of human agency:

The Arian Controversy (Edinburgh: T&T Clark, 1988), 446–58.

12   Grillmeier, *Christ in Christian Tradition*, 315.

13   Hanson, *The Search for the Christian Doctrine of God*, 451–52.

14   Adolf Von Harnack, *History of Dogma* (London: Oxford, 1898), 4:45.

15   Hanson, *The Search for the Christian Doctrine of God*, 448–51.

16   Torrance, "Athanasius," in *Theology in Reconciliation*, 225; Torrance, *Divine Meaning*, 189.

17   Charles S. Twombly, "The Nature of Christ's Humanity: Study of Athanasius," *Patristic and Byzantine Review* 8 (1989): 238–40.

Redemption was not accomplished just by a downright *fiat* of God, nor by a mere divine "nod", but by an intimate, personal movement of the Son of God himself into the heart of our creaturely being and into the inner recesses of the human mind, in order to save us from within and from below, and to restore us to undamaged relations of being and mind with himself. Thus throughout his earthly life Christ laid hold of our alienated and darkened human mind in order to heal and enlighten it in himself. In and through him our ignorant minds are brought into such a relation to God that they may be filled with divine light and truth. The redemption of man's ignorance has an essential place in the atoning exchange, for everything that we actually are in our lost and benighted condition has been taken up by Christ into himself in order that he might bring it under the saving, renewing, sanctifying, and enlightening power of his own reality as the incarnate wisdom and light of God.[18]

The firm evidence of Christ's human activity lies in his restoration of the human mind and soul through his earthly life. Torrance's intention here is not to challenge Grillmeier's position that Christ assumed only human flesh without human soul and mind – such an endeavor would mean for him to seek a proper solution to a false problem.[19] Rather, he shows Athanasius taught that Christ healed the darkened mind by his human agency and not merely by an immediate act of divine power.

For Torrance the origins of dualistic tendencies in modern Athanasian scholarship do not lie in its indebtedness to pre-Nicene Greek patristic concepts, but in the adoption of the Tertullianic and Augustinian dualism so evident in the clear-cut distinction between Incarnation and Redemption present in post-Reformation theology.[20] Torrance himself attempts to bridge this gap between Incarnation and Atonement that was opened up by post-Reformation theology. Though he does not directly mention R. P. C. Hanson's position concerning Athanasius' Christology, which propagated this rift between Incarnation and Redemption, nevertheless he strongly refutes it. By emphasizing that the human agency of Christ is evident in his role of High Priest, Torrance offers a response to Hanson's allegations that Athanasius' doctrine of Incarnation almost swallowed up his doctrine

---

18   Thomas F. Torrance, *The Trinitarian Faith* (Edinburgh: T&T Clark, 1988), 187–8.

19   Torrance, "Athanasius," *Theology in Reconciliation,* 230.

20   Ibid., 230.

of Atonement.[21] According to Torrance, the human priesthood and the saving mediation of Jesus Christ in and through his kinship with humankind are the crucial elements that witness in favor of Christ's active humanity.[22] Torrance rejects Hanson's view that the redemption in Athanasius is accomplished simply by the act of the Logos assuming human flesh. According to Torrance, the saving economy of the Incarnation for Athanasius entails a threefold atoning exchange or reconciliation: a) ransom, b) the redemption of suffering, and c) deification or *theopoiesis*.[23] Hanson's insistence only on the *redeeming* aspect of the Incarnation completely overlooks the other two features emphasized by Torrance. Deification aside, Torrance's elaboration of Athanasius' treatment of the vicarious role of Christ suggests a response to Hanson's claim that despite his belief in the atonement Athanasius cannot really explain why Christ should have died. Relying on Athanasius' assertion that "our resurrection is stored up in the Cross,"[24] Torrance states that the profound interaction between incarnation and atonement in Jesus finalized and sealed the ontological relations between him and every human being, for he "has anchored human nature in his own crucified and risen being."[25]

This highlighting of atoning exchange or reconciliation, which according to Torrance features strongly in Athanasius' theology, is something that is evidently lacking in other scholarly approaches to the bishop of Alexandria. According to Torrance, Athanasius' theology, enriched with the Christology of Cyril of Alexandria, may serve as a platform for the ecumenical reconciliation of Orthodox, Monophysite, Roman Catholic and Evangelical churches, precisely because of its reconciling capacity in overcoming not only ancient, but also modern dualisms.[26] This makes Athanasius a figure of central significance for the unity of the Church and the main subject of our current investigation.

---

21 Hanson, *The Search for the Christian Doctrine of God*, 450.

22 Torrance, "Athanasius," *Theology in Reconciliation*, 228.

23 Torrance, *The Trinitarian Faith*, 181–90.

24 Athanasius, *Contra Arianos* 1.43.

25 Torrance, *The Trinitarian Faith*, 182–3.

26 Torrance, *Theology in Reconciliation*, 8–9.

The Incarnation of the Logos in the Created Order

Since the topic of the Incarnation of the Logos in the created order requires a lengthy exposition, this portion of our investigation will be limited solely to the place of human rational capacities within the created order. The common presupposition concerning this issue is that the human mind and soul have been sanctified and renewed in the Incarnate Logos. Thus, by restoring in his own human mind and soul the paradisiacal state, Jesus Christ has removed any stain of the fall from human intellectual faculties as such. As a consequence of this, human nature is able by progressing toward deification to embrace God fully, and the human mind is able to perceive God. However, Torrance approaches this issue from a different perspective.

Torrance begins by pointing to two important features, not only of human nature, but also of every created nature: (a) its correspondence with truth and (b) its dynamic character. Firstly, Torrance claims, for Athanasius nature (φύσις) is equivalent to truth (αλήθεια). Thus, to think "in accordance with [the] nature" (κατα φύσιν) of things, a phrase frequently employed by Athanasius, means to think truly (αληθως) about them.[27] Secondly, according to Torrance, the notion of human or created nature in Athanasius differs from the corresponding notion in pagan philosophy, the latter being characterized by unchanging static patterns and immutable relations.[28] Human nature and its intellectual capacities are in a state of flux. According to Torrance, this departure of Athanasius from the Greek conceptual framework led him to abandon the abstraction of form from being in favor of a concept of nature that refers beyond itself.[29] This implies that the proper understanding of human nature is not to be acquired by abstracting from all its particular features that constitute it, but rather precisely the opposite: to consider all these particular, sometimes conflicting, moments of human existence as reconciled in reference to its final state. The truth about the created natures is also the truth about their final destiny, enabling every particular being to test in regard to that truth whether its existence is "in accordance with nature" (κατα φύσιν). Torrance maintains that God through creation has conferred intelligibility on the world of created being in such a way that form inheres in being, and logos inheres in human being. This unity

27   Torrance, "Athanasius," *Theology in Reconciliation*, 247–8.

28   Ibid., 248.

29   Ibid., 249.

between logos and being imposed by God on creation actually resembles the unity of Logos and Being in God.[30] Even before his historical incarnation, the divine Logos is present as reflected in the cosmic order of created beings through this metaphysical principle of unity between being and logos.

By relying on this principle Athanasius claims in the opening lines of Contra Gentes that to reveal the purpose of our godliness and to obtain the true knowledge about everything one does not need instruction from human beings, as both may be attained on their own terms.[31] The purpose of human godliness may be attained by itself, but this does not mean that worship, prayer and godly life have their purpose in themselves, but rather in something beyond them. Athanasius continues by saying that the purpose of godliness is revealed through the teaching of Christ. This means that Christ, as the Incarnate God, and his teaching, is the purpose of godliness – or, as the apostle put it, that the mystery of godliness (τῆς ευσεβείας μυστήριον) is revealed in the incarnation of God in the flesh (1 Tim 3:16).[32] The Pauline term ευσεβείας is a synonym to the term θεοσεβείας used by Athanasius. By following Athanasius here, Torrance couples θεοσεβείας with θεολογία. Although Athanasius does not use the term θεολογία in Contra Gentes, it is not difficult to conclude that for him the "true knowledge of all'" (τῆς τῶν ὅλων αληθείας γνωσις) may be only attained by theology. Torrance defines the exact purpose of theology for Athanasius:

> Theology is concerned to penetrate into the inherent order, the innate coherence, the essential pattern of God's self-communication to us in revelation and reconciliation, and in and through that to rise in the Spirit to an understanding of God in his Triune Being (as far as that is allowed for finite creatures) which Athanasius called *theologia* in its strictest sense (εν τριάδι η θεολογία τελεία εστι) (Contra Arianos 1.18, 4).[33]

Thus, both godliness as worship, prayer, and godly life, and theology as the means to acquire the knowledge of everything, including God, serve

---

30 Ibid., 249.

31 Contra Gentes 1.1–3 in Athanasius: Contra Gentes and De Incarnatione, ed. Robert Thomson (Oxford: Clarendon Press, 1971), 2–3.

32 Cf. Torrance's essay "Logic and Analogic of Biblical and Theological Statements," in Theology in Reconstruction (London: SCM Press, 1965), 30–45; reprinted in Divine Meaning, 374–91, especially 378.

33 Torrance, "Athanasius," Theology in Reconciliation, 250.

the purpose of knowing God as Trinity and of being reconciled with Him. The human capacities of worshiping and knowing God are inseparable, since genuine knowledge of God may be reached and maintained only in the context of continuous worship.[34] In his later article "The Doctrine of the Holy Trinity according to St. Athanasius," Torrance actually claims that *theologia* is equated by Athanasius with the knowledge and worship of God "both as he is known through Jesus Christ and in the Holy Spirit and as he is eternally in himself, with the doctrine of Trinity."[35] Further, in *Contra Gentes*, while Athanasius acknowledges the significance of both Scripture and the treatises of Church authors in revealing the truth of Christian religion, he chooses to rely only on the knowledge that derives from the faith in Christ (κατα τον Χριστον πίστιν), in order to prove the genuine correspondence between knowledge and faith.[36] The knowledge of God, which brings with it knowledge of everything else, is inseparable from faith in God, just as θεοσεβείας is inseparable from θεολογία. Moreover, the ground for θεοσεβείας is actually in the faith (πίστις) that Jesus Christ is Son of God, the Incarnate Logos, inasmuch as the true knowledge of God and His creation provides the basis for the true θεολογία. Regarding θεολογία, Torrance is very clear that true theology begins with the orderly structure of the saving *oikonomia* (or the "economic" Trinity) and proceeds further to the inner relations of God in himself (or to the "ontological" Trinity or the "immanent" Trinity.)[37] This is a daring statement, since it (a) opens the possibility to the human mind to penetrate the inner relationship between the Persons of the Trinity, a domain considered by many theologians as inaccessible; and (b) it implies a certain analogy between the economic and ontological Trinity. We will leave the matter of "the ontological Trinity" for a moment and return to it while discussing Torrance's view on the Incarnation of the Logos in Jesus Christ. For now, it must simply be noted that in Torrance's view, the saving *oikonomia* includes the orderly created structure of the cosmos as well as the revelation of God through other means.

One may reflect further on the features and structure of the divine economy. If godliness, as a crucial dimension of true theology, is the way by which the Old Testament Jews expressed their relationship with God,

---

34   Ibid., 248.

35   Thomas F. Torrance, "The Doctrine of the Holy Trinity according to St. Athanasius," *Anglican Theological Review* 71 (1989): 395.

36   Athanasius, *Contra Gentes* 1.13–16.

37   Torrance, "Athanasius," *Theology in Reconciliation*, 250.

then the pagan theology that recognizes the fundamental ontological structure of cosmos as entailing a genuine correspondence between being and logos was a model with which God chose to guide the Greeks and others who did not revere Him on the basis of the common covenant. Actually, the purpose of Athanasius' *Contra Gentes* is to show to the Greeks that Christian faith is not only rational, but that it is actually based on this genuine correspondence between being and logos, which resembles the same correspondence of Logos and Being in God and which is implanted in the creation. Therefore, understanding of the saving economy includes two features: first, the recognition of the *logoi* of the Logos in created beings; and second, the revelation of the Trinity in the economy *strictu sensu*.

However, this does not imply that nature and revelation are identical, nor that the Logos, together with the *logoi*, constitutes an intervening divine element between God and the world. For indeed, the Logos, the Mind and the Word of God, is identical with Jesus Christ, the Incarnate Son of the Father.[38] Thus, Torrance claims that the knowledge of God and the purpose of His creation embedded in the *logoi* of creation, derived from cosmological systems, may not be "attained prior to or independently of the knowledge of God as the Father of Jesus Christ."[39] Θεοσεβείας is an inseparable part of θεολογία, since the faith in God through Christ is the precondition for penetrating into the intrinsic order and intelligibility, first of the cosmos and then further of the Trinity on both economic and ontological levels.[40] According to Torrance, faith and obedience to God in Jesus Christ actually yields the knowledge of things "in their own compulsive movement and in their innate coherence."[41]

Athanasius develops the Stoic argument that the order (τάξις) of the cosmos indicates that it has a creator:

> For seeing the circling of heaven and the course of sun and moon, the positions and revolutions of the other stars, which are opposed and different but in their difference all keep a common order, who would not think that they do not order themselves but that there is another who orders them and who made them?[42]

---

38 Torrance, "Hermeneutics of Athanasius", *Divine Meaning*, 229–30.

39 Torrance, "Athanasius," *Theology in Reconciliation*, 255.

40 Ibid., 255.

41 Ibid., 256.

42 Athanasius, *Contra Gentes* 35.30–4.

However, a common order reveals more than just the existence of a creator. In accordance to λόγου ὄντος φυσικου,[43] "the intrinsic rationality of things"[44] or the "rational law,"[45] the common order is not one of many, but is actually the *one* common order. The one common order implies that there is only one cosmos, which is the creation of one, and not of many creators.[46] Moreover, according to Athanasius, due to the orderly movement of the cosmos, one may also conclude that it is led by one Lord and King and not by many (ενα και μή πολλους).[47] The fact that the world is both created and governed by one and the same Creator and Ruler, points to a certain divine purpose (σκοπος) conceived before the beginning of creation. According to Athanasius, this purpose is revealed in the Incarnation of the Logos as the mystery of Christ (το Χριστου μυστήριον).[48] Thus, the demarcation line between nature and revelation, but also their meeting point, is the Incarnation of the Logos, which restored the unity of the creation.[49] The rationality that has been embedded in the cosmos is the guarantee of the unity of the creation. This unity of the cosmos, given in potentiality through the rational order, is fully realized in the Incarnation of the Logos, when God became man.

Human intellectual capacities may lead one just to conclude that the one single order of the cosmos refers to one creator and ruler, but this creator and ruler becomes known as the all-holy Father of Christ only by the Incarnation of the Logos.[50] The unity of the cosmos is fully realized only as the unity of many *logoi* in the Logos of God revealed in Christ. For Athanasius, the Logos of God, or the Son of the Father, revealed Himself as the Creator and the Provider by His incarnation:

> The Father calls him King in regard to his works in time, lest anything in the measured character of the Incarnation should detract from the glory that inheres in him by nature. For even after his economy he remains no less in him, begotten of his Royal

43   Ibid., 39.24.

44   Torrance, "Athanasius," *Theology in Reconciliation*, 257.

45   Athanasius, *Contra Gentes*, 109 (Thomson).

46   Athanasius, *Contra Gentes*, 39.

47   Ibid., 38.44-47; 39.33-35.

48   Athanasius, *Expositiones in Psalmos*, 27.112c.

49   Torrance, "Athanasius," *Theology in Reconciliation*, 7.

50   Athanasius, *Contra Gentes* 40.11–16.

Father, and as King and God, he is said to enter in his Royal Rule through becoming flesh.[51]

For Torrance, Athanasius' view of the cosmos – its origin, history, and purpose – as well as metaphysics and ontology, natural philosophy and cosmology, become linked to a distinctive Christological and soteriological perspective. However, this Christological perspective, evident in both *oikonomia* and *theologia* also has a Trinitarian character, since the knowledge of the Son, which is only possible in the Spirit, leads further to the Father:

> As by looking up to heaven and seeing its order and the light of the stars one can form an idea of the Word who sets their order, so when thinking of the Word of God one must also think of his Father, God, from whom he proceeds and is therefore rightly called the interpreter and messenger of his Father. One can see this from what happens with us. For if, when a word is spoken by men, we think that its source is the mind and, concentrating on the word, we perceive by reasoning the mind which it reveals, all the more, by a greater and far superior effort of the imagination, when we see the power of the Word we form an idea of his good Father.[52]

Torrance develops Athanasius' analogy between divine and human uttered word by directing the whole christological issue to the purpose of Father's utterance of His Word. Thus, the love of God toward human beings, as the inner reason for the Incarnation of the Logos, has a twofold purpose: (a) to restore the unity of creation, and (b) to reconcile the creation, particularly humankind with the Father. Myk Habets aptly remarks that to acknowledge the unity of the creation by referring to one Creator is "one, but not the highest step."[53] The highest step is to acknowledge the Creator as Father and to call and know him as Father of the Son.

At the level of the human intellectual faculty the restoration of the creation to its previous state took place as restoration of human rationality through and in the Logos.[54] The practical display of this restored human rationality is the acknowledgement of the one Creator

51 Athanasius, *Expositiones in Psalmos*, 27.565a in Thomas F. Torrance, "Hermeneutics of Athanasius," 269.

52 Athanasius, *Contra Gentes* 45.1–10.

53 Myk Habets, "How 'Creation is Proleptically Conditioned by Redemption," *Colloquium* 41 (2009): 8.

54 Torrance, "Athanasius," *Theology in Reconciliation*, 262.

beyond the created order and the realization that the purpose of the creation is not in itself, but in something higher. However, while this saves one from attempting to seek the meaning of the universe in the created order, without elevating one's mind beyond it, the entire purpose of the Incarnation of the Logos remains unfulfilled. According to Torrance, Christ achieved the reconciliation with the Father for human beings and *from the side of* human beings through His crucifixion and resurrection. The cross and resurrection, as the reconciliation of humanity with the Father, are not only sufficient to understand the Incarnation; they are also the realization that every concrete human being might be reconciled with the Father only by following in Christ's footsteps and by being with Christ in the Spirit.[55] Thus, by being led by Christ's example restored human rationality realizes the purpose of the universe in general and the meaning of every concrete human existence in particular. In short, for Athanasius, the Mystery of Christ is stored up in the intrinsic rationality of things (λόγου οντος φυσικου) revealed in the general order as well as in the profound interaction between the Logos of God and the logos of every human being.

The Incarnation of the Logos in the Scriptures

Athanasius' approach to the Scriptures was a long-lasting inspiration to Torrance. John Webster argues that Torrance's view of Scripture is structured with two movements, from (a) a trinitarian and incarnational theology of revelation, through (b) an ontology of the prophetic and apostolic texts to (c) a hermeneutics of repentance and faith.[56] This is the exact structure of Torrance's dealing with Athanasius' scriptural account. Moreover, a similar structure may be noticed in Torrance's view of creation, since the understanding of the *logoi* or the words of the Scripture corresponds to the understanding of the *logoi* or the rational principles of the creation, in that both are acquired in relation to Logos:

> That is the *Logos*, God himself speaking to us and acting upon us in Jesus Christ, whom we must hear and understand if we are to interpret the divine words of Holy Scripture according to their proper sense and nature. Apart from the *Logos* of God

55 Ibid., 262–4.

56 John Webster, "T. F. Torrance on Scripture," *Scottish Journal of Theology* 65 (2012): 37.

there is no truly *logical* thinking or speaking for the Logos is the source of all rationality in thought and speech. Applied to the interpretation of the Holy Scripture, that means that only when we discern the relation between the words (λόγοι) and the Word (Λόγος) are we engaged in the rational exegesis in accordance with the speaking and acting of God upon us in Jesus Christ.[57]

The basic center of reference of the Scriptures is Jesus Christ, both as the originator of the words (λόγοι) of Scripture and as Scripture's final scope and *telos*.[58] This is not to oppose Christocentrism to the Trinitarian pattern in the understanding of the Scriptural message. Torrance claims that the essential conceptuality of Scripture in its basic form of thought and speech as derived from the *oikonomia* of the Logos of God is founded in and through the Logos in the *theologia* or the Being of the triune God.[59] Similar to the rationality of the Logos embedded in the creation as part of the divine economy, the *logoi* of Scripture are economical embodiments of the Logos in the form of thought and speech. Again, Torrance points out the analogy of *oikonomia* with *theologia*. The words of Scripture do not reflect only the rationality of the Logos[60] – they also lead the human mind to penetrate into the inner relations of the Persons of the Holy Trinity. Torrance maintains that the incarnation of the Logos actually discloses the impossibility for the human mind to penetrate by its own power into the Mystery of God. At the same time, however, it makes possible the knowledge of God through the Logos in the form of thought and speech.[61] This knowledge of God through the Logos is possible only in the Spirit, since for Torrance Athanasian Christocentrism implies "the intrinsic mutuality of the indwelling between the Son and the Spirit, each receiving from the other."[62] Torrance applies the Athanasian principle of "coordination and unity," which describes God's activity as moving through the Son in the Spirit,[63] to the proper understanding of the scriptural message as shaped within the Spirit-led Church:

57   Torrance, "Hermeneutics of Athanasius," *Divine Meaning*, 234.

58   Ibid., 240.

59   Ibid., 270.

60   Ibid., 274.

61   Ibid., 286.

62   Torrance, "Athanasius," *Theology in Reconciliation*, 254.

63   Ibid., 251.

> It was out of this corporate reciprocity centred in and creatively controlled by Christ through the outpouring of his Spirit of Truth upon it that the New Testament Scriptures were born and took shape within the church. They constitute, therefore, the divinely-provided and inspired linguistic medium which remains of authoritative and critical significance for the whole history of the church of Jesus Christ. Its purpose in this written form . . . is to enable us to stand with the original witnesses under the creative impact of the Word which they received and obeyed, and to be drawn into the sphere of its effective operation in the world.[64]

The words of the Scriptures are the divinely inspired medium through which God acts upon us. The Spirit commences the effective divine operation by relating divine words to divine acts. The divine operation of the Spirit of Truth, who inscribes the Logos in the hearts of the interpreters, leads from a Trinitarian and incarnational theology of divine self-revelation to an ontology of the written text. This connection of the texts with the divine actions of God's Spirit opens up the possibility for understanding the *logoi* of scripture as true *reality*, which Torrance equates with truth (αλήθεια) itself.[65]

Torrance here makes a shift from the economic and theological dimensions of God's self-revelation to the ontological or paradigmatic significance of the scriptural account. According to Torrance, there exists an analogy between the nature (φύσις) or the reality (αλήθεια) of the scriptural statements (λόγοι) and the nature of the created beings. One should understand the scriptural statements in accordance with their correspondence with divine realities and their dynamic character. The scriptural statements are equivalent to truth (αλήθεια) if they point to divine realities, or have an *ostensive* function.[66] For Torrance, theological statements, as derived from the message and the content of the statements of Scripture, can be considered true only "when they manifest in themselves a 'logic' that corresponds with the actual way which the Word of God has taken in becoming flesh among us, and so raises us up to communion with the eternal God."[67]

---

64   Thomas F. Torrance, *Reality and Evangelical Theology: The Realism of Christian Revelation* (Eugene, OR: Wipf and Stock, 2003), 92–3.

65   Torrance, "Hermeneutics of Athanasius," 232.

66   Ibid., 253, 257; Thomas F. Torrance, "Logic and Analogic of Biblical and Theological Statements," *Divine Meaning*, 376.

67   Torrance, *Divine Meaning*, 378.

This leads to the second feature of the scriptural statements: their dynamic character. Torrance claims that there is no allegorical and tropical interpretation of the Scriptures, since the scriptural statements are pointers to the dynamic divine acts.[68] In other words, the common meanings of the scriptural words are abstracted from their ordinary experience, by referring upward (ανα) to God. Thus, they attain their meaning within the scope of divine Being.[69] Torrance relies here mostly on Athanasius' distinction between biblical terms that refer to both human and divine realities:

> And if so be the same terms are used of God and man in divine Scripture, yet the clear-sighted, as Paul enjoins, will study it, and thereby discriminate, and dispose of what is written according to the nature of each subject (κατα την ἑκάστου τών σημαινομένων φύσιν τα γεγραμμένα διαγινώσκειν), and avoid any confusion of sense, so as neither to conceive of the things of God in a human way, nor to ascribe the things of man to God.[70]

Nevertheless, Torrance brings the biblical figures used to discern the divine realities into close relation with the economic divine self-revelation or, to use the language of Athanasius, illustrations (παραδείγματα) of these images. These illustrations are not human similes or metaphorical devices, but the means of divine economy to refer to something beyond created nature. As such they open up the possibility for human beings to know God.[71] Since these illustrations have a common point of reference, which is the Incarnation of the Logos, they provide the knowledge of God just in the context of divine *oikonomia*. The knowledge of God is not acquired by human intellectual capacities and presented in the form of statements, but God communicates it in the dim form of illustrations to those who may discern their spiritual sense

---

68   Torrance, "Hermeneutics of Athanasius," 232.

69   Torrance, "Logic and Analogic of Biblical and Theological Statements," 377.

70   Athanasius, *De Decretis Nicaenae Synodi* 10.6 in H. G. Opitz, *Athanasius Werke*, vol. 2.1 (Berlin: De Gruyter, 1940). The English translation from A. Robertson, *St. Athanasius. Select Works and Letters.* A Select Library of Nicene and Post-Nicene Fathers of the Christian Church, 2nd ser., ed. H. Wace and P. Schaff (Edinburgh: T&T Clark, Grand Rapids: Eerdmans, 1987), 4:156.

71   Torrance, "Hermeneutics of Athanasius," *Divine Meaning*, 255; Torrance, "Logic and Analogic of Biblical and Theological Statements," *Divine Meaning*, 376. Cf. also Athanasius, *De Decretis* 12.3.

and their cryptic character. The spiritual understanding of the Scripture as distinct from the profane character of the biblical terms is possible only through the Incarnate Logos in the Spirit, and also requires religious experience based on faith and godly and reverent reasoning (εν πίστει καί εύσεβεί λογισμω μετ᾽ εύλαβείας).[72]

According to Webster, the hermeneutics of faith occupies the third and the last level in Torrance's structuring of Athanasian scriptural account, immediately after the ontology of biblical text.[73] For Torrance the connection between the knowledge of the divine nature (φύσις) – for Athanasius, synonymous with reality (αλήθεια)[74] – and faith (πίστις) and godliness (εύσεβείας), is also substantiated by the scriptural account. In his exegesis of the Old Testament meaning of the Hebrew term ᵉmeth, Torrance concludes:

> The usual translation of ᵉmeth in the LXX is aletheia, but aletheia is not used to signify abstract or metaphysical truth, but what is grounded upon God's faithfulness, i.e. truth not as something static, but as active, efficacious reality, the reality of God in covenant-relationship. It is the steadfastness or the reality of God which is the ground of all truth. Primarily, truth is God's being true to Himself, His faithfulness or consistency. God's Truth means, therefore, that He keeps truth or faith with His people and requires them to keep truth or faith with Him. Thus the Hebrew ᵉmeth is translated not only by aletheia but also by pistis and dikaiosune.[75]

Torrance relies on A. G. Herbert's claim that in the biblical usage the term "faith" does not refer to some human capacity or virtue, but it refers to the tendency in human nature to take refuge from human frailty and instability in God who is firm and steadfast.[76] However, Torrance points out that the Old Testament concept of faith differs from the one proclaimed by the Gospels since in the latter the steadfast faithfulness

---

72   Torrance, "Hermeneutics of Athanasius," *Divine Meaning*, 243–244. Cf. Athanasius, *Epistulae quattuor ad Serapionem* 1.20 in K. Savvidis, *Athanasius: Werke, Band I. Die dogmatischen Schriften, Erster Teil, 4. Lieferung* (Berlin and New York: De Gruyter, 2010).

73   Webster, "T. F. Torrance on Scripture," *Scottish Journal of Theology* 65, 37.

74   Torrance, "Athanasius," *Theology in Reconciliation*, 247–8.

75   Thomas F. Torrance, "One Aspect of the Biblical Conception of Faith," *The Expository Times* 68 (1957): 112.

76   A. G. Herbert, "'Faithfulness' and 'Faith'," *Theology* 424 (1955): 374.

of God has achieved its end in righteousness and truth in Jesus Christ, because truth has been actualized in Him as Truth and fulfilled in our midst.[77] This statement of Torrance perfectly corresponds with his view of Athanasius' scriptural interpretation as operating "within the scope of faith, under the direction of the Word made flesh and in accordance with His truth."[78] From his earliest works Athanasius consistently claimed that the study and true knowledge of Scripture is inseparable from godliness and faith:

> But in addition to the study and true knowledge of the Scriptures are needed a good life and pure soul and virtue in Christ, so that the mind, journeying in this path, may be able to obtain and apprehend what it desires, in so far as human nature is able to learn about God the Word.[79]

There is no doubt for Torrance that Athanasius keeps to the scope of the Scripture by keeping within the scope of faith.[80]

The relationship between the interpretation of the Scriptures and the faith, however, is one of the most criticized aspects of Torrance's method of biblical exegesis. Thus, James Barr refutes Torrance's metaphysical-theological type of approach to scriptural thought-structures as evidencing an inability to keep to linguistic method strictly and to see and present linguistic evidence properly. According to Barr, Torrance, in his exegetical method, expresses a tendency to replace linguistic analysis with theological and philosophical argumentation.[81] Darren Sarisky suggests that Barr's criticism of Torrance might be summed up by the words of Barr's follower John Barton:

> One cannot establish what the Bible means if one insists on reading it as necessarily conforming to what one already believes to be true – which is what a theological reading amounts to.[82]

---

77 Torrance, "One Aspect of the Biblical Conception of Faith," 113.

78 Torrance, "Hermeneutics of Athanasius," *Divine Meaning*, 238.

79 Athanasius, *De Incarnatione* 57.1–5.

80 Torrance, "Hermeneutics of Athanasius," *Divine Meaning*, 279.

81 James Barr, *The Semantics of Biblical Language* (London: Oxford University Press, 1962), 204–05.

82 John Barton, *The Nature of Biblical Criticism* (Louisville: Westminster John Knox, 2007), 164. See also Darren Sarisky, "T. F. Torrance on Biblical Interpretation," *International Journal of Systematic Theology* 11 (2009): 336.

In his attempt to respond to Barton's comment in defense of Torrance's view of Scripture, Sarisky emphasizes that the interpretative framework is not constituted by some subjective belief of the interpreter, but rather by the ultimate faith in the Holy Trinity.[83] This is evident in Torrance's treatment of Athanasius' interpretative method:

> Thus while Athanasius is not a Biblicist, yet he appeals to the Scriptures for the demonstration of the faith . . . He treats biblical statements, however, not as embodying the truth in themselves, but as pointing, under the direction of the Spirit by whose inspiration they were uttered, to the words and acts of Christ who is himself the Truth.[84]

The interpretative framework within the scope of faith in the Holy Trinity is actually the result of divine self-revelation, as much as the particular forms of thought and speech that express the divine realities are generated by the self-revealing Trinity.[85] Torrance maintains that Athanasius' contribution is crucial to the hermeneutical method that subjects terms to the realities to which they refer, instead of subjecting realities to the terms which refer to them as Barr does.[86] Moreover, the scriptural statements or *logoi* as embodiments of the Logos not only provide the understanding of the realities to which they refer, but also lead one to move toward their *telos*. Thus, Torrance argues, for Athanasius divine self-revelation and his saving activity operate as one movement of self-communication to human beings.

This movement of God as revealer and reconciler toward human beings, however, is located within a specific ecclesial context, which allows us to establish a proper link between the general framework of revelation and individual divine acts, between reality and the scriptural forms of thought and speech, and between historical and ontological factors of divine self-communication. Torrance maintains that it is only *in the Church* that "the faith and language and mind are brought in the

---

83   Sarisky, "T. F. Torrance on Biblical Interpretation," 336.

84   Torrance, "Hermeneutics of Athanasius," *Divine Meaning*, 284.

85   Thomas F. Torrance, *The Christian Doctrine of God: One Being, Three Persons* (Edinburgh: T&T Clark, 1996), 21.

86   Thomas F. Torrance, *Royal Priesthood: A Theology of Ordained Ministry* (Edinburgh: T&T Clark, 1993), x. Cf. also Thomas F. Torrance, *The Hermeneutics of John Calvin*, (Edinburgh: Scottish Academic Press, 1988), 50; and "Hermeneutics of Athanasius," 274.

conformity with the nature of Christ."[87] Thus, not individual belief, but the coherent ecclesial faith in Christ as the interpretative scriptural framework, may provide proper reception of his revealing and reconciling deeds. The same is applicable to the language or text of the Bible. Only within the scope of faith do the common human terms used in the Scripture acquire the spiritual or ecclesiastical sense, which prevails over existing human conceptions.

Thus, finally, the true ecclesiastical understanding of the *logoi* of Scripture allows us to recover the properly disposed *mind*. This is not a natural process, but one of the fruits of the Incarnation of Logos, who restored human nature to its previous state. The proper understanding of Scriptural *logoi* results in acquiring the mind remade and renewed in Christ (αλλα τον έν Χριστω κτισθέντα και ανακαινισθέντα νουν).[88] The main feature of this ecclesiastical mind is to discern the divine acts within the historical, prophetic and apostolic framework of Scripture. This mind does not divorce the Scriptural *logoi* from their historical actuality, but rather penetrates the surface of both biblical syntax and historical events in order to discern the deeper history of revelation. Therefore Torrance, following Athanasius, refers here to this ecclesiastical mind also as the "apostolic mind."[89]

Torrance expresses the mutual relationships that exist among *logoi* of Scripture, the properly disposed mind, and faith and piety in the conclusion to his essay on Athanasian hermeneutics:

> But when in accordance with true piety we allow our thoughts to take forms in accordance with what is given to us from God, so that our minds are opened out towards his self-revelation, then we are in a position to read the Scriptures and listen to what they have to say, and through rational reflection upon their message formulate trains of thought which may provide a medium through which the Scriptures may continue to reflect their meaning, and reflect it ever more profoundly.[90]

It should be carefully noted here that the triadic structure of Torrance's scriptural interpretation proposed by Webster corresponds exactly with

---

87 Torrance, "Hermeneutics of Athanasius," *Divine Meaning*, 241.

88 Athanasius, *Ad Serapionem* 1.9.

89 Torrance, "Hermeneutics of Athanasius," *Divine Meaning*, 288. Cf. Athanasius, *De Synodis* 5, in *Athanasius Werke*, ed. H. G. Opitz, vol. 2.1 (Berlin: De Gruyter, 1940).

90 Torrance, "Hermeneutics of Athanasius," *Divine Meaning*, 288.

the structure previously observed in Torrance's view of divine rationality embedded in the created order. Thus, the interpretation of both created order and the Scripture are structured around three basic principles: (a) divine self-revelation, displayed through cosmological, scriptural and incarnational activity; (b) genuine correspondence between divine realities on the one hand, and cosmological and rational arrangement, scriptural syntax and historical deeds of the Incarnate Logos on the other hand; and (c) the role of faith and piety in the process of understanding and appropriating the Mystery of Christ and, through Christ, the Mystery of the Holy Trinity.

The Incarnation of the Logos in the God-man Jesus Christ

One may presume that the general triadic pattern of Torrance's interpretation of both the rational order of cosmos and the Scripture applies also in his description of the embodiment of the Logos in the Person of Jesus Christ. Moreover, as both the rationality embedded in cosmos and the Scripture serve as *signa* to the Incarnation of the Logos, it is highly unlikely that the Incarnation of the Son of God in the Person of Jesus Christ refers just to itself. Therefore, it would be pertinent to explore whether for Torrance the Incarnation of the Logos is a *signum* of some higher reality.

In his analysis of Athanasius' thought, Torrance emphasizes the importance and centrality of the Incarnation for the Alexandrine bishop. Before embarking on investigation of the various implications that the Incarnation has for Athanasius, it would be more relevant to define first what is meant here by Incarnation. For Torrance, the Athanasian identification of God the Son, the eternal Logos, with Jesus Christ represents the crucial contribution in relation to previous theological developments.[91] Moreover, in order to refute some modern misinterpretations of Athanasius' view of Incarnation, such as the above-mentioned stances of Grillmeier and Hanson, Torrance emphasizes that God the Son was not simply incarnated *in* human being, but *as* human being. For Torrance this fact actually refers to the double role of the Incarnation, since Jesus Christ, the eternal Logos of God, *"ministered not only of the things of God to man but ministered of the things of man*

---

91 Torrance, "Athanasius," *Theology in Reconciliation*, 227.

to God.[92] Torrance signifies the latter implication of the Incarnation by
what he calls the "vicarious humanity" of Christ. The vicarious humanity
of Christ presupposes a certain reciprocity. On the one hand, God the
Son appropriates the fullness of fallen humanity.[93] On the other hand,
by his saving deeds God the Son has exalted humanity to the extent
of being deified and adopted by the Father, in the Holy Spirit.[94] By his
role both as a High Priest taken from among human beings and as
an Apostle from God,[95] Christ accomplishes the saving work which,
according to Torrance, consists of the following: atoning expiation,
priestly propitiation, substitutionary sacrifice and victory over the forces
of evil, sanctifying exaltation and finally deification or *theopoiesis.*[96]
While many of these categories are really developed in later works such
as *Contra Arianos,* Torrance also states that the most important elements
of Athanasius' soteriology such as the doctrine of deification are already
present in *De Incarnatione*:

> For he [the Word of God] became man (ανηνθρώπησεν) that we
> might become divine (θεοποιηθώμεν); and he revealed himself
> through a body that we might receive an idea of the invisible
> Father; and he endured insults from men that we might inherit
> incorruption (αφθαρσίαν).[97]

This renowned passage from *De Incarnatione* 54 reveals how deep
and subtle was Torrance's reading of Athanasius. First, accenting the
reciprocity of inhomination and deification, Torrance emphasizes the
double role of Christ, who as God becomes human being, and as human

---

92 Torrance, "Athanasius," *Theology in Reconciliation,* 228, emphasis original. On
the basis of *Contra Arianos,* 1.4. 50, 2.7, 12, 50, 65, 74, 3.30, 38, 4.6.

93 The question of Christ's appropriation of "fallen" humanity remains an open
one for theology. Torrance followed Barth on this point in arguing for an assumption
of "fallen" humanity, but it seems that he was open to reconsider and accommodate
as well the patristic account and the stance of his former supervisor Hugh R.
Macintosh, who in his *The Doctrine of the Person of Jesus Christ* (Edinburgh:
T&T Clark, 1913) stressed the sinlessness of Christ's humanity as well. See the
lecture of George Dion. Dragas, "T. F. Torrance a Theologian for Our Times:
an Eastern Orthodox Assessment," 2012 Annual Meeting of the T. F. Torrance
Theological Fellowship, http://www.youtube.com/watch?v=Frhvk-MY3dg (accessed
on May 3, 2013).

94 Torrance, "Athanasius," *Theology in Reconciliation,* 230.

95 Athanasius, *Contra Arianos* 2.9.

96 Torrance, "Athanasius," *Theology in Reconciliation,* 228–30.

97 Athanasius, *De Incarnatione* 54 in Thomson, 268–9.

being becomes God – corresponding also to His "double account" (διπλῆν ἀπαγγελίαν).[98] For Torrance, this means that the God who became human was the only one able to elevate humanity to union with God, on account of the deification of Christ's "vicarious humanity" in the hypostatic union of divine and human natures. The Incarnation of the Logos actually yielded and secures the human receptivity of deification.[99] The deification of mankind is not automatic or natural because of Christ's introduction of human nature into the life of the Holy Trinity, but it is made possible by the grace of God through Christ and in the Holy Spirit.

Secondly, Torrance pays considerable attention to the end of this chapter from *De Incarnatione*, where Athanasius claims that the achievements of the Lord effected through His incarnation are as the innumerable waves of the ocean that are impossible to grasp by one single gaze. According to Torrance, the metaphor applied by Athanasius actually suggests not only the multiform activities of the Logos that are impossible to seize, but also the dynamic of the divine economy manifested in Christ's deeds. Thus, Torrance states:

> Theology that proceeds strictly by thinking κατα φύσιν of God in his economic condescension to us in Jesus Christ, cannot proceed by determining certain fixed positions and then arguing deductively from them as axioms in the old Euclidean or Aristotelian way, for that would involve operating with a kind of necessity which is alien to the nature of God and the activity of his Spirit.[100]

However, Torrance argues further, "some way must be found to discern the coherent relation or chain of connection in God's saving *economy*."[101] In fact, the previously quoted passage suggests precisely such a possible chain of connection. Before turning to his metaphor of the multiplicity of the waves and to the inability of the human gaze to comprehend them, Athanasius mentions two fruits of the Incarnation: (a) the knowledge of the Father and (b) the inheritance of incorruption. While the knowledge of the Father is certainly only possible through the Son, the state of incorruption is something that humanity already possessed,

---

98   Athanasius, *Contra Arianos* 3.29.

99   Myk Habets, *Theosis in the Theology of Thomas Torrance* (Farnham, England: Ashgate, 2009), 80.

100   Torrance, "Athanasius," *Theology in Reconciliation*, 260.

101   Ibid.

lost and regained in Christ. Thus, the knowledge of the Father, as Myk Habets points out, is not the knowledge of God as creator, but rather the knowledge of the Father through His intimate relationship with the Son.[102] The new relationship between God and mankind is no longer exhausted in the relationship between the Creator and the creation, but is elevated to a new level as the relationship between God the Father and His children through Christ in the Holy Spirit. Thus, even incorruptibility, while being a fruit of the Incarnation, should not be understood as the pinnacle of salvation. According to Torrance, the chain of relation within the divine economy "reaches back to the original order of creation and far transcends it in the amazing purpose of the divine love, as the order of the new creation."[103] The appropriation of incorruptibility does not presuppose automatic deification as the so-called "physical redemption" theory implies; rather, it represents the first step on the long road of deification that necessarily includes the life in the Spirit.[104]

Torrance's intention is to develop both the soteriological aspect of Incarnation that sums up its anthropological consequences, as well as the *theological* or strictly Trinitarian aspect. Concerned with both epistemological and ontological dimensions of the Incarnation, Torrance focuses his interest on the relation among the divine persons within the Holy Trinity first in *oikonomia* and next toward *theologia*.[105] According to Torrance, the relation between the Father and the Incarnate Son constitutes the epistemological heart of Athanasius' theology,[106] because the revelation of the Father through the Son is crucial for the human understanding of the relations in the Holy Trinity. Thus, Torrance heavily relies on Athanasius' insistence on this relationship for theological understanding: "It is more godly and accurate to signify God from the Son and call him Father, than to name him from his works and call him unoriginate."[107] Torrance draws from this the conclusion that the

---

102 Habets, "How 'Creation is Proleptically Conditioned by Redemption," 8.

103 Thomas F. Torrance, *Conflict and Agreement in the Church*, vol. 2, *The Ministry and the Sacraments of the Gospel* (London: Lutterworth, 1960), 15.

104 Habets, *Theosis in the Theology of Thomas Torrance*, 57–8.

105 Torrance, "Athanasius," *Theology in Reconciliation*, 250.

106 Ibid., 240.

107 Athanasius, *Contra Arianos* 1.34, in K. Metzler & K. Savvidis, *Athanasius: Werke, Band I. Die dogmatischen Schriften, Erster Teil, 2. Lieferung* (New York: De Gruyter, 1998); *De Synodis* 48 in Opitz 2.1. Here we make use of Torrance's English rendering from "The Doctrine of the Holy Trinity according to Athanasius," 396.

knowledge of the Son leads to the knowledge of the Father, and that the knowledge of the Father is the knowledge of his own essential Nature, which provides the knowledge of God in the internal relations of his eternal Being.[108]

Here Torrance distinguishes three levels of knowledge of God. The first is the knowledge that one derives from the revealing and saving acts of God in the "incarnate parousia" of his only begotten Son in Jesus Christ. The second is the knowledge of God that is revealed through the relationship between the Father and the Son, described by the Nicene formula *homoousios to Patri*. The third and final is the knowledge of the eternal relations and distinctions within one Being of the Godhead.[109]

Since Torrance exposed this view in the context of the official international dialogue between Reformed and Orthodox theologians as an implication of Athanasian theology that might serve as a basis to attain ecclesial unity, I would dare to comment on it from an Orthodox perspective. While the first two claims are undisputable, the third – knowledge of internal relations – is highly problematic, implying not only that human beings may know the divine essence, but also a questionable use of analogy between the Holy Trinity in the divine economy and the Holy Trinity in their innate relations within the Godhead.

First, before insisting on the primacy of the Father-Son relation over the Creator-creation relation, Athanasius makes two distinctions: (a) between the originate and the creator or the maker of what is originate;[110] and (b) between the *being* and the *will* of God.[111] It is important to emphasize that the distinction between the creator of what is originate and the originate[112] does not coincide with the distinction between originated and unoriginate,[113] because the former implies dependence of the originate on the grace and will (χάριτι καὶ βουλήσει) of the creator.[114] The nature of the things originated is restrained by

---

108   Torrance, "The Doctrine of the Holy Trinity according to Athanasius," *Anglican Theological Review* 71, 396.

109   Ibid., 396-7.

110   Athanasius, *Contra Arianos* 1.20.

111   Ibid. 2.2.

112   Ibid. 1.20: οὐδὲν ὅμοιον κατ' οὐσίαν ἔχει πρὸς τὸν πεποιηκότα.

113   Khaled Anatolios, *Athanasius: The Coherence of His Thought* (London and New York: Routledge, 1998), 103.

114   Athanasius, *Contra Arianos* 1.20.

their creator and restricted by their "beginning,"[115] as well as their proper limits (οροις ἰδίοις).[116] By stressing that the omnipotent and perfect (ὁ παντοδύναμος καὶ παντέλειος) Logos of the Father himself is present in all things and extends his power everywhere, Athanasius actually argues in favor of the Logos' *complete unlikeness* to the world. Athanasius expresses this unlikeness between the world and the Logos by claiming that the Logos, as the Father's power in creation, possesses all the properties of the Father, not by participation like the rest of creation, but absolutely.[117] Therefore, the Son of God does not participate in the Father, but rather the creation is related to God through participation in His Logos and the Son.[118]

By the second distinction pointed above, between the divine being and divine will, Athanasius strengthens the relationship based on likeness between the Father and the Son, both *ad intra* and *ad extra*. Athanasius describes the relationship between the Father and the Son *ad intra* or within the divine being in terms of nature and not of will, since the Son is the offspring of the Father's own essence. Claiming further that "as far as the Son transcends the creature, by so much does what is by nature transcend the will,"[119] Athanasius does not downgrade the divine will, but establishes the priority of the Son over the world and his difference from it.

Regarding the Father-Son relations *ad extra*, i.e. in the creation, by giving the examples of Genesis 1:26 and Proverbs 8:27, Athanasius emphasizes that the creation of the world is the willing action of both the Father and the Son.[120] This not only proves the genuine intention of God to create; it also shows (a) that the act of creating was agreed upon between the Father and the Son, and (b) that this same act was granted by the Father to the Son. By giving power to things to come into existence, the Son created, formed and ordered the universe.[121]

---

115 Georges Florovsky, "The Concept of Creation in St. Athanasius," *Studia Patristica* 6 (1962): 32–57. Reprinted in Florovsky, *Aspects of Church History*, vol. 4, *Collected Works* (Belmont, Mass.: Nordland, 1975), 39–62.

116 Athanasius, *Contra Gentes* 42 in Thomson, 114–17.

117 Athanasius, *Contra Gentes* 46.52-60 (Thomson, 130–131).

118 Anatolios, *Athanasius: The Coherence of His Thought*, 105.

119 Athanasius, *Contra Arianos* 3.62: ὅσῳ οὖν τοῦ κτήματος ὁ υἱὸς ὑπέρκειται, τοσούτῳ καὶ τῆς βουλήσεως τὸ κατὰ φύσιν.

120 Athanasius, *Contra Gentes* 46.52-60 (Thomson, 130–31).

121 Athanasius, *Contra Gentes* 46.47-50 (Thomson, 128–131).

Athanasius also emphasizes the role of the Son as the provider of the creation. As in the case with the creation of the world, in exercising this role the Son is always with the Father and there is no distance that separates them. Athanasius claims not only that there is no interval or distance between the Father and the generation of the Son, but also that the Son's active involvement in creating and governing the world does not separate him from the Father.

The other possible implication of the relationship between the Father and the Son *ad intra* and *ad extra* is the distinction between the divine being and the divine will. Here, one has to recognize the basic difference between the divine *theologia*, i.e. the inter-Trinitarian relations among the persons, and the divine *oikonomia*, i.e. the relationship of God with the creation, in Athanasius. As Khaled Anatolios suggests, the essence-power distinction parallels the nature-works distinction.[122] This does at all not mean, however, that the divine power is an accidental exposition or display of divine being in a form of created grace. On the contrary, the divine power essentially belongs to the divine being, or the divine essence. By denying the interval in the act of creation, Athanasius not only claims that there is no distance or interval between the power of the Son and the Father, since it is one and the same power or will or energy springing from the divine essence, but also that there is no interval between the divine being or essence and the divine power employed in creating and governing the world. On one hand, Athanasius contrasts the divine will to the divine nature in order to emphasize the ontological differences between the Son as the product of the nature and the world as the product of the will. On the other hand, Athanasius differentiates the divine will from the temporal process of the divine economy, by claiming that the creative act remains timeless and mysterious.

All that has been said above inevitably leads to the conclusion that Athanasius attempted to show the bond of the Son to the Father within the divine essence on the one hand, and to differentiate ontologically God as creator from the creation on the other hand. Athanasius denies the existence of any distance between the Father and the Son, claiming the existence of an inseparable divine unity, without mediation or distance. Likewise, the Alexandrine bishop goes a step further, arguing for the lack of distance between the Father and the Son in creating and governing the world. Thus, while the Son is the Father's will and tool in

---

122   Anatolios, *Athanasius: The Coherence of His Thought*, 46.

creation, He remains inseparably united to the Father. If the difference between the divine being and divine will and power is acknowledged in Athanasius, it is possible to discern both the lack of distance between the Son and the Father in the divine power or energy, and the absence of any interval that may separate God's essence from the divine power employed in the temporal order of the world. The divine activity may appear as temporary since it is revealed to us in a chronological sequence, but it is the everlasting expression of God's activity *ad extra*.

We may draw two conclusions that are relevant for the present study. First, Athanasius' intention is not to claim the ultimate understanding of the Father through the Son, but by connecting closely the being of the Son with the being of the Father he argues against the Arian tendency that equates the Son with a creature.

Torrance states that, as the controlling centre of Athanasius' thought, the term *homoousios* carries the conception of coinherent relation or mutual indwelling of each divine Person in the other two.[123] Torrance emphasizes the strategic importance of the concepts of *homoousios* and *perichoresis* for Athanasius, because they help him to move from the second level dealing with the economic Trinity to the third level of the ontological Trinity.[124] However, thorough analysis of Athanasius' corpus does not substantiate Torrance's claim that the concept of *homoousios* occupies the controlling centre of Athanasius' thought. Lewis Ayres lists the historical reasons why *homoousios* can hardly be described as fundamental to Athanasius' theology.[125] Athanasius neither uses the term *homoousios* to describe relations within the Trinity nor the Father's relationship to the Son. He applies the term almost exclusively to the relationship of the Son to the Father.[126] Apart from applying *homoousios* with a strictly traditional Eusebian argument, which intends to secure only the Son's being from God and distinguish it from

123   Torrance, "The Doctrine of the Holy Trinity according to Athanasius," Anglican Theological Review 71, 397.

124   Kris Miller, "Participating in the Knowledge of God: An Engagement with the Trinitarian Epistemology of T. F. Torrance," (PhD Diss., Durham: University of Durham, 2013), 115.

125   Lewis Ayres, "Athanasius' Initial Defense of the Term Ὁμοούσιος: Rereading the De Decretis," *Journal of Early Christian Studies* 12:3 (2004): 337–39.

126   Ibid., 358. On the basis of Christopher Stead, "Homoousios dans la pensée de Saint Athanase," in *Politique et théologie chez Athanase d'Alexandrie*, ed. Charles Kannengiesser (Paris: Beauchesne, 1974), 231–53.

the creatures,[127] Athanasius introduced principles of divine immateriality and indivisibility, none of them dealing strictly with Trinitarian issues. Therefore, the view that as the negative term *homoousios* does not disclose, but preserves divine nature impenetrable by pointing that it differs from created nature,[128] would be the main Orthodox objection to Torrance's understanding of *homoousios*.

Moreover, later, especially Cyrillian and Maximian, development of *homoousios* proves that the term is more pregnant with economical than with Trinitarian implications. The doctrine of Christ's "double consubstiantiality," based on the claim of the Council of Chalcedon that Christ is "consubstantial with the Father" and "consubstantial with us,"[129] neither reveals the content of divine nor the content of human nature, but it rather affirms the reciprocity between the human and divine nature in Christ. It may be the case that Torrance has been reading these later developments into the term, because the Athanasian theological vision can hardly be pressed into such a static notion as *homoousios* was in the fourth century.

One may draw the same conclusion from the concept of *perichoresis*. With the concept of double *perichoresis* or coinherence this term ceases to express the static aspect of union of two persons or two natures, but it acquires the meaning of an active reciprocity.[130] As Andrew Louth points out "the tendency to interpret Christological terminology in terms of Trinitarian terminology, and vice versa, was by no means well-established, or even commonplace, in the century before Chalcedon."[131] Thus, one should not expect to find in Athanasius consistent terminology that is applicable in both Christological and Trinitarian contexts. However, it would be wrong to accuse Torrance for attributing something to Athanasius that was not in his work. Torrance rightly sensed the general direction of Athanasius' main theological endeavors, but he wrongly

---

127   Ayres, "Athanasius' Initial Defense of the Term Ὁμοούσιος," 358–59.

128   Cf. John Zizioulas, "The teaching of the 2nd ecumenical council in the historical and ecumenical perspective" in *Credo in Spiritum Sanctum: Atti del Congresso Teologico Internazionale di Pneumatologia* (Rome: Libreria, Editrice Vaticana 1983), 32.

129   *Decrees of the Ecumenical Councils*, ed. N. P. Tanner, 2 vols. (London: Sheed & Ward, and Washington DC: Georgetown University Press, 1990), 86–7.

130   Lars Thunberg, *Microcosm and Mediator: The Theological Anthropology of Maximus the Confessor* (Chicago and La Salle: Open Court, 1995), 28–9.

131   Louth, *Maximus the Confessor*, 49.

tried to capture them with two notions that underwent significant development in centuries after Athanasius.

Second, by denying any separation in nature and will between the Father and the Son, Athanasius actually rejects any separation between the divine essence and activities. By acknowledging that the Holy Trinity is homogenous and unitary, not only in the oneness of his activity, but also in the indivisibility of his eternal being,[132] Torrance draws an analogy between the divine activity and being. The lack of separation between the divine being and will led Torrance to conclude that theology may smoothly progress from the "economic Trinity" into "ontological Trinity."[133]

Torrance understands the identification of the economic Trinity with the immanent Trinity in the sense that all knowledge of God proceeds from God's saving activities in the economy.[134] Thus, all the knowledge of God is acquired in and through the economic Trinity, yet without being restricted to the economic Trinity advances toward the immanent Trinity. If one acknowledges that the basic duality between economic and ontological Trinity is rooted in the distinction between God's essence and activities, then the knowledge of the ontological Trinity is somehow higher than the knowledge of the economic Trinity, since the divine essence is ontologically prior to the divine activities. However, the distinction between the higher, ontological knowledge of God and the lower, economic knowledge of God may appear as a hindrance for progressing in apprehension of God. This view is evident in Maximus the Confessor who claims that "the affirmation of the knowledge of what is ranked above is a negation of the knowledge of what is ranked below, just as the negation of the knowledge of what is below implies the affirmation of what is above."[135] Thus, the analogy between the economic and the immanent Trinity implies the reversed analogy between the knowledge of economic and the knowledge of the

132 Torrance, "The Doctrine of the Holy Trinity according to Athanasius," Anglican Theological Review 71, 398.

133 Torrance, "Athanasius," Theology in Reconciliation, 253.

134 Molnar, Thomas F. Torrance:, Theologian of the Trinity (Farnham: Ashgate, 2009), 68.

135 Ambiguum ad Joannem 20 (PG 91:1240d). The English translation of Brian E. Daley is available in H. U. von Balthasar, Cosmic Liturgy. The Universe According to St. Maximus the Confessor (San Francisco: Ignatium Press, 2003), 93.

immanent Trinity, since the latter is negation of the former and vice versa. It is highly unlikely that Torrance had this in mind.

Another solution is to reject the claim that distinction between the divine essence and energies serves to distinguish between the ontological and the economic Trinity and further between the knowledge of both. Then, we figuratively speak of the two levels of knowledge, since the process of apprehension of God is not a successive two-stage process, but rather a simultaneous process comprising two components. The first component consists in establishing God as the object of knowledge by acknowledging his saving economy, while the second component includes rejecting a duality between "I" as the subject of knowledge and God as the object of knowledge by rushing into simple union with Him. By relying on Athanasius, Maximus the Confessor developed the view of a knowable God who transcends knowledge. The previous sections of this study thoroughly elaborates the basic Athanasian pattern, pointed to by Torrance, in which reason (λόγος) empowered by faith (πίστις) leads to the divine reality or Truth (αλήθεια), which is synonymous to the knowledge of the divine nature (φύσις).[136] The aforementioned elements such as reason (λόγος), faith (πίστις), knowledge (γνώσις), truth (αλήθεια) and nature (φύσις) or essence are present in Maximus, but structured in two simultaneous and mutually dependent processes, one leads to God as essence (ουσία), and another to God as energy (ενέργεια). For Maximus, the grace of the apprehension of the divine essence is granted to the mind (νους), while the reason (λόγος) is endowed with the knowledge of divine energy.

Reason (λόγος) proceeds toward God by its power, habit, and action. The power (δύναμις) of reason is prudence (φρόνησις), the habit (έξις) of reason is action (πράξις), and the activity (ενέργεια) of reason is virtue (αρετή). The inward and unchangeable bond of prudence, action, and virtues as the power, habit, and activity of reason generates faith (πίστις). Faith leads reason further toward God as Good (τό αγαθόν), which is the energy (ενέργεια) of God.[137]

In a similar vein, the power (δύναμις), the habit (εξις), and the activity (ενέργεια) of mind (νοῦς) are wisdom (σοφία), contemplation (θεωρία), and knowledge (γνώσις). By actualising its potency in wisdom, by discovering its habit in contemplation, and by performing its activity

---

136   Torrance, "Athanasius," *Theology in Reconciliation*, 247–8.

137   *Mystagogia* 5.10–11 (PG 91:677CD).

in knowledge, the mind ends in enduring knowledge (αλητος γνώσις).[138] The enduring knowledge is "the perpetual and unceasing movement" of wisdom, contemplation, and knowledge as potency, habit, and activity of mind around the essence (οὐσία) of God as the Truth (ἀλήθεια).

Finally, Maximus concludes that by the grace of Holy Spirit and its own work, every soul can unite mind with reason into reasonable mind, wisdom with prudence into prudent wisdom, contemplative with practical activity into an active contemplation, knowledge with virtues into virtuous knowledge, and finally faith with enduring knowledge into enduring knowledge which is faithful and unchangeable.[139] Thus, the two processes are genuinely one since there is no real differentiation between essence and activity in God, nor differentiation between the two kinds of knowledge.

By acknowledging the interdependence of θεοσεβεία and θεολογία in Athanasius, Torrance anticipated the Maximian solution. Nevertheless, Torrance expressed his position (a) by claiming that the movement of knowledge is the reversed movement of God himself from the ontological Trinity through the economic Trinity,[140] and (b) by considering the concepts of homoousios and perichoresis as the linkage between the economic and immanent Trinity. While the latter has been proved to be problematic, especially in regard to Athanasius' thought, the former may be considered not as false, but rather as an optional reading of Athanasius.

According to Torrance, the order of deification or the elevation of human beings to the Father through (and with) the Son, in the Holy Spirit, is actually the reversed order of the divine activity in the world, which is always from the Father, through the Son, in the Holy Spirit.[141] This so called organic structure of Athanasius' theological understanding allowed Torrance to conclude that there must be coordination between the concrete pattern of divine condescension and the inherent order in the Trinitarian relations in the Godhead.[142]

Contrary to Torrance, Justin Popovich, an Orthodox theologian of the twentieth century, fits human deification into the classical paradigm, that

138 *Mystagogia* 5.8–9, (PG 91:676C–677A).

139 *Mystagogia* 5.13, (PG 91:680A).

140 Miller, "Participating in the Knowledge of God: An Engagement with the Trinitarian Epistemology of T. F. Torrance," 120.

141 Torrance, "Athanasius," *Theology in Reconciliation*, 251–53.

142 Ibid., 251.

is, from the Father, through the Son, in the Spirit. Popovich's interpretation of Athanasius goes further towards a dynamics of love that is untypical to a closed circular model advocated by Torrance, in which the divine operation descends from the Father, while the human action, through worshiping, ascends again to the Father. Torrance's closed model describes to a certain extent the Incarnation and deification as the two paradigmatic processes, by being in accordance with Athanasius' axiom that God became man that man might become God,[143] but it does not portray the Trinitarian life of the deified creation.

Popovich's insistence on the classical formula from-through-in (εκ-δία-εν) actually describes a new reality. As he insists that the Incarnation of the Logos of God signifies a new reality, which by its value surpasses both the divine and human values, the Trinitification of the creation brings a new reality that is constantly renewing and it makes new.[144] The newness, which arises from a new life in Christ, is a continuous growth of deified beings in love within the relationship of the Holy Trinity. Thus, the love of the Father to the Son, perfected and confirmed by the Holy Spirit, is transferred to us and continually renews us and makes us new through the process of deification (θέωσις) understood as Athanasian θεοποίησις, theo-humanization, Christification and Trinitification.[145] Deification as θεοποίησις does not only mean that human beings are called to become gods, but also requires their active participation in the very process of being made gods themselves. The fullness of deification is in Christification, because Christification implies the introduction into the eternal loving union of the three divine persons. The goal toward which created beings strive for is the Trinitification, as admittance in the beginningless and endless love of the Holy Trinity. However, this is not the end of deification, but always a new beginning and renewal.

The problematic of divine being and divine activity leads to another significant issue in Torrance's approach to Orthodox theology by way of Athanasius. Taking a critical attitude toward the Cappadocian distinction between divine *ousia* and energies, Torrance argues that

143 Athanasius, *De Incarnatione Verbi* 54 (Thomson, 268–9).

144 Justin Popovich, *Pravoslavna Filosofija istine: Dogmatika* (Valjevo: Manastir Ćelije, 1978), 3:91.

145 Letter of Justin Popovich to a student, Nov. 19, 1968, "Bogočovečanska evolucija," in Justin Popovich, *Na bogočovečanskom putu* (Beograd: Manastir Ćelije, 1980).

any diversity in energies would endanger the unity of divine Being supposed by Athanasius.[146] Moreover, he proposes that for the purpose of ecumenical unity the Orthodox should renounce the stance that the aforementioned distinction between the essence and energies in God is a faithful development of Athanasius.[147] It seems that we deal here with Torrance's failure to properly understand the Cappadocian contribution. Like some modern scholars, Torrance perceives the divine energies as diverse and possibly temporary.[148] In the Orthodox understanding, however, the divine energies are acts by which God reaches down to creatures and manifests himself to them, and they are certainly not "automatic" emanations from the essence, nor by-products of the internal activity, but are based on the deliberate choice of God to act *ad extra*. The divine foreknowledge of creation, as well as the creative and providential activities, is clearly dependent on God's will to create and govern his creation. The divine names "creator" and "provider" designate these activities and these activities may be considered as the features that necessarily accompany any manifestation of God, but they also do not constitute the divine essence.

The ways in which God chooses to reveal himself through his activities to human beings may be as various as the names that derive from these activities. If one acknowledges that the divine names refer to various divine energies and that divine energies are God Himself, then Torrance's claim that the unity of the divine being might be at risk would be logical. However, if one presupposes that the divine names do not refer to particular energies, but instead are *derived from* particular energies, then we have a different picture regarding diversity. For example, both Basil of Caesarea and Gregory of Nyssa maintain that God's goodness and wisdom, as observed from the created order, reveal God as the Creator, or, to be more precise, reveal His creative activity. Thus, divine goodness and wisdom are not necessarily the divine energies, but they are more aspects of God's creative activity. One may make a similar remark in regard to other activities of God and to the way in which they are perceived. The distinction between the divine names that *are* divine activities and the divine names that *derive from* the divine activities points out the distinction between the names that have the same point

---

146   Torrance, "Athanasius," *Theology in Reconciliation*, 236.

147   Torrance, *Theology in Reconciliation*, 9.

148   Cf. Lewis Ayres, *Nicaea and its Legacy: An Approach to Fourth-Century Trinitarian Theology* (Oxford: Oxford University Press, 2004), 196.

of reference and the names that do not necessarily have the same point of reference. By referring clearly to the divine creative and providential activities, divine names such as "creator," "provider," or "judge" have God as the only point of reference. Thus, the identification of these names with the divine activities seems to be justified. Other divine names, such as goodness and justice, observed by people from the created order and from the Scriptures refer actually to divine creative and providential activities and not to the divine activities of goodness and justice, because divine goodness and justice are the features that people attribute to the creative and providential energies of God. The point of the diversity of the energies in God may be only applicable if it is considered that every divine name refers to a different specific activity of God. If, however, the diversity of names is derived from the creative, providential and other essential activities of God toward the world, then Torrance's objection is not valid, because it is one and the same energy of God directed toward the creation. This one energy of God, manifested as foreknowledge before the creation, as creative activity during the creation, as providence while preserving the world in its existence, and as divine judgment at the end of the world, is actually simultaneous and eternal divine activity *ad extra* since God is not subjected to time.

There are two more issues that Torrance allegedly draws from Athanasius and raises in his approach to the Orthodox that are problematic. By the identification of the Being of God with the divine "I am," Torrance intends to equate the Holy Trinity not with some impersonal essence, or abstract generic notion of being, but with the active self-revelation of God as "he who is who he is."[149] For some Orthodox theologians, Torrance's proposal may resemble the approach of Fr. Sergius Bulgakov, who also embarked on the refutation of the Aristotelian concept of substance as philosophical abstraction,[150] and propagated a more dynamic concept of divine *ousia*, which introduces creation in the life of the Holy Trinity. Bulgakov developed his Sophiology by substituting the philosophical concept of the essence of God as something hidden by the essence of God as the self-revelation in love or Sophia-Ousia, which allows the whole creation to participate in the very life of God, without sharing its tri-hypostatic nature. The Orthodox Church has not accepted Bulgakov's

---

149   Thomas F. Torrance, "The Doctrine of the Holy Trinity according to Athanasius," *Anglican Theological Review* 71, 403.

150   Sergius Bulgakov, *The Wisdom of God* (Hudson, NY: Lindisfarne Press, 1993), 46.

Sophiological project, which received the official condemnation of the Moscow Patriarchate and the Synod of the Russian Orthodox Church Abroad in 1935. Georges Florovsky, in one of his letters to Torrance, accused both Bulgakov and Karl Barth as having "attempted to *rationalize* the antinomic mystery, and then the Timeless is *ontologically* involved in the Time-process."[151] By referring to Bulgakov's and Barth's failures in the rationalization of the mystery, in my opinion, Florovsky implies that he and Torrance may also be liable to such a failure if they do not preserve this antinomy-mystery intact.

Another problematic issue is the rift that Torrance opens in the theology of the Cappadocians in regard to the *monarchia* of the Father. It seems that Torrance here fights some modern interpretations of the Cappadocian view on the monarchy of the Father.[152] Even though all three Cappadocian Fathers share the general view on *monarchia* of the Father, their motifs for introducing the notion are different, if not divergent. Thus, for Basil the concept of *monarchia* served to establish the unity of God on the causality of the Father, while for Gregory of Nyssa it helps to distinguish between the persons of the Trinity.[153] Although for Gregory the Theologian the *monarchia* is the root of both the oneness of the Trinity and uniqueness of the persons,[154] some scholars consider that Gregory applies this term not to the Father, but to the divine essence.[155] Thus, not only alleged Athanasian causeless equality of the divine persons, but also Nyssen's interpretation of *monarchia* of the Father as a means to distinguish between the divine persons and Nazianzen's view of *monarchia* of the divine substance avoid any of Torrance's feared

---

151   Georges Florovsky to T. F. Torrance, Oct. 21, 1973. Thomas F. Torrance Manuscript Collection, Princeton Theological Seminary Library, 104.

152   Cf. John D. Zizioulas, *Communion and Otherness* (London: T&T Clark, 2006), 113– 54.

153   Michel R. Barnes, "Divine Unity and Divided Self," *Modern Theology* 18 (2002): 483–84. Vladimir Cvetković, "St. Gregory's Argument Concerning the Lack of *Diastema* in divine Activities from *Ad Ablabium*" in *Gregory of Nyssa: The Minor Treatises on Trinitarian Theology and Apollinarism*, ed. V. H. Drecoll and M. Berghaus (Leiden: Brill, 2011), 369–82.

154   *Oratio* 20.6, (*PG* 35:1072D). Cf. Christopher A. Beeley. "Divine Causality and Monarchy of God the Father in Gregory of Nazianzus," *Harvard Theological Review* 100 (2007): 204–08.

155   Richard Cross, "Divine Monarchy in Gregory of Nazianzus," *Journal of Early Christian Studies* 14 (2006): 116, Ayres, *Nicaea and Its Legacy: An Approach to Fourth-Century Trinitarian Theology*, 244-45. Mainly on the basis of Gregory's *Oratio* 31.14.

subordinationism within the Trinity. Therefore, from the Orthodox perspective, the main objection to Torrance in regard to *monarchia* would be that instead of grasping this richness of the internal dynamism and variety of the respective theologies of the Cappadocians[156] in the light of their indebtedness to the Athanasian contribution, he embraced the view that causeless ontological equality as supposedly advocated by Athanasius is the only viable form of Orthodoxy.

In spite of these minor obstacles – which are perhaps due more to the inconsistencies of Orthodox theologians with their own tradition[157] than to Torrance's failure to grasp the importance of this same patristic tradition – Torrance's intention to develop an ecumenical theology of reconciliation on the basis of Athanasius and Cyril deserves great respect from all sides that participate in the dialogue.

The references to Maximus the Confessor proved to be useful, since the salient points on which Torrance built his understanding of Athanasius underscores the theology of the Byzantine monk. The Athanasian doctrine of the intrinsic rationality of things, which reveals the Logos of God in the general order, is developed by Maximus as the doctrine of the *logoi* of creation. The scriptural statements or *logoi*, similarly to the intrinsic rationality embedded in the cosmos which provide the understanding of the divine realities and lead human beings toward their *telos*, deeply resemble Maximus' view on Scripture. Finally, the Mystery of Christ for both Athanasius and Maximus is seen in the context of the preconceived divine plan of the Incarnation of the Logos in human nature, who introduces the assumed humanity into the life of the Holy Trinity and opens up the way to salvation and deification for humankind. Moreover, Maximus' theology contains the full realization of the Athanasian ideas on which Torrance heavily relied.

Issues, such as the analogy between God *in se* and God *ad extra*, or between one divine being and diversity of energies that are mentioned above as potential problems in the interpretation of Athanasius, find

---

156   Najeeb G. Awad, "Between Subordination and Koinonia: Toward a New Reading of the Cappadocian Theology," *Modern Theology* 23 (2007): 181–204.

157   One of the main inconsistencies of modern Orthodox theologians with their own tradition is overstating some elements from the tradition, while understating the other. Thus, Bulgakov overstated divine essence at the expense of the energy of the divine persons, Florensky overstated Trinitarian theology at the expense of Christology, Lossky overstated epistemological apophaticism at the expense of ontological encounter and Zizioulas overstated person at the expense of grace.

their successful handling in Maximus. By his doctrine, Maximus not only gathered various contributions of Athanasian, Cappadocian, and Cyrillian theological endeavours in one perfect synthesis, but also built one overall theology that might serve as a point of unity and reconciliation for disparate confessional strands.

It is a pity that Torrance, apart from some slight indications of a sporadic reading of Maximus, never engaged the Byzantine monk in any serious way, especially given that so much of his reading of Athanasius, and his theology as a whole, intuitively converges with the Maximian development. Torrance's theological legacy will undoubtedly play a significant role for understanding the ecumenical reconciliation in a broader perspective of the reconciliation of the creation with the Father in the Mystery of Christ. Moreover, his theological intuition, which sometimes inclined toward rationalization of the Mystery, may be of greater importance, because in accordance with his method, it opens up the right path to encounter and to know the incomprehensible God.

Chapter 5

Theological Realism in St. Ephrem the Syrian and T. F. Torrance[1]

Mark Mourachian

There can be no doubt about who the chief patristic figures were that shaped T. F. Torrance's theology. That Torrance's theological contributions lean heavily on the "Athanasius-Cyril axis" is, of course, well known;[2] to them one would quickly add the names of Hilary of Poitiers and Irenaeus of Lyons.[3] This essay, however, brings Torrance into conversation with a figure less known to many of his readers: Ephrem the Syrian, the masterful poet-theologian of fourth-century Mesopotamia. What Torrance has written about theological method and epistemology bears striking resemblance in several respects to the methodological and epistemological framework of the Syrian Father's conception of symbolic knowing and divine revelation. With respect to Torrance, the aim of this essay is to broaden, if only a little, the patristic basis on which his articulation of theological realism rests; for readers of Ephrem, the aim is to offer further evidence that he can be of service to contemporary theological endeavors and of interest outside the realm of strictly historical or literary studies, to which some may wish to relegate him. Indeed, examining the continuities that obtain between Ephrem and Torrance is enriching for readers of both, and the normative status of Nicene theology for all Christian thought is

---

1 This essay is adapted from a chapter from the author's Ph.D. dissertation, "Human Freedom in the Context of the Theological Anthropology of St. Ephrem the Syrian" (Washington, DC: Catholic University of America, 2012).

2 Thomas F. Torrance, *Theology in Reconciliation* (Grand Rapids, MI: Eerdmans, 1975), 9.

3 See, e.g., Torrance's essays on those two Fathers in his *Divine Meaning* (Edinburgh: T&T Clark, 1995) and Matthew Baker, "The Place of St. Irenaeus of Lyons in Historical and Dogmatic Theology according to Thomas F. Torrance," *Participatio* 2 (2010): 5–43.

reaffirmed by drawing attention to the unqualifiedly Christocentric nature of both theologians' conceptions of theological knowing and the demands it entails.[4]

The present study first examines Ephrem's working conception of revelation and of the knowledge of God offered to us by means of it. Ephrem's theological epistemology then comes into sharper focus by way of contrast with the method and presuppositions entailed in "investigation,"[5] the theological epistemology exemplified first and foremost by Arianizing Christians. Ephrem remains the major focus throughout this study. Nevertheless, affinities and continutities between him and Torrance are drawn out where they are most striking.

Media of Divine Revelation

> If you look anywhere, His symbol is there,
>
> and wherever you read, you will discover His types.
>
> For all creatures were created by Him,
>
> and He inscribed his symbols upon His possessions.
>
> Behold, when He created the world,
>
> He looked upon it and adorned it with His images.
>
> Fountains of His symbols were opened; they flowed and poured forth
>
> His symbols upon its members.[6]

4   For some relatively recent discussions of Ephrem as "Nicene" or "anti-Arian" see, e.g., Lewis Ayres, *Nicaea and Its Legacy: An Approach to Fourth-Century Trinitarian Theology* (Oxford: Oxford University Press, 2004), 229–35; Christine Shepardson, "Ephrem, Athanasius, and the 'Arian' Threat," in *Anti-Judaism and Christian Orthodoxy: Ephrem's Hymns in Fourth-Century Syria* (Washington, DC: Catholic University of America Press, 2008), 106–56; and Kees den Biesen, *Simple and Bold: Ephrem's Art of Symbolic Thought* (Piscataway, NJ: Gorgias, 2006), 77–85, and 293–307, where the author examines Paul S. Russell's *St. Ephraem the Syrian and St. Gregory the Theologian Confront the Arians* (Kottayam: St. Ephrem Ecumenical Research Institute, 1994).

5   There are at least three semantically related terms relevant here: *ᶜuqqābā*, *bṣātā*, and *bᶜātā* (all nouns, but their related verb forms are implicated here as well). They share a common notion of "investigation" or "inquiry." Den Biesen states that while the first two often have negative connotations in Ephrem's works, there are passages in which they have a positive sense (*Simple and Bold*, 194n147). The last term, he says, is neutral in itself; its shades of meaning are determined by the contexts in which it is used (ibid., 135n82).

6   Ephrem, *Hymns on Virginity* (hereinafter *Virg*) 20.12. Edmund Beck, the editor of the Syriac text, refers the reader to Ephrem's *Hymns on Faith* (hereinafter *HdF*)

So ends one of Ephrem's *Hymns on Virginity*. In stanzas like this one we find evidence of the way images, types, and symbols function in Ephrem's theology. The Syriac term most frequently and intimately connected with this foundational aspect of Ephrem's thought is *rāzē*, mystery-bearing symbols laden with divine meaning.[7] In the verses quoted above we read of a two-fold act of creation: God does not merely constitute created things in being as such, but stamps upon them the distinctive marks of their divine Craftsman. The fountains of symbols that gushed forth upon the creation recall the fountain of waters in Genesis 2:6, which "on the day that God made heaven and earth . . . rose up and watered all the face of the earth."[8] Those twin aspects, bringing into being and stamping, jointly constitute God's act of creation. For Ephrem, God does not create anonymously, nor would he. It is inconceivable that the loving Creator would so withhold his goodness and grace from his creatures by de-personalizing his creative act. The very act of creating, from which the act of inscribing in creation chosen symbols of himself is inseparable, betokens God's establishment of a relation with that which is other than himself. That holds true above all with respect to human persons. It is the living God who creates, and his act of creating human persons flows from his personal subjectivity, which could not be rendered impersonal or anonymous.

So the fact that God impresses his seal upon all that he brings into being in no way implies a bifurcation in the nature or meaning of creatures, as though the divine imprint were something added to them over and above some independently coherent and complete meaning they might otherwise enjoy or had previously enjoyed. In bringing them into being, God constitutes his creatures as objectively

76.12 and *Virg* 21.10 for parallels. All translations of Ephrem's works in this article, unless otherwise noted, are the author's and are based on the Syriac text of the CSCO editions. Available modern language translations were consulted: Beck's German translations in the CSCO volumes; Kathleen McVey, *Ephrem the Syrian: Hymns* (New York: Paulist Press, 1989); and Paul S. Russell, Ephraem the Syrian: Eighty Hymns on Faith (unpublished, 1995).

7 For a discussion of *rāzē* and other terms involved in Ephrem's symbolic theology, see Tanios Bou Mansour, *La pensée symbolique de saint Ephrem le Syrien* (Kaslik, Lebanon: Université Saint-Esprit, 1988), 23–71.

8 As quoted in Ephrem's *Commentary on Genesis* 26:12–15. If Ephrem intends to echo Genesis 2:6 in *Virg* 20.12, then the latter is just one example of the rich poetic exegesis, whose symbolic repertoire ranges far and wide, that Ephrem applies to the same scriptural passages he interprets in his prose according to the "plain sense" of literal, historical meaning.

meaningful with ultimate reference to himself, and this is so for a specific reason. Creation is endowed by God with symbolic significance precisely in order to reveal something of himself to mankind. Torrance makes much the same point, based on Barth's distinction between God's primary and his secondary form of objectivity.[9] According to the latter:

> God objectifies Himself for us within the world of our natural objects, and so clothes His ultimate and divine objectivity with the kind of objectivity with which we are familiar in creation, in Israel, among men, in history, in our common human life – that is to say, within the space and time of this world.[10]

The loving relationship that God establishes with his human creatures is one in which he invites them to discover him through the whole panoply of created realities. And those created media of divine revelation do not impose their symbolic meaning on their observers by sheer force. Human persons are urged to discover their ultimate meaning in freedom, by an effort of the will and mind on the ground of faith.[11]

Of immeasurable importance among those created realities, the two biblical testaments together occupy a unique place in Ephrem's understanding of the way God reveals himself to humanity. The Bible is unique among the *loci* of God's self-revelation in that there divine truth is conveyed by means of the human word, whereas nature, of itself, is silent and can only come to verbal expression by way of human interaction with it, reflection upon it, and articulation of it.[12] One must make the

9 See Karl Barth, *Church Dogmatics*, ed. G. W. Bromiley and T. F. Torrance (London: T&T Clark, 2004), 2:1.16–18.

10 Thomas F. Torrance, *Theological Science* (Oxford: Oxford University Press, 1978), 43.

11 See ibid., 36, where Torrance illuminates the paradoxical relationship between freedom and the demands of objectivity in a manner consonant with Ephrem's thought.

12 Perhaps Ephrem would have considered this task part of the priestly function of human persons – he certainly saw it as part of his own work as a theologian and poet. Torrance viewed the task of the scientist along similar lines. For him, "the pursuit of science is one of the ways in which man exercises the dominion in the earth which he was given at his creation." T. F. Torrance, "Newton, Einstein and Scientific Theology," *Religious Studies* 8 (1972): 233. Explaining Bacon's understanding of the work of natural science and the natural scientist, Torrance continues: "Science is a religious duty, while man as scientist can be spoken of as *the priest of creation*, whose task it is to interpret the books of nature, to understand the universe in its wonderful structures and harmonies, and to bring it all into orderly articulation, so that it fulfills its proper

effort to engage mute nature so that, as the whole of Ephrem's literary corpus exemplifies, one can grasp its divine meaning and be able to give it a material voice by way of the written or spoken word, to the glory of God and for the benefit of others.

While they are distinct in that regard, the Bible and the natural world are nevertheless coordinated such that they confirm and shed light upon one another. Recall the opening of *Virg* 20.12: "If you look anywhere, His symbol is there, / and wherever you read, you will discover His types." As den Biesen rightly points out, the "anywhere" may refer to the whole creation, and the "wherever" to the whole Bible.[13] It is telling that Ephrem places the two side by side in his presentation of the way God manifests himself, since, as Robert Murray notes, biblical types do not constitute an entirely independent mode of revelation: "[Ephrem] never treats the biblical text as a world on its own: rather, the Bible, as a work of God in human imagery and language, is a part, as well as a special interpreter, of the whole world and its history."[14] Murray identifies in Ephrem's thought the mutual influence and consonance of the Bible and the natural world. They help to interpret and confirm each other, all under the watchful eye enlightened by faith. And as we will see in the course of this study, the fact that both nature and the Bible are *created* means of God's self- revelation is essential to Ephrem's polemic against those who are guilty of the sin of investigation. Working in tandem, nature and Scripture are unified in their purpose: to bear witness to God in order to glorify him and to facilitate our knowledge of him who is the Truth, should we engage them appropriately and follow where they lead us.

Though we engage them differently – "using" nature, but "reading" Scripture, as Ephrem says[15] – the two witnesses are harmonized with one another. A beloved image of Ephrem's for that harmony is that

---

end as the vast theatre of glory in which the creator is worshipped and praised. Nature itself is dumb, but it is man's part to bring it to word, to be its mouth through which the whole universe gives voice to the glory and majesty of the living God" (ibid.).

13 den Biesen, *Simple and Bold*, 25.

14 Robert Murray, "The Theory of Symbolism in St. Ephrem's Theology," *Parole de l'Orient* 6/7 (1975–76): 5. If nature and Scripture help to interpret each other more fully, that function is secondary to their primary function of witnessing to the Lord of them both. According to Bou Mansour, Ephrem was not of the opinion that the witness of nature has the Bible or its truth as its proper object: "Bien au contraire, nature et Ecriture sont orientées toutes les deux vers l'attestation de la vérité du Créateur" (*Pensée*, 125).

15 Ephrem, *Hymns on Paradise* (hereinafter *Parad*) 5.2.

of the harp, which serves two basic purposes. On the one hand, the harp, as an image of the vehicles of divine revelation, is that which God uses to communicate himself to us;[16] on the other hand, the three harps are the God-given instruments on which believers freely play to him in response.[17] Ephrem's harps are the created means for man's encounter with his Creator – an encounter initiated by God (in the act of creating in the first place) and taken up and reciprocated by human persons in their free response of faith and love.[18]

Up to this point, our discussion of Ephrem's understanding of divine revelation has focused on the manifest things of God, that which he has planted in the midst of creation voicelessly, and that which he has conveyed through the Bible by means of human language. It is necessary, though, to appreciate the correlate to Ephrem's emphasis on God's self-manifestation: his stress on God's hiddenness. In one of his *Hymns on Faith* Ephrem writes:

> Indeed, who is able to comprehend the Lord of natures,
>
> to inquire into His Being and to investigate His Fatherhood,
>
> and to explore His Greatness and to say how It is?
>
> For, behold, in all those respects He is hidden from all,
>
> and unless He wants to make Himself plain to us
>
> there is nothing in Creation that is able to interpret Him.[19]

The core assumption at work here – indeed, everywhere in Ephrem's theology – is that between the Creator and the creation there yawns a gaping chasm, a "great, boundless gulf" over which no created thing may cross.[20] Any and all knowledge of God is fundamentally dependent upon God's good pleasure in revealing himself as he sees fit. Note the last two verses in the stanza quoted above: God is altogether hidden, and no created thing can interpret him, *unless* he wills it do so. He has so willed, and his very act of creating the natural world and taking on human

---

16 *Virg* 30.1.

17 *Virg* 27.4.

18 See Bou Mansour's comments (*Pensée*, 125–26) on the *taxis* Ephrem maintains between Scripture and nature as means of God's self-revelation (*pace* Beck, who, Bou Mansour says, thought that Ephrem placed the witness of nature and that of Scripture on the same level).

19 *HdF* 44.7.

20 *HdF* 15.5. It should be noted that the chasm is not the result of man's disobedience and sin; it exists simply by virtue of the Creator-creation distinction.

language is sufficient evidence of that claim's truth. Yet as near as God may draw, through the created means he chooses for his self-revelation, he nevertheless remains infinitely transcendent. He is at once very close and immeasurably far.[21]

Sebastian Brock uses the category of perspective to explain this example of Ephrem's habit of thinking through polarities.[22] From our perspective, all created things are of revelatory significance, and we understand them as just that, God's self-revelations in and through his handiwork. But from the perspective of divine reality itself, God has *hidden* something of himself in created things, pointing "to something that will one day be revealed: what is 'hidden' in the symbols of Nature and of Scripture is revealed in Christ at the Incarnation; what lies hidden in the Sacraments will be revealed at the eschaton, in Paradise."[23] Even when we come to see the symbolic significance of all that God has imprinted of himself in created realities, he yet remains hidden, which fact is all the more apparent in view of the ontological divide between God and creation: nothing finite could ever manifest completely the infinite, inimitable majesty of God as he is in himself.

While Brock's explanation of the polarity between the hidden and the revealed is helpful, there is one point on which his language is potentially misleading. He speaks of the human perspective as "subjective," while the divine perspective enjoys objectivity.[24] By "subjective" he means that "every individual will approach God's hiddenness by way of a different set of *galyata*, or points of revelation."[25] That is so because all the instances of God's self-revelation are differentiated, and that to which they all point in their manifold ways, God himself, is infinitely greater than the sum of revelation's parts: "the revelation is always partial."[26] His explanation of what he deems the "subjective" character of the human perspective is certainly true to Ephrem, but his choice of the term "subjective," in contrast to "objective," is open to misinterpretation. To the modern ear those terms typically register in ways that are contrary to Ephrem's thinking and are commonly understood against the background of

21 See *HdF* 72.23–24.

22 See his discussion in his *Luminous Eye: The Spiritual World Vision of Saint Ephrem the Syrian* (Kalamazoo, MI: Cistercian Publications, 1992), 27–29.

23 Ibid., 28–29.

24 Ibid., 27–28.

25 Ibid., 27.

26 Ibid.

a dualist framework in which *subjectivism* is pit against claims to an accessible objective reality – not with reference to *subjectivity*.

Brock surely does not foist on Ephrem some radical disconnect between knower and known, or between the content of one's thought and the reality it appears to intend, such as a dualist epistemology would entail. His exposition of Ephrem shows no marks of that kind of crippling of the human capacity for real knowledge. But it bears repeating that, for Ephrem, it is God who implanted in creation reliable indications and symbols of himself, constituting them to function as the faithful mind of the believer understands them to function. In that respect, both the divine and the human perspective are objective: they are grounded in and intend the objective reality that God is, albeit in radically different ways. God makes created symbols to correspond in a contingent, creaturely way to the truth that he himself is in a non-contingent, uncreated way.

It is better to consider the terms "subjective" and "objective," as applied to Ephrem's theology, from within the realist framework that Torrance so clearly articulated. In Torrance's description, realism is:

> the orientation in thought that obtains in semantics, science, or theology on the basis of a nondualist or unitary relation between the empirical and theoretical ingredients in the structure of the real world and in our knowledge of it. This is an epistemic orientation of the two-way relation between the subject and object poles of thought and speech, in which ontological primacy and control are naturally accorded to reality over all our conceiving and speaking of it.[27]

It is critical to appreciate how much a realist Ephrem actually is. In no way whatsoever does Ephrem allow for a theory of meaning as subjectively constructed out of whole cloth and totally dependent on the idiosyncrasies and fantasies of the mind unmoored from objective reality. The media through which God reveals himself to us, and the specific content of those manifestations, are objectively determined by God to be what they are and to function as they do. When we exert the effort to engage those media and discern their function and their hidden, divinely bestowed content, that experience yields results that are real yet, as Brock rightly notes, always and necessarily partial – partial in each

---

27 Thomas F. Torrance, *Reality and Evangelical Theology* (Philadelphia: Westminster Press, 1982), 60. See also Torrance's essay "Theological Realism," in *The Philosophical Frontiers of Christian Theology*, ed. Brian Hebblethwaite and Stewart Sutherland (Cambridge: Cambridge University Press, 1982), 173.

individual instance and in the aggregate. What that fact implies is that the revelation of God is always and everywhere new, and the particulars of its manifestations are unexpected. As Michael Polanyi avers:

> To hold knowledge is indeed always a commitment to indeterminate implications, for human knowledge is but an intimation of reality, and we can never quite tell in what new way reality may yet manifest itself. It is external to us; it is objective; and so its future manifestations can never be completely under our intellectual control.[28]

While we are free to discover the coherence and meaning of divine revelation through created things, we are not free to construct it. In other words, the fundamental structure, manner, and content of divine revelation are not subject to human control and determination: the structure, because the Creator orders all things; the manner, because he reveals himself *as* he wills; and the content, because the real, ultimate content of his self-revelation is the person of the incarnate Word, who reconciles us with the Father and gives us his Spirit to guide us "into all truth."[29]

Jesus Christ, "the Lord of Symbols"[30]

Since God wishes to reveal himself to us, he has both endowed created things with revelatory significance and enabled us to discover their meaning. He is unceasing in his efforts to win mankind over, and so from the beginning he has offered us, as an invitation, pathways to knowledge of him in the created world. Extending the invitation further, and making it more fully revelatory of himself, God communicates with his word-endowed creatures by means of Scripture:

> He drew near to us by means of what belongs to us.
> He put on names that belong to us so that He might clothe us
> with the manner of life that belongs to Him.
> He borrowed our form and put it on,
> and as a father with his infants, so He spoke with our childishness.[31]

---

28 Michael Polanyi, "Faith and Reason," *Journal of Religion* 41 (1961): 244. See also Torrance's discussion of open concepts (*Theological Science*, 15), with respect to which "the reality conceived keeps on disclosing itself to us in such a way that it continually overflows all our statements about it."

29 John 16:13.

30 *HdF* 9.11.

31 *HdF* 31.2.

In condescending to the level of the written and spoken word, God sanctified the use of human language to refer to himself. The events related in the Old Testament, his dealings with his beloved Israel, as well as the written biblical testimonies themselves, manifest divine *kenosis* already before the Incarnation – the verses quoted just above make that plain. One could even say that God's gracious condescension was begun with the act of creation itself, since he has woven telltale signs of his truth into the very fabric of creation.[32]

Yet the ultimate revelation of God at the center of all created realities comes in the Incarnation of the Son of God in the person of Jesus Christ, when, no longer putting on names and metaphors only, the Lord "put on the body," "put on Adam."[33] In taking on our flesh the Son made himself the sole bridge over the chasm separating God and creation. If any creature is to have access to the Father, it is only in and through the incarnate Lord. Ephrem hymns the glorious name of Jesus, calling it "the hidden bridge that leads / from death to life."[34] He prays:

> Be the bridge for my speech;
>
> may it cross over to Your truth.
>
> Make Your love a bridge for Your servant;
>
> let me cross over You to Your Father.[35]

The perfect visible image of the invisible God, Christ is both the source and the fulfillment of all types, images, and symbols, the fountainhead of all the streams of created manifestations of God – most clearly those found in the Bible – and the vast sea where they all converge:

> Christ conquered and surmounted the symbols by His interpretations,
>
> the parables by His explanations. Just like the sea, He receives within Himself
>
> all the rushing streams . . .
>
> For Christ is the one who perfects [the Scriptures'] symbols by His cross,
>
> their types by His body, their adornments by His beauty,
>
> and all of them by all of Himself.[36]

---

32 See *Virg* 20.12.

33 See Ephrem, *Hymns on the Nativity* (hereinafter *Nat*) 9.2, 23.13.

34 *HdF* 6.17.

35 Ibid.

36 *Virg* 9.10, 15. See Murray, "Theory of Symbolism," 7–9, where he offers an explanation and schematic illustration of the network of symbolic relations at

Ephrem's entirely Christocentric understanding of biblical revelation brings to mind Torrance's own scriptural hermeneutic, according to which Christ is God's Word addressed to man, as well as man's word of response to God.[37] Torrance writes:

> *The real text* of New Testament revelation is *the humanity of Jesus*. As we read the Old Testament and read the New Testament and listen to the Word of God, the real text is not documents of the Pentateuch, the Psalms or the Prophets or the documents of the Gospels and the Epistles, but in and through them all the Word of God struggling with rebellious human existence in Israel on the way to becoming incarnate, and then that Word translated into the flesh and blood and mind and life of a human being in Jesus, in whom we have both the Word of God become man and the perfect response of man to God offered on our behalf. As the real text of God's Word addressed to us, Jesus is also the real text of our address to God. We have no speech or language with which to address God but the speech and language called Jesus Christ. In him our humanity, our human understanding, our human word are taken up, purified and sanctified, and addressed to God the Father for us as our very own – and that is the word of man with which God is well pleased.[38]

In both Ephrem and Torrance we find the two-fold meaning of God's *self-revelation* at work: both theologians stress, first, the fact that it is with God himself that all revelation originates and, second, the all-important truth of the Incarnation, whereby God himself, in the person of the Word, reveals himself.[39] In the latter respect the strongly Nicene thrust of both theologians' concepts of revelation is clearly at the fore.

---

work in Ephrem's theology, in which Christ is "the term of all symbols, towards whom they home in from every side" (Ephrem, *Commentary on Tatian's Diatessaron*, 1.1, quoted in ibid., 7).

37 See *HdF* 6.17, quoted above, and Torrance, *Theological Science*, 45.

38 Thomas F. Torrance, *The Mediation of Christ*, 2nd ed. (Colorado Springs: Helmers & Howard, 1992), 78–79 (emphasis original). See also Torrance, *Reality and Evangelical Theology*, 93–94; and *Theological Science*, 45, where Torrance states that since Christ "is the concrete embodiment of knowledge of God within our humanity," then "it is by positive and concrete reference of all our theological knowledge to Him . . . that we have genuine knowledge of God."

39 See, e.g., Torrance, *Reality and Evangelical Theology*, 23.

"Everything depends on faith"[40]

The pervasive emphasis in Ephrem's works on the concrete reality of God's self-revelation in the midst of the world he created may incline some of his readers to consider him a natural theologian of sorts.[41] The corrective to that misreading is Ephrem's equally persistent stress on the priority of faith in Christ as that which enables human persons to read nature and Scripture rightly, to find in them what God has veiled. The notion that natural knowledge serves as the necessary propaedeutic for the reception of divine revelation given in Christ and in the biblical testimonies to him is certainly alien to Ephrem's way of thinking.

Faith is the requisite lens through which the human person is able to perceive the truth of God to which all the natural world and all the Bible bear witness in symbolic fashion. It is faith that transforms the believer's eye into the instrument by which the opacity of created realities is changed to a transparency opening out onto God. More accurately, it is faith in the incarnate Word and the life-giving relation into which he draws the believer that make proper vision, perceptive hearing, and true knowledge possible: "With faith gaze upon Him, / upon the Lord of symbols, who gives you life."[42]

Since truth, for Ephrem, is ultimately hypostatized in the person of the Word,[43] our relation to the truth consists in our relation to him. The source of all true knowledge and that of life are one and the same, the person of the incarnate Lord, and our relation to him is given life by way of faith in him – Ephrem considers faith a "second soul," enlivening our soul which, in turn, enlivens our body.[44] All theological knowing is actualized in relation to Christ and through the dynamism of faith in him. The mind possessed of faith is enabled by God to bear the fruit of a godly life in freedom on the basis of knowledge of truth.[45]

---

40 *HdF* 7.9.

41 That is, according to a conception of natural theology as an antecedent and completely independent field of inquiry that requires the bracketing of faith, not altogether unlike the kind that, according to Torrance, Barth strongly rejected: see his *Transformation and Convergence in the Frame of Knowledge* (Grand Rapids, MI: Eerdmans, 1984), ix.

42 *HdF* 9.11.

43 See, e.g., Ephrem, *Hymns against Heresies* (hereinafter *HcH*) 2.18.

44 *HdF* 80.1. See also *HdF* 80.2–3.

45 *HdF* 80.7–8.

Torrance points to the same interpenetration of faith, true knowledge, and life lived according to the truth:

> The very passion of faith is the opening up of the knowing subject to the most objective of all realities, God Himself as He actively communicates Himself to us in Jesus Christ. To know the truth is to be in a right relation to Him, to be in the truth with the Truth. To know this Truth in a medium appropriate to Him is to do the truth and to live the truth, to be true.[46]

For Ephrem, the process of coming to know the truth (coming to know God), and living in accordance with the truth (leading a godly life according to the pattern of Christ, who is the Truth) are the flowering of God's bestowal of his divine image in the creation of human persons.[47] Being formed in the image of God is partly what we are already, and partly what we are to become; it is at once a gift and a calling. Both the epistemic and ascetical dimensions of the human vocation are radically dependent upon the free, loving, and obedient activity of a faithful mind whose limpid eye is able to discover God where and how he reveals himself – ultimately in the person of his incarnate Son.

The Nature of Investigation

The preceding sections of this study have laid the groundwork for a discussion of Ephrem's polemic against the Arians, his chief adversaries within the Church.[48] It is not so much the content of their doctrine as

46 Torrance, *Theological Science*, 6. His comments there stem from his reading of Kierkegaard. See also T. F. Torrance, *The Trinitarian Faith* (London: T&T Clark, 2000), 38, where he discusses the connection between knowledge of God and a godly life in the thought of Origen.

47 See Ephrem's *First Discourse to Hypatius* (hereinafter *Hyp* 1), 22.8–11 (J. Josephus Overbeck's edition, 1865, using his page and line numbers): "If Adam was the image of God by virtue of his authority (šulṭānā), it is very praiseworthy when, by means of knowledge of the truth and true conduct, a man becomes the image of God, for indeed, that authority consists in these [two]."

48 Problems related to a proper taxonomy of the various groups and movements commonly collected under the label "Arian" are beyond the scope of this study. Neither does this study assess the accuracy of Ephrem's estimation of Arian doctrine and theological method. What is important here is the profile of what Ephrem deems a threat to orthodox faith and life, not whether he properly understands his opponents' ways of thinking.

such that is of most interest here as much as their theological method and epistemology – that is, the way in which they believed, according to Ephrem, that they could arrive at the knowledge of God, and what theological knowledge they assumed was open to them and was subject to their inquiry.

Ephrem's most frequently repeated charge against the Arians is that of the sin of "investigation."[49] In his examination and rejection of that epistemological method, Ephrem decries the rationalistic hubris that arrogates to itself the power to penetrate into the hidden things of God "behind the back of Jesus Christ"[50] and to speak plainly of that which is in fact immeasurably beyond the capacities of the creaturely mind and of the language used to express what it knows. Ephrem insists on thinking and speaking through God's chosen symbols and names, taking them as trustworthy signs of divine truth, but the investigators refuse to be content with that mode of thought and speech: symbolic and metaphoric expression gives way to univocal speech. As Ephrem sees it, they blindly attempt to circumvent God's chosen means of self-revelation in preference for an allegedly direct (i.e., unmediated) apprehension of God as he is in his essence and apart from his self-revelation. As Torrance so keenly put it:

> We find and know God where He has sought us and condescended to communicate Himself, in His objectivity in Jesus Christ. We cannot seek to know Him by transcending His condescension or objectivity, or by going behind it, for that would be to go where God has not given Himself to be the object of our knowledge.[51]

Ephrem characterizes the investigator's attempt at totally unmediated knowledge as the vain effort to "pry into" (*bṣā*)[52] the things of God. In Torrance's language, the investigator violates one of the fundamental

---

49 See footnote 5 above for the relevant Syriac terms.

50 The phrase is Torrance's. See his *The Trinitarian Faith*, 135. The phrase is there set, aptly enough for the present discussion, in the context of arguing for the indispensability of the Nicene confession and its significance for a proper understanding of divine revelation: "'The *homoousion* asserts that God *is* eternally in himself what he *is* in Jesus Christ, and, therefore, that there is no dark unknown God behind the back of Jesus Christ, but only he who is made known to us in Jesus Christ."

51 Torrance, *Theological Science*, 51.

52 This is a verb form of *bṣātā* mentioned in footnote 5 above.

principles of realism, that one's "method of knowledge must correspond to the nature of the object."[53] Torrance writes:

> [God] does not give Himself to us as a mere object subjected to our knowing, but as Subject who maintains Himself in implacable objectivity over against us, objecting to any attempt on our part to subject Him to our knowing. This is an objectivity that is the antithesis of all objectivism, for objectivism treats the object merely as an object and prescinds the relation of the knowing subject to the object in such a way that the relation of the subject to the object becomes purely theoretical or logical, i.e. an abstraction.[54]

For Ephrem, the way of investigation is not, however, only a lamentable error of the intellect that tries to subjugate the truth of God to the dictates of its own logic. In the Arians it is a mutation of the same fatal disease that so plagued the Greeks at Athens that they rejected both Paul's preaching and the medicine of life.[55] Ephrem's case against the investigators marshals a vast array of arguments against their many ills and vices. Among its other faults, investigation constitutes a sure sign of bad faith; willful disregard for the limitations inherent in human nature, and the neglect of an appropriately measured search for the knowledge of God; a complete distortion of the character of appropriate speech and appropriate silence; profound ignorance of the nature of God's self-revelation and of the proper response to it; and evidence of a divisive and contentious spirit that wreaks havoc in the churches. In all those respects, investigation and the cognate sin of "inquiry" (bṣātā) stem directly from the free choices made by the guilty parties. In no way whatsoever are they compelled to seek after the knowledge of God in the way they do. God freely and lovingly reveals himself to his human creatures for their own good, and he bids them to use the reason and freedom he gave them to apply themselves to the task of discovering his truth and of allowing themselves to be formed by it in turn. That task is, for Ephrem, an ascetic discipline to which the mind and will must commit themselves in faith and in freedom. Knowledge of God cannot be gained in any other way.

---

53 Torrance, *Theological Science*, 38.

54 Ibid., 38–39.

55 *HdF* 47.11.

Investigation as a Sign of Bad Faith

One of the most damning accusations that Ephrem brings against the investigators is that in seeking knowledge of God in the way they do they have chosen the way of unbelief. The following stanza is typical of Ephrem's manner of taking them to task:

> Seal our mouth, O Lord! For, if even Your revelation
>
> bewildered the cunning, since they were unable to comprehend
>
> Your birth from Mary, the bookish called Your generation into doubt
>
> by their contentions. And if men do not grasp even Your humanity,
>
> who indeed can comprehend Your divine birth? Glory to Your Begetter![56]

Time and again Ephrem argues that it is futile to engage in investigation and that such a theological method could only spring from insolence and presumption.[57] The "bookish" Arians, unable to wrap their minds around the divine generation of the Son, reject God's self-revelation as untrustworthy and look for names other than "Son" by which to refer to Christ.[58] Yet God himself revealed that name; the faithful, who believe in the name, find their way to the knowledge of God unobstructed:

> Vouchsafe to me also, O Lord, that I may walk in that fear,[59]
>
> and that I may dread lest I cross the boundary of my faith.
>
> Your truth is level and straight. To the faithful it is even,
>
> and to the perverse it is rough.
>
> The simple go straight and proceed;
>
> the bookish go astray and fall into the abyss of investigation.
>
> May our Lord draw them out! Glory to Him who can do all things![60]

All that the investigator has to offer as the fruit of his labors is something alien to the true faith, an innovation, to which the believer must respond, "My faith is complete, my pearl is perfect; your embellishment is not accepted."[61] Ephrem can urge us to rebuke, not merely to correct, the presumptuous innovator because the latter's own bad faith and his

---

56 *HdF* 51.4.

57 See, e.g., *HdF* 1.16, 3.14, 7.1, 28.9–11, 28.13.

58 See *HdF* 51.7–8. See also *HdF* 44.1.

59 I.e., of death, mentioned in the preceding stanza.

60 *HdF* 51.11.

61 *HdF* 51.13.

attempt to pervert the faith of others are the results of his preference for the path that leads to ruin. The possibility for praise or blame rests on the recognition that we are accountable for the ways in which we exercise our freedom.[62] Ephrem's reproach only makes sense in the context of that recognition. Likewise, his exhortation to his readers that they "abide with [the Lord] in faith"[63] only has meaning if he understands the choice to preserve faith or to engage in investigation to be just that – a free choice.

We have already seen how crucial the medium of the natural world and that of the Bible are to Ephrem's doctrine of divine revelation. In his infinite freedom, God made the world as he did and condescended to the level of human language in order to invite his human creatures into a life-giving relationship with him. They have every means and ability to respond and to engage him, but they cannot approach him by any means other than those he provides. They cannot disregard his "hidden manifestations" in created nature and spurn the Scriptures[64] and still expect to come to know him. Ephrem's emphasis is on God's *self*-revelation, actualized and made sufficient by him alone and through the instruments that he chooses: "Without Him you would not even be able to know / that He exists"[65] – as Torrance put it, "We cannot know God against His will, but only as He wills to reveal Himself."[66] So when Ephrem interprets one of the symbols in the natural world – in *HdF* 73, for example, Ephrem writes of the Father, Son, and Holy Spirit as imaged, respectively, in the sun, its light, and its heat – his conviction is that the likeness is real and is intended by God to be an aid for coming to know him, but that that is God's doing. We are not free to construct any path to divine truth that God did not establish as such.[67]

---

62   See *HcH* 5.8.

63   *HdF* 72.4.

64   It is important to note that for Ephrem, receiving God's self-revelation through the Scriptures is always an ecclesial act. When he talks about the Bible, it is the Bible as proclaimed and preached in the true Church that he has in mind. There is private reading of Scripture, but the results of any reading must be assayed in the crucible of Christ in his Church.

65   *HdF* 72.5.

66   Torrance, *Theological Science*, 41. See ibid., 31–32, where, in his discussion of Schleiermacher, Feuerbach, and anthropologizing approaches to theology, Torrance cites Camfield, saying that God's Word "declares to us what we are utterly incapable of learning and declaring to ourselves."

67   See Torrance's plea (*Theological Science*, 33–32) for testing every claim to theological knowledge "by referring it to the concrete reality of the object known"

It takes concerted effort to learn what nature has to teach us, and everyone learns in proportion to their abilities and to the measure of their labors. But if one does not so apply himself and does not submit himself to the One who teaches all things, he is duly called "one who is led astray by his freedom," as Ephrem says.[68] Submission to the divine Teacher necessitates submission to the ways and means he has chosen to teach us, nature being the most ubiquitous means of instruction.

Ephrem also urges his readers not to neglect the other harp (or *harps*) of revelation beside that of nature. He urges them to stay close by the Scriptures and not to wander where they do not lead – unlike the investigators, who by choice "have gone forth outside the Scriptures, / to wander around in a pathless desert waste, and have deserted the [New] Testament, the path to the Kingdom."[69] The faithful and obedient mind seeking the knowledge of God must hold fast to the Scriptures as both complete and trustworthy. If we readily place our confidence in our physicians, Ephrem wonders, and submit to their remedies without any questioning or reluctance, however painful they may be, why is it that "the books of God are not to sufficient to convince / about His Son that He is His Begotten?"[70] Who are we to judge the "words of Him who judges all" or to "reproach the voice of Him who reproaches all?"[71]

For Ephrem, the Bible, along with the symbolic meaning inherent in nature (properly interpreted), is the criterion by which all our language referring to God is judged. He calls Scripture a "furnace" for testing the "names and distinctions" that we would ascribe to God.[72] Ephrem's reverence for Scripture both binds him to what it contains and preserves him from straying outside its scope.[73] The following stanzas,

---

on the conviction that theological thinking is positive, *a posteriori*, and empirical: it is "verifiable by reference to its divine ground in the actual region of experience in which knowledge of Him has arisen."

68 *HdF* 48.5.

69 *HdF* 65.1.

70 *HdF* 56.12.

71 *HdF* 56.11. See T. F. Torrance, *Theology in Reconstruction* (Grand Rapids, MI: Eerdmans, 1965), 121, where he notes the effrontery of any kind of questioning that tries to drag the truth of God "down within our dividing and compounding dialectic in order to be controlled by us." He concludes: "In the last resort it is we who are questioned by the Truth, and it is only as we allow ourselves to be questioned by it that it stands forth before us for our recognition and acknowledgment."

72 *HdF* 44.1.

73 It is worth noting that Ephrem nevertheless feels free to expand on the biblical

worth quoting in full, give expression to some of the issues at the heart of Ephrem's polemic and bring much of the foregoing exposition into sharper focus:

> Is anyone able to tell me whence you know
> the nature of the Lord of all? God forbid that I should ever profess
> to know! His books proclaim Him,
> and because it is fitting that we should firmly believe in God,
> I listened and firmly believed Him, and by my faith I restrained
> the inquiry of my audacity.
>
> For I have never drifted along after [other] people
> that I might speak as they speak, for I have seen that
> by other names that are not written do they call our Savior.
> I have forsaken what is not written, and I have instructed [others]
> in that which is written,
> lest on account of these things that are not written
> I should bring to naught the things that are written.
>
> He created water and gave [it] to the fish for [their] benefit;
> He set down the books and gave [them] to men for [their] benefit.
> And they bear witness to one another, for if fish cross
> the boundary of their course, their leaping is also [their] suffering,
> and if men cross the boundary of the books,
> their investigation is [their] death.[74]

These stanzas show that Ephrem is keen to root his own manner of speech about God firmly in the Scriptures, to strictly observe their measure, and to avoid at all costs the deadly presumption he finds in the investigators: their trust in their own intellectual resources to the extent that they attempt to bypass God's self-revelation and acquire knowledge of him on their own terms. Ephrem credits his faith with sparing him from the death that comes in the wake of investigation beyond or behind the God-given biblical medium.

It is worth noting, too, that the passage ends with an illustration of nature's cooperation with Scripture. Here it is not the various books of the Bible that bear witness to one another, although Ephrem would

---

text in targumic fashion, one could say – wherever he deems it necessary or helpful.

74   *HdF* 64.10–12.

surely affirm that. Rather, it is the natural fact that the life-sustaining environment for a fish has its boundaries that bears witness to the presence of boundaries no seeker of knowledge may cross and live. For Ephrem, faith rooted in biblical revelation is what keeps us from killing the spirit by trying to know what is not given us to know. In other words, Ephrem insists that we must choose biblical faith over the ruinous attempt at intellectual mastery over the truth of God. Whether one chooses to trust in the veracity of Scripture is central to Ephrem's anti-Arian polemic, since it is Scripture that, over and above the testimony of nature, offers knowledge of both Christ's humanity and his divinity.[75] Notwithstanding the preeminence of Scripture over nature, Ephrem urges his audience to trust not in themselves, as the investigators do, but in the testimony given by both harps of revelation, or more precisely, in the one to whom they all testify.

The material presented in the preceding several pages has shown that the Arians' epistemological method is, in Ephrem's view, inimical to the way of faith in God's self-revelation delivered through nature and Scripture and safeguarded in the Church that adheres to the Nicene confession. Only by the faith that Ephrem commends to his audience does God draw near to the one who seeks to know him; if we scrutinize him, we stray far from him.[76] Because the sin of investigation does not merely weaken or injure the faithful mind but kills it, accusing the investigators of "bad faith" turns out to be too imprecise. If we follow Ephrem's train of thought, we recognize that inasmuch as his opponents engage in investigation, to that same extent they reject faith – not only the true faith, but the very category of faith.[77] Investigation is the willful attempt to ground belief on something other than that which we are given to believe, which amounts to the rejection of the possibility of faith altogether.[78]

75 HdF 65.2. This passage lends weight to Bou Mansour's argument, mentioned in footnote 18 above, that Ephrem maintains a *taxis* between nature and Scripture.

76 HdF 72.2.

77 Shepardson (*Anti-Judaism*, 116n34) cites two passages relevant here: Ephrem's *Homilies on Faith* 2.501–4, 3.69–70.

78 Torrance wrote that faith is, at least in part, "the orientation of the reason towards God's self-revelation, the rational response of man to the Word of God . . . faith is a 'condition of rationality'" (*Theological Science*, 33). While Torrance's manner of expression is not Ephremian, the substance of his statement is surely of a piece with Ephrem's theological epistemology. Ephrem pits faith against audacious investigation; but faith, as he understands it, is anything but irrational or antirational.

Measure and Limits

Part and parcel of the investigator's rejection of faith as the only way to knowledge of God is his willful disregard for the proper measures, limits, and order inherent in the natures of things. At the heart of Ephrem's polemic against investigation, as well as his positive doctrine of divine revelation through created realities, is his conviction that God, and he alone, is the author of all order, measure, and limit.[79] As the Lord and Maker of all things, God sets the boundaries and measures of created realities, and he orders them to the good. Only when the mind and the will work in harmony with the structures of created reality do they act to the benefit of the whole person and in a godly manner.

Yet the order that God establishes is not only that which obtains within creation but also the order of its relation, as a whole, to him. Freedom is oriented not only toward the order evident in creation; its proper exercise is predicated on the proper relation between it, a created reality, and its Maker. In terms of human knowledge, that means that we are free to inquire only into that which God gives us to know. We must recognize and abide by the limits inherent in our nature and in the natures of all created things. The investigator acts otherwise. He foolishly yet freely commits himself to a hopeless quest for that which lies infinitely beyond his creaturely measure. Underlying this aspect of Ephrem's polemic is, of course, the fact of the ontological chasm separating the created from the uncreated, and the fact that no created thing can comprehend the uncreated. Investigation entails the presumption that a creature can cross the chasm by some means other than the bridge that Christ is, and that a created vessel, by an exercise of intellectual mastery, can contain (conceptually) the infinitely transcendent God.[80] The Arians' presumption is, in Beck's words, "eine

---

Right theological knowing and thinking, using our God-given reason for that for which it was created, is of the very substance of faith. These comments anticipate the discussion of a positive form of inquiry below.

79   *HdF* 28.4.

80   See, e.g., *HdF* 50.3. See also Torrance's distinction between closed and open concepts (*Theological Science*, 15) and his closely related discussion of cataleptic apprehension and cataphatic comprehension. Thomas F. Torrance, *God and Rationality* (Edinburgh: T&T Clark, 1997), 22–23. Ephrem's different ways of conceiving and speaking of God span the whole spectrum of natural and biblical symbols, and yet he takes none of them as comprehensive, only apprehensive. The elasticity and great variety of images and metaphors in his theological discourse

Erbschaft der Verwegenheit Adams":[81] as Adam tried to arrogate the status of divinity, so the Arians try to seize divine knowledge beyond their measure, grossly exaggerating the strength and reach of their own intellectual resources. Arguing the point that the "the begetting of the Son is above and beyond man's query,"[82] Ephrem uses the image of a clumsy archer: if he cannot hit even a target "large, obvious, and near" (comprehending Christ's humanity), how could he be so foolish as to think he could hit one far off (comprehending Christ's hidden divinity)?[83] Since his choice for unmeasured inquiry was freely made, it stands to reason that things could have been different for him and, perhaps, still could: "If he had shaken off his wine and recognized that he is mortal, / he would have kept silence and observed the measure of mortals."[84]

The specifically Nicene dimension of Ephrem's polemic against investigation emerges by way of his contrast between what we can know of God – that is, the measure of theological knowing proper to human nature – and what the Son knows. The chasm provides the framework for the contrast:

---

are not simply poetic niceties but evidence of his rejection of univocal speech about God. A further connection obtains here with what Torrance has to say about images in *Theological Science*, 20. There Torrance apparently sides with the patristic concept that "images have to be taken, not in a descriptive but in a *paradeigmatic* sense, that is, as aids to our human weakness in apprehending the indescribable God, to point him out in such a way that we may have some hold in our thought upon His objective reality, but without actually imaging Him. As Hilary expressed it, the likeness or comparison the images entail is to be regarded *as helpful to man rather than as fitted to God*, since they suggest or indicate and do not exhaust Him." When Torrance agrees with Hilary, he agrees with Ephrem as well.

81 Edmund Beck, *Ephräms Reden über den Glauben, ihr theologischer Lehrgehalt und ihr geschichtliche Rahmen* (Rome: Herder, 1953), 70. See Torrance, *Theological Science*, 53: "God is present to us, and gives Himself to our knowing, only in such a way that He remains the Lord who has ascendency over us, who distinguishes Himself from us, and makes Himself known in His divine otherness even when He draws us into communion with Himself. He is present to us in such a way that He never resigns knowledge of Himself to our mastery, but remains the One who is Master over us, who resists, and objects to, every attempt on our part to subdue or redact the possibility of knowledge grounded in His divine freedom to an immanent and latent possibility which we deem ourselves to possess apart from Him in virtue of our own being."

82 *HdF* 1.3.

83 *HdF* 7.2. See also *HdF* 27.8.

84 *HdF* 47.9.

> Behold, all eyes and all minds
> are far too weak in comparison with that strength
> of the Godhead.
>
> That Ray that shines forth from It
> comprehends It; the Light that It begets
> knows It.[85]

Only the uncreated Word of God, whose revealed name "Son" betokens his divine generation, can know fully and directly the uncreated Father,[86] for it is in the hiddenness of God that the Son's generation is grounded. All creaturely knowing falls infinitely short of that mark and must freely, humbly, and obediently keep to its own measure.

An essential part of keeping to our own measure is the recognition that the criterion for the truth or falsity of our thoughts lies not in us but in God. We are not the crucible for assaying the metal of our own or others' teachings, says Ephrem; God alone is.[87] Christ is the crucible. Torrance likewise called for this kind of critical assessment, affirming that

> we are really able to put false objectivities to a decisive test – in Jesus Christ. It will be through the ruthless and relentless Christological criticism of all our knowledge of God that we may be able to distinguish, as far as possible, between genuine and false objectivity.[88]

For Ephrem, God is the balance in which we must weigh our thoughts and our wills; he employs just the right weight for each thing according

---

85   *HdF* 71.19–20.

86   See, e.g., *HdF* 26.12, 27.3. Matt 11:27 and Lk 10:22 obviously come to mind here. See Paul D. Molnar's comments on the importance of those Gospel passages in Torrance's thought, along with relevant citations from Torrance's works, in his *Thomas F. Torrance: Theologian of the Trinity* (Farnham: Ashgate, 2009), 60. The fact that those passages connect so strongly with the *homoousion* and that they root our knowledge of God in the person of his Word makes it clear why Torrance thought them so important. Likewise for Ephrem, while only the Son can know the Father in the depths of his hiddenness, we are brought to a nevertheless real knowledge of God in and through his Word.

87   *HdF* 12.2, 48.2–3.

88   Torrance, *Theological Science*, 43.

to its nature.[89] The inquirers are found wanting, and yet God may have mercy on them for their being too light in the balance.[90]

Elsewhere Ephrem points to scriptural examples of limits not to be crossed – the cherub with the flaming sword guarding the boundary of Paradise, and God's command that no one but Moses ascend Sinai – as metaphors for the limits of theological inquiry.[91] God set a boundary around the mountain for a day, but the height of his hiddenness is bounded off forever; death by stoning was the sentence for the one who crosses the limit imposed around Sinai, Gehenna for the one who tries to cross the limit of God's hiddenness.[92]

Ephrem's convictions about the injurious effects of unmeasured inquiry are all predicated on his belief that the investigator freely chooses his path. The same holds true for Ephrem's exhortations to know our proper measure and observe its limits,[93] to not lead ourselves astray and scrutinize our God:

> Let us temper our minds and measure our thoughts as well,
> and let us recognize [about] our knowing that
> it is far too small and wretched to inquire into the One who knows all.[94]

Ephrem's plea for self-restraint and sober reflection on the limits of human knowing is charged, through and through, with moral urgency. One who chooses to step over the limit and exceed his God-given measure does so at his own peril. His choice does not lead him to the deep truth of God but traps him within the circuit of his own feeble mind and the absurd fictions it takes for theological knowledge. He hems himself in by his own ignorance and perversion and cuts himself off from the gift of God's self-revelation, refracting all that he is actually given to know of God through the prism of his own investigation, the structure of which he alone determines:

> O blind congregation of inquirers,
> they stand in the midst of the light and seek it . . .
> Each one, as he imagined,
> took and depicted the light in his mind.

89 *HdF* 12.3.
90 See *HdF* 12.5.
91 *HdF* 28.8.
92 Ibid.
93 See, e.g., *HdF* 72.1.
94 *HdF* 25.3.

The investigator so deludes himself that he thinks he actually strikes his external, objective target while his vain inquiry, in point of fact, has only turned his mind back upon itself.[95] He generates a mental image and takes it for the Light itself. Indeed, the link between investigation and idolatry is a strong one, as Ephrem sternly warns:

> Rebuke your thought, lest it commit adultery and beget for us
>
> a Messiah that does not exist and deny the one that does exist!
>
> Beware not to make an idol by your investigation.
>
> Beware not to fashion with your intellect
>
> an omen of your mind and an offspring of your thought.
>
> Let the Offspring of the True One be depicted in your thought![96]

Torrance makes a similar connection between the cardinal sin of idolatry and what is essentially a projection into God of our own ideas. If God did not speak his Word to us (or if we reject the Word he did speak, as the investigators do), then:

> we are thrown back upon ourselves to authenticate His existence and to make Him talk by putting our own words into His mouth and by clothing Him with our own ideas. That kind of God is only a dumb idol which we have fashioned in our own image and into whose mouth we have projected our own soliloquies . . . In other words, we have no genuine knowledge of God at all, for we are left alone with our own thoughts and self-deceptions.[97]

Binding himself, by his abuse of freedom, to the idols fashioned by his own intellect, the investigator cuts himself off from the revealed truth of God and sows controversy and division among others. The alternative to investigation that Ephrem offers is one that works toward the reintegration of the person, both as a whole person and as a member of the Church.

---

95 See Torrance, *Theology in Reconstruction*, 125, where he states that because of our empty theologizing, "the questions we direct come bouncing inexorably back upon us to reveal that they are but empty and deceptive moments of inquiry."

96 *HdF* 44.10. See also *HdF* 42.6, where Ephrem makes the related yet more basic point that natures are not what they are because of the working of our will: they are what they are independent of our knowing or acting, and we must accept reality as it is.

97 Torrance, *Theological Science*, 31. See also his comments in ibid., 42, about the need "to distinguish divine objectivity from all idolatry."

Right Theological Inquiry in and with the Church

One of the most pernicious effects of unmeasured investigation is the disturbance and confusion it engenders in the churches. For Ephrem, this is not only a matter of right doctrinal profession over against error; it has direct bearing on the very life of the body of believers and troubles its peace.[98] Investigation and contentious disputation go hand in hand, and together they wreak havoc on the life of faith lived in ecclesial unity which Ephrem so ardently commends to his audience. Several passages in the *Hymns on Faith* speak about the scourge of controversy, offer prayers for peace and unity among believers, or tout the advantage that Ephrem's own undivided congregation enjoys.[99]

And yet it is important to recognize that Ephrem, while he castigates the insolent investigators and their divisiveness, nevertheless concedes a proper method of inquiry for believers. Much more than a concession, in fact, the right way of questioning reality is the path to the knowledge of God about which Ephrem speaks so eloquently. Essential to this healthy type of inquiry is the humble recognition of natural limits and the strict observance of measure. The faithful inquirer is careful to discern the right balance between questioning and silence, between pressing on to a deeper knowledge of God through God's chosen media of self-revelation and restraining himself, all through faith, obedience, and trust in God. Numerous passages talk of right speech and right silence, the proper use of the mind and tongue, and even an appropriate form of disputation for the sake of edification.[100] The necessary condition for such healthy inquiry and debate is faith firmly rooted in the life of the Church, which presupposes a trusting obedience to the specific means God has chosen to reveal himself. The limits of those means provide the framework within which Ephrem encourages believers to exert their efforts in coming to know God more deeply. Only by the right use of freedom in accepting as the foundation of one's inquiry and debate what the true faith presents can one rightly exercise one's

---

98 This is not to imply that Ephrem would separate those two concerns at any great distance. Quite the contrary, Ephrem's thought evinces a strong and intimate connection between what one thinks or professes, on the one hand, and the character of one's moral and ecclesial life as a whole, on the other hand.

99 See, e.g., *HdF* 47.12, 48 refrain, 52.15, 53.2–3.

100 See, e.g., *HdF* 2 passim, 4.1, 4.13–14, 23 passim, 24.6–7, 38.8–10, 50.2–4, 58.7, 67.25.

freedom in forging ahead with any theological investigation. It would be better to say, rather, that the life of faith is not only the foundation of proper theological investigation but also its abiding guide and standard. Healthy inquiry can only be carried on by one whose whole disposition is oriented by the orthodox faith, which comes to expression in the Church's worship. As faith and love are intimately bound up with each other,[101] so love and truth are yokefellows who jointly prepare the way for concord and peace.[102] The orthodox believer engages in theological inquiry within the strict compass of the faith-love-truth nexus preserved whole and entire in the Church, and only there. So when Ephrem writes that "the faithful never debate or investigate / for, they have faith in God,"[103] the reader must balance that statement with the following:

> In the Church there is
>
> inquiry such that you may investigate things revealed –
>
> not such that you may pry into things hidden.[104]

Several polarities have already been brought together, all in relation to theological inquiry: the revealed and the hidden, faith and unbelief, humility and presumption, measure and excess. To those we should now add, in connection with the quotation just above, the polarity between rationality and rationalism, since that pairing takes account of much of what Ephrem puts his finger on in his contrast between proper and improper investigation. Clearly Ephrem does not repudiate the exercise of reason, the God-given "word" (*melltā*), but exhorts his audience to recognize and observe the limits of human reason dictated by human nature and ultimately by God himself. The difference between rationalism (exemplified by excessive, presumptuous investigation) and rationality (exemplified by measured, humble inquiry) is not merely one of degree; they are entirely different in their foundation, orientation, and end.[105]

---

101   See *HdF* 80.3.

102   See *HdF* 20.12. See also Torrance *Theological Science*, 12n4, where he quotes John Macmurray: "The capacity to love objectively is the capacity which makes us persons. It is the ultimate source of our capacity to behave in terms of the object. It is the core of rationality." J. Macmurray, *Reason and Emotion* (New York: D. Appleton-Century, 1937), 32.

103   *HdF* 56.8.

104   *HdF* 8.9.

105   In at least one passage, however, Ephrem presents the notion of intelligent discernment as a middle way: "It is right for us to cultivate neither simple-mindedness

The former is an abuse of freedom and, in effect, the frustration of the human desire to know, since it does not terminate upon any objective reality at all but generates mental fictions that supplant the truth of God: it ends in irrationality and idolatry. The latter, however, is exercised in accord with the *telos* of human freedom, exercising the authoritative mind according to its given nature, and in accord with the nature and means of God's self-revelation.

It is also exercised in accordance with the nature of its object, which is not revelation itself as such, but God, whom we know in and through his self-revelation.[106] One of the pillars of Torrance's realist epistemology is the principle that "reason is the capacity to behave in terms of the nature of the object."[107] In Ephrem's thought we see that principle at work insofar as the kind of theological inquiry he advocates and exemplifies is one that measures the knowing subject's limitations against the infinite excess of the object's reality and rationality and behaves accordingly. In other words, to behave in terms of the object's nature is the only reasonable thing to do in light of the chasm that separates them, taking jointly into account the nature of the subjective pole and of the objective pole in all theological thinking. The correspondence between human rationality, the event and means of revelation, and the object of theological inquiry accounts for the real progress that the faithful inquirer achieves on his path to the knowledge of God: they are all attuned to one another, since God, in his grace, structures the first two and *is* the last. It is clear, then, how Ephrem can condemn one type of investigation and, at the same time, advocate another.

The way of theological knowing that Ephrem describes – sometimes positively and explicitly, other times implicitly and negatively, by way of his polemic against unhealthy investigation – has a three-fold nature. First, it takes on the character of ascetic discipline. The humble, obedient mind and tongue learn to control themselves as they should, restraining

nor deep investigation, but discernment between-these-two-extremes, sound and true," *Hyp* 1, 29.26–30.1, translated by den Biesen in *Simple and Bold*, 228.

106 See Torrance, *Theological Science*, 54: "Knowledge of God does not entail any diminishing of our rational powers, but the very reverse, for in requiring of us sober and critical judgements of our own powers and possibilities, it does so through requiring us to be obedient to the rational Word of God and to acknowledge that we are face to face with a Reality which we cannot rationally reduce to our own creaturely dimensions."

107 Ibid., 11–12.

the insolence of their inquiry by faith.[108] They curb the wayward and overbold tendencies of their thoughts and words and achieve a disciplined balance of action and rest.

Second, it is inherently dialogical. It seeks converse with God, not theft of his hidden mysteries.[109] Unlike presumptuous investigation, faithful inquiry does not try to bypass the given content and structure of God's self-revelation in order to discover what in fact cannot be discovered. Rather, it responds to God's invitation according to the terms in which it was delivered, taking up the harps that God has ordained for that purpose, and meeting him where he approaches us – this encounter is most fully realized in the Church.

Finally, and closely related to the second point, it is doxological by nature. Inquiry is no end in itself but only a means to a more profound knowledge of God. One who inquires rightly will take up Ephrem's prayer that the Lord make his tongue a pen for God's glory and that he should sing what is right with his harp.[110]

That last point about the character of proper inquiry raises the issue of Ephrem's preferred idiom for theological discourse. By far, his most frequently chosen literary form is the *madrāšā* (hymn, or teaching song) – second to that is the *mēmrā* (metrical homily).[111] These are liturgical compositions, intended for public performance in the context

108   See *HdF* 64.10. To this Torrance would add the related ideas of conversion and repentance, pointing out the need "for radical change even in the inner slant of our mind, and in the structural capacities of our reason" (*Theological Science*, 49).

109   See Torrance, *Theological Science*, 39: "But God gives Himself to be known as personal Subject, as the one Lordly Subject who approaches us and assumes us into personal relation with Him as subjects over against His own divine majestic Subjectivity. Apart from being a primary element in the objectivity of theological knowledge, this means that our cognitive relation to the object is essentially and unceasingly dialogical. At no point can theological knowledge step outside this dialogical relation, without abstracting itself from the object, without falsifying itself, or without retreating into unreality. Thus theological knowledge is . . . reflection upon the object of faith in direct dialogical relation with that object, and therefore in faith – i.e. in conversation and communion with the living God who communicates Himself to us in acts of revelation and reconciliation and who requires of us an answering relation in receiving, acknowledging, understanding, and in active personal participation in the relationship He establishes between us."

110   *HdF* 51.5–6.

111   See Sidney Griffith's remarks in his essay "Ephraem, the Deacon of Edessa, and the Church of the Empire," in *Diakonia: Essays in Honor of Robert T. Meyer*, ed. T. Halton and J. P. Williams (Washington, DC: Catholic University of America Press, 1986), 45.

of his community's worship. So, for Ephrem, speech about the mysteries of God finds its proper place in the liturgical life of the Church because that is the context in which the truth of God, knowledge of which is grounded on the *terra firma* of orthodox faith in the eternal Word of God become man in Jesus, is most fully appropriated and celebrated. Right belief, freely appropriated and nurtured, issues forth in right worship freely offered; right worship is the fullest exercise of rational faith and freedom, the only fitting human response to God's self-revelation in nature, in Scripture, and, above all, in Jesus Christ. There is a strong connection here with Torrance's stress on the communal dimension of theological knowing. As he so eloquently states:

> The implication of this is that we know God and interpret his self-revelation only in the attitude and context of worship and within the fellowship of the church, where to the godly reason God is more to be adored than expressed. It is only as we allow ourselves, within the fellowship of the faith and through constant meditation on the Holy Scriptures, to come under the creative impact of God's self-revelation that we may acquire the disciplined spiritual perception or insight which enables us to discriminate between our conceptions of the Truth and the Truth itself. This is not a gift which we can acquire and operate for ourselves alone but one which we may have only as we share it with others in common listening to God's Word and in common adoration and worship of God through the Son and in the one Spirit.[112]

All knowing is oriented toward the worship of God, and when we discover the truth of God, as he makes himself accessible to faithful and discerning minds, our response of worship gathers up and presents to him the best that we can offer in the best way we can offer it: in rational faith and obedience; according to the measure appropriate to us, recognizing our creaturely limits; using fitting speech sanctified by God, while observing proper silence; from within the context of a life lived according to the truth of God revealed in Christ; avoiding all divisiveness; and as the most profound expression of human freedom. For Ephrem, human freedom is ultimately the freedom given by God to know and worship him rightly and, in so doing, to become fully a human person. Rational freedom, in other words, enables us to fulfill our

112 Torrance, *Reality and Evangelical Theology*, 119–20.

shared priestly vocation and so to become saints gathered in Christ in his Church, an image of Paradise.[113]

Concluding Remarks

It goes without saying that Ephrem and Torrance worked in radically different contexts and idioms. The liturgical compositions of a fourth-century Mesopotamian poet would not immediately appear to be fit companions for the philosophical and systematic works of a twentieth-century Reformed theologian with a heavy interest in the hard sciences. And yet there are strong continuities between them that attest both to the perennial status of the theological vision they share, and to their contributions to what Fr. Georges Florovsky called an "ecumenism in time." If one reads deeply in Ephrem, it takes only a cursory reading of Torrance's *Theological Science*, for example, to discover deep affinities between those two realist theologians. The tie that binds them in perhaps the most fundamental way is the Nicene confession and its implications for all theological thinking. The status of the incarnate divine Word and Son as the inimitable self-revelation of God, in whom all theological knowing is actualized, and with reference to whom all that claims to be theological knowing is tested, is paramount in the thought of both theologians.

Their realism is an incarnational realism that, in different yet consonant ways, takes full account of the Logos as the basis of all rationality. Torrance, of course, is impacted by and responds to many of the developments in science, philosophy, and theology that occurred in the centuries that separate him from Ephrem. It stands to reason, then, that the conceptual and linguistic equipment that Torrance employs would be markedly different than Ephrem's. Behind and beneath all such differences, though, there lies enough agreement in substance to consider them strong allies and co-workers in the Church's mission to help all men acquire "the mind of Christ."[114]

---

113   *Parad* 6.8, 10.
114   1 Cor. 2:16.

Chapter 6

Justification in St. Cyril of Alexandria, with Some Implications for Ecumenical Dialogue[1]

Donald Fairbairn

It goes without saying that T. F. Torrance was a giant of twentieth-century British theology. His range was extraordinary – from patristics to Barth, from core doctrinal developments to theology's interaction with modern science, from the Reformed tradition to ecumenical dialogue with Eastern Orthodoxy. Torrance was also a kind encourager of young scholars, and I remember with fondness his correspondence with me about Cyril of Alexandria while I was doing my PhD in Cambridge in the late 1990s. That encouragement and his perspective on the development of Greek patristic theology have had a profound influence on my own interpretation of the great doctrinal developments of the fourth through sixth centuries. Torrance impressed on me the importance of what he called the "Athanasian-Cyrillian axis" as a way past the rocks on which East-West dialogue often runs aground, and my own work on Cyril and in patristics in general has reflected that impress. Indeed, I am honored that several colleagues, without knowing my history, have nevertheless recognized in my own work the influence of T. F. Torrance.

The subject for my essay was suggested to me by Matthew Baker, who noted that Torrance once commented that no one had better expounded the evangelical doctrine of justification by grace than Cyril of Alexandria. Baker pointed out to me that nowhere in Torrance's corpus does he elaborate on this cryptic comment and asked me whether I would be willing to do so. I eagerly agreed, not only because I believe Torrance's brief remark is correct, but also because I think Cyril's particular understanding of justification is one from which both Protestant and Eastern Orthodox theology can learn.

1 I would like to thank my research assistant, Thomas Hill, for his assistance in the background study for this essay.

In this essay, I will address Cyril's understanding of justification by doing five things. First, I will briefly discuss Torrance's comment about Cyril's doctrine of justification and the possible reason for the under-emphasis on this aspect of his thought in patristic scholarship. Second, I will summarize and categorize the various words and phrases Cyril uses for justification and describe some of the implications of this vocabulary. Third, I will describe in some depth Cyril's exegesis of four key biblical passages related to justification. Fourth, I will suggest a way of understanding the relation between justification and sanctification in Cyril's thought. Finally, I will draw some conclusions about the way Cyril's understanding of justification can both provide common ground for dialogue between Protestants and the Orthodox, and offer a challenge to both groups to sharpen their own thinking about salvation.

The Apparent Under-emphasis on Justification in Cyril's Writings

Torrance's reference to justification in Cyril comes as he explains the Protestant Reformation to Orthodox readers in a 1983 article. He writes:

> The Reformation was an attempt against the hard structure of Roman canon law to recover the essential nature and form of the ancient Catholic Church by calling for a Christological correction of its doctrinal innovations and its ecclesiastical structure. For it called for a recovery of the evangelical doctrine of justification by grace (nowhere better expounded in all the history of theology than by the impeccably orthodox Cyril of Alexandria), a liberation of the doctrine and practice of the Eucharist from the hard crust of Aristotelian notions of causality, and an emancipation of the ministry and the nature of its authority from the patterns assimilated into the Church from the Roman Empire and its replacement by the ancient patristic and conciliar concept of ministry and authority through communion of *koinonia* which took an essentially corporate form.[2]

Torrance argues further that this effort to reform Christianity around Christ himself was trapped by the rising nationalisms of Europe and cut off from essential input from the Orthodox Churches. Now (in 1983), Torrance

---

2 Thomas F. Torrance, "The Orthodox Church in Great Britain," *Texts and Studies* 2 (1983): 254.

claims, it is possible to gain such input and to complete the needed reform that the Protestant Reformation brought about only incompletely.

Torrance's claim holds forth promise for ecumenical dialogue, but at the same time his comment about Cyril's view of justification would seem to offer a surprising and poor starting place for such conversation. Not only does Cyril never use the exact phrase "justification by grace,"[3] but he is one of the Greek church's foremost champions of the doctrine of θέωσις or deification, and thus of a participatory concept of salvation, rather than the forensic understanding that undergirds the classical Protestant idea of justification. Furthermore, Cyril regards δικαιοσύνη and ἁγιασμός as virtual synonyms,[4] a fact that appears to fly directly in the face of the classical Protestant distinction between justification and sanctification.

Indeed, Cyril's persistent link between δικαιοσύνη and ἁγιασμός would seem in and of itself to invalidate Torrance's claim. Daniel Keating argues:

> In Cyril's narrative account of salvation, divine initiative is primary. Salvation and life are properly from God alone, and even the virtues that obtain in us are seen primarily as gifts of God, not as objects of our attainment. Yet in Cyril's view we are actively engaged at every stage, from the first signs of faith to mature conformity to Christ. There is no marking off of justification from sanctification as distinguishable stages in our attainment of divine life. Nor does Cyril appear to indicate a distinction between our part in justification and our part in sanctification, initial or ongoing. Faith and love are the co-ordinate responses to *each* encounter with God, and both secure our possession of the divine life and cause us to cling to Christ, the source of that life. In the end, the gracious activity of God precedes and grounds our response of faith and love. Even faith itself is described as the preeminent gift of grace.[5]

3 He does, however, use a variety of related expressions, as we shall see below.

4 As Daniel Keating helpfully summarizes, "Cyril typically groups together as the characteristics of baptism into new life what later theology has at times more clearly distinguished: justification by faith, sanctification of body and soul, elevation to the status of divine sonship, and participation in the divine nature. While these are distinguishable in Cyril, he does not order these elements sequentially, either temporally or theologically, in the description of our entrance into new life through baptism." Daniel A. Keating, "Divinization in Cyril," in *The Theology of St. Cyril of Alexandria: A Critical Appreciation*, ed. Thomas G. Weinandy and Daniel A. Keating (London: T&T Clark, 2003), 161n30.

5 Daniel A. Keating, *The Appropriation of Divine Life in Cyril of Alexandria*, Oxford Theological Monographs (Oxford: University Press, 2004), 141.

In this excellent summary of Cyril's soteriology, Keating emphasizes that Cyril does not distinguish justification and sanctification because he does not attempt to sort out "distinguishable stages" in Christian life or even distinguishable roles assigned to God and to humanity. He views all aspects of salvation in terms of divine life, and he views the whole of an individual's salvation as the work of both God and that individual. There is, or at least there seems to be, no hint of any focus on an initial declaration by God and an on-going active holiness in which the Christian cooperates. How then can one even speak of a concept of justification in Cyril?

At first, it would seem that one cannot speak of any such concept. Given that the Greek word δικαιοσύνη can and usually does mean simply "righteousness," if one does not distinguish this kind of righteousness from the holiness produced gradually in sanctification then one can hardly be said to espouse the Protestant understanding of justification. To say it differently, if δικαιοσύνη is the same as holiness, then it is not "justification" and should not even be translated as such. Accordingly, most theologians who *do* emphasize justification in the Protestant sense distinguish it sharply from other aspects of salvation, with justification as a passively-received righteousness accomplished by grace through faith, and sanctification as a cooperatively-produced holiness/righteousness in which the believer's active effort plays a major role. As Keating makes clear, Cyril does not make this distinction. Furthermore, most theologians who emphasize justification in the Protestant sense regard it as very central to their soteriology – in contrast to Cyril for whom it is merely one emphasis among several, and hardly the main one. Because Cyril does not do either of these things, scholars can be excused for thinking that justification is not a major aspect of his thought, and the lack of scholarly attention to a concept of justification in his writings is thus perfectly understandable.

Nevertheless, Keating's statement quoted in the previous paragraph also indicates something else that is very important to Cyril – something that makes his view of justification worth exploring. The *reason* he does not distinguish justification and sanctification is not that he collapses justification into sanctification by seeing both as an actively-produced righteousness, that is, as something that God produces *within* the Christian through the believer's cooperation with the work of grace. Rather, I think the reason is that he sees both justification and sanctification – and indeed all aspects of salvation – flowing directly from God himself and as given to the Christian by God *from the outside*. This is not to say that Cyril ignores the necessity of inward transformation in the life of a Christian; he does not. Rather, he sees such inward transformation as the manifestation of the Christian's new identity as a child of God, an identity that is given through the believer's union to Christ, the true Son. This identity is given from without, and as a result the righteousness/holiness that accompanies it is, at the most basic level, given from the outside, not so much produced from within. It seems to me that Cyril's concept of a righteousness given from without means that he does have a discernible idea of justification with some affinities to the Protestant understanding. And this, I suggest, has important implications for Protestant-Orthodox dialogue.

Cyril's Vocabulary of Justification/Righteousness

Because the Greek word δικαιοσύνη can mean simply "righteousness," a mere listing of the passages in which Cyril uses the word (1214 instances, according to a TLG search) would tell us relatively little about whether he teaches anything resembling the Protestant sense of justification. More fruitful for our purposes is the fact that Cyril frequently uses a variety of expressions that link δικαιοσύνη to faith or to grace, and that indicate that God, Christ, or grace is the direct source of our righteousness.

Cyril uses the actual phrase δικαιοσύνη ἐν πίστει only nine times in his writings (once in *De ador.*, twice in *Glaph. Pent.*, once in *Expos. Psalm.*, once in *Com. Is.*, three times in *Com. Johan.*, and once in *Frag. Rom.*).[6] But he uses the essentially equivalent phrase δικαίωσις εν πίστει 17 times (twice in *De ador.*, three times in *Glaph. Pent.*, twice in *Expos. Psalm.*, four times in *Com. Is.*, once in *Com. proph. min.*, four times in *Com. Luc.*, and once in *Ep. pasch.*). In all 26 of the passages where he uses one or the other of these phrases, Cyril employs the preposition ἐν with the anarthrous form πίστει, never the arthrous form τῇ πίστει or the anarthrous πίστει without a preposition.

Cyril uses phrases equivalent to "justified by faith" 75 times in his writings (24 times in *De ador.*, 23 times in *Glaph. Pent.*, twice in *Expos. Psalm.*, eight times in *Com. Is.*, twelve times in *Com. proph. min.*, once in *Com. Johan.*, once in *Frag. Rom.*, once in *Frag. Heb.*, and three times

---

6 Throughout this essay, I refer to Cyril's works by abbreviations of the Latin titles. The full titles and the location of the best text for each work are found in the table at the end of the essay.

in *Trin. dial.*). These are passages where a passive participle or passive infinitive of the verb δικαιόω is used to describe Christians, usually in connection with ἐν πίστει, or rarely τῇ πίστει or even simply πίστει. Furthermore, Cyril uses a passive form of δικαιόω with χάριτι eleven times in his writings (once in *De ador.*, once in *Expos. Psalm.*, twice in *Com Is.*, once in *Com. Johan.*, twice in *Frag. Rom.*, three times in *Ep. pasch.*, once in *Hom. div.*). Thus, there are 86 passages in which he refers to Christians as "justified by faith" or "justified by grace." In all of these cases, the passive verb forms suggest that we are the recipients of a righteousness that originates outside of ourselves, rather than being the producers of such righteousness. This external righteousness comes to us by faith or by grace.

Even more striking than the passive expressions described in the previous paragraph are active constructions. Cyril uses the expression ἡ δικαιοῦσα χάρις (a present active participle of which χάρις is the subject) 24 times (once in *De ador.*, four times in *Glaph. Pent.*, once in *Expos. Psalm.*, six times in *Com. Is.*, once in *Com. proph. min.*, twice in *Com. Luc.*, five times in *Com. Johan.*, three times in *Frag. Rom.*, and once in *De dog. sol.*). Similarly, in 60 places Cyril uses an active verb form (sometimes an active participle, sometimes an active indicative, subjunctive, or even optative form) with "Christ" or "God" as the subject – expressed or implied (five times in *De ador.*, three times in *Glaph. Pent.*, eleven times in *Expos. Psalm.*, 15 times in *Com. Is.*, nine times in *Com. proph. min.*, twice in *Com. Johan.*, twice in *Com. Luc.*, three times in *Frag. Rom.*, four times in *Trin. dial.*, five times in *Ep. pasch.*, and once in *Hom. frag.*). Thus, there are 84 passages in which Cyril uses various expressions indicating that grace/God/Christ is the active source of the Christian's righteousness. Interestingly, this is almost exactly the same number as the 86 times when he uses passive constructions of which Christians are the subjects.

Furthermore, among the 60 passages that contain expressions indicating that God or Christ justifies the Christian, there are 43 in which τῇ πίστει (or more rarely, ἐν πίστει or πίστει) also occurs (three of the five in *De ador.*, two of the three in *Glaph. Pent.*, ten of the eleven in *Expos. Psalm.*, ten of the 15 in *Com. Is.*, all nine in *Com. proph. min.*, both of the two in *Com. Luc.*, one of the three in *Frag. Rom.*, one of the four in *Trin. dial.*, four of the five in *Ep. pasch.*, and the one in *Hom. frag.*) Also, among these 60 passages that contain expressions indicating that God or Christ justifies the Christian, there are seven in which the word χάριτι occurs as well (one in *Frag. Rom.*, one in *Frag. Heb.*, one in *Glaph. Pent.*, and four in *Com. Is.*). Cyril strengthens the idea that God or Christ is the active, direct source of the believer's righteousness by indicating that such righteousness comes to a Christian by grace or by faith.

In summary, the language of justification is quite prominent in the Cyrillian corpus, and he carefully uses active and passive verb forms to indicate that God produces this righteousness and that believers receive it by grace and faith. The direct source of the righteousness is God, Christ, or grace. This does not mean that inward transformation is unimportant, and it certainly does not mean that the believer plays no role in such a transformation. But it does mean, I think, that at the most basic level, the righteousness of the Christian is an external righteousness received by faith, rather than an internal righteousness produced cooperatively.

It is also noteworthy that almost all of the passages in which Cyril discusses justification occur in his exegetical writings, most of which pre-date the outbreak of the Nestorian controversy in AD 428. Cyril's justification language is thus part of his general theology of salvation which he articulates in his broad exegetical-theological corpus before his attention turns more narrowly to Christology during the struggle with Nestorius. Perhaps another part of the reason this justification language gets so little attention from scholars and churchmen is simply that Cyril's exegetical corpus in general gets relatively little attention in comparison with the substantial scholarly focus on his polemical Christology from the time of the controversy. But justification is an important part of Cyril's soteriology that informs the Christology for which he is much more famous.

Justification/Righteousness in Cyril's Exegesis of Four Illustrative Biblical Passages

Now that we have seen Cyril's general patterns for using justification language, I would like to illustrate his understanding more fully by discussing four examples. These come from Cyril's comments on Isaiah 1 (in which Cyril uses the text's proclamation of Judah's sinfulness to discuss justification by faith rather than by our own actions), on Habakkuk 2 (with its well-known assertion that the righteous will live by faith), on John 8 (in which Cyril links Jesus' identity as the "I am" to justification, among other salvific benefits) and on Romans 3–5 (the *locus classicus* for the Protestant understanding of justification). Looking at Cyril's exegesis of these key passages will flesh out our understanding of his concept of justification.

Isaiah 1

Cyril prefaces his commentary on Isaiah by stressing that even though the prophet points out the sins of Judah repeatedly, he also returns often to the theme of redemption. Cyril writes:

> At every point, however, there is mention of redemption through Christ (τῆς διὰ τοῦ Χριστοῦ λυτρώσεως); it says that in due course on the one hand Israel would be expelled from its relationship with God, and on the other the multitude of the nations would be admitted by being justified through faith in Christ (δικαιουμένη διὰ τῆς πίστεως τῆς ἐν Χριστῷ). And so it seems to me that the blessed prophet Isaiah is awarded the crown, not only of Old Testament grace but also of New Testament privilege; he here acts as both Old Testament and New Testament author, and will deliver words of his own composition that are not bereft of the splendor of the evangelical proclamation.[7]

This passage touches on one of Cyril's most common themes, the contrast between Jews and Christians. Cyril, like other church fathers, sees the entire Jewish nation in a way similar to the way John the evangelist sees the Jewish leaders – as people who have thoroughly rejected Christ. Cyril often and forcefully contrasts Jews who rely on the Law for salvation and believers who rely on Christ.[8] Here, as part of that distinction, he contrasts being expelled from a relationship with God because of one's breaking the Law and being justified through faith in Christ.

Later, commenting on Isaiah 1:3 ("the ox knows its owner, but Israel does not know me"), Cyril explains that the words should be applied to Christ, whom Israel does not know because it focuses only on the law. He continues:

---

7 *Com. Is.* Preface, in Migne, *Patrologiae cursus completus, series Graeca* (Paris: Migne, 1857–1866), 70.13. This English translation is from Robert C. Hill, trans., *Cyril of Alexandria: Commentary on Isaiah, Vol. 1: Chapters 1–14* (Brookline, Mass.: Holy Cross Orthodox Press, 2008), 19–20.

8 The classic treatment of this theme in Cyril's writings is Robert L. Wilken, *Judaism and the Early Christian Mind: A Study of Cyril of Alexandria's Exegesis and Theology* (New Haven, Conn.: Yale University Press, 1971). See Wilken's conclusion on p. 227: "Cyril's points of reference are so Jewish because he is so deeply rooted in the biblical tradition, and it is because he is so concerned with Judaism that the Bible is the chief source of his theology. He knows no other way to interpret Christianity than in relation to Judaism and no other way to view Judaism than as an inferior foreshadowing of Christianity."

The Law was also imposed up to the time of correction, as Scripture says. But since it was not possible for the shadow to justify us (ἀνέφικτον δικαιοῦν ἡμᾶς δύνασθαι τὴν σκιὰν), the only-begotten Word of God appeared to us in the flesh so as to justify by faith those approaching him (ἵνα δικαιώσῃ τῇ πίστει τοὺς προσιόντας αὐτῷ), and rid them of death and sin.[9]

Here Cyril stresses the fact that the Law was a shadow of what was to come, and the shadow cannot make people righteous. Instead, the incarnate Word himself directly justifies those who approach him.

While commenting on Isaiah 1:15 (God will hide his eyes and ears from Israel because of their sins), Cyril argues that the Lord's statement through Isaiah, "I shall no longer tolerate your sins," applies to Israel after the crucifixion of the Savior. He continues, "The fact that they [the Jews] would have mercy shown to them eventually, in fact, when justified by grace in Christ with us (τῇ εἰς Χριστὸν χάριτι μεθ' ἡμῶν δικαιούμενοι), the sacred text proclaims, although as I said the period of their subjection to wrath lasted longer than before."[10] Shortly after this, he explains the statement "wash, make yourselves clean" (Is. 1:6) as a reference to faith and baptism: "It was as a gift they were justified not from the works of the Law but rather by faith and holy baptism (δικαιουμένου δωρεὰν καὶ οὐκ ἐξ ἔργων νόμου. Μᾶλλον δὲ διὰ τῆς πίστεως, καὶ τοῦ ἁγίου βαπτίσματος)."[11]

Later in the discussion, while commenting on Isaiah 1:25–28 (a prophecy of destruction on those who forsake the Lord), Cyril writes that Jerusalem rejected God's Son when he was sent from heaven and insulted him, "despite his justifying the offender and ridding it of former sins through faith (καίτοι δικαιοῦντα τὸν ἀσεβῆ, καὶ τῶν ἀρχαίων πλημμελημάτων ἀπαλλάττοντα διὰ τῆς πίστεως)."[12] Shortly after this, Cyril comments that the judgment Isaiah foretells is aimed at those who "are addicted to foolish and sacrilegious living, with no regard for Christ, who can save them, forgive their sins, and justify them by grace (καὶ Χριστοῦ μὴ πεφροντικὸς τοῦ σώζειν εἰδότος, καὶ ἀνιέντος ἐγκλήματα καὶ δικαιοῦντος τῇ χάριτι)."[13]

Thus we see that Cyril's extended discussion of Isaiah 1 is (among other things) a vehicle for contrasting a life devoted to the Law and the

---

9   Com. Is. 1 (PG 70:20) (Hill, Commentary on Isaiah, 1:25).

10   Com. Is. 1 (PG 70:37) (Hill, Commentary on Isaiah, 1:39).

11   Com. Is. 1 (PG 70:40) (Hill, Commentary on Isaiah, 1:40).

12   Com. Is. 1 (PG 70:57) (Hill, Commentary on Isaiah, 1:55).

13   Com. Is. 1 (PG 70:61) (Hill, Commentary on Isaiah, 1:58).

life that flows from devotion to Christ. In the process, Cyril emphasizes that our righteousness comes directly from Christ, from grace, and that it is received by faith. It is a righteousness given to us from the outside, not ultimately one that is accomplished by us or even within us through our cooperation with grace.

Habakkuk 2

Habakkuk 2:2-4 refers to the fulfillment of the prophet's vision and encourages the hearers to wait patiently. In Cyril's version of the text, the hearers are to wait not for "it" (the fulfillment of the vision), but for "him."[14] Cyril points out that in the short term, the referent of the word "him" is Cyrus who will deliver the Jews from the Babylonian captivity, but ultimately, the referent of "him" is Christ. Thus, the one who shrinks back in 2:3 is the one who rejects faith in Christ and offends God, whereas the righteous one who lives by faith in 2:4 is the believer in Christ. Of the latter, Cyril writes:

> The one who overcomes lethargy and delay, on the other hand, and introduces into their mind and heart love and faith in him, enjoys a reward for such an attitude, namely, the special privilege of an uncurtailed life, rejection of sin, and sanctification through the Spirit (τὸν διὰ Πνεύματος ἁγιασμόν). We have, in fact, been justified (δεδικαιώμεθα) "not by the works of the Law," as Scripture says, but by faith in Christ (διὰ πίστεως δὲ μᾶλλον τῆς εἰς Χριστόν); while "the Law brings wrath," summoning transgressors to retribution, grace offsets wrath, undoing the offenses.[15]

Cyril continues with a long comparison of the Babylonians and Satan, and he refers Habakkuk's declaration in 2:8 that the surviving peoples will despoil Babylon to the despoiling of Satan by believers. Cyril describes

---

14   Here the Hebrew verbs and pronouns in question are masculine singular, as is the word for "vision." In Greek, the word for "vision" is neuter plural, yet in the LXX the pronouns and verbs are still masculine singular. The translators of the LXX thus see a shift in the focus of this passage from the vision itself to a person who is to come. Cyril follows the LXX in this and interprets the coming person as both Cyrus (the near deliverer) and Christ (the messianic fulfillment of the prophecy).

15   *Com. Hab. 2*, in P.E. Pusey, *Sancti patris nostri Cyrilli archiepiscopi Alexandrini in xii prophetas* (Oxford: Clarendon Press, 1868), 2:95. English translation in *St. Cyril of Alexandria: Commentary on the Twelve Prophets, Volume 2*, Fathers of the Church, trans. Robert C. Hill (Washington, D.C., Catholic University of America Press, 2008), 116:350.

these believers as "those justified by faith through Christ and sanctified by the Spirit (τῶν ἐν πίστει δεδικαιωμένων διὰ Χριστοῦ καὶ ἡγιασμένων ἐν Πνεύματι)."[16] In this passage, like the longer one quoted in the previous paragraph, Cyril writes not only of justification by faith in Christ, but also of sanctification through (or "in") the Spirit. Here we see the linking of justification and sanctification that Keating has noted and that I have mentioned above. I will return to this link between the two later in this essay.

John 8

In book 5 of *Com. Johan.*, Cyril comments on John 8, in which Jesus three times uses the phrase "I am" (εγω ειμί) to refer to himself (John 8:24, 28, 58) and explains his identity in contrast to Abraham. Cyril's comments as we have them today end with John 8:43 and thus do not include Jesus' climactic affirmation in 8:58, "Before Abraham was, I am." But as Cyril comments on 8:24 ("For unless you believe that I am, you will die in your sins"), he writes:

> He makes the way of salvation crystal clear and shows them what road to travel to ascend to the life of the saints and to arrive at the city above, the heavenly Jerusalem. Not only must one believe (πιστεῦσαί), he says, but he insists that one will have to believe in him (εἰς αὐτὸν). For we are justified when we believe in him as God from God (δικαιούμεθα γὰρ πιστεύοντες εἰς αὐτὸν ὡς εἰς Θεὸν ἐκ Θεοῦ), as Savior and redeemer and king of all and truly Lord.[17]

At the beginning of this passage, the fact that Cyril mentions the way of salvation and a road to travel might lead the reader to expect some sort of requirement that we actively fulfill in order to achieve our salvation. Indeed, if Cyril had understood salvation/righteousness primarily in terms of an inward transformation in which the believer's active cooperation played a major part, this would have been a very natural place for him to discuss that role. But he does not do this. Instead, he follows this statement with the present passive verb form δικαιούμεθα

---

16 *Com. Hab.* 2, in Pusey, *Cyrilli in xii prophetas*, 2:102; FOTC 116:355.

17 *Com. Johan.* 5.4, in *Sancti patris nostri Cyrilli archiepiscopi Alexandrini in D. Joannis evangelium*, ed. P. E. Pusey (Oxford: Clarendon Press, 1872), 2:19. English translation in *Cyril of Alexandria: Commentary on John, Volume I*, Ancient Christian Texts, trans. David R. Maxwell (Downers Grove, Ill.: IVP Academic, 2013), 334.

in connection with the present active participle πιστεύοντες. What we do – the road we travel – is to believe in Christ, but what happens as we believe is that we are justified (passive) with a righteousness that comes from outside ourselves.

Somewhat later in this discussion, while he comments on John 8:32 ("And you will know the truth, and the truth will set you free"), Cyril contrasts the Law with Christ who is the Truth. He writes:

> True salvation, then, is not in them (in the ordinances of the law, I mean). Nor could one gain from there the thrice longed-for freedom (from sin, I mean). But when we leap just above the types and focus on the beauty of worship in the spirit and recognize "the truth," that is, Christ, we are justified through faith in him (διὰ τῆς εἰς αὐτὸν πίστεως δικαιούμεθα). And when we are justified (δικαιούμενοι), we pass over to true freedom, no longer ranked as slaves, as we were before, but as children of God.[18]

Here again, we see that Cyril links justification to a faith that is specifically *in Christ*. His point is not that faith is an action that makes us righteous, but that faith is the channel for justification if that faith focuses on the correct object, Christ himself. Notice also that justification is linked to the freedom that comes with being children of God rather than slaves. For Cyril, justification is closely tied to adoption, which is of course a major theme in all his writings.[19]

Shortly after this, as he comments on John 8:33 (in which the Jews claim that they are Abraham's children and have never been slaves), Cyril writes that Abraham was illustrious not by his human birth, but through faith in God. Cyril quotes Gen. 15:6 and continues:

> His faith was reckoned to him as righteousness (ἐλογίσθη δὲ αὐτῷ ἡ πίστις εἰς δικαιοσύνην), and the righteousness that comes from faith (ἡ ἐκ πίστεως δικαιοσύνη) has become his basis for freedom before God. Therefore, when he was justified by believing (ὅτε πιστεύσας ἐδικαιώθη), that is, when he shook off the low birth that is from sin, then he shone forth illustrious, noble and free. Foolishly, then, the Jews reject the grace that

---

18 *Com. Johan.* 5.5, in Pusey, *Cyrilli in Joannis evangelium*, 2:61–2 (Maxwell, 354).

19 For my summary of this important aspect of Cyril's thought, see Donald Fairbairn, *Grace and Christology in the Early Church*, Oxford Early Christian Studies (Oxford: University Press, 2003), 76–8.

frees the very founder of their race and advance only to the one who was freed by it.[20]

In this passage we see again that justification is connected to spiritual freedom and that this righteousness/freedom comes through faith. Notice also that the source of this righteousness and the accompanying freedom is grace. It is ironic in Cyril's eyes that the Jews attach themselves to Abraham who was righteous/ free through faith, even as they reject the grace that produced his righteousness/ freedom.

Cyril concludes his discussion of Abraham's slavery and subsequent freedom/righteousness by writing:

> The Lord was hinting that the blessed Abraham himself, who was once enslaved to sin and was set free through faith alone in Christ (διὰ μόνης τῆς εἰς Χριστὸν πίστεως ἐλευθερωθεὶς), was not sufficient to pass on this spiritual nobility (πνευματικὴν εὐγένειαν) to others, since he is not authorized with the power to free others when he did not on his own put off the slavery of sin. Nor did he bestow freedom on himself; he received it from another, namely, from Christ himself, who justifies (παρ' ἑτέρου δὲ ταύτην λαβὼν, αὐτοῦ δηλονότι τοῦ δικαιοῦντος Χριστοῦ).[21]

In this passage Cyril links another idea – spiritual nobility – to the ideas of freedom and righteousness he has been developing. And here again his emphasis is that Abraham received all of these things from another, from Christ who justifies. With respect to the broader concerns of Cyril's theology, the point here is that one who receives grace/freedom/ righteousness/nobility cannot pass these on to others. Only the one who is the source of these qualities can give them to others, and Christ can be this source only because he is by nature God's Son.[22] With regard to the specific focus of this essay, it is clear here that Cyril sees righteousness not as something we accomplish, nor even something that God helps us accomplish or accomplishes in us with our cooperation. Rather, righteousness is something given to us by another – by Christ who justifies us. This righteousness comes to us only through a faith whose object is the Christ who alone can make us righteous.

---

20   *Com. Johan.* 5.5, in Pusey, *Cyrilli in Joannis evangelium*, 2:63 (Maxwell, 354), translation slightly modified.

21   *Com. Johan.* 5.5, in Pusey, *Cyrilli in Joannis evangelium*, 2:65 (Maxwell, 355).

22   See chapter four of Fairbairn, *Grace and Christology in the Early Church,* for my explication of these themes.

Therefore, Cyril's extended discussion of John 8 ties justification or righteousness to the broader themes of freedom, nobility, and adoption, all of which are given to us by Christ, God's Son. In connection with these broader themes, righteousness for Cyril is not a human achievement, or even an achievement wrought jointly by God and human beings, but rather something that Christ directly gives the Christian from without.

Romans 3–5

Unfortunately, Cyril's commentary on the Pauline epistles survives only in fragments. With respect to Romans 3–5, these fragments include comments on 3:21, 3:27, 3:31, 4:2, 5:11, 5:13–18, and 5:20. Thus we do not have Cyril's comments on the most central passage of all, Romans 3:24–25, although he alludes to this passage in his comments on 3:21 and 3:27. In spite of the fragmentary nature of our evidence, there is enough material available for us to be confident about the way Cyril handles this *locus classicus* for justification.

In a substantial fragment on Romans 3:21 ("But now, apart from the Law a righteousness of God has been revealed"), Cyril contrasts the Jews, who trust in the righteousness that comes through the keeping of the Law, with Paul, who declares that he counts all such righteousness to be rubbish in comparison with knowing Christ (Phil. 3:8), who regards the ministry of justification to be far more glorious than the ministry of the Law that brings condemnation (2 Cor. 3:9), and who refuses to impose on Gentiles a yoke that the Jews themselves are not able to bear (Acts 15:10). Cyril continues:

> Therefore, since the Gentiles were under sin as those who were ignorant of the Creator, but the Jews were guilty as transgressors of the Law, the people on earth were in absolute need of Christ who justifies (ἐδέησεν ἀναγκαίως τοῖς οὖσιν ἐπὶ τῆς γῆς τοῦ δικαιοῦντος Χριστοῦ). For we have been justified (δεδικαιώμεθα) "not from works that we ourselves have done in righteousness (ἐν δικαιοσύνῃ), but according to the riches of his mercy" (Tit. 3:5). For he was the one who spoke long ago through the voice of the prophets, saying, "I am the one who will blot out your transgressions . . . and I will remember them no more" (Is. 43:25). For justifying grace (ἡ δικαιοῦσα χάρις) comes upon all equally, that is, upon Jews and Gentiles, because "all have sinned and lack God's glory" (Rom. 3:23).[23]

23 *Frag. Rom.*, in P. E. Pusey, *Sancti patris nostri Cyrilli archiepiscopi Alexandrini in D. Joannis evangelium* (Oxford: Clarendon Press, 1872), 3:178–79 (my translation).

Here we see a sharp contrast between a righteousness that we (Jews or Gentiles) could hypothetically achieve ourselves, and a righteousness that comes from Christ, from grace. Since no one – even one who is blameless according to the Law – is actually righteous in and of himself, we all need justification from without. Notice also that in this passage, Cyril's accent is not primarily on justification itself, but on who justifies us. We do not merely need righteousness; we need the Christ who justifies, the grace that justifies. In Cyril's thought, justification is never an independent concept but is directly connected to Christ who provides it.

The next fragment we possess from Cyril's Romans commentary deals with Romans 3:27 ("Where then is boasting? It is excluded"). Cyril writes:

> For who will boast at all, or on what grounds, given that all have become worthless and have been shut out from the straight path, and there is absolutely no one who does good (cf. Rom. 3:12)? Therefore he says that boasting is excluded, that is, it is cast out and carried away, since it has no place among us. On what grounds is it excluded? [On the grounds that] we have been made rich by the passing over of previous sins (Rom. 3:25), having been justified as a gift by mercy and grace in Christ (ἐλέῳ καὶ χάριτι δικαιούμενοι δωρεὰν ἐν Χριστῷ – cf. Rom. 3:24).[24]

Here again we see that Cyril draws a strong contrast (just as Paul does) between any righteousness we might be able to achieve and the righteousness Christ provides for us. Our righteousness – such as it is – is worthless, and we have no reason to boast. But we have been enriched by being justified in Christ by both mercy and grace.

In a long fragment on Romans 5:11 ("And not only this, but we also boast in God"), Cyril quotes John 3:16 and emphasizes that the one whom God sent was truly his own Son, the Logos made flesh. He stresses that the atonement Christ accomplished defeated death and corruption, both of which were controlled by Satan, and he quotes Hebrews 2:14–15 in the process of making this argument. Cyril then anticipates the second half of Romans 5 by discussing the condemnation that came to all through the sin of Adam, and he states:

> For the Son came down out of the heavens, dissolving the charges [of the Law against humanity], justifying the ungodly one by faith (δικαιῶν ἐν πίστει τὸν ἀσεβῆ), and as God transforming

24 Ibid., 179 (my translation).

the nature of man into incorruption and raising it up to what
it had been at first. For whatever is in Christ is a new creation
(cf. 2 Cor. 5:17), because a new root has also been planted.
He has also become the second Adam, not like the first one
who was the source of wrath and rejection from above for
those who came forth from him, but rather the protector and
the grantor of communion with God (δοτὴρ τῆς πρὸς Θεὸν
οἰκειότητος), through sanctification and incorruption and
the righteousness that comes by faith (δι᾿ ἁγιασμοῦ τε καὶ
ἀφθαρσίας καὶ τῆς ἐν πίστει δικαιοσύνης).[25]

In this passage, Cyril links justification to two major themes of his
soteriology that I have not yet mentioned in this essay – salvation as
a return to a previously incorruptible condition,[26] and salvation as
communion with God.[27] He also (as elsewhere) links justification to
sanctification, and again, I will return to this connection later. Here
as elsewhere, it is clear that the righteousness Cyril has in mind is one
that Christ directly gives the Christian, from the outside.

The most extended extant fragment of Cyril's comments on these
chapters concerns Romans 5:13–18, and a fairly lengthy portion of
this fragment is worth citing here. As Cyril comments on Romans
5:16 ("And the free gift is not like what came through the one man's
sin"), he asks rhetorically:

> For if it was necessary, as he [Paul] says, that from one man,
> or rather through one man, Adam's condemnation passed
> through to all men in accordance with their likeness to
> him (for as I said, he was the root of the race that suffered
> corruption), how would it not also come about, in the case of
> a man acceptable and beloved to God by faith, that the many
> must be justified (δικαιοῦσθαι πολλούς) from the righteous act
> of that one man following the many transgressions (τὸ δεῖν
> ἐξ ἑνὸς δικαιώματος ἐκ πολλῶν παραπτωμάτων δικαιοῦσθαι
> πολλούς)?[28]

Shortly thereafter, Cyril writes:

25 Frag. Rom., in Pusey, Cyrilli in Joannis evangelium, 3:182 (my translation).

26 For my explication of this aspect of Cyril's thought, see Fairbairn, Grace and
Christology in the Early Church, 64–9.

27 The word Cyril uses here for "communion" is οἰκειότης, which is one of his
favorite words in his exegetical writings. See my discussion in Fairbairn, Grace and
Christology in the Early Church, 83–103.

28 Frag. Rom., in Pusey, Cyrilli in Joannis evangelium, 3:185 (my translation).

Therefore, just as Christ the second Adam has been justified, he will walk at first in the way by which justification (ἡ δικαίωσις) will surely come to us. But when we say that Christ has been justified (δεδικαιῶσθαι), we do not mean this as if he were once made unrighteous, and through a free gift had gone before us into a better condition, that is, justification (δικαίωσιν). Instead, we mean that he was himself the first and only man upon the earth who "did no sin, nor was any deceit found in his mouth" (Is. 53:9).[29]

This passage is the only one I have found in the Cyrillian corpus that uses a passive form of the verb δικαιόω to refer to Christ. Under the influence of the Adam-Christ comparison, Cyril describes both Christ and believers as "justified" (passive). But he clarifies his meaning by spelling out that Christ is not justified in the same way we are. He is justified because he is sinless, but we are justified because righteousness comes to us as a free gift through the righteous act of Christ. Through this clarification, Cyril renders even more apparent his constant insistence that righteousness comes to *us* from the outside. Furthermore, Cyril also indicates that Christ's obedience/ sinlessness is the direct source of both his righteousness and ours. He is just because – considered as a man, as the second Adam – he perfectly obeyed God and committed no sin. In contrast, we are justified because the second Adam who obeyed perfectly grants us his own righteousness.

These passages from Cyril's comments on Romans 3-5 build upon and add to the picture of justification he develops in the other passages we have seen in this section. It is clear that, in Cyril's mind, justification is something that Christ actively accomplishes, something that comes to Christians from outside ourselves. Likewise, Cyril's emphasis is not on the concept of justification per se, or even on the Christian's state of justification, but on the one who justifies us: only God's natural Son, who alone is righteous in himself, could grant us this righteousness. Furthermore, Cyril ties justification closely to other themes of his soteriology – adoption as children of God, sanctification or holiness, freedom from death and condemnation, and restoration to mankind's originally incorruptible condition.

29   Ibid., (my translation)..

Justification/Righteousness and Sanctification in Cyril

We have seen that Keating argues that Cyril does not distinguish between justification and sanctification, and in the previous section, we saw that in two of the passages I considered (on Hab. 2 and Rom. 5), Cyril directly links the two concepts. In fact, Cyril's writings contain 82 passages in which he connects the two by using the words (either verb or noun forms) in parallel (four in *De ador.*, ten in *Glaph. Pent.*, five in *Expos. Psalm.*, 13 in *Com. Is.*, 13 in *Com. proph. min.*, one in *Com. Matt.*, four in *Com. Luc.*, nine in *Com. Johan.*, three in *Frag. Rom.*, one in *Frag. Heb.*, seven in *Thes.*, one in *Trin. Dial.*, three in *De dog. sol.*, three in *Resp. Tib.*, and five in *Ep. pasch.*). As I have indicated above, the prevalence of this link between δικαιοσύνη and ἁγιασμός in Cyril's writings would seem to imply that his understanding of δικαιοσύνη is not similar to that of classical Protestantism, in which justification and sanctification are sharply distinguished. It is important to recognize, however, that Cyril's understanding of sanctification is not, at heart, a concept of an active process of becoming holy, in which the Christian collaborates with the Holy Spirit. Instead, Cyril regards sanctification most fundamentally as a participatory holiness that is granted to the believer when he/she is united to the Holy Spirit.[30] A look at three illustrative passages should serve to illustrate the way Cyril understands sanctification and its relation to justification.

Commenting on Isaiah 8:14–16 (which, in the LXX contrasts the house of Jacob that will be crushed with those who keep the Law under seal so as not to learn it), Cyril describes in his typical fashion the difference between Jews and Christians. He asks who those who keep the Law under seal are, and he answers:

> Those justified and sanctified in Christ through the Spirit (Οἱ ἐν Χριστῷ δηλονότι δεδικαιωμένοι τε καὶ ἡγιασμένοι διὰ τοῦ Πνεύματος), to whom could be applied the statement, "Let the light of your face be shown to us, O Lord"; the Son is the image and likeness and as it were the face of the God and Father. Light sent from him on us is the Holy Spirit, through whom we are sealed by being conformed to the original image through sanctification (πρὸς εἰκόνα τὴν πρώτην ἀναμορφούμενοι δι'

---

30 For my brief discussion of this concept in Cyril's writings, see Fairbairn, *Grace and Christology in the Early Church*, 65, 76.

ἁγιασμοῦ), for we have been made "in the image and likeness" of God the creator.[31]

Here we see that sanctification, as Cyril understands it, is directly tied to Christ and consists of conformity to him. It is not so much a process of becoming holy as it is a present sharing in Christ's holiness. And here, as elsewhere, Cyril treats justification and sanctification as synonyms. Neither is a righteousness or holiness that the Christian achieves (with or without the help of grace); both are a participation in the righteousness/holiness of another: Christ. Cyril continues by contrasting those who live in a Jewish manner with those who live by faith, and he concludes: "In living by the Law you have fallen away from grace. For by faith we wait for the hope of righteousness (διὰ πίστεως ἐλπίδα δικαιοσύνης ἀπεκδεχόμεθα)."[32] Here Cyril indicates that the posture of the Christian life, the posture of one living by grace, is one of waiting and hoping for a righteousness that comes from Christ.

In his commentary on Micah 7:16–17 (which declares that the nations will be ashamed of their might), Cyril writes:

> By *nations* here he means the loathsome and unclean herds of demons; when they *see* those called in Christ to justification, to sanctification, to redemption, to sonship, to incorruptibility, to glory (τοὺς ἐν Χριστῷ καλουμένους εἰς δικαίωσιν, εἰς ἁγιασμὸν, εἰς ἀπολύτρωσιν, εἰς υἱοθεσίαν, εἰς ἀφθαρσίαν, εἰς δόξαν), to a life that is unconstricted and free, then it is that they will *be ashamed*.[33]

In this passage one should notice that justification is linked not only to sanctification but to redemption, sonship, etc. Justification and sanctification are not discrete states but rather are synonymous aspects of a multi-faceted salvation. Furthermore, we can recognize that just as sonship, incorruptibility, and glory belong to Christ and become ours by participation, so also – in Cyril's mind – righteousness and holiness belong to Christ and become ours as we participate in him. Shortly after this, Cyril writes that the demons are right to feel ashamed when they see Christians, because the news about us is extraordinary. This news is that Christ has died for the ungodly (Rom. 5:8):

---

31 *Com. Is.* 8 (*PG* 70:236) (Hill, *Commentary on Isaiah*, 1:193).

32 *Com. Is.* 8 (*PG* 70:236) (Hill, *Commentary on Isaiah*, 1:194; translation slightly modified).

33 *Com. Mic.* 7, in Pusey, *Cyrilli in xii prophetas*, 1:736; FOTC 116:275.

in order that we who were formerly guilty of terrible and insupportable failings should now be sanctified (νῦν ὦμεν ἡγιασμένοι), "not by works of righteousness that we ourselves have performed (Οὐκ ἐξ ἔργων δικαιοσύνης ἃ ἐποιήσαμεν ἡμεῖς), but" (Tit. 3:5) through mercy and grace (ἐλέῳ καὶ χάριτι), so that we who were formerly distressed and devoid of all hope should now be loved, the cynosure of all eyes, "heirs of God and co-heirs with Christ" (Rom 8:17).[34]

One should note that here, Cyril specifically denies that our sanctification or holiness comes about by righteous acts that we might have done. Sanctification comes by mercy and grace, and it focuses on who we are in Christ – his co-heirs and beloved ones. Sanctification, like justification, is something Christ directly gives us when we participate in him.

As Cyril comments on John 6:69 (in which Peter affirms that Christ is the holy one of God), he commends the faith of the apostles and explains that believing and coming to know are the same thing because the great truths of the faith are apprehended by faith. He argues that faith comes first as a foundation, and that knowledge is built on that faith. He then asserts, "Christ is for us a beginning and a foundation for sanctification and righteousness (ἀρχὴ γὰρ ἡμῖν καὶ θεμέλιος εἰς ἁγιασμὸν καὶ δικαιοσύνην ὁ Χριστὸς), through faith, that is, and in no other way. For that is how he dwells in us."[35] From this point Cyril goes into one of his common explanations of the difference between Christ and Christians – he is the true Son of the living God, but we are adopted sons of God by grace. By preceding that familiar refrain with the statement quoted just above, Cyril shows that only the true Son of God can be a beginning and foundation for our salvation. Again he links sanctification and justification and he emphasizes that *both of them* come to us through the indwelling of the true Son, which happens as we believe.

These passages are illustrations of a consistent pattern that Cyril employs in discussing justification and sanctification. He connects the two, not because he believes that justification is something we achieve, but because he believes that even sanctification is something given to us from the outside, by Christ through grace. Righteousness and holiness are very similar concepts, and Cyril treats both of these as properties of Christ, the righteous and holy one, just as he treats sonship as a property of Christ, God's unique and true Son. We become righteous and holy in the same

---

34 *Com. Mic.* 7, in Pusey, *Cyrilli in xii prophetas*, 1:737; FOTC 116:276.
35 *Com. Johan.* 4.4, in Pusey, *Cyrilli in Joannis evangelium*, 1:576 (Maxwell, 257).

way we become sons/daughters of God, through participation in the one who possesses these properties by nature. In Cyril's understanding, it is not just justification, but also sanctification and adoption, that are by grace through faith.

Here it is also worth elaborating on a related issue that the previous discussion has highlighted: the relation between Cyril's Christology and his understanding of justification/sanctification. One could argue that just as Cyril rejects a separation between divine and human action in Christ's person, so also he rejects a separation between divine (justifying) action and human (cooperating) action in the believer's salvation. This statement is true, but it does not quite go far enough. The point of Cyril's Christology is not merely – and not primarily that divine and human action are inseparable in salvation. It is that God the Son became human precisely so that he, God, could do *as man* something for human beings that we could not do for ourselves.

This Christological emphasis dovetails closely with the idea that Christ gives the believer a righteousness from without. For Cyril, even the human side of salvation is not primarily *our* human action; it is *Christ's* human action. In order for that human action to accomplish our salvation, it had to be human action performed by God the Son. Throughout Cyril's struggle against Nestorianism, he argued against an understanding of Christ as a divinely-indwelt man who could lead us in doing what we needed to do for our salvation. Leaving aside the question of whether Cyril understood Nestorius correctly, his own point was clear: we *cannot* do what is necessary for our salvation, and so we need a Savior who is more than just a divinely-indwelt leader. We needed God himself to do as man what was necessary but what we human beings could not do. The "asymmetry" of Cyril's Christology – in which Christ is fully human, but his humanity subsists in the hypostasis of the Logos is directly related to this understanding of our inability to save ourselves. And it leads Cyril to a corresponding asymmetry in soteriology – at the most fundamental level, we do not *produce* righteousness within ourselves, nor do we even cooperate with grace in producing such inward righteousness. Rather, most fundamentally, we *receive* another's righteousness – the righteousness of God's Son who became human in order to unite us to himself and thus to give us his righteousness.

Conclusions

From what I have written, it is clear that there are important similarities and differences between Cyril's understanding of justification and that of Protestantism. Cyril repeatedly writes of the believer's righteousness as one that is given by another, by Christ, from the outside. This emphasis on Christ as the source of the Christian's righteousness is similar to the Protestant understanding of the *passive* nature of the Christian's righteousness. Cyril, as much as Luther or any Protestant subsequently, sees the righteousness or holiness of the Christian as that which *belongs to Christ* and which Christ *actively* grants to the believer, who *passively* receives it through faith and grace. But as we have seen, there are also differences between Cyril and many classical Protestant writers. Cyril does not adopt a forensic framework as the dominant aspect of his soteriology. He does not distinguish justification and sanctification to any great degree at all. And he certainly does not make justification the central idea of his soteriology. Thus, Cyril stands as a caution against the potential dangers of a theology that is too exclusively forensic or makes the justification/sanctification distinction too sharply.

When one examines Cyril's relation to modern Eastern Orthodoxy, we find that there are also similarities and differences. The participatory nature of salvation shines very clearly in both Cyril and modern Orthodoxy. But on the other hand, two things about Cyril's understanding of participation stand in partial contrast to some expressions of modern Orthodoxy. First, the basis for Cyril's understanding of participation is not the *qualities* of God (whether they be the energies, as in later Palamite theology; qualities such as incorruption and immortality that dominate the attention of many Greek patristic writers; or even qualities like righteousness and holiness on which this essay has focused), but the *person* of Christ. For Cyril, participation is at heart personal. We become righteous when we are personally united to the one who is righteous, to Christ. (Notice again that this exactly parallels the fact that we become sons of God when we are united to Christ, the true Son.) Second, the very fact that participation is at heart personal means that it is not fundamentally gradual or progressive. The outworkings of union with Christ are indeed gradual, but union with Christ himself, effected in baptism at the very beginning of Christian life, lies at the heart of Cyril's concept of participation. To say this even more directly, for Cyril even deification is primarily the present state of the believer, rather than the culmination of a process, and his teaching on justification undergirds this fact.

At this point, readers from both Protestant and Orthodox traditions may object that their tradition does in fact emphasize personal union with Christ. This is true. There are some – perhaps many – voices within both traditions that possess such an emphasis. But my point is that in both Protestantism and Orthodoxy, the centrality of personal union with Christ tends to be obscured by these other emphases: forensic justification in Protestantism and a more mystical and/or progressive approach to union with God in Orthodoxy. I ask my readers to recognize these tendencies, even though the mistakes to which they can lead are sometimes successfully avoided.

With that caveat registered, I suggest that as one looks at these two sets of similarities and differences between Cyril on one hand and either Protestantism or Orthodoxy on the other, they expose a false dichotomy that has perhaps hindered dialogue between the two groups. Protestants, schooled in on-going disputes with Roman Catholicism, are often quick to point out the difference between imputed righteousness and imparted or infused righteousness, and the classical Protestant concept of justification is closely tied to the first of these, in opposition to the second. It seems to me, though, that Protestants sometimes extend this dichotomy into an opposition between imputed righteousness and participatory righteousness, thus unhelpfully applying concepts borrowed from anti-Catholic polemic to anti-Orthodox polemic. (Whether those concepts are appropriate even in dialogue with Roman Catholics is another question, but one I will not address here.) I believe Cyril's thought demonstrates that this is a false dichotomy. Instead, Cyril teaches us that participatory righteousness – or better, our participation in the one who is himself righteous – is the very heart of imputed righteousness. To say this in Protestant terms, the righteousness of Christ is imputed to the Christian when the Christian is united to Christ, who is the righteous one. But to say the same thing in Orthodox terms, participation in Christ, because it is a personal participation granted to the believer at the beginning of Christian life, implies that his righteousness becomes ours.

As a result, I suggest that a deeper consideration of Cyril's doctrine of justification can both challenge Protestants and the Orthodox, and help to uncover latent common ground between them. Protestants need to recognize that justification is not merely or even mainly transactional, but primarily personal and organic. We are united to Christ as a person, and as a result, his righteousness is imputed to us. The forensic crediting of righteousness grows out of the personal union. At the same time, the Orthodox need to recognize that the gradual process of deification (even the continual reception of life-giving grace through the Eucharist, one of Cyril's greatest emphases) is grounded in an initial personal union with Christ, and thus, both righteousness and deification are at heart gifts that Christ gives us when he gives himself to us. Perhaps both Protestants and Orthodox can then recognize that as Christians, we are righteous, holy, and even divine, because – and only because – we are in Christ. And if we are righteous, holy, and divine in Christ, then throughout Christian life we will progressively become more and more who we already are.

Cyril's Works Cited in this Essay

Abbrev. Title	Full Title	Location of Best Greek Text
De ador.	*De adoratione et cultu in spiritu et veritate*	J.-P. Migne, *Patrologiae cursus completus, series Graeca* (Paris: Migne, 1857–1866), 68:132–1125.
Glaph. Pent.	*Glaphyra in Pentateuchum*	J.-P. Migne, *Patrologiae cursus completus, series Graeca* (Paris: Migne, 1857–1866), 69:9–677.
Expos. Psalm.	*Expositio in Psalmos*	J.-P. Migne, *Patrologiae cursus completus, series Graeca* (Paris: Migne, 1857–1866), 69:717–1273.
Com. Is.	*Commentarius in Isaiam prophetam*	J.-P. Migne, *Patrologiae cursus completus, series Graeca* (Paris: Migne, 1857–1866), 70:9–1449.
Com. proph. min.	*Commentarius in 12 prophetas minores*	P. E. Pusey, *Sancti patris nostri Cyrilli archiepiscopi Alexandrini in xii prophetas*, 2 vols. (Oxford: Clarendon Press, 1868).
Com. Matt.	*Commentarii in Matthaeum*	J. Reuss, *Matthäus-Kommentare aus der griechischen Kirche, Texte und Untersuchungen* (Berlin: Akademie Verlag, 1957), 61:153–269.

Com. Luc.	Commentarii in Lucam	J. Sickenberger, *Fragmente der Homilien des Cyrill von Alexandrien zum Lukas-evangelium*, Texte und Untersuchungen 34 (Leipzig: Hinrichs, 1909), 76–107.
Com. Johan.	Commentarii in Joannem	P. E. Pusey, *Sancti patris nostri Cyrilli archiepiscopi Alexandrini in D. Joannis evangelium*, 3 vols. (Oxford: Clarendon Press, 1872).
Frag. Rom.	Fragmenta in sancti Pauli epistulam ad Romanos	P. E. Pusey, *Sancti patris nostri Cyrilli archiepiscopi Alexandrini in D. Joannis evangelium* (Oxford: Clarendon Press, 1872), 3:173–248.
Frag. Heb.	Fragmenta in sancti Pauli epistulam ad Hebraeos	P. E. Pusey, *Sancti patris nostri Cyrilli archiepiscopi Alexandrini in D. Joannis evangelium* (Oxford: Clarendon Press, 1872), 3:362–423
Trin. dial.	De sancta trini-tate dialogi 7	G.-M. de Durand, *Cyrille d'Alexandrie: Dialogues sur la Trinité*, 3 vols., Sources chrétiennes 231, 237, 246 (Paris: Éditions du Cerf, 1976, 1977, 1978).
Thes.	Thesaurus de sancta et consub-stantiali trinitate	J.-P. Migne, *Patrologiae cursus com-pletus, series Graeca* (Paris: Migne, 1857–1866), 75:9–656.
Ep. pasch.	Epistulae pas-chales	J.-P. Migne, *Patrologiae cursus com-pletus, series Graeca* (Paris: Migne, 1857–1866), 77:401–981.
De dog. sol.	Tractatu de dog-matum solutione	P. E. Pusey, *Sancti patris nostri Cyrilli archiepiscopi Alexandrini in D. Joannis evangelium* (Oxford: Clarendon Press, 1872), 3:549–566
Resp. Tib.	Responsiones ad Tiberium diaco-num sociosque suos	P. E. Pusey, *Sancti patris nostri Cyrilli archiepiscopi Alexandrini in D. Joannis evangelium* (Oxford: Clarendon Press, 1872), 3:577–602.
Hom. div.	Homiliae diver-sae	J.-P. Migne, *Patrologiae cursus completus, series Graeca* (Paris: Migne, 1857–1866), 77:1096–1100.
Hom. frag.	Homiliarum incertarum frag-menta	P. E. Pusey, *Sancti patris nostri Cyrilli archiepiscopi Alexandrini in D. Joannis evangelium* (Oxford: Claren-don Press, 1872), 3:461–468, 470–475.

Chapter 7

The Theology of Baptism in T. F. Torrance and its Ascetic Correlate in St. Mark the Monk

Alexis Torrance[1]

The Theology of Baptism in the Writings of T. F. Torrance

Torrance develops his theology of baptism most fully in a lecture delivered to the *Académie Internationale des Sciences Religieuses* in 1970, subsequently forming chapter two of *Theology in Reconciliation* and entitled "The One Baptism Common to Christ and His Church."[2] The current essay will depend in large measure on his thought as it is found there, although insights from elsewhere in Torrance's *oeuvre* will not be overlooked. Torrance begins by emphasizing the need in theology "to give more rigorous attention to the humanity of Christ," a frequent concern of his.[3] When we turn to the sacraments, he argues, we must begin with "the primary *mysterium* or *sacramentum*" who is "Jesus Christ himself."[4] Baptism must be grounded so firmly and objectively in the historic work of Christ "that it has no content, reality, or power apart from it."[5] This standpoint leads Torrance to distinguish baptism, properly speaking, from any ritual

---

1   I would like to thank Matthew Baker for his invaluable help in the preparation of this essay. I should also point out that, despite my name and my patristic sympathies, I am no immediate relation of the Torrance theological dynasty.

2   T. F. Torrance, "The One Baptism Common to Christ and His Church" in *Theology in Reconciliation: Essays towards Evangelical and Catholic Unity in East and West* (Grand Rapids, MI: Eerdmans, 1976), 82–105.

3   Torrance, "The One Baptism," 82. For another more recent turn to this issue, see Patrick Henry Reardon, *The Jesus We Missed: The Surprising Truth About the Humanity of Christ* (Nashville, TN: Thomas Nelson, 2012).

4   Torrance, "The One Baptism," 82.

5   Ibid., 83.

act or ethical "response of man," putting the emphasis wholly on the "power of [Christ's] vicarious life, death, and resurrection" which alone effects the baptism of the faithful, albeit through the sacramental actions of his Body, the Church.[6] The *baptisma* of Christians refers to Christ's own baptism, which in turn refers not only to the events at the River Jordan, but to the entirety of Christ's life, conceived as a baptism undergone "for our sakes in the whole course of his redemptive life."[7] The key for Torrance is the vicariousness of Christ's actions for our humanity: his obedience, humility, and submission to the Father as man dignifies human nature with the honor of sonship: "Jesus was baptized with the baptism of our humanity that was anointed by the Spirit and consecrated in sonship to the Father."[8] It is this baptism of our humanity unto God in Christ that constitutes the meaning of "the one baptism." It is this baptism that the Church undergoes in Christ, but in a qualified sense. As Torrance puts it, "Christ and his Church participate in the one baptism in different ways – Christ actively and vicariously as Redeemer, the Church passively and receptively as the redeemed Community."[9] But while the means of participation is different, the content is the same: "As Jesus Christ is, so are we in this world, for what happened to him as Head of the Body happens to us also who are members of the Body."[10]

Having established an identity between the baptism of Christ and the baptism of the faithful, Torrance moves on to unpack the sacramental question. He repeatedly attacks what he sees as a post-Augustinian "sacramental dualism" in the West between water-baptism and Spirit-baptism, which in itself divides the one baptism of the Church. He insists instead on the need for a "stereo-understanding" of the one baptism, which includes water and Spirit, and which is wholly God's work in us.[11] But parts of the early church, he claims, fell prey in their understanding of baptism to "a syncretistic Gnosticism", "a mystical notion of redemption," and "mythico-ritualistic modes of initiation and participation in the divine", i.e. to a Neo-Platonizing travesty which ultimately does away with the vicarious work of Christ for us.[12]

6   Ibid.
7   Ibid.
8   Ibid., 86.
9   Ibid., 87.
10   Ibid., 89.
11   Ibid., esp. 92–9.
12   Ibid., 94.

Although there are some heroes in his story, namely Irenaeus, Athanasius, and the early pro-Nicenes, all of whom refused to create a sacramental theology based on the division between the noetic/intelligible and sensible realms rather than the work of Christ, these heroes appear few and far between. While Augustine is commended for his "Irenaean Christocentricity" in expounding the doctrine of baptism, his thought falls short of the mark for its persistent "dualism between the intelligible and sensible worlds," which shifts our gaze away from the "mighty acts of God in Christ" to the workings of grace in the human soul.[13] The mention of grace brings Torrance to the crux of his argument: it is the Western doctrine of supernatural grace mediating between the intelligible and sensible worlds that undermines and ultimately destroys the Christian doctrine of baptism. What is needed is a total re-orientation back to the redemptive acts of God in Christ for us: only then can our theology of baptism be placed on surer footing. Torrance invites us to marvel at the sheer grandeur of baptism's true meaning as compared with an impoverished notion of created and mediating grace: "That is what will always baffle us about the saving act of God in us: it is the direct activity of God in which he is personally and immediately present in his own transcendent being, and is not just some created relation effected between us by his divine causality."[14]

The emphasis in the closing pages of his essay is placed squarely on this sovereign and free gift of Christ's divine life to the faithful in baptism: "in Jesus Christ God has once and for all assumed human nature into that mutuality [between Father and Son] and opened his divine being for human participation. This took place vicariously and redemptively, for it was *our* human nature which God assumed in Jesus Christ."[15] The vicariousness of Christ's life for our salvation is given a supreme status, and any hint of a Christian's own activity in this salvation is forcefully denied, insofar as "his act of grace remains sovereignly free and is not trapped within a reciprocity between man and God that begins with man and ends with man."[16] Thus in receiving baptism, we rely "upon Christ alone and his vicarious faithfulness."[17]

13   Ibid., 97–8.
14   Ibid., 101.
15   Ibid., 101–02.
16   Ibid., 103.
17   Ibid., 104.

The themes Torrance develops in his essay "The One Baptism" just discussed are scattered throughout his writings, and it is evident that he held dearly to the principle of Christ's vicarious humanity in his understanding of both baptism and the Church. It is no surprise that his thoughts regarding baptism should re-surface in some detail in his essay "The One Church," which analyzes and expounds the final lines of the Nicene-Constantinopolitan Creed.[18] Here the significance of baptism as being in the Name of the Trinity is stressed as the incontrovertible basis for the Trinitarian faith of early Christians and the development of Trinitarian theology in the fourth century.[19] In discussing this significance, Torrance turns once again to the relationship between the baptism of Christ and the baptism of the faithful. His words, which give an eloquent summary of his theology of baptism, are worth citing at length:

> Baptism in the name of the Father, Son, and Holy Spirit initiates people into the sphere in which all the divine blessings of forgiveness of sins, resurrection, and eternal life are bestowed and become effective, but does the emphasis fall on baptism as an objective event in Christ or as a subjective event in our experience of Christ through the Spirit? No doubt baptism properly understood involves both, but a noticeable difference in emphasis already arose in the early Church, for example in the teaching of Cyril of Jerusalem compared to that of Athanasius. With Cyril there was clearly a greater stress upon baptism as a mystical replica of what took place in Christ, an interiorisation in the soul of the spiritual reality signified by baptism. With Athanasius, however, there was a considerable stress on the fact that even when we consider our adoption in Christ to be sons of God as taking place in the Spirit, we must think of that not as viewed in ourselves, but as viewed in the Spirit who is in God. For Athanasius the decisive point, to which we have referred already, was that in his baptism in the Jordan the incarnate Son of God received the Spirit upon the humanity he had taken from us, not for his own sake,

18 T. F. Torrance, *The Trinitarian Faith: The Evangelical Theology of the Ancient Catholic Church* (New York: T&T Clark, 1991), 252–301. The lines from the Creed he deals with are: "I believe in One, Holy, Catholic, and Apostolic Church. I confess one baptism for the remission of sins. I look for the resurrection of the dead, and the life of the world to come."

19 Torrance, *The Trinitarian Faith*, esp. 256, 264. This idea recurs in *The Trinitarian Faith*: see, for instance, 45, 193, 196, 230–31, etc.

but for our sake. That is to say, it was our humanity that was baptised, anointed, sanctified and sealed in him. Thus when he was baptised for us we were baptised in him. Our baptism in the name of the Holy Trinity, therefore, is to be understood as a partaking through the Spirit in the one unrepeatable baptism of Christ which he underwent, not just in the Jordan river, but throughout his life and in his death and resurrection, on our behalf. That vicarious baptism was the objective truth behind the ἕν βάπτισμα of the Creed in which its depth of meaning was grounded.[20]

And again, a little further he writes:

When he died for us and was buried, we died and were buried with him, and when he rose again from the grave, we were raised up with him – that is the truth sealed upon us in "one baptism." Jesus Christ underwent that one baptism vicariously as Redeemer, but by uniting us to himself through his Spirit he makes us participate in it receptively as those whom he has redeemed. The central truth of baptism, therefore, is lodged in Jesus Christ himself and all that he has done for us within the humanity he took from us and made his own, sharing to the full what we are that we may share to the full what he is. Baptism is the sacrament of that reconciling and atoning exchange in the incarnate Saviour. When we understand baptism in that objective depth, we are directed away from ourselves to what took place in Christ in God. Hence St Paul was accustomed to speak of our dying and rising in Christ in the aorist tense. However, if we think of baptism not objectively as βάπτισμα but subjectively as βαπτισμός, then the only meaning we can give to it will be in terms of what we do or experience, or in terms of the efficacy of its valid performance as a rite.[21]

Before turning to the theology of baptism in St. Mark the Monk, and from there comparing and contrasting the two theologians, I would like to highlight an interesting and important element in these passages from Torrance. As seen in his article "The One Baptism," the objectivity and subjectivity of baptism are distinguished. What is interesting here, however, is that Torrance initially admits that "no doubt baptism properly understood involves both," and yet he goes on to challenge if not dismiss any understanding of baptism – even that of Cyril of Jerusalem – which

20   Torrance, *The Trinitarian Faith,* 292–93.
21   Ibid., 293.

is not wholly focused on the *objective* aspect (i.e. the historic work of God in Christ for us). All subjective readings are viewed, it appears, with the utmost suspicion. This is a significant point that will re-emerge in the last part of our discussion.

The Theology of Baptism in the Writings of St Mark the Monk

It may initially come as a surprise that the theology of T. F. Torrance should be brought into conversation with that of a fifth-century ascetic, whose writings, moreover, were perhaps entirely unknown to Torrance. Yet in the writings of St. Mark, particularly his treatise *On Baptism*, we find numerous grounds for fruitful dialogue between the Greek-speaking Christian ascetic tradition and Torrance's patristically-minded Reformed theology.

The precise identity and date of Mark the Monk (also known as "the Ascetic," "the Egyptian," and "the Hermit") remains unsolved, although a placement somewhere in the first half of the fifth century with at least some link to Egypt is probable.[22] His popularity amongst subsequent generations of Eastern Christian ascetics is significant, crystallized to a certain extent in recent centuries by the inclusion of three of his works in the first volume of the *Philokalia*, a now classic compendium of ascetic texts first published by Sts. Nikodemus of the Holy Mountain and Makarios of Corinth at Venice in 1782.[23] He can thus safely be employed as a representative of Eastern Christian

---

22 For a discussion and relevant bibliography, see Alexis Torrance, *Repentance in Late Antiquity: Eastern Asceticism and the Framing of the Christian Life* (Oxford: Oxford University Press, 2013), 88–95. The best general analysis of Mark's theology remains the unpublished dissertation by (Kallistos) Timothy Ware, "The Ascetic Writings of Mark the Hermit" (DPhil thesis, University of Oxford, 1965). For Mark's view of baptism, see (Kallistos) Timothy Ware, "The Sacrament of Baptism and the Ascetic Life in the Teaching of Mark the Monk," *Studia Patristica* 10/1 (1970): 441-52 and Torrance, *Repentance in Late Antiquity*, 92–4, 100.

23 The three works included are: *On the Spiritual Law, On those who think they are made righteous by Works,* and *Letter to Nicholas the Solitary.* An English translation of these works can be found in *The Philokalia*, trans. G. Palmer, P. Sherrard, and K. T. Ware (London: Faber and Faber, 1977), 1:110–160. A complete English translation of his works has now been made: T. Vivian and A. Casiday, trans., *Counsels on the Spiritual Life*, 2 vols. (Crestwood, NY: St Vladimir's Seminary Press, 2009). There is likewise a critical edition of his writings: Marc le Moine, *Traités*, ed. G. de Durand, 2 vols. (*SC* 445, 455; Paris: Cerf, 1999–2000). Translations here are my own.

ascetic thought, which in turn will allow us to use the dialogue between Torrance and Mark as a dialogue between Torrance's thought and Eastern Christian ascetic theology more broadly. When Mark the Monk turns to the issue of baptism, he is doing so within a particular context of theological debate. While for Torrance the debates fuelling his theology of baptism revolve around sacramental dualism and the Trinitarian and Christological basis of the Church's and each Christian's life, for Mark, the debate is more ascetically-oriented. Specifically, Mark appears (especially in his treatise *On Baptism*) to be countering Messalian tendencies or groups within the ascetic Christian movement. I say "appears" because he never overtly identifies his foes, but it is almost certain that he had Messalian theology in mind. The debate for Mark centers on the nature and efficacy of baptism: in short, is baptism a secondary facet of the Christian life, subservient to the ascetic struggles of the Christian in the quest for salvation (the Messalian position), or does baptism freely confer the foundation and goal of the Christian life, the content of salvation, which is lovingly responded to and experienced through the keeping of Christ's commandments (St. Mark's position)?

We might be tempted to draw a neat parallel here with the struggles of the Reformation – salvation by works (Messalian/Roman Catholic) versus salvation by faith or grace alone (Markan/Protestant) – and indeed, St. Mark figured conspicuously in several Reformation and post-Reformation debates. Lutherans were particularly drawn by his treatise, *On those who think they are justified by works*.[24] But imposing such an anachronistic bifurcation on the fourth century ascetic debates would be misguided. The gratuitous nature of the divine grace conferred in baptism is never conceived by Mark as a substitute for struggle, but rather as the *enabling and sustaining* factor of the Christian (read "ascetic") life, a life that is fulfilled in the keeping of Christ's commandments. The value of asceticism (or the active Christian life) on the path of salvation, in other words, is never in question: what is at stake is the placing of asceticism within a correct dogmatic framework, which for Mark must revolve around, and be grounded in, the person and work of Jesus Christ.

---

24 For a summary of how the works of St. Mark were brought into Protestant and Roman Catholic debates from 1531 onwards (with Protestants being generally favorable and Roman Catholics generally cautious), see T. Vivian and A. Casiday, *Counsels on the Spiritual Life*, 32–3.

The treatise *On Baptism* takes the popular form of a question-and-answer dialogue (erotapokriseis). It opens with a question regarding the nature of baptism: does baptism bring perfection of itself, obliterating original/"ancestral" sin, or must this be achieved through struggle after baptism? The rest of the treatise is essentially made up of a series of back-and-forth questions and answers stemming from this initial question. St. Mark's position has already been summarized: baptism does indeed freely convey perfection, clothing us with Christ, the perfect God and perfect man. Crucially, however, this imputed perfection from Christ to the faithful is never dissociated, logically or otherwise, from the active Christian life.

Early on Mark writes: "Holy baptism is perfect, but it does not render perfect the one who does not keep the commandments."[25] He goes on: "For faith is not only to be baptized into Christ, but to keep his commandments."[26] The concept of the commandments (particularly Christ's New Testament commandments) lies at the heart of Mark's theory of the Christian life. Just as baptism is "of Christ," so are his commandments, and to set them aside or relegate their significance is to insult Christ. Conceptualizing Christian salvation apart from the keeping of Christ's commandments is also an affront to baptism itself, since baptism provides all the means (or grace) necessary to keep the commandments. This understanding of the grace of baptism allows Mark to insist on the importance of the ascetic life without considering that life a "work" of salvation in itself (and indeed, he repeatedly shuns such a notion as a "lie"). As he puts it in one place, the commandments themselves can only be fulfilled "by the mercies of our Lord Jesus Christ."[27]

But that there is a *need* for every Christian to strive to keep the commandments is without question in Mark's mind. Christ's vicarious work, imputed in its perfection to the Christian in baptism, introduces and equips the Christian for "the law of liberty," which is the path of the commandments.[28] This point is worthy of note, as it touches on the nature of the human will. Contrary to the popular perception of Eastern Christian thought on this matter, namely that human beings have an inherently free

25 *On Baptism* 2 (*SC* 445:298).

26 *On Baptism* 2 (*SC* 445:298–300).

27 *On the Spiritual Law* 30 (*SC* 445:82).

28 On the "law of liberty" in Mark, see especially *On Baptism* 2 (*SC* 445:300–304); also *On the Spiritual Law* 28, 30 (*SC* 445:82); and *On those who think they are made righteous by works* 16 (*SC* 445:134).

will from birth, Mark is a little more nuanced. Before baptism, there is a definite "bondage of the will" in human beings that cannot be freed by human effort. It is bondage, however, of *inclination*, not of *necessity*: the will inclines more easily to evil, but does not necessarily commit evil. What it cannot do of itself is properly keep the commandments of Christ. Part of the gift of baptism is to free the will and give it the opportunity and strength to walk in the statutes of the Lord. To turn away from the commandments is to submit the will to bondage once again, and thus to slight the gift of baptism.[29]

Baptism, then, conveys the fullness of grace, the fullness of Christ's salvific work, and yet this fullness is only experienced or lived out through the keeping of the commandments. To reconcile such a tension, Mark introduces a distinction between the full and true incorporation into Christ at baptism, which occurs μυστικῶς (mystically or secretly), and the experience of that incorporation ἐνεργῶς (actively) through keeping to the "law of liberty."[30] In one sense, a parallel can legitimately be drawn between the μυστικῶς-ἐνεργῶς distinction in Mark and the "stereo-understanding" of baptism seen in Torrance. Both are, after all, attempting to keep the work of Christ (our adoption as sons of God through him in the Spirit) front and center within the sacramental act of baptism, although the emphasis falls rather differently in each case. For Mark, the revelation (ἀποκάλυψις) of the baptismal gift through the active Christian life is of paramount importance, without which Christians effectively cheat the great gift given them, whereas for Torrance, it is mainly a proper understanding of the grandeur of Christ's baptism in itself that is the focus.[31]

---

29 Among the main passages relating to this point regarding the human will in Mark are: *On Baptism* 2 (*SC* 445:302), 3 (*SC* 445:306), 9 (*SC* 445:358), and 13 (*SC* 445:374); in this context see also *On those who think they are made righteous by works* 178 (*SC* 445:186).

30 Mark gives the most direct and comprehensive summary of his μυστικῶς-ἐνεργῶς teaching on baptism at *On Baptism* 5 (*SC* 445:324–348); for his teaching in a nutshell, see *On those who think they are made righteous by works* 85 (*SC* 445:156): "all that have been baptized in an orthodox manner have received the whole of grace mystically, but they afterwards receive full assurance through the keeping of the commandments." The distinction is discussed at greater length in Ware, "The Ascetic Writings of Mark the Hermit," 227–40.

31 For a more detailed analysis of the active revelation of baptism in the Christian life according to Mark, in terms of purification (καθαρισμός), freedom (ἐλευθερία), and indwelling (ἐνοίκησις), see Ware, "The Sacrament of Baptism."

We have spoken much of Mark's insistence on linking baptism with the keeping of the commandments without elaborating on which commandments he means in particular. This is not the place to explore the matter in detail, but one or two points should be made.[32] Firstly, he does not frequently elaborate on which commandments he is referring to, but in one passage of *On Baptism* he demonstrates that he means primarily the directives of the New Testament.[33] The one treatise where the "content" of the commandments is the center of attention is his work *On Repentance*. The opening words (and the opening commandment) of Christ's public ministry, to "repent for the kingdom of heaven is at hand," is understood by Mark to be the supreme commandment in which all other commandments are summed up and contained. In a manner not altogether dissimilar from the opening sentences of Luther's *Ninety-Five Theses*, Mark associates repentance with the Christian life in its totality, a continuous conforming of the Christian mind to the mind of Christ. Repentance refers, as Luther puts it, "to the whole life of believers."[34]

Given the status of repentance as the commandment of Christ *par excellence*, the intimate link between baptism and the commandments for Mark inevitably implies a similar link between baptism and repentance. And indeed, Mark is explicit that "in all our activity, there is but one foundation of repentance – and that is the one baptism in Christ."[35] This is a crucial statement for the current discussion. Instead of being based in the concept of sin, repentance is grounded instead in the work of Christ. Baptism inaugurates a life of lived repentance, a repentance linked with Christ's own life. Linking repentance with Christ is obviously a delicate matter, since Christ "committed no sin" (1 Peter 2:22) and "knew no sin" (2 Corinthians 5:21). But Mark capitalizes on the fact that Christ was "made sin for us," taking upon

32 For more on the concept of the commandments in Mark's theology, see Torrance, *Repentance in Late Antiquity*, 95–102.

33 The commandments he refers to (as examples, not as an exhaustive list), are prayer, fasting, watchfulness, sharing, renouncing oneself, suppression of thoughts (Paul's λογισμῶν καθαίρεσιν, usually translated "destroying arguments"), dying, being crucified, acting with virtue in any circumstance, and struggling without turning back: *On Baptism* 3 (*SC* 445:308).

34 Martin Luther, *The Ninety-Five Theses*, Thesis 1 in *Works of Martin Luther*, trans. and ed. A. Spaeth, L. D. Reed, H. E. Jacobs et al (Philadelphia, PA: A. J. Holman Company), 1:29.

35 *On Repentance* 7 (*SC* 445:238).

himself the sins of the world. Christ is thus the vicarious penitent for all humanity. In a beautiful elaboration of this concept, Mark writes (in question-and-answer form):

> "Tell me, those who fall into debt because of their own borrowing, are they alone debtors or are their guarantors (ἐγγυώμενοι) also?"

The subordinate answered saying: "their guarantors also of course." The old man went on:

> Know it well that in becoming our guarantor, Christ constituted (καθίστημι) himself a debtor according to the Holy Scriptures: "the lamb of God who takes away the sin of the world" (John 1:29), "the one who became a curse for us" (Galatians 3:3), "the one who took upon himself the death of all and died on behalf of all" (cf. 2 Corinthians 5:14).[36]

Christ is here the guarantor of humanity, the one who stands as debtor in our place, and heals the debt. This vicarious understanding of Christ's work, and its implications for Mark's theology of baptism, are significant, and bring us to the most striking, fruitful, but also potentially distancing element in the comparison with Torrance. For as with all of Mark's theology of Christ's work for us, the vicarious repentance of Christ is at once salvific and *actively participable* among the faithful by virtue of their baptism. In other words, the baptized Christian is called, as a corollary of keeping the commandments, to share in the vicarious work of Christ, standing surety for others just as Christ stands surety for all. The repentance of the faithful, then, includes not simply repentance for oneself, but among those who live in concert with the perfection of grace imputed to them in baptism, it includes repentance for one's neighbor as well.[37]

What binds Mark the Monk and T. F. Torrance here is the insistence on the vicariousness of Christ's work, of his baptism, which is the sole basis for salvation. The "vicarious humanity" and "vicarious obedience" of Christ described by Torrance sits very comfortably within Mark's framework. Their common Christocentrism, however, reveals a common tension, to which I would like to turn.

---

36 *Causid* 15.12–23 (*SC* 455.70).

37 On this concept of "Christ-like repentance" in Mark, see Torrance, *Repentance in Late Antiquity*, 109–12. The key relevant passages in Mark's writings include *On Repentance* 11 (*SC* 445:250) and *Discussion with a Lawyer* 18–20 (*SC* 455:78–88).

Two Theologians Divided by a Common Christocentrism

The theology of baptism in Mark, it has been argued, is thoroughly Christocentric. From the Reformed perspective, however, one might be tempted to view the tendency in Mark to move imperceptibly from the gift of Christ conferred in baptism to the keeping of Christ's commandments as simply a dressed-up version of works-righteousness. How far Reformed theology in general can ultimately countenance the position of Mark remains to be seen, but a key common element must be acknowledged: the primacy of the work of Christ in the affair of salvation. As we have seen, however, a common element such as this, crucial though it is, does not necessarily yield an identical result. The chief question that must be asked, then, is whether or not the differences between T. F. Torrance and Mark the Monk reflect an insurmountable theological divide, or whether the differences rather than being substantial, reflect more the dissimilarity of the theological debates being engaged with in each case.

To this reader, despite the similarities between the two thinkers, there is a feature of Torrance's theology of baptism that may betray more than just a superficial difference of emphasis. I have in mind what Torrance sees as the wholly passive nature of the baptism of Christ received by the Church *as opposed to* an active understanding of that baptism. Mark, and the Eastern Christian tradition in general, would agree with the basic point being made, namely that Christ is the active giver of baptism, but that would not be grounds in his mind to absolutize the passivity of the faithful. In fact, to separate the gift of baptism from any "activity" on the part of the Christian, or to "objectify" the reality of baptism *at the expense of* the subjective or mystical experience of (or communion with) that reality through the keeping of the commandments would in Mark's mind be tantamount to insulting and even undoing the objective value of baptism itself. We saw that Torrance could concede that baptism properly understood includes both objective and subjective categories, but his priorities lead him to diminish any place for a "subjective" understanding to such an extent that one wonders if his theology can really accommodate it. To find the beginnings of a solution, one needs to look elsewhere in Torrance's *oeuvre*, particularly his elaboration of the notion of knowledge and the knowledge of God in *Theological Science*, where the concept of the active Christian life is developed with depth and elegance.[38]

---

38 T. F. Torrance, *Theological Science* (Edinburgh: Continuum, 1996). On one

We have seen that in his theology of baptism proper, Torrance is reluctant to afford any place to the Christian's active participation in the gift of Christ given in baptism. But when we turn to *Theological Science* in which he provides an analysis of the knowledge of God and the role of the human subject in that knowledge, Torrance speaks in terms strikingly reminiscent of St. Mark and the Greek ascetic tradition. In the original preface to that book, he writes with intimacy about encountering God: "His presence presses unrelentingly upon me through the disorder of my mind, for He will not let Himself be thwarted by it, challenging and repairing it, and *requiring of me on my part to yield my thoughts to His healing and controlling revelation.*"[39] The action of God in our knowledge of him is rightly prioritized, and yet in this process of knowledge space is likewise given to the active yielding of one's thoughts to the Almighty.

This sentiment is developed more fully in the book's second chapter. Framing a discussion of the place of the human subject's knowledge of God in terms of the Reformed doctrines of accommodation and election, Torrance turns his attention to the same theme that lies at the heart of his theology of baptism: the historic humanity of Christ. Since God himself assumed the fullness of our humanity (excepting sin) through the Incarnation, his humanity has become part of the knowledge of God:

> It is because God has become man in Jesus Christ and our knowledge of God is rooted and grounded in Christ and shaped through conformity to Him that the very humanity embedded in our knowledge of God is an essential part of that knowledge, for it belongs to the essential nature of the Truth.[40]

Torrance then turns immediately to our acquisition of this knowledge (my italics): "Thus the *active obedience and conformity of the human mind to the Word of God* is part of the full content of our knowledge of God."[41] He later states (again, my italics): "To know the Truth is thus to be

occasion, Torrance even spoke positively of a need for "ascetic theology," but the idea is left undeveloped: see T. F. Torrance, *The Mediation of Christ* (Colorado Springs: Helmers & Howard, 1992), 26. I am grateful to Matthew Baker for this reference.

39   Torrance, *Theological Science*, ix (my italics).

40   Ibid., 86–7.

41   Ibid., 87.

actively participant in it."[42] Of course, throughout this analysis, Torrance places the priority squarely on the God who accommodates, elects, and reconciles, but he never allows this priority to eclipse or deny the definite role of the human subject in knowing God. There is, as he puts it, a "real interplay between human subject and divine Object."[43] While it is God who acts upon us to bring us to knowledge of himself,

> He acts upon us in such a way that He does not negate but rather posits and fulfills our subjectivity. We are never allowed to impose ourselves with our notions upon Him, but we are freed and lifted up as rational subjects in communion with God, and summoned to decisions and acts of volition in that communion, so that knowledge of Him arises and increases out of obedient conformity to Him and the way He takes [*sic*] with us in revealing Himself to us.[44]

The very fact that Torrance speaks of "obedient conformity to" and "active participation in" God's Truth freely given strikes an immediate chord with the theology of baptism found in Mark. What brings them closer still is Torrance's discussion of this conformity of mind and participation in knowledge in terms of *repentance* (μετάνοια):

> The subject is given freedom and place before God and yet …
> is summoned into such communion with Him that he can only
> engage in it with self-criticism and repentance (μετάνοια), that
> is, through an alteration in the structure of his consciousness,
> in which he is brought into conformity with the Truth. Nowhere
> more than in Christian theology does knowledge involve such
> a profound change in the attitude of man, or such a radical
> break in the structure of his natural mind, or such a complete
> reorientation in his life. That is to say theological knowledge
> takes place only through a critical reconstruction of subjectivity
> in accordance with the nature of the object.[45]

As we saw, the whole of Mark's theology of baptism and the Christian life revolves around the concept of repentance, which ultimately is a striving to assimilate and remain faithful to the gift of Christ, the person and work of the Incarnate Lord. Although not in the context

---

42 Ibid.

43 Ibid., 97.

44 Ibid.

45 Ibid., 98.

of a discussion of baptism, nevertheless Torrance here betrays a near-identical sentiment: we can truly know God only insofar as we submit in repentance to his will and actions for us, his unwavering and faithful presence in our lives.

Conclusion

If we are to take Torrance's theology of baptism in isolation and compare it with that of St. Mark the Monk, we are confronted with disagreements. They are disagreements, however, which may begin to be worked out and resolved through Torrance's concept of knowledge. Whether Torrance himself would agree to connect his theory of theological knowledge with his theology of baptism is an open question. Certainly from this writer's perspective Torrance's theology of baptism remains incomplete without a clarification of the meaning and import of its "subjective" sense. In turning to Torrance's most sustained analysis of subject-object relations in theology (found in *Theological Science*), the beginnings of such a clarification can be uncovered, though they are not explicitly brought to bear on the concept of baptism.

In the writings of Mark the Monk we find a means of bridging and retaining the "objective" and "subjective" elements in the theology of baptism more directly through a sustained commitment to the role of Christ's commandments in the Christian life, and the baptismal mode of their fulfillment. Baptism frees, enables, and strengthens the faithful to practice the commandments (summed up in the commandment of repentance), in the practice of which Christ hidden in the baptized heart is found.[46] The one objective vicarious baptism of Christ remains the focus here, the axis and focal point of all Christian endeavor. Its outworking, however, is not *only* objective, not *only* passive, since the goal of the baptism of Christ is to lead not to a dictated or mechanistic renewal of humanity, but to the "glorious liberty of the children of God" in the keeping of his commandments. It is a theology of baptism that both agrees with and challenges that of Torrance. The agreements, challenges, and possible solutions to those challenges discussed in this paper hopefully serve to bring into sharp relief the wider need for continued constructive and honest ecumenical discussion between Christian theologians.

---

46   See *On the Spiritual Law* 191 (SC 445:124): "the Lord is hidden in his own commandments, and he is to be found there in the measure that he is sought."

Chapter 8

T. F. Torrance, John Zizioulas, and the "Cappadocian" Theology of Divine Monarchia: A Neo-Athanasian or Neo-Cappadocian Solution?

Nikolaos Asproulis

It is no exaggeration to say that Trinitarian theology is currently a point of deep interest and theological creativity amongst the most eminent of modern theologians across the Christian traditions. However, the method of interpreting this fundamental doctrine of faith and the implied understanding of its consequences that follow from different methodologies have rendered this doctrine a primary point of divergence between Eastern and Western Christianity. Since Theodore de Regnon's schematic and superficial definition of the radically different approach to Trinitarian theology,[1] this – one may dare say – "gulf" between the two traditions has been conceived as a sort of metaphysical argument. Even today this quite simplistic understanding of the doctrine of the Trinity is still taken for granted to some extent.

In this paper a study is conducted of the work of two well-known Trinitarian theologians, T. F. Torrance (1913–2007)[2] and John Zizioulas (1931–),[3] and the ongoing debate between them, regarding their reading

---

1   See Theodore de Regnon, *Etudes de théologie positive sur la Sainte Trinite*, 3 vols. (Paris: Victor Retaux et Fils, 1892). In his he argued that the West began its reflection about the Trinity with the common essence, while the East with the different persons. See also the interesting discussion and re-assessment of de Regnon's thesis in Michel René Barnes, "De Regnon Reconsidered," *Augustinian Studies* 26 (1995): 51–79.

2   For an overview of his thought and an extensive bibliography of his work see Alister McGrath, *T. F. Torrance. An Intellectual Biography* (Edinburgh: T&T Clark, 1999).

3   For an overview of his thought and an extensive bibliography of his work see Aristotle Papanikolaou, *Being with God: Trinity, Apophaticism, and Divine-Human Communion* (Notre Dame, IN: University of Notre Dame Press, 2006) and

of the patristic, but especially Cappadocian, doctrine of the *monarchy of the Father*, in relation to fundamental issues having to do with the proper theological *method* of Christian theology and patristic *interpretation*.

Sources, Conceptual Tools, and Motives

T. F. Torrance is widely considered as one of the most creative minds in modern Trinitarian theology. In several of his writings on Trinitarian doctrine, he provided extensive historical and systematic reading of patristic theology regarding the Church's Trinitarian faith.[4] The basic guide for Torrance's interpretation of Trinitarian doctrine is, without doubt, the patristic theology of the fourth and fifth-centuries: the Cappadocians, with priority given to Gregory of Nazianzus; Cyril of Alexandria, and Epiphanius of Salamis. The pre-eminence, however, goes to the thought of Athanasius of Alexandria – doubtless the key lens through which Torrance approaches the whole tradition.[5]

If one looks over the chapters of his books that deal with this issue, one sees from the outset that the *Athanasian-Nazianzen* axis is the dominant platform upon which he bases his Trinitarian thinking. However, Torrance will also take into account the "evangelical" roots of the Trinitarian doctrine.

Torrance's close devotion to Athanasius explains to some extent his pre-occupation with the term *homoousion*[6] – once sanctified by the Nicene Council – as his almost unique conceptual tool in dealing with the issue of divine *monarchia*.[7] But how in fact does Torrance understand the meaning of *homoousion*?

Paul McPartlan, *The Eucharist Makes the Church: Henri de Lubac and John Zizioulas in Dialogue* (Edinburgh: T&T Clark, 1993).

4 See Thomas F. Torrance, *The Christian Doctrine of God: One Being, Three Persons* (Edinburgh: T&T Clark, 1996); *The Trinitarian Faith*, 2nd ed. (Edinburgh: T&T Clark, 1997); and *Trinitarian Perspectives*, 2nd ed. (Edinburgh: T&T Clark, 2000).

5 For contrast, see Colin Gunton, "Eastern and Western Trinities: Being and Person. T. F. Torrance's Doctrine of God," in *Father, Son & Holy Spirit: Towards a Fully Trinitarian Theology* (Edinburgh: T&T Clark, 2003), 51, who argues critically that it is in fact really Augustine that lies behind Torrance's Trinitarian theology.

6 E.g. Torrance, *The Trinitarian Faith*, 110–145, where he describes the hermeneutical and evangelical importance of the "homoousion."

7 As has been recently stated [Victor Shepherd, "Thomas F. Torrance and the Homoousion of the Holy Spirit," *Participatio* 3 (2012): 108], "Thomas F. Torrance has

From the outset, Torrance makes a methodological comment: with the "aid of the *homoousion* and the *perichoresis* our understanding of God's self-revelation to us is lifted up from the economic Trinity to the ontological Trinity, yet paradoxically, without leaving the economic Trinity behind."[8] Moreover, this concept identifies the Son within the divine *ousia*, a term which, according to Torrance, is used to denote the "Being of God" and, further, expresses the reality of "the identity of being (ταυτότης της οὐσίας) between the Father, the Son and the Holy Spirit," as manifested by God's self-revelation in history. Following Athanasius, Torrance will question any use of *ousia* that is preoccupied by a preconceived idea or definition of being, such as the metaphysical and static sense of being in Aristotle's *Metaphysics* and (supposedly) scholastic theology.[9] Torrance argues that "the doctrine of the *homoousion* was as decisive as it was revolutionary: it expressed the evangelical truth what God is toward us and has freely done for us in his love and grace and continues to do in the midst of us through his Word and Spirit, he really is in *himself . . .*"[10] What is at stake here are the *soteriological* implications of the proper conceptualization of the relationship between God and the world, following what might be called the "grammar of the Realism of Revelation."[11]

In this context, Torrance makes use of another closely related concept, that of *perichoresis*, which could be understood as a necessary "deepening" of the understanding of the *homoousion*.[12] Making use of this concept introduced by Pseudo-Cyril and John of Damascus, Torrance aims to give

> expression to the dynamic Union and Communion of the Father,
> the Son and the Holy Spirit with one another in one Being in such
> a way that they have their Being in each other and reciprocally

become notorious for his insistence on the *homoousion* (of the Son) as essential to any sound doctrine of the Trinity, arguing that the *homoousion* safeguards . . . the Trinity against any form of Sabellianism or modalism, and the doctrine of God against any form of Unitarianism or polytheism."

8   Torrance, *The Christian Doctrine of God,* 110.

9   Cf. Aristotle, *Metaphysics,* 1028b quoted in ibid., 116. See Athanasius, *Contra Gentes,* 2 and 40 quoted in idem, 116.

10   Torrance, *The Christian Doctrine of God,* 130.

11   Colin Gunton ("Eastern and Western Trinities: Being and Person. T. F. Torrance's Doctrine of God," 50), in his critical approach to the theology of Torrance refers to a sort of "homoousial revelation" in order to highlight the importance of *homoousion* for his entire argumentation.

12   Torrance, *The Christian Doctrine of God,* 168.

> contain one another, without any coalescing . . . *Perichoresis* has
> essentially a *dynamic* and not static sense . . . [i]t imports a mutual
> movement as well as a mutual indwelling.[13]

In this respect, "the mystery of *perichoresis*" is "not a speculative concept. It expresses the soteriological truth of the identity between God himself and the content of his saving revelation in Jesus Christ and in the Holy Spirit." Torrance emphasizes that *perichoresis*, "[t]ogether with the conception of the *homoousion* . . . enables us to read back the interrelations between the Father, the Son and the Holy Spirit in the economy of salvation into the eternal relations immanent in the one Being of God."[14] Finally, *perichoresis* in conjunction with *homoousion* allows one to apprehend the *order* or τάξις, the equality and the distinction of the Trinitarians persons.[15]

What is it that motivates Torrance's insistence on the *homoousion*? It is evident throughout his writings that Arianism is considered as the most serious primitive heresy,[16] the *context* from which the proper Trinitarian formulations emerged. If one would like to "translate" this in a more systematic way, one could find the same *soteriological* motivation lying in the background of his conception, inasmuch as Arianism was the most serious threat against the confession of the *divine* nature of the Son and Logos of God, an idea with profound and explicit implications for the very reality of the salvation of man and the created order as a whole.

John Zizioulas is widely recognized as the most representative Orthodox theologian in recent times and an original, although in some respects controversial, spokesman of the Cappadocian legacy. In various *ad hoc* publications, Zizioulas highlights the importance of Cappadocia as a *third* – so to say, alternative – way[17] of doing theology against the dominant discourse of Alexandria and Antioch.

It is noteworthy that Zizioulas, unlike Torrance, does not make use of the biblical narrative as his starting point. Instead, he draws his theological reasoning almost exclusively from the Cappadocian

---

13   Ibid., 170–171. Cf. Ps-Cyril, *De Sacrosancta Trinitate*, 10 and 23, (*PG* 77.114D and 1164B); John of Damascus, *De fide orthodoxa* 1.8, and 1.11 quoted in idem, 170.

14   Torrance, *The Christian Doctrine of God*, 172.

15   Ibid., 172–73.

16   Gunton, "Eastern and Western Trinities: Being and Person. T. F. Torrance's Doctrine of God," 38.

17   John Zizioulas, "The Father as Cause: Personhood Generating Otherness," in *Communion & Otherness* (Edinburgh: T&T Clark, 2006), 124.

Fathers[18] (especially Basil the Great and Gregory Nazianzen) of the late fourth century (and subsequently on the Creed of the Second Ecumenical Council and also Maximus the Confessor), while at the same time offering important exemplary lessons regarding how one might go beyond the *merely historical* study of texts to a more *systematic* one.[19]

If the recovery of the importance of the Cappadocian patristic theology was a major achievement of Zizioulas, his ontology of personhood seems to be the axis upon which he founds his whole theological argument. Since the beginning of his career Zizioulas has focused on the importance of the concept of personhood both as a *conceptual* tool for the conceptualization of the doctrine of the Trinity and as the very *soteriological* reality of Christian faith, the fulfillment of *theosis*. As he puts it, "the concept of person with its absolute and ontological content was born historically from the endeavor of the Church to give ontological expression to its faith in the Triune God."[20] Highlighting the "revolution" inherent in the Cappadocian identification of *personhood* (a relational concept) with *hypostasis* (an ontological concept), Zizioulas asserts that personhood, despite its dominant understanding as *mask* (*prosopeion*) in earlier ages, should be now conceived as an ontological concept, belonging to the very core of being.[21]

Zizioulas articulated his theology of personhood for the first time with reference to the *Eucharistic* context. He repeatedly argues that personhood is "an identity that stems from a relationship." This does not mean, however, that person should be assimilated to an abstract relationality, like the "in–between" of Martin Buber or the

18 The title "Cappadocian Fathers" seems to be a misleading caricature, insofar as it assimilates the theological and philosophical variety of thought of the three Fathers, to the extent that they appear to share the same vision and methodology of doing theology without contradistinctions or differences. In this direction, see for instance the very important work of Christopher Beeley, *Gregory of Nazianzus on the Trinity and the Knowledge of God* (Oxford: Oxford University Press, 2008), 271–324. I owe particular thanks to my good friend Matthew Baker for bringing to my attention Beeley's work on the Cappadocians and in particular Gregory of Nazianzus.

19 John Zizioulas, *Lectures in Christian Dogmatics* (Edinburgh: T&T Clark, 2008) ix–x.

20 John Zizioulas, *Being as Communion* (Crestwood, NY.: St Vladimir's Seminary Press, 1985), 36.

21 Ibid., 39.

modern "metaxology" of W. Desmond,[22] which then might acquire primordial ontological status along the lines of the essence or substance of ancient Greek and medieval philosophy, defined as a necessary entity. Rather, Zizioulas considers personhood as a *relational, unique,* and *concrete* identity having *ontological priority* over substance, a priority that bestows the person with absolute freedom and relationality. *Communion* and *otherness* are the fundamental aspects of the concept of personhood. Grounded in the Eucharistic experience of the Church, the Cappadocian Fathers elaborated an original Trinitarian theology of personhood which implies that "the person rests in the fact that [it] represents two things simultaneously which are at first sight in contradiction: particularity and communion."[23] For Zizioulas, the person is in fact the soteriological outcome of the doctrine of the Trinity, the necessary concept for conceptualizing the divine-human communion in terms of freedom, love, constant relationship, and uniqueness.[24]

If for Torrance the fundamental threat to orthodoxy was the heresy of Arianism, in the case of Zizioulas, Eunomianism occupies the central place. Yet the central issue here is again the divine nature of the Son of God. The Cappadocians had to wrestle with the Eunomian identification of the essence of God with the Father alone, which downgraded the divine status of the Son to that of a creature with a different essence than the Father. Again, the problem was soteriological.

Methodology

In discussing the methodological parameters[25] of Trinitarian theology, Torrance is adamant that "the movement from economic to ontological relations in our formulation of the doctrine of the Holy Trinity must be taken seriously, for only in the Lord Jesus Christ . . . are we really in touch with God, and through him with the Trinitarian relations

22   William Desmond, *God and the Between* (Oxford: Wiley-Blackwell, 2008); Christopher Ben Simpson "Theology, Philosophy, God and the Between", *Radical Orthodoxy: Theology, Philosophy, Politics,* 1:1–2 (August, 2012): 262–279.

23   Zizioulas, *Being as Communion,* 105.

24   John Zizioulas, *Communion & Otherness* (London: T&T Clark, 2006), 9–11.

25   For a detailed analysis of the epistemological levels of Torrance's "Trinitarian mind," see Gunton, "Eastern and Western Trinities: Being and Person. T. F. Torrance's Doctrine of God," 36–38, where he clearly presents the three epistemological levels in Torrance's thought: 1) experience, 2) economy, and 3) Theology.

of love immanent in God." And further, conversely, "the formulation of the doctrine of the Trinity through the unfolding of its stratified structure reinforces our basic evangelical conviction that theological understanding and doctrinal formulation are properly grounded in God's unique self-giving to us in the Lord Jesus Christ."[26] In this respect he follows Athanasius,[27] who seems to legitimate the "godly contemplation and humble worship of the Holy Trinity and the reverent formulation of the doctrine,"[28] not primarily because of the threat of heresy, but mainly because of the soteriological fact that it was the *Word* that was made flesh and has made God known (Jn. 1:14, 18).

While strongly emphasizing that it is only from and through the economic self-manifestation of the triune God in Christ that one can begin reflection on the immanent Trinity, Torrance is at the same time quick to secure the ontological priority of the transcendent or ontological Trinity and the unity of both levels in Christ, since it is "on the ontological Trinity that the evangelical nature of the economic Trinity entirely depends."[29] It is clear that Torrance's methodology of elaborating his Trinitarian perspective is based on a firm economical-evangelical account that takes quite seriously God's great will to reveal himself in the person of Jesus Christ in history, as the only legitimate starting point of doing theology. While Zizioulas himself considers the question of "theological presuppositions" of profound importance for theological discourse in ecumenical perspective, since the "latter are only logical developments of the former,"[30] he very rarely, if ever, demonstrates explicitly his starting point of doing theology. Claiming to follow the methodological premises implied in Basil's introduction of a new doxology in the Liturgy ("Glory be to the Father with the Son, with the Holy Spirit" instead of "Glory be to the Father through the Son, in the Holy Spirit"),[31] Zizioulas, according to his own account, opts for a *meta*-historical, liturgical and eschatological starting point in theology, which goes beyond the dominance of a propositional understanding of Revelation to focus on *Theologia* (God *ad intra*) in a manner that

26 Torrance, *The Christian Doctrine of God*, 109–10.

27 Ibid., 111.

28 Ibid.

29 Ibid., 109.

30 John Zizioulas, *The One and the Many. Studies on God, Man, the Church and the World Today* (Alhambra, CA.: Sebastian Press, 2010), 136.

31 Basil, *De Spiritu Sancto* 1.3, 7.16 (Ibid., 160), 25.58 (Ibid., 220).

seems to put aside the methodological priority of God's self-revelation in history. In this light, the Eucharist renders possible the participation by communion in the very life of God, which is communion of persons caused by the person of the God the Father. In Zizioulas' understanding, this communion legitimates discussion about God's very being, the question of *how* God is – his *personal* mode of existence – rather than the *what* of the ineffable divine *ousia*. Therefore in virtue of his Eucharistic methodology and his concern for ontology, Zizioulas is able to reflect on the personal "aspect" of God's very being, supposing that believers participate by communion and acquire real knowledge of the Trinitarian personal life, as manifested in this ecclesial communion.

T. F. Torrance on the Monarchy of the Father

From the outset, Torrance makes a bold statement about the monarchy, which he claims follows the viewpoint of Athanasius: "the *Mone Arche* (μόνη Ἀρχή or Μοναρχία) is identical with the Trinity, the *Monas* with the *Trias* . . . and it is precisely in the *Trias* that we know God to be *Monas* . . . The *Monarchia* or the *Monas* is essentially and intrinsically Trinitarian in the inner relations of God's eternal *Ousia*."[32] For Torrance, there is only one understanding of the monarchy and that is a *Trinitarian* one. Here he also refers to Epiphanius of Salamis, who argues that "in proclaiming the divine *Monarchia* we do not err, but confess the Trinity, and Trinity in Unity, one Godhead of the Father, Son and the Holy Spirit."[33] Torrance is clear in making a very subtle distinction between two understandings of the divine Fatherhood. As he puts it:

> when the Father is considered relatively, that is *ad alios* in relation to the Son and the Holy Spirit, he is thought of as the Father of the Son, but when the Father is thought of absolutely, that is *in se*, as God himself (Αὐτόθεος), the name "Father" is often applied to God . . . or the Godhead . . . The name "Father", then, may refer to the one Being or οὐσία of God, but it may also refer to the Person or ὑπόστασις of the Father . . . When considered absolutely God the eternal Father is the one Principle of Godhead, the μόνη Ἀρχή, Μοναρχία, or the Monarchy, but when the Father is considered in his inseparable

---

32 Athanasius, *Contra Arianos* 4.1,3; *De Decretis* 26; etc., quoted in Torrance, *The Christian Doctrine of God*, 183.

33 Epiphanius, *Haereses* 62.3, quoted in ibid., 184.

oneness in Being with the Son and the Spirit, as One Being (μια οὐσία), then the Monarchy . . . is to be thought of as identical with the Holy Trinity.[34]

On the one hand, there is a kind of an *ad intra* monarchy of the Father, as regards his inner relationship to the Son (Father of the Son), following in this respect the well-known passage from Gregory of Nazianzus: "The Father is a name neither of *ousia* nor of *energeia* but of *schesis* and of *how* the Father relates to the Son or the Son to the Father."[35] Torrance argues that this first way "does not mean, however, that the Son is to be thought of as proceeding from the *Person* of the Father . . . but from the *Being* of the Father . . . as in the pronouncement of the Council of Nicaea."[36]

On the other hand, as regards the *ad extra* relationship and providence of God toward humanity and creation, there one should apply the concept of monarchy to the *Trinitarian* God, as a whole. In other words one would say that for Torrance there is a "Trinitarian Monarchy" (τριαδική ἀρχή). Beginning with Nicaea and the Athanasian "axiom" that "whatever we say of the Father we say of the Son and the Spirit except 'Father,'" Torrance holds that "since the whole Godhead is in the Son and in the Spirit, they must be included with the Father in the one originless Source or Ἀρχή of the Trinity."[37]

In order to understand his position better, it is necessary to follow the chain of his argument for a Trinitarian monarchy from the beginning. In virtue of his methodological presuppositions, Torrance asserts that it is necessary to "think of the economic Trinity and the ontological Trinity together or conjunctively as a whole."[38] In this perspective, following the Nicene endeavor to clarify the status of the Son against the Arian challenge, he notes that "what is at stake here was the essential oneness in Being and Act between the economic Trinity and the ontological Trinity." This essential oneness, in Torrance's view, was upheld by the adoption of the Nicene *homoousion*, underscoring that God is indivisibly and eternally in himself the same one indivisible

34 Torrance, *The Christian Doctrine of God,* 140–41.

35 Gregory Nanzianzus *Theol. Orat.* 3.16, quoted in *Communion and Otherness,* 126.

36 Torrance, *The Christian Doctrine of God,* 141.

37 Ibid., 181.

38 Ibid., 114.

Being in three coequal persons that he is toward us in the redemptive missions of the Son and his Spirit.[39]

It is important to note that for Torrance *ousia* is used in view of *identity of Being* (ταυτότης της ουσίας),[40] as this concept was re-interpreted under the impact of divine revelation. Following this *grammar of revelation*, Torrance couples the "I am of Yahweh and the 'I am' of our Lord together." This conjunction, he says, gives rise "to an onto-relational and fully personal conception of the being of God, and indeed to the understanding of the Being of God as Communion, for the three divine Persons in their communion with one another are the Triune Being of God."[41] With reference to Basil's conception of the Trinity as *communion*[42] and Gregory Nazianzen's application of the *homoousion* to the Holy Spirit,[43] Torrance argues strongly for the oneness of God's Being in his interior relations, as the communion of the three divine persons with one another.

In his attempt to outline the "Trinitarian mind" Torrance gives priority to the one being (*ousia*) of God and then talks subsequently about the Trinitarian persons. This approach follows from his understanding of the self-revelation of God in history which reveals the triune Fatherhood whereby the Son and the Holy Spirit are "included within God's Fatherhood of all creation and his covenant people."[44] This understanding is further underwritten by the concept of *homoousion* in order to show the unity of God both *ad intra* and *ad extra* and also to insist on the soteriological importance of the divine nature of the Son. At the same time, Torrance thinks of *homoousion* as an adequate concept to demonstrate also "the eternal distinctions and internal relations in the Godhead wholly and mutually interpenetrating one another in the one identical Being of the Father, the Son and the Holy Spirit,"[45] since

---

39   Ibid., 115.

40   Ibid., 116.

41   Ibid., 124.

42   Basil, *De Spiritu Sancto* 45 (CCEL 200): "εν τη κοινωνία της Θεότητας εστίν η ένωσις."

43   Gregory Nazianzus, *Fifth Theol. Orat.* 31.10.

44   Benjamin Dean, "Person and Being: Conversation with T. F. Torrance about the Monarchy of God," *International Journal of Systematic Theology* 15 (2013): 65.

45   Torrance, *The Christian Doctrine of God*, 125.

(following here Epiphanius) "one Person cannot be *homoousios* with himself."[46]

Turning to the intra-Trinitarian relations, Torrance makes use of the concept of *person*, following his reading of Gregory of Nazianzus,[47] "as substantive relations (in preference to the concept of 'modes of being' developed by the other Cappadocians)." In other words, person is "an onto-relational concept,"[48] since the relations between the divine persons belong to what they are *as* persons, i.e. they are constitutive onto-relations.[49] It is in this same light that Torrance, following again Gregory of Nazianzus, brings to the fore also the relevance of *perichoresis,* as a concept identifying at once: (a) the τάξις "that obtains between the Father, the Son and the Holy Spirit in their relations with one another;"[50] (b) the full equality of the three divine persons as "whole God," "whole from whole," in order to express their indivisible nature and essential equality in Being;[51] and finally (c) the distinctions between the persons.

Torrance is known for his robust critique of the "Cappadocian settlement," which identified the monarchy exclusively with the person of the Father and introduces causal relations within the Holy Trinity: the Cappadocians "sought to preserve the oneness of God by insisting that God the Father, who is himself without generation or origination, is the one Principle or Origin and Cause of the Son and the Spirit."[52] Torrance strongly questions the Cappadocian understanding of the distinction between *ousia* (denoting what is *common*) and *hypostaseis* (signifying the *particular*) in God's being,[53] insofar as this understanding entails a radical differentiation between the three *hypostaseis* due to their distinct modes of existence (Father unbegotten, Son begotten, and Spirit sending forth). Torrance is concerned here to avoid any suggestion of

46   Epiphanius, *Anchoratus* 6.8; *Haereses* 57.10 etc. quoted in Torrance, *The Christian Doctrine of God,* 126.

47   Gregory Nazianzus, *Third Theol. Orat.* 29.16 (CCEL 616). Cf. Torrance, *The Christian Doctrine of God,* 157; Torrance, *The Trinitarian Faith,* 239–240, 319.

48   Torrance, *The Christian Doctrine of God,* 157.

49   Ibid., 157.

50   Ibid., 176.

51   Gregory Nazianzus, *Orationes* 36.15; Athanasius, *Ad Serapionem* 1.16 quoted in ibid., 175.

52   Torrance, *The Trinitarian Faith,* 237.

53   E.g. Basil, *Ep.* 234.4: "I shall state that *ousia* has the same relation to *hypostasis* as the common has to the particular."

tritheism and, on the other hand, a subordinationism of the Origenist type. With the Cappadocians, he claims, the two "senses of Paternity were completely conflated," and the "emphasis upon the ὁμοούσιος, as the key to the identity, intrinsic oneness, and internal relations of the Holy Trinity" shifted "to emphasis upon the three diverse ὑποστάσεις, as united through the Μοναρχία of the Father."[54] This development, Torrance feels, "was done at the cost of cutting out the real meaning of οὐσία as being in its internal relations, and robbing οὐσία of its profound personal sense which was so prominent at Nicaea," suggesting instead "a hierarchical structure within the Godhead."[55]

According to Torrance, the introduction of such a hierarchical and subordinationist structure, following from the priority of the person of the Father as the "cause" of the Godhead and the one principle of Trinitarian unity, constitutes the main thrust of the Cappadocian teaching.[56] This, however, threatened the affirmation of the oneness of God's being and the equality of the Trinitarian persons. According to Torrance, the perception of ἀρχή as the cause of deity was an explicitly Origenist concept. Torrance acknowledges that the Cappadocian Fathers (especially Gregory of Nazianzus as president) did play a decisive role in the formulation of the Trinitarian doctrine at the Second Ecumenical Council of Constantinople (381). Yet he insists – without much evidence – that "the main development did not follow the line advocated by the Cappadocians in grounding the unity of Godhead in the person of the Father as the unique and exclusive Principle of the Godhead, but reverted to the doctrine of the Son as begotten of the Being of the Father."[57] In this respect he singles out Athanasius, Gregory of Nazianzus, Epiphanius, Cyril, and Augustine for praise for their supposed support of a wholly Trinitarian view of the monarchy, which "may not be limited to one person."[58] As Benjamin Dean states clearly, "the coequality of Father, Son and Spirit – together the one eternal Being of God – renders

---

54 Torrance, *The Trinitarian Faith*, 240–41.

55 Ibid., 242. Also *The Christian Doctrine of God*, 182.

56 Torrance, *The Christian Doctrine of God*, 181.

57 Ibid., 182.

58 Gregory Nazianzus, *Third Theol. Orat.* 29.2, 31.14. Cf. also Torrance, *The Christian Doctrine of God*, 182–184.

this trinitarianly construed monarchy intrinsically Trinitarian and thereby, on Torrance's reckoning, the perfection of divine triunity."[59]

Paradoxically enough, as we have already seen, Torrance praises Gregory of Nazianus, one of the Cappadocian Fathers, who according to his reading, while he "offered much the same teaching as his fellow Cappadocians," nevertheless "exercised more flexibility in the use of theological terms, and had a more Athanasian conception of the unity of God and of the Godhead as complete not primarily in the Father but in each Person as well as in all of them."[60] Bringing Gregory Nazianzen into conflict with his Cappadocian colleagues, Torrance admits that while Gregory does at times speak of the Father as *arche* or *aitia* within the Trinity, this perception really refers to *scheseis* in God that are "beyond all origin (ἀναρχος), and beyond all cause (ἀναίτιος)."[61] Torrance's reading of a few important passages of Gregory could be considered one-sided, and not absolutely accurate in his perception or usage of Gregory's texts. However, one should give merit to his patristic scholarship, especially as he provides a theological interpretation of the texts that move beyond the narrowly historicist approach evident in much Anglophone patristic scholarship.[62]

In general Torrance attempts to stay close to the *grammar of revelation*, which according to him, gives a sort of monarchical *priority* to the person of the Father on the level of *economy*, yet does not allow that this priority should be read back into the intra-Trinitarian life, where the absolute oneness of God's being and coequality of the persons renders impossible any kind of one-sidedly asymmetrical relationship of the person of the Father towards the other persons. It seems that it is only in this perspective, of *order* in the economy, that Torrance would be able to attribute a monarchical sense to the Father alone who, through his "two hands" of the Son and the Spirit, works toward the salvation of the created order.

---

59 Dean, "Person and Being: A Conversation with T. F. Torrance about the Monarchy of God," 61.

60 Torrance, *The Trinitarian Faith*, 239.

61 Gregory Nazianzus, *Third Theol. Orat.* 29.2.

62 For this see Alan Brown, "On the Criticism of *Being as Communion* in Anglophone Orthodox Theology," in *The Theology of John Zizioulas. Personhood and the Church,* ed. Douglas Knight (Farnham: Ashgate, 2007), 35–78.

John Zizioulas on the Monarchy of the Father

Since his early work, Zizioulas has repeatedly expressed his insistence on the *causal priority* of the Father within the Trinitarian life. He presents his position as follows:

> Among the Greek Fathers the unity of God, the one God, and the ontological "principle" or "cause" of the being and life of God does not consist in the one substance of God but in the *hypostasis,* that is *the person of the Father.* The one God is not the one substance but the Father, who is the "cause" both of the generation of the Son and of the procession of the Spirit. Consequently, the ontological "principle" of God is traced back, once again, to the person. Thus when we say that God "is" we do not bind the personal freedom of God . . . but we ascribe the being of God to His personal freedom. In a more analytical way this means that God, as Father and not as substance, perpetually confirms through "being" His *free* will to exist . . . Thus God as person – as the hypostasis of the Father – makes the one divine substance to be that which it is: the One God.[63]

Zizioulas distinguishes between two opposite ways of defining the unity or oneness of God: (a) by way of the divine *substance,* a position which Zizioulas attributes to the Augustinian and in general the western (medieval or modern) tradition; and (b), by way of the *hypostasis* of the Father, which is the dominant if not the exclusive perception of the unity of the God in the Greek patristic tradition. The issue at stake here for Zizioulas concerns no less than the very heart of *Monotheism* – as well as, on a more philosophical level, the ontological ultimacy of *otherness* in the doctrine of the Trinity. It is true that Zizioulas is searching for a kind of correlation (as in Tillich) of biblical faith with the "existential" needs of modern humanity, following the patristic ethos and way of bringing the Gospel in a transformative dialogue within their context.

Zizioulas traces the location of the unity of God in the *hypostasis* of the Father in relation to the monistic attitude of the Greek ontology with which the Cappadocian Fathers were in continuous struggle. Much of the introductory chapter in Zizioulas' celebrated *Being as Communion* is focused on the position and the perception of the concept of person within the various trends of Greek philosophy, in order to show that there was always a tendency towards a monistic and

---

63 Zizioulas, *Being as Communion,* 40–41.

necessary substance-ontology. This was the dominant way of approaching the being of God in both Sabellianism and Arianism, against which the Greek Fathers had to wrestle. But, according to Zizioulas, this same *tendency* is evident even in the western Christian tradition, Roman Catholic and Protestant, especially following Augustine who, according to him, radicalized the "priority of substance over against the personal relations in Trinitarian theology,"[64] leading to the predominance of *De Deo Uno* over *De Deo Trino* in western theology.[65] In this respect Zizioulas adopts, on the one hand, De Regnon's well-known assertion, while on the other hand, he praises Karl Barth and especially Karl Rahner for their efforts to raise a voice against this predominant approach.

Zizioulas's argument in favor of the sole monarchy of the Father is articulated in a *threefold* thesis. As he puts it:

> By making the person of the Father the expression of the one ontological ἀρχή in God, we make otherness ontologically constitutive in divine being. Equally by attributing divine being to a personal cause rather than substance, we elevate particularity and otherness to a primary ontological status. Finally, by attributing primary ontological causation to only one person of the Trinity, we affirm that the "One" of the platonic and Greek ontology does not ontologically precede the "Many" but is itself "One" of the "Many" . . . The ontological Monarchy of the Father, that is of a *relational* being, and the attachment of ontological causation to him, serve to safeguard the coincidence of the One and the Many in divine being.[66]

Working out the implications of this three-fold affirmation, one should highlight two fundamental dimensions of Zizioulas' thought. First, there is the dialectic relationship between *ousia* (a monistic category by definition) and *hypostasis* or person (which is inconceivable without relationship)[67] – or, in other words, between necessity (divine being

---

64 Zizioulas, *Communion and Otherness*, 33, following in this respect the interpretation of J. N. D. Kelly, *Early Christian Doctrines* (London: A&C Black, 1977), 272; also, Harry A. Wolfson, *The Philosophy of the Church Fathers* (Harvard: Harvard University Press, 1956), 326. Zizioulas seems, throughout his work, to lack a first hand and comprehensive reading of the work of Augustine or even of the recent secondary literature, following in an uncritical way the far outdated work of otherwise eminent patristic scholars.

65 Zizioulas, *Being as Communion*, 40.

66 Zizioulas, *Communion and Otherness*, 35.

67 Ibid., 34–35.

without cause, that is self-explicable and thus logically necessary) and freedom (divine being attributed to a radically other person yet in relation to radically other persons, which causes otherness, freedom and its ontological content). Second, there is his view that

> the idea of God as Father did not arise as a speculative reflection about God, but emerged from ecclesial experience. Only in and through incorporation into the ecclesial community can there be recognition of God as Father. This is what the baptismal origin of the idea of divine Fatherhood implies.[68]

As already mentioned, Zizioulas speaks of an ontology emerging from the *Eucharistic* experience of the Church and guiding the Fathers "in working out their doctrine of the being of God."[69] While the concept of personhood occupies a central place in his work, this should be explained by attributing *communion* and *otherness* as the necessary content and components of this personalistic ontology.

However – and this is a decisive point in understanding his view – though he assigns to communion an ontological ultimacy, Zizioulas is quite cautious in not attributing to communion an ontological priority over the persons. Rather, it is the person "which makes something really be." As he puts it:

> the fact that God owes His existence to the Father, that is to a person, means a) that His "substance", His being, does not constrain Him . . . and b) that communion is not a constraining structure for His existence . . . The fact that God exists because of the Father shows that His existence, His being is the consequence of a free person, which means . . . that not only communion but also freedom, the free person constitutes true being.[70]

While Zizioulas is more a systematic theologian than a historian of doctrine, he does attempt to trace the historical roots and basis of his argument. Taking as his starting point the early Creeds, he highlights the importance of the old creedal statement: "I believe in God the Father Almighty." The crucial exegetical problem in this case is the question of whether the word "Father" should be understood as attached primarily

---

68   Zizioulas, *Communion and Otherness*, 113; Zizioulas, *Being as Communion*, 16–17.

69   *Being as Communion*, 17.

70   Ibid., 17–8.

to "Almighty" or to "God." Following the frequent biblical reference to "God the Father" (Gal. 1:1–3; 1 Thess. 1:1, etc.) and the early Fathers,[71] Zizioulas argues for the latter.

In his attempt to follow the philosophical consequences of this primal conjunction of "Father" to "God," Zizioulas distinguishes between "the ontological and the moral content of divine Fatherhood."[72] He stresses that, while all the old creeds "relate divine Fatherhood . . . to creative power," one should avoid a possible confusion of divine Fatherhood "with some of divine energy," something that is an inherent danger in the western prioritization of the moral content of the Fatherhood, at least according to Zizioulas' reading of Tertullian, Cyprian, and Augustine.[73] In this regard, following the original sense of "Almighty" found in the Greek Fathers as παντοκράτωρ, rather than παντοδύναμος, Zizioulas attributes priority to an *ontological* understanding of divine Fatherhood – God is Father because he has a Son – instead of the *moral* connotation of creative and providential relationship toward creation. In virtue of this bold distinction between God's being *ad intra* and his *ad extra* action, Zizioulas argues for the necessary distinction between *being* and *act*. Nevertheless, as we have seen above, in the Eucharistic context, one participates within the very life of God – and so it might be said: in his personal being, not just his act.

Zizioulas acknowledges that by adding the word "one" before God the Father, the Eastern Creeds highlighted the problem of divine *unity*. As he puts it: "if God = Father, as is the case already with the Roman creed and if now, in the case of the Eastern creeds, God is 'one,' it follows that only the Father can properly be called 'God.' The phrase 'one God the Father' seems to attach divine unity to the divine Fatherhood."[74] Following Zizioulas' argumentation, one sees which two alternatives were left to early theology in order to solve the problem of divine unity:[75]

71 E.g. Cyril of Jerusalem, *Catech.* 7.4, 33, 608–10: "only by a misuse of language …can the word 'Father' be understood as referring to God's relation to mankind; it properly belongs to God in virtue of his relation to the Son" quoted in Zizioulas, *Communion and Otherness*, 114.

72 Zizioulas, *Communion and Otherness*, 114.

73 Ibid., 114–15.

74 Ibid., 117.

75 If we also add the more or less variation of the communion model in place of substance we will have in front of us the threefold spectrum of possible responses to the problem of divine unity as this has been considered by Zizioulas.

either (1), a "radical departure" from the biblical association of God with Father, giving priority to divine substance and assigning to it the role of expressing the divine unity; or else (2), the more eastern, Cappadocian way of dealing with the Arian challenge, maintaining the bold biblical equation between God and the "Father."[76] In his case, following Gregory of Nazianzus[77] especially, Zizioulas argues that although the Fathers do speak of divine substance in relation to the oneness of God, nevertheless "the ground of unity" is "the Father, out of whom and towards whom the subsequent persons are reckoned."[78]

Two specific points that have been introduced by the Cappadocian Fathers are of great importance for the development of Zizioulas' argument. One the one hand, the clear distinction, especially in Basil, of the concepts of *person* or *hypostasis* and *substance* or *ousia* will facilitate the prioritization of personal language and causation in the divine being, since the Cappadocians would give to being a sort of double definition beyond the monistic substantialism of Greek philosophy. In this emerging personalistic ontology, not only *ousia* (τι ἐστιν) but also *personhood* (πως ἐστιν) acquires *ontological* status.[79] On the other hand, it is claimed that the Cappadocian Fathers in general, especially Gregory Nazianzus, contributed to the introduction of the idea of ἀρχή in the sense of both a *personal* ontological origination (referred to the Father) and a *movement* (from the *one* to the *Three*), as well a *causal relationship* between the divine persons.

Interpreting Gregory in this regard, Zizioulas states that this kind of causation "takes place (a) before and outside time[80] . . . and (b) on the hypostatic or personal level and not on that of *ousia*,[81] which implies *freedom* and *love*."[82] This is opposed to the Greek, especially neo-platonic, perception of the *arche* in a substantialistic sense.[83] Zizioulas highlights in this perspective the necessity of distinguishing between the level of *nature* or *ousia* and that of *person* or *hypostasis* in divine being.[84] Thus,

76   Ibid., 117–18.

77   Gregory Nazianzus, *Orat.* 42.15.

78   Zizioulas, *Communion and Otherness*, 118.

79   Basil, *C. Eun* 1.14–15; Gregory Nazianzus, *Orat.* 3.16.

80   Gregory Nazianzus, *Orat.* 42.15.

81   Basil, *C. Eun.* 1.14–15; Gregory Nazianzus *Orat.* 3.15–6.

82   Zizioulas, *Communion and Otherness*, 119.

83   Ibid., 127–28.

84   Ibid., 128–29.

Zizioulas argues, according to this development of the Cappadocian theology,

> what the Father "causes" is a transmission not of ousia but of personal otherness . . . the Father as "cause" is God or *the* God in an ultimate sense, *not because he holds the divine essence and transmits it . . . but because he is the ultimate ontological principle of divine personhood* . . . in fact, the equality of the three persons in terms of substance is not denied by the Father's being the cause of personhood; it is rather ensured by it.[85]

Hence, for Zizioulas, "the idea of cause was introduced...in order to indicate that in God there is not only substance, relational and dynamic, but also otherness, which is also dynamic," implying a movement within the divine being. This, however, is not a movement of the divine substance or the three persons altogether; rather, "it is the one, the Father, that moved to threeness," according to the famous passage of Gregory Nazianzen.[86]

In stressing the distinction between *ontological* understanding of the divine *monarchia* and any understanding of this monarchy in exclusively moral or cosmological terms, Zizioulas brings evidence from Basil[87] and Gregory Nazianzen[88] in order to highlight that the Greek Fathers, while informed of both meanings of ἀρχή, distinguish carefully between them, attributing the divine *monarchia* exclusively to the Father as regards the ontological realm.

On the other hand, Zizioulas also stresses the relevance of the monotheism of the *lex orandi*, especially the Eucharistic prayers, which were addressed to the Father, in order to strengthen his argument as regards the simultaneity of the one and the triune God, "thanks to not an impersonal relationality or 'Tripersonality'[89] but to an *hypostasis*, which

---

85   Zizioulas, *Communion and Otherness*, 130. In this respect, Zizioulas strives against Lossky's reading of John of Damascus, who seems to identify the divine ousia with the Father, implying that the Father "confers His one nature upon the Son and upon the Holy Spirit." See Vladimir Lossky, *Mystical Theology of the Eastern Church*, 60, quoted in Zizioulas, *Communion and Otherness*, 129n52.

86   *Orat.* 3.2.

87   *C. Eun.* 2.22.

88   *Orat.* 3.2.

89   Against Dumitru Stăniloae, who prefers the expression "Tripersonality" as quoted in Zizioulas, *Communion and Otherness*, 134n63.

is both particular and relational."[90] Far from jeopardizing the co-equality and communion of the three persons, the confession of the monarchy of the Father preserves both the ontological *primacy* of the Trinitarian communion of the divine persons and the ontological *ultimacy* of the person of the Father, "without projecting into God subordinationist notions," as would be the charge of those who do not follow the relevant distinction between personhood and substance in the divine being. Recalling again Gregory Nazianzen,[91] Zizioulas argues that a sense of the reality of *order* within the life of the Trinity is always taken for granted. This *order* is not referred only to the economic manifestation and soteriological function of the Trinity, as many theologians hold, implying thus a dissociation of the *economic* Trinitarian from God's eternal being.[92] Based on his *Eucharistic* methodology, Zizioulas follows the "Basilian" axiom that "every movement in God, ad extra as well as ad intra, begins with the Father and ends with him."[93] This means that the "order" applies both to the *immanent* and the *economic* Trinity, in both cases assuming a *personal* initiative – that of the Father who is "moved as the Begetter (γεννήτωρ) and Emitter (προβολεύς), of whom the others are the one begotten and the other the emission (των δε, το μεν γέννημα, το δε πρόβλημα)."[94]

As Zizioulas clarifies his provocative and often misunderstood claim for the personal character of God's being,

> in saying that God as person – as the hypostasis of the Father
> – makes the one divine substance to be that which it is: the
> one God[95], we automatically exclude the priority of substance
> over personhood . . . The co-emergence of divine nature with
> the Trinitarian existence initiated by the Father implies that the
> Father too "acquires" so to speak, deity "as" the Son and the Spirit
> are in existence . . . Thus the Father is shown to be "greater" than
> the Son . . . not in nature, but in the way . . . the nature exists,
> that is, in the hypostatization of nature . . . Trinitarian ordering

90   Zizioulas, *Communion & Otherness,* 137.

91   Gregory Nazianzus, *Orat.* 42.15.

92   Zizioulas is referring here to Vladimir Lossky, Colin Gunton, and T. F. Torrance, in Zizioulas, *Communion and Otherness,* 138n75.

93   Ibid., 138.

94   Gregogy Nazianzus, *Orat.* 3.2. Cf. Zizioulas, *Communion and Otherness,* 133.

95   Zizioulas, *Being as Communion,* 41.

(τάξις) and causation protect rather than threaten the equality and fullness of each person's deity.[96]

In close relation to this understanding of *order*, Zizioulas derives the lesson that divine causality

> teaches us . . . that personal otherness is not symmetrical but a-symmetrical. There is always in this otherness a "greater" one (Jn. 14.28), not morally or functionally but ontologically. Otherness is, by definition "hierarchical", in spite of the pejorative sense that this concept has acquired in modern times.[97]

Despite recent important critiques of the radical way that Zizioulas understands the concept of divine *monarchia* and ἀρχή in God's being,[98] one should at least acknowledge that his contribution on the issue is of profound importance and has various implications on anthropology, ecclesiology and in Christian life in general.

The Debate between Torrance and Zizioulas and the Neo-Cappadocian Solution

It is not my intention here to deal in detail with the latent debate between Torrance's family tree[99] and Zizioulas on the understanding of the monarchy of the Father and all the implied issues, or regarding the importance and the development of the "Cappadocian settlement." This "Cappadocian settlement" has been more recently considered as more or less a *construction* of patristic scholarship rather than a conscious achievement of the Fathers. One should, however, argue that appreciation of the Cappadocian contribution should not primarily be focused on the classic formula "one *ousia*, three persons," which modern scholarship has attributed to Augustine,[100] but rather on the introduction of the concept

96 Zizioulas, *Communion and Otherness*, 140.

97 Ibid., 143.

98 E.g. Alan Torrance, *Persons in Communion: Trinitarian Description and Human Participation* (Edinburgh: T&T Clark, 1996).

99 It is noteworthy that not only T. F. Torrance but also his brother James Torrance and his nephew Alan Torrance as well have been involved implicitly or explicitly in this debate with Zizioulas regarding the relevance of the Monarchy of the Father.

100 Cf. Joseph T. Lienhard, SJ, "Augustine of Hippo, Basil of Caesarea, and Gregory Nazianzen," in *Orthodox Readings of Augustine*, ed. A. Papanikolaou and G. Demacopoulos (Crestwood, NY: St Vladimir's Seminary Press, 2008), 81–99; and

of ἀρχή, as meaning the personal *origination* and *causation*, attributed to the person or hypostasis of the Father as the *ultimate* origin, cause, source and "ontological principle" of the divine being. Moreover, it is not hard to see that the debate between the Torrances and Zizioulas revolves around this prioritization of *personhood* over *substance* in Trinitarian ontology.

Following the previous presentation of Torrance's and Zizioulas' conception of divine *monarchia*, I would like to highlight now some fundamental methodological points of divergence between the two and also provide some hermeneutical comments on several passages from the Cappadocian Fathers – especially the most disputed, Gregory of Nazianzus – that seem to be the cause, or rather the *alibi*, of their dispute.

Historical Revelation vs. Eucharistic Experience

Undoubtedly one would agree from the outset that the most fundamental opposition between Torrance and Zizioulas is related to the starting point of doing theology. Torrance, on the one hand, adamantly follows the biblical narrative regarding the self-revelation of God in history and his "evangelical acts" and elaborates his theological enterprise in accordance with a grammar derived from this history; Zizioulas, on the other hand, concentrates his thought on the *Eucharistic* experience of the early Christian communities that provided them with the capacity to "communicate by participation" in the very life of God, acquiring thence knowledge of the personal mode of being. Despite the definition of Torrance's model of revelation as *homoousial* and Zizioulas' as *communal*,[101] one could argue that Christian theology should be articulated in keeping with the methodological priority of the self-revelation of God in Christ, as narrated in the Bible, without prioritizing ecclesial experience as the exclusive way of reception of this self-revelation of God. While it is true that this ecclesial experience could be interpreted, as has been done by Georges Florovsky,[102] in a historical perspective, there is always the danger in downplaying the methodological (not exclusively

---

"Ousia and Hypostasis: The Cappadocian Settlement and the Theology of 'One Hypostasis,'" in *The Trinity: An Interdisciplinary Symposium on the Trinity*, ed. S. T. Davies et. al. (Oxford: Oxford University Press, 1999), 99–121.

101   Alan Torrance, *Persons in Communion*, 299.

102   On this see Matthew Baker, "Theology Reasons" – in "History: Neo-patristic Synthesis and the Renewal of Theological Rationality," Θεολογία 81 (2010): 81–118.

epistemological) priority of revelation in doing theology in a Christian, that is biblical, manner.

Although Torrance, due to his commitment to the biblical *grammar of revelation*, would stress the unity between the economic and transcendent Trinity, or in other words between *ontology* and *soteriology, being* and *act*, he did not follow this close connection through to its full implications. In this respect, on the issue of the monarchy of the Father, he refused to follow the *economic order* as indicated in the biblical narrative of the self-revelation of God and the divine deeds, to the *ontological* order. This entails, in my view, a logical inconsistency in his thought, insofar as he prioritizes the use of a substantialistic language that seems to downplay the Trinitarian persons and their respective roles. On the other hand, Zizioulas in virtue of his Eucharistic methodology and ontological pre-occupation (or "personalistic foundationalism")[103] seems to make a *leap* within the ontological Trinity, attempting to define in detail the intra-Trinitarian life in an abstract and metaphysical manner. This way of reasoning implies a radical departure from the biblical *grammar of revelation*, and subsequently implies a more or less diminution of the unity between economy and theology, if not always without important qualifications due to his Eucharistic and (according to him) "meta-historical" methodology.

In other words, it seems that both Torrance and Zizioulas do not avoid *confusion* between the ontological priority of the transcendent Trinity (Zizioulas) and the methodological priority of the economic Trinity (Torrance). This is too subtle a point to be dealt with here in detail, but it indicates the profound relevance of *methodology* in theology, something almost neglected in modern Orthodox theology.

Athanasius, Cappadocians, and the Contextualization of the Fathers

A careful reading of Torrance's Trinitarian *magnum opus* would indicate that Athanasius is celebrated as his patristic hero to which the whole patristic (and Reformation – mainly Calvin and Barth – as well) tradition should be fitted, toward the theological enterprise of clarifying the Christian faith. At the same time, the Cappadocians, especially Basil and Gregory of Nazianzus, constitute the ever-privileged partner

103 Alan Torrance, *Persons in Communion*, 300.

of Zizioulas' program, in his attempt to articulate a comprehensive and promising *personalistic* ontology. While, in most cases, Zizioulas bases his argument on a limited reading of the work of the three Cappadocians and related secondary literature and has also been accused of inaccurate historical use of his sources, his interpretation indicates a profound originality and a commitment to the "patristic ethos": to theologize creatively *ad mentem patrum* without the restrictive obligation to be in literal, textual or linguistic continuity with the earlier tradition.

However, what is at stake here, at least in my view, is the crucial issue about the proper way of approaching the Fathers, in the attempt to avoid various dangers of historical anachronism, homogenization, or abstract and romantic readings of them, outside of their historical and theological context. The discussion that opened following the provocative conference organized in Volos (Greece) 2010, on the question "Can Orthodox Theology be Contextual?"[104] should be understood as an indication of the urgent importance of the questions regarding patristic authority and patristic interpretation, in view of the danger of the so-called "patristic fundamentalism."[105] I would not argue here that one can see this danger in Torrance's absolutization of Athanasius' legacy or in Zizioulas' reduction of the three Cappadocians to one single voice. However, one must question the lack of a contextual reading in both cases. To argue for an Athanasian axis as the predominant starting point of reading the whole Christian tradition, against the subsequent conceptual and doctrinal development (of the Second Ecumenical Council, the concepts of *hypostasis* and *personhood*, the theory of the *logoi* of Maximus, etc.), or to try to combine the thought of the three Cappadocian Fathers, as if they represent a unique and single theological reasoning of the Greek patristic tradition, against the whole western tradition, and despite the latent differences (if not oppositions) that each of them evidence with one other on various points,[106] seems to be a historiographical error, one

104   On June 3–6, 2010, the Volos Academy for Theological Studies in cooperation with the Orthodox Christian Studies Program at Fordham University, the chair of Orthodox Theology at the University of Münster, and the Institute for Inter-Orthodox, Interfaith and Inter-Christian Studies of Cluj-Napoca, Romania, organized an international conference entitled "Neopatristic Synthesis or Post-Patristic Theology? Can Orthodox Theology be Contextual?" For the conference program, see www.acadimia.org.

105   Pantelis Kalaitzidis, "From the 'Return to the Fathers' to the Need for a Modern Orthodox Theology," *St. Vladimir's Theological Quarterly*, 54 (2010): 5–36.

106   Following in this respect the recent patristic scholarship one might speak

that could be the cause of a distortion of the ideal and often constructed image of a *single* and *undifferentiated* Christian tradition.

Ousia vs. Person

It seems that the basic motive that lies behind the theses of the two thinkers under review has to do with their differing conceptions of the being of God. Following his methodological prerequisites, Torrance seems to hold a single and undifferentiated understanding of the divine Being simply as *ousia*, as suggested in the subtitle of his book, *The Christian Doctrine of God: One Being, Three Persons*. This may be read as an exaggeration and hasty reading of his corpus. However, there is evidence that because of his absolute focus on the equality and *homoousial* relationship of the Trinitarians persons within the divine being, Torrance tends to downplay the distinctions between the persons, particularly since he believes that the concept of *homoousion* is enough to safeguard the particularity of the persons in place of any causal relations between them, which would compromise their inner equality. Torrance's definite distinction between the *being* and *person* of the Father could recall modalistic connotations, something that is obscured probably due to his diminution of the subsequent doctrinal development beyond Athanasius. While both Zizioulas and Torrance appear to agree more or less on a firm distinction between the *ontological* and *moral* (Zizioulas) or *absolute* or *relative* (Torrance) conception of Fatherhood, it is not clear what is the *role* of the Trinitarian *persons* in Torrance's essentialist account. On the other hand, although Zizioulas recognizes a distinction between *person* and *ousia* in the divine being, attributing ontological priority to personhood, he seems simply to invert the coin, prioritizing the personal aspect of divine life at the expense of the *ousia*, which is more or less marginalized. This is a very subtle issue since there is always the danger either to downplay the importance of the Trinitarian persons in the sense that they are swallowed by the *ousia* – in which case our prayers should be addressed to the divine substance as such! – or else to imply a disharmony within the divine life because of a dialectic relationship between *ousia* and *person*. This appears also to be a tendency in modern patristic scholarship, for example on Gregory

also of variety of voices even within a single Father. Cf. e.g. Beeley, *Gregory of Nazianzus on the Trinity and the Knowledge of God*.

of Nazianzus, where it is argued that what the Trinitarian persons commonly share is finally the Father's divine being.[107] This actually is not very far from the understanding of Eunomius, who identified the Father with the substance of God. The basic argument of Torrance against understanding the divine *monarchia* as located in the person of the Father provides thus an alternative perspective. However, as Zizioulas has pointed out, this is the only solution, if the causation is considered on the level of personhood and not of nature, in which case any kind of Origenistic subordination is excluded from the divine life, since the Father does not possess the divine substance prior to the other persons and then transmit it to them, but rather causes only their personal otherness, while safeguarding the common possession of the divine substance.

Zizioulas' motivation to assign absolute freedom to the divine being in virtue of the *monarchia* of the Father could suggest the necessary simultaneity of monarchy and consubstantiality, if Zizioulas had only avoided the projection to the Trinitarian life of an *a priori* dialectical relationship between *ousia* and *person,* as two opposite aspects of divine being.[108] In order to go beyond any sort of impasse that would render "theologizing" a mere metaphysical and superficial abstraction, which is a tendency in Zizioulas' work, one should give greater recourse to the biblical grammar of revelation, which provides us with a profound Trinitarian structure and order that represents not only God in his economic manifestation but also in his divine life.

Gregory of Nazianzus vs Gregory of Nazianzus

The deep differentiation between these two eminent ecumenical figures is closely related to their different readings of the textual evidence

---

107   Ibid., 211.

108   It is noteworthy that in recent publications Zizioulas has attempted to give a more balanced understanding of the relation between *ousia* and *person* within the divine being, see John Zizioulas, "Trinitarian Freedom: Is God Free in Trinitarian Life?" in *Rethinking Trinitarian Theology: Disputed Questions and Contemporary Issues in Trinitarian Theology,* ed. Giulio Maspero and Robert Wozniak (London: T&T Clark, 2012), 193–207; and "Person and Nature in the Theology of St. Maximus the Confessor," in *Knowing the Purpose of Creation Through the Resurrection: Proceedings of the Symposium on St. Maximus the Confessor,* ed. Maxim Vasiljević (Alhambra, CA.: Sebastian Press and The Faculty of Orthodox Theology of the University of Belgrade, 2013), 85–113.

mostly of the same Fathers. The reading of Gregory of Nazianzus appears to be the most fundamental point of divergence.[109] Torrance utilizes Gregory in opposition to the other two Cappadocian Fathers and in supposed continuity with Athanasius, in order to argue against the attribution of divine *monarchia* to the person of the Father alone. In contrast, Zizioulas sees Gregory as in accordance with his Cappadocian colleagues and constituting together with them the "Cappadocian legacy" in which priority of the person is underscored.

In view of this impasse, I would like, by way of conclusion, to comment on two important passages from Gregory that have been used by both Torrance and Zizioulas to opposing ends. The first passage is from the *Fifth Theological Oration* 31.14:

> What is our quarrel and dispute with both? To us there is One God, for the Godhead is One, and all that proceedeth from Him is referred to One, though we believe in Three Persons. For one is not more and another less God; nor is One before and another after; nor are They divided in will or parted in power; nor can you find here any of the qualities of divisible things; but the Godhead is, to speak concisely, undivided in separate Persons; and there is one mingling of Light, as it were of three suns joined to each other. When then we look at the Godhead, or the First Cause, or the Monarchia, that which we conceive is One; but when we look at the Persons in Whom the Godhead dwells, and at Those Who timelessly and with equal glory have their Being from the First Cause – there are Three Whom we worship.[110]

One is obliged here to discern between two different meanings of *monarchia*. One the one hand, one can see that Gregory first refers to the entire Godhead as *monarchia*: first cause in relationship to creation, whereby the *ad extra* action is undivided, even if differentiated according to the specific mission and role undertaken by each person in the economy. In that case there is "one mingling of Light" that shines toward the created order (although "three suns joined to each other") with common power and will. At the same time however, and within the same passage, Gregory is adamant to make a subtle distinction of

---

109 One should apply the same hermeneutical and exegetical perspective in similar important passages of the other Cappadocians, as well: e.g., Basil, *De Spiritu Sancto* 45; and Gregory Nyssa, *Great Catechism* 3.2; and *On Not Three Gods: To Ablabius*.

110 Gregory Nazianzus, *Fifth Theo. Orat.* 31.14.

this *ad extra* divine *monarchia*, assigned to Godhead as a whole, from the *ad intra* divine *monarchia*, referred now to the *how* the Son and the Spirit "have their being" – not to the creative power and providence of God towards his creation. Therefore, it is clear from this passage that Gregory does not negate outright the personal cause and origination, or order within the Trinity, as Torrance claimed. It is also evident, however, that in this passage at least, it is only with great difficulty that one could attribute this same order (from the Father . . .) to the economic manifestation of God, as Zizioulas claims is the case with the entire Cappadocian theology. It seems paradoxically that each theologian read in the text only the half of Gregory's argument in order to fit his interpretation to his own respective theological rationale.

The *second* passage I would like to comment on is again from Gregory *Oration* 42.15:

> That which is without beginning, and is the beginning, and is with the beginning, is one God. For the nature of that which is without beginning does not consist in being without beginning or being unbegotten, for the nature of anything lies, not in what it is not but in what it is. It is the assertion of what is, not the denial of what is not. And the Beginning is not, because it is a beginning, separated from that which has no beginning. For its beginning is not its nature, any more than the being without beginning is the nature of the other. For these are the accompaniments of the nature, not the nature itself. That again which is with that which has no beginning, and with the beginning, is not anything else than what they are. Now, the name of that which has no beginning is the Father, and of the Beginning the Son, and of that which is with the Beginning, the Holy Ghost, and the three have one Nature – God. And the union is the Father from Whom and to Whom the order of Persons runs its course, not so as to be confounded, but so as to be possessed, without distinction of time, of will, or of power. For these things in our case produce a plurality of individuals, since each of them is separate both from every other quality, and from every other individual possession of the same quality. But to Those who have a simple nature, and whose essence is the same, the term One belongs in its highest sense.[111]

111   Ibid, 777.

In this passage Gregory becomes more analytical. Again he appears to combine both meanings of divine *monarchia*, with no *a priori* dialectical relationship (if not radical *existentialist* opposition) between *ousia* and *person* such as we find in modern interpretations. It is clear from the outset that Gregory advocates the *causal* relations and the *order* between the Trinitarian persons and especially the *causal priority* of the Father, who "is the union . . . from Whom and to Whom the order of Persons runs its course . . . without distinction of time, of will or of power." The Father is considered in this perspective the "ground" of the unity of the three persons within the divine life. At the same time (note the evident subsequent order of the argument), Gregory, when he turns to the created order, attributes the concept of *monarchia* to the Trinity as a whole due to the "simple nature . . . and same essence." One should also mention the effort of Gregory to define with caution the distinctive characteristics (*idiomata*) of the Persons, as *without beginning* (Father), *from the beginning* (Son), and *with the beginning* (Holy Spirit). *Pace* Torrance, Gregory affirms the causal priority of the Father regarding the *how*, the mode of existence,[112] of the divine Persons.

   On the other hand, although Zizioulas claims that the name "Father" is a relational concept (there is no Father without his Son), there seems little in Gregory to support an exaggerated patrocentrism sometimes suggested by Zizioulas' work, as if the other persons do not play any constitutive role in the divine life. The one God is the Father as cause of the *Son* and the *Spirit*, but insofar as all three share the *common* divine *substance*. Therefore, in my reading of these two indicative passages of Gregory, there is a *personal* initiative and causation, to the extent that this has taken place *within* and not in opposition to the *ousia* or outside the divine being. The distinction suggested by Zizioulas between a *personal* and *substantial* level in the Trinity is legitimate insofar as both levels play an ultimately *in*stitutive (common *ousia*) and logically primary *con*stitutive (person of the Father in relation to the Son and Spirit) role in divine being as both one and the many, the one Triune God of our biblical faith.

---

112   Although Torrance argues that Gregory "would have nothing to do with his fellow Cappadocians' description of the divine Persons as 'modes of Being,'" (Torrance, *The Christian Doctrine of God*, 127), this is not enough to argue that Gregory finds himself in opposition to his colleagues regarding the attribution of divine *Monarchia* within the Godhead to the person of the Father.

Conclusions

As has been shown, the debate surrounding the divine *monarchia* implies a great variety of consequences for fundamental issues in theology, concerning both the *lex credendi* and *lex orandi*. In this paper an attempt was made, with a view to the work of two ecumenical thinkers, Torrance and Zizioulas, to re-assess the whole debate on a methodological level. The idea of divine *monarchia* should not be considered as a secondary one, insofar as, even more than the *filioque,* it seems to be a basic point of divergence not only between East and West, but also within single traditions: as evidenced, for instance, in the work of late Colin Gunton, a Western advocate of the "Basilian" understanding of monarchy of the Father, as well as in the late Fr Dumitru Stanilaoe or Fr Nikolaos Loudovikos within the East, both of whom represent different understandings of the issue than what it found in Zizioulas.

These divisions might be overcome in the light of the above analysis, which suggests that one should distinguish between the *methodological* priority of the economic Trinity and the *ontological* priority of the transcendent Trinity. Further, following the *grammar of the revelation* as recorded in the Bible, one should be able to affirm the person of God the Father as the origin, source, cause and "ontological principle" of the intra-Trinitarian life, to the extent that this same God the Father with his "two hands" (the Son and the Spirit) is working toward the salvation of the created realm. Such a perspective would preserve both the *soteriological* unity between economy and theology but also the *ontological* difference between them, finding the meeting point of both in the *person* and the *work* of Jesus Christ. Following this way of reasoning – a sort of "Trinitarian Christology" – one would avoid confusing the two levels into one, as well as projecting into the divine life suppositions quite apart from what the self- revelation of God in history, as attested to us in Scripture, would have to say.

The fact that both theologians, Torrance and Zizioulas, would agree that theology has to do with *realities* and not just with names, and with the *presuppositions* that lie behind the issues and not primarily the theses, constitutes a promising hope for the future of Christian theology to regain its *biblical* and *apostolic* roots in the faith of God the Father, Son and the Holy Spirit. Toward this end, one should study very carefully the patristic texts and especially the Cappadocian legacy, without projecting on them *a priori* philosophical or other premises, and without compromising their *distinct* voices. Rather than a univocal foundation for different theological visions, ever shifting according to the will and the motivations of each theologian, the Fathers in all their variety should be treated as pointers and witnesses to the revealed truth, the reality of the incarnate Logos of God.

Chapter 9

The Concept of Energy in T. F. Torrance and in Orthodox Theology

Stoyan Tanev

Introduction

The distinction between the essence and energy of God is a basic principle of the Trinitarian thinking of the Eastern Church.[1] While some tend to associate it exclusively with the works of St. Gregory Palamas and the theological controversies of 14th century Byzantium, Gregory himself considered his theological efforts as a direct elaboration on the dogmatic definitions of the 6th Ecumenical Council (Constantinople III, 680/681), referring back to the works of St. Athanasius and St. Cyril, the Cappadocian Fathers, St. Cyril of Alexandria, St. Maximus the Confessor, and St. John of Damascus. Recent scholarship has demonstrated the link between Palamas' teaching and the Greek Fathers before him, as well as the early Christian appropriation and transformation of Hellenic philosophical understandings of *energeia*.[2] The fall of Byzantium to the Ottoman Turks initiated centuries of struggle during which Orthodox theology, in particular the teaching on the divine essence and energies, did not find a strong, articulate voice. However, the theology of Palamas was "rediscovered" in the first half of the 20th century. The rediscovery was initiated by the theological controversies associated with some Russian monks on Mount Athos who were accused of claiming that the name of God is God Himself (the so-called Name-worshipers or *Imiaslavtzi*), and

---

1 See Amphiloque (Radovic) du Montenegro et du Littoral, *Le Mystère de la Sainte Trinité selon Saint Grégoire Palamas* (Paris: Les Editions du Cerf, 2012).

2 Jean-Claude Larchet, *La théologie des Energies Divines des origines* à *saint Jean Damascène* (Paris: Editions du Cerf, 2010); David Bradshaw, *Aristotle East and West: Metaphysics and the Division of Christendom* (Cambridge: Cambridge University Press, 2004).

whose teaching was associated with the theology of St. Gregory Palamas.[3] This rediscovery, together with the controversy revolving around the sophiology of Fr. Sergii Bulgakov,[4] is of particular interest, as it initiated a renewal of Orthodox theology by reopening some key theological themes, including the essence-energies distinction, which have impacted Orthodox theology to the present.[5]

In parallel to the Orthodox theological renewal in the first half of the 20th century there were ongoing inter-confessional debates (predominantly between Orthodox and Roman Catholics) focusing on the relevance of the theology of St. Gregory Palamas. These debates emerged within theological circles associated with the Russian diaspora in France and clearly contributed to the rediscovery and the appropriation of the teaching on the distinction between divine essence and energies.[6] This distinction has become quite a sensitive topic in inter-confessional discussions ever since, due to its relation to all-important chapters of Christian theology as well as to such controversial issues as the *filioque*. According to Duncan Reid, the distinction between essence and energies

---

3 See Catherine Evtuhov, *The Cross and the Sickle: Sergei Bulgakov and the Fate of Russian Religious Philosophy* (Ithaca: Cornell University Press, 1997); Hilarion Alfeyev, *Le Mystère sacré de l'Église – Introduction à l'histoire et à la problématique des débats athoniques sur la vénération du nom du Dieu* (Fribourg: Academic Press Fribourg, 2007); Stoyan Tanev, "ΕΝΕΡΓΕΙΑ vs ΣΟΦΙΑ: The Contribution of Fr. Georges Florovsky to the Rediscovery of the Orthodox Teaching on the Distinction between the Divine Essence and Energies," *International Journal of Orthodox Theology* 2, No. 1 (2011): 15–71; and Stoyan Tanev, "The Theology of Divine Energies in 20th Century Orthodox Thought" (Phd Diss., Sofia University, 2012).

4 For a summary of Bulgakov's sophiological doctrine, see Sergius Bulgakov, *Wisdom of God: A Brief Summary of Sophiology* (New York: The Paisley Press–Williams and Norgate, 1937).

5 Here the following works are representative and of special historical importance: Georges Florovsky, "'Tvar' I tvarnost'," Pravoslavnaya Mysl' 1 (1928): 176–212; and "L'idée de la création dans la philosophie Chrétienne," Logos: Revue Internationale de la Pensee Orthodoxe 1, (1928): 3–30; Vasily Krivocheine, Aspeticheskoe i bogoslovskoe uchenie svyatogo Grigoriya Palamy (Praha: Seminarium Kondakovianum 8, 1936); Dumitru Stăniloae, Viata și învatatura Sf. Grigorie Palama. Cu trei tratate traduse (Sibiu: n.p. 1938); Vladimir Lossky, Essai sur la Théologie mystique de l'Église d'Orient (Paris: Aubier, 1944); Jean Meyendorff, Introduction à l'Etude de Grégoire Palamas (Paris: Editions du Seuil, 1959); John Romanides, The Ancestral Sin: A comparative Study of our Ancestors Adam and Eve according to the Paradigms and Doctrines of the first-and second-century Church and the Augustinian Formulation of original Sin (Ridgewood: Zephyr, 2002).

6 See the Introduction to Jean-Claude Larchet, *La théologie des* énergies *Divines des origines* à *saint Jean Damascène* (Paris: Editions du Cerf, 2010).

runs "directly contrary, it seems, to one of the basic principles of the Western Trinitarian tradition, viz. 'that we have no formula for the being of God in Godself other than the being of God in the world.'"[7] In Reid's view, the Western position is an "*a priori,* though not always acknowledged, methodological principle," while in the East it is "a recognized doctrine, confirmed by ecclesiastical synods, that has in turn certain methodological ramifications."[8] Here Reid refers to the relevance of the Church councils in 14th century Byzantium that provided the most explicit doctrinal articulation of this teaching. The importance of these councils for Orthodox theology is well expressed by a statement of Fr. Georges Florovsky:

> This basic distinction (i.e., between divine essence and energies) has been formally accepted and elaborated at the Great Councils of Constantinople in 1341 and 1351. Those who would deny this distinction were anathematized and excommunicated. The anathematisms of the council of 1351 were included in the rite for the Sunday of Orthodoxy, in the Triodion. Orthodox theologians are bound by this decision.[9]

The motivation to focus on this theme of divine energy in a special volume dedicated to Thomas F. Torrance and his theological relations with Orthodoxy is fourfold. First, it is to emphasize the fact that this teaching is an integral part of Orthodox theology, and second, to provide an initial analysis of why Torrance did not adhere to it. Third, I hope that the discussion suggested here will help in correcting certain erroneous perceptions regarding Orthodox theology put forward by scholars who have already discussed Torrance's view on the essence and energies distinction in its relation to deification or theosis. Fourth and finally, the motivation for the present paper is to suggest an analysis demonstrating the correlation between Torrance's engagements with particular themes in modern physics and the content of his theological positions. This last analysis is of particular relevance since it is directly associated with his interpretation of the distinction between essence and energies.

---

7 Duncan Reid, *Energies of the Spirit: Trinitarian Models in Eastern Orthodox and Western Theology* (Atlanta: Scholar Press, 1997), 3, referring to F. D. E. Schleiermacher, *Der Christliche Glaube,* ed. M. Redeker (Berlin: de Gruyter, 1960), 2:589.

8 Ibid., 4.

9 Georges Florovsky, "St. Gregory Palamas and the Tradition of the Fathers," in *Bible, Church, Tradition: An Eastern Orthodox View, The Collected Works of Georges Florovsky* (Vaduz, Europa: Buechervertriebsanstalt, 1987), 1:105–20.

Torrance against dualisms

Before going into the details of Torrance's views on the essence-energies distinction, it is worth highlighting one major aspect of his theological preoccupations – his passion for addressing theological and scientific dualisms. This is a major point since, as it will be shown later, it provides a key for understanding Torrance's view on the relationship between science and theology. Torrance repeatedly highlighted the struggle of the Church throughout all her history with cosmological and epistemological dualisms that threaten to destroy the meaning of the Gospel. The Christian doctrine of the incarnation was articulated against a philosophical background characterized by a fundamental disjunction between the real world of the intelligible and the shadowy, less real world of phenomenal or sensible.[10] In Torrance's own words:

> The Church found itself struggling with two powerful ideas that threatened to destroy its existence: *(a)* the idea that God himself does not intervene in the actual life of men in time and space for he is immutable and changeless, and *(b)* the idea that the Word of God revealed in Christ is not grounded in the eternal Being of God but is detached and separated from him and therefore mutable and changeable.[11]

According to Torrance the split between God and the world in modern thought has been most damaging following Kant's arguments for an axiomatic distinction between unknowable things in themselves and what is scientifically knowable, i.e. the things as they appear to us. In other words, for Kant knowledge was limited to the appearances of things without any grounding in their inner dynamic nature and the lack of grounding severed the connection between science and faith, depriving faith of any objective or ontological reference and emptying it of any real cognitive content.[12]

10   Thomas F. Torrance, *Theology in Reconstruction* (London: SCM Press, 1965), 34, 175, 211; Thomas F. Torrance, *Space, Time and Incarnation* (Edinburgh: T&T Clark, 1997), 15, 43; Thomas F. Torrance, *The Trinitarian Faith: The Evangelical Theology of the Ancient Catholic Church* (Edinburgh: T&T Clark, 1995), 47, 275; Thomas F. Torrance, *Theology in Reconciliation* (Grand Rapids: Eerdmans, 1976), 224. For more insights on Torrance's view on dualisms, see Andrew Purves, "The Christology of Thomas F. Torrance," in *The Promise of Trinitarian Theology*, ed. Elmer Colyer (Lanham, MD: Rowman and Littlefield, 2001), 52.

11   Torrance, *Theology in Reconstruction*, 261.

12   Thomas F. Torrance, *Ground and Grammar of Theology* (Charlottesville:

According to Colin Gunton, Torrance's concern with dualism has two distinct aspects.[13] First, there is the division between the world of sense and the world of intellect, which deprives modern intellectual life of its basis in material being. The continuity of the human mind with the material world is essential for the integration of thought and experience, without which neither natural nor theological science can operate. According to Gunton, Torrance's approach generates a realist parallel to Kant's essentially idealist epistemology, since for Torrance all theological concepts must have a corresponding empirical grounding in order to be a theology rooted in the Gospel.

The second dualism with which Torrance is concerned regards the relation between the being and act of God.[14] Interestingly, Torrance associates this dualism with what he calls "'the Latin Heresy': for in theology at any rate its roots go back to a form of linguistic and conceptual dualism that prevailed in Patristic and Mediaeval Latin theology."[15] According to Torrance, this heresy has entrenched in the tradition the breach between the act of God (what he does) and his being (what he is) leading to a radical distinction between the person and work of Christ. Torrance seeks to avoid this dualism and its resultant external, transactional notion of redemption through the adoption of an incarnational model of atonement.[16] Further, Torrance's Trinitarian theology appears to be a continuous effort to overcome the same dualism. For him the danger of the dualistic disconnect between God and man requires a knowledge of Jesus Christ on his own ground as he reveals Himself to us and according to His nature *(kata physin)* within the objective frame of meaning that he has created for the church, through the apostolic testimony to him. Here Torrance follows the basic Barthian axiom that God's being is known only through his act, and that the person and work of Christ are inseparable.[17]

University of Virginia Press, 1980), 26–7.

13   Colin Gunton, "Eastern and Western Trinities: Being and Person. T. F. Torrance's Doctrine of God," in *Father, Son & Holy Spirit* (London: T&T Clark, 2003), 34.

14   Ibid., 35.

15   Thomas F. Torrance, "Karl Barth and the Latin Heresy," *Scottish Journal of Theology* 39 (1986): 461–82.

16   Myk Habets, *Theosis in the Theology of Thomas F. Torrance* (Farnham, UK: Ashgate, 2009), 50.

17   Torrance, *The Doctrine of Jesus Christ*, 150.

In Torrance's own words, "Christ is what he does, and does what he is."[18] If the identity and mission of Jesus Christ form a coherent whole, then it is both the person and the work that have redemptive significance. "The Redemption is the Person of Christ in action; not the action itself thought of in an objectivist impersonal way."[19]

One should point out that the above statements manifest Torrance's unwarranted preoccupation with the danger of a potential disjunction between person and agency, as if personal acts and activity may exist somehow independently of the person itself. Such preoccupation may be explained with Torrance's predominant focus on the theology of St. Athanasius and the Christian theological debates of the 4th and the 5th centuries, when the distinction between essence (*ousia*), nature (*physis*), person (*hypostasis* or *prosopon*) and activity (*energeia*) was not fully articulated yet. It is undisputed that Torrance's argumentation against dualism never loses its basis in the Arian controversy and Nicene theology.[20] For Torrance the coexistence of the divine and human natures in the person of Christ is not a dualism but "the only way to safeguard a real, dynamic, and open (that is, free of deterministic causalities) relationship between God and the world."[21] For him dualism does not consist in a mere appearance of two poles but in the specific understanding of the nature of the relation between the two poles involved. His emphasis on the *homoousion* is an expression of a realism that could be applied to both theology and science: "what is observed is of the same being with reality itself so that an observation does not relate to a superficial phenomenon only but to reality in its ontological depth. Apparent phenomena and reality, then, do not live their own separate lives but are actually one and the same."[22] In this way the link between theology and science in Torrance's thought emerges not as mere academic endeavor but as part of an integrated vision of God, man, and the world. This point should help later in clarifying part of the motivation for his critique of the distinction between essence and energies.

18   Ibid., 150, 165.

19   Ibid., 151.

20   Tapio Luoma, *Incarnation and Physics: Natural Science in the Theology of Thomas F. Torrance* (Oxford: Oxford University Press, 2002), 90.

21   Ibid.

22   Ibid., 91.

Distinction Between Theologia and Oikonomia

Torrance equates the distinction between the being of God (what he is) and his act (what he does) with the patristic distinction between *theologia* and *oikonomia,* and emphasizes that this distinction should not be understood dualistically: "Due to the epistemological dualism (*chorismos*) pervading Hellenistic thought the Church had constantly to struggle against a threat to *sever* 'economy' from 'theology' (*oikonomia* from *theologia*), for it would have done away with the ontological reference of the Gospel and of faith to any real ground in the being and activity of God."[23] Here Torrance refers positively to Florovsky's essay "The Concept of Creation in Saint Athanasius" for support; yet it is interesting that in this paper Florovsky expresses exactly the *opposite* concern.[24] In Florovsky's words:

> In fact, St. Athanasius carefully eliminates all references to the *oikonomia* of creation or salvation from his description of the inner relationship between the Father and the Son. This was his major and decisive contribution to the Trinitarian theology, in the critical situation of the Arian dispute. And this left him free to define the concept of creation properly. *Theologia*, in the ancient sense of the word, and *Oikonomia* must be clearly and strictly distinguished and delimited, although they could not be separated from each other. But God's "Being" has an absolute and ontological priority over God's action and will . . . There are two different sets of names which may be used of God. One set of names refers to God's deeds or acts – that is, to His will and counsel – the other of God's essence and being. St. Athanasius insisted that these two sets of names had to be formally and consistently distinguished. And, again, it was more than just a logical or mental distinction. There was a distinction in divine reality itself. God is what He is: Father, Son, and the Holy Spirit. It is an ultimate reality, declared and manifested in the Scriptures. But Creation is a deed of the divine will, and this is common to and identical in all Three Persons of the One God . . . the actual mystery is double. There is, indeed, the mystery of the divine Being. But there is another mystery of the divine *oikonomia*. No

---

23   Torrance, *The Christian Doctrine of God: One Being, Three Persons,* 7.

24   A similar point was made by Matthew Baker, "The Eternal 'Spirit of the Son': Barth, Florovsky, and Torrance on the *Filioque*," *International Journal of Systematic Theology* 12 (2010): 382–402.

real advance can be achieved in the realm of "Theology" until
the realm of "Oikonomia" had been properly ordered.[25]

Florovsky points out here that the difference between divine generation, as
an effect of nature, and creation, as an effect of will, is one of the distinctive
marks of Eastern theology, which was systematically elaborated later
especially in the theology of St. Gregory Palamas. St. Gregory's emphasis
that "unless a clear distinction had been made between the 'essence' and
'energy' of God, one could not distinguish also between 'generation'
and 'creation' . . . was a true Athanasian motive," says Florovsky. "Not
only do we distinguish between 'Being' and 'Will'; but it is not the same
thing, even for God, 'to be' and 'to act.' This was the deepest conviction
of St. Athanasius."[26] In his earlier essay "Creation and Creaturehood,"
Florovsky elaborated on this theme even further, pointing out that the
"life- giving acts of God in the world *are God Himself* – an assertion which
precludes separation but does not abolish distinction."[27] One can see how
in Florovsky the fear of dualism is replaced by a subtle understanding
of the important distinction between *theologia* and *oikonomia*, divine
nature and will, divine being and act, divine essence and energies. It is the
perception of this subtlety that provides a hint of the dynamic apophatic
realism[28] of divine-human communion.

Torrance's concerns, however, go in the opposite direction, stressing
the identity of *oikonomia* and *theologia*:

> While for Athanasius *economy* and *theology* (*oikonomia* and
> *theologia*) must be clearly distinguished, they are not to be
> separated from each other. If the economic or evangelical Trinity
> and the ontological or theological Trinity were disparate, this
> would bring into question whether *God himself* was the actual
> content of his revelation, and whether *God himself* was really in

25   Georges Florovsky, "The Concept of Creation in Saint Athanasius," *Studia
Patristica* 4, (1962): 48, 54.

26   Ibid., 56–7.

27   Georges Florovsky, "Creature and Creaturehood," in *Creation and
Redemption*, Collected Works (Belmont, Mass: Nordland, 1976), 3:65–6 (a careful
examination of part III and IV of Florovsky's "Creature and Creaturehood" will
illustrate its relevance to the topic and its relation to the teaching on the divine
essence and energies).

28   The term was recently discussed by Haralambos Ventis, "Toward Apophatic
Theological Realism: An Orthodox Realistic Critique of Postmodernism with
Special Attention to the Work of George Lindbeck" (PhD Diss., Boston University,
2001).

> Jesus Christ reconciling the world to himself . . . The economic Trinity and the ontological Trinity overlap with one another and belong to one another, and can no more be separated than the Act of God can be separated from his Being or his Being from his Act. It is in that interrelation between the two that the redemptive significance and evangelical relevance of the Holy Trinity become disclosed.[29]

What is important here for the present study is that Torrance directly associates the discussion of the distinction/identity of the ontological and economic Trinity to the distinction between divine essence and energies:

> The question must be asked how far the Byzantine elaboration of the distinction between the uncreated energies (*energeiai, dunameis*) and the Being (*ousia*) of God retreats from the Athanasian position as to the real knowability of God, and how far it bars the way in an intelligible movement from the Economic Trinity to the Immanent Trinity . . . The Byzantine thesis that all we can say positively of God manifests not his Nature but the things about his Nature[30] seems to put a question mark before any doctrine of oneness between the Immanent or Ontological Trinity and the Economic Trinity.[31]

Torrance on the Teaching Regarding Divine Essence and Energies

The theological insights of Thomas Torrance can be closely associated with his inspiration from two major theologians: Karl Barth and St. Athanasius of Alexandria. According to Colin Gunton,

> Athanasius served Torrance as a theologian of God's being as Barth served as a theologian of his act (though the greatness of both is that they integrated the two) and it would be difficult to exaggerate the importance for him, in all aspects of his work, of the principle of the *homoousion*.[32]

29 Torrance, *The Christian Doctrine of God: One Being, Three Persons*, 7–8.

30 This is a reference to John of Damascus' interpretation, *De fide orthodoxa*, 1.4, of Gregory Nazianzen's words in *Oratio* 38.7. Torrance considers this interpretation as inappropriate and misleading.

31 Thomas F. Torrance, *Theology in Reconciliation* (Grand Rapids: Eerdmans, 1976), 222, 237.

32 Gunton, "Being and Person: T. F. Torrance's Doctrine of God," 116.

It is against this background that one should examine Torrance's comments about the distinction between divine essence and energies.

Discussing John of Damascus' use of Athanasius, Torrance points out that "God is so wonderfully and transcendentally free in his own eternal Being that he can do something new without changing in his *ousia* and can go outside of himself in the Incarnation without ceasing to be what he is eternally in himself in his own ineffable Being, for his *energeia* inheres in his eternal *ousia*." In Athanasius, the Greek notion of *energeia* was Christianized under the transforming impact of the biblical conception of the creative and providential activity of the living God:

> The Athanasian view of God was one in which activity and movement were regarded as intrinsic to his very being as God. God is never without his activity, for his activity and his being are essentially and eternally one. The act of God is not one thing, and his being another, for they coinhere mutually and indivisibly in one another. Hence far from God being inactive in his inner being, it belongs to the essential and eternal nature of his being to move and energise and act.[33]

However, according to Torrance, this "is an entirely different conception of God from that which developed in later theology when the *energeia* of God was distinguished from his *ousia*,"[34] as, for instance, in the Cappadocians and in St. John of Damascus.

Torrance is fully aware of the evolution of Greek philosophical terminology, in which the "meanings of *ousia* and *hypostasis, logos* and *energeia*, underwent a radical change through the use to which they were put in the hermeneutical and theological activity of the Church." In particular he believes that the Nicene *homoousios* marked a significant redefinition of *ousia*:

> The *homoousios to Patri* was revolutionary and decisive: it expressed the fact that what God is "toward us" and "in the

---

33 Thomas F. Torrance, *Trinitarian Faith: The Evangelical Theology of the Ancient Catholic Church* (Edinburgh: T&T Clark, 1995), 74–5. It is worth comparing this last statement to Florovsky's statement that "Not only do we distinguish between 'Being' and 'Will'; but it is not the same thing, even for God, 'to be' and 'to act.'" As we have already seen, for Florovsky "this was the deepest conviction of St. Athanasius": Florovsky, "The Concept of Creation in Saint Athanasius," *Studia Patristica* 4 (1962): 56–7.

34 Thomas F. Torrance, *Divine Meaning: Studies in Patristic Hermeneutics* (Edinburgh: T&T Clark), 187–88.

midst of us" in and through the Word made flesh, he really is *in himself;* that he is in the *internal relations* of his transcendent being the very same Father, Son, and Holy Spirit that he is in his revealing and saving activity in time and space toward mankind. In precise theological usage *ousia* now refers to being not simply as that which is but to what it is in respect of its internal reality . . . If God is in himself what he is in the Person and activity of his incarnate Word and Son, then the being or *ousia* of God must be understood in a very un-Greek way. Applied to God *enousios logos* and *enousios energeia* express the fact that the being of God is not intrinsically empty of word or activity, not mute or static, but is essentially eloquent and dynamic.[35]

Moreover, Torrance repeatedly points out that "If the Word (*Logos*) and activity (*energeia*) of God manifest in the Gospel are not inherent (*enousioi*) in his eternal being, as Athanasius had insisted, then we cannot relate what God is toward us in his economic self-revelation and self-giving to what he ever is in himself or *vice versa.*" However, in Torrance's view, this was precisely "the danger that lurked in the Basilian distinction between the divine being and the divine energies, which had the effect of restricting knowledge of God to his divine energies, and ruling out any real access to knowledge of God in the intrinsic relations of his eternal triune being."[36] According to Torrance, the approach of St. Athanasius was quite different:

> In speaking of the being or *ousia* of God, Athanasius used the term in its simplest sense as that which *is* and subsists by itself, but allowed that to be changed and transformed by the nature of God. Thus the *ousia* of God as Athanasius understands it is both *being* and *presence,* presence in being, and *being* and *activity,* activity in being, the transcendent Being of God the Creator who is actively, creatively present in all that he has made, upholding it by the Word of his power and by *his* Spirit.[37]

Here one clearly finds articulated one of Torrance's main concerns with the essence-energies distinction, the introduction of which he blames on St. Basil the Great and St. Gregory of Nyssa. For Torrance, the distinction

35 Torrance, *Trinitarian Faith,* 130–32.

36 Ibid., 335–36.

37 Torrance, "Athanasius: a Study in the Foundations of Classical Theology," in *Divine Meaning,* 182.

restricts the knowledge of God to his energies, which are something else than what God is in himself, i.e. not God himself. The distinction therefore rules out any real access to the knowledge of God in the intrinsic relations of his eternal triune being. This opinion of Torrance again goes against some of the key points of Florovsky in his papers "The Concept of Creation in Saint Athanasius"[38] and "Creature and Creaturehood,"[39] where it is stressed that the divine essence is God's inherent self-existence and the energies are his relations towards the other:

> God *is* Life, and *has* life; *is* Wisdom, and *has* wisdom; and so forth. The first series of expressions refers to the incommunicable essence, the second to the inseparably distinct energies of the one essence, which descend upon creation. None of these energies is hypostatic, nor hypostasis in itself, and their incalculable multiplicity introduces no composition into the divine Being. The totality of the divine "energies" constitutes His pre-temporal will, His design, His good pleasure – concerning the "other," His eternal counsel. This is God Himself, not His Essence, but *His will*. The distinction between "essence" and "energies" – or, it could be said, between 'nature' and 'grace' [φύσις and χάρις] corresponds to the mysterious distinction in God between 'necessity' and 'freedom,' understood in a proper sense.[40]

"Translating" the distinction between essence and energies to the distinction between necessity and will could be helpful in identifying the hidden dangers in Torrance's terminology. Although emphasizing the understanding of divine *ousia* as being and presence, presence in being, and being and activity in the transcendent being of God the Creator who is actively and creatively present in all that he has made, is a wonderful way of expressing the dynamically active nature and presence of God in the world, it could be misinterpreted as referring to the assignment of necessity and homogeneity to the divine activity in the world. This danger seems to emerge from the predominant emphasis on preserving the divine unity expressed in Torrance's energetic terminology. This emphasis explains Torrance's focus on the epistemological and soteriological role of the *homoousion*. However, it leaves open the question about the

---

38 Florovsky, "The Concept of Creation in Saint Athanasius," *Studia Patristica* 4 (1962): 36–57.

39 Florovsky, "Creature and Creaturehood," 43–78.

40 Ibid., 68–9.

specificity of the divine activity within the created order. As Florovsky points out:

> Out of eternity God sees and wills, by His good pleasure, each and every being in the completeness of its particular destiny and features, even regarding its future and sin . . . "Christ will behold all the numberless myriads of Saints, turning His glance away from none, so that to each one of them it will seem that He is looking at him, talking with him, and greeting him," and yet "while remaining unchanged, He will seem different to one and different to another."[41] God, in the counsel of His good pleasure, beholds all the innumerable myriads of created hypostases, wills them, and to each one of them manifests Himself in a different way. And herein consists the "inseparable distribution" of His grace or energy, "myriadfold hypostatic" in the bold phrase of St. Gregory Palamas, because this grace or energy is beneficently imparted to thousands upon myriads of thousands of hypostases. Each hypostasis, in its own being and existence, is sealed by a particular ray of the good pleasure of God's love and will. And in this sense, all things are in God – in "image" *but not by nature,* the created "all" being infinitely remote from Uncreated Nature.[42]

In this paragraph one may sense the advantage of the essence-energy distinction in providing a more subtle picture of divine-human communion.

As we have seen, Torrance's main objection to the essence-energies distinction is that it appears to suggest that "we cannot know God through the immediate activity of his Being, or according to what he is in himself, but only through mediating forces emanating from him, and not according to what he is in himself."[43] However, drawing on Florovsky's subtle reading of Athanasius and other Greek Fathers – a reading to which Torrance himself appeals as authoritative – we can also see that Torrance's reading is not quite satisfactory or accurate on this point. To repeat Florovsky's unpacking of the essence-energies distinction: "The

---

41 Here Florovsky refers to St. Symeon the New Theologian.

42 Florovsky, "Creature and Creaturehood," 72–3.

43 Thomas F. Torrance, "The Doctrine of the Holy Trinity in Gregory Nazianzen and John Calvin," in *Trinitarian Perspectives: Toward Doctrinal Agreement* (Edinburgh, T&T Clark, 1994), 38.

life-giving acts of God in the world *are God Himself* – an assertion which precludes separation but does not abolish distinction."[44]

Remarkably, Torrance suggested that the specific use of the "Basilian" distinction between essence and energies by Sts. Maximus the Confessor, John of Damascus, and Gregory Palamas had the effect of introducing into Byzantine theology a "damaging dualism of an Augustinian kind."[45] This is a serious and very unfortunate (and un-historical) claim, which only demonstrates that Torrance did not have the chance to seriously engage with later Byzantine thought articulated, for example, in the dogmatic formulations of the 5th, 6th and 7th ecumenical councils. Unfortunately, by keeping himself so restrictively to the theological legacy of Sts. Athanasius and Cyril, he framed himself within pre-Chalcedonian terminology, missing the opportunity to enjoy the subtleties of its later theological refinement in the works of Maximus the Confessor, John of Damascus, and Gregory Palamas. Undoubtedly, there were understandable reasons for this, since his main audience consisted of fellow Reformed Christians, and he may have used his interaction with the Orthodox Church as a way for the careful initiation of a respectful and very much needed renewal of his own tradition.[46] Perhaps it was some awareness of this limitation that allowed him on occasion to be soberly insightful about the value of the Orthodox teaching on the divine essence and energies, as in one place he admits, reflecting a more accurate understanding:

> Yet Orthodox theology does not rest content merely with an Economic Trinity, for the uncreated energies through and in which God makes himself known to us are proper to and inseparable from the divine Being who nevertheless remains unapproachable and unknowable in his innermost essence. The distinction is intended to reject any surrender of God's transcendence, while maintaining an ontic relation between God's economic self-revelation and what he is inherently in himself . . . It is the essence of the Being (or Essence) of God that we can never know, but in *God* the Son and in *God* the Spirit we really are given to know God in his Being or *Ousia*, for in them God really reveals *himself through himself.*[47]

---

44 Florovsky, "Creature and Creaturehood," 65–6.

45 Ibid., 38.

46 An idea suggested in private conversation with Fr. George D. Dragas, one of the Orthodox students of Thomas Torrance.

47 Torrance, *Theology in Reconciliation*, 222, 237.

A Science and Theology Interlude

One of the most popular themes in Torrance's works is related to the theological importance of the relational understanding of space. Why is the relational notion of space so important for Torrance? Because, according to him, the Newtonian understanding of space as static and absolute would shut God out of the world in a way that he could not enter into any relation with his creation. For Torrance, therefore, the discussion of the relational character of space has a definite epistemological import, since it is related to his understanding of divine activity as a way for God to manifest himself and act in the world. "If we are really to have knowledge of God we must be given a point of access to him which is both in God himself and in our creaturely existence."[48] The actuality and the reality of the presence of the incarnate God in space and time enabled the Fathers of the Church to develop relational conceptions of space and time applying them in different ways to God and to created beings: "to God in one way in accordance with his transcendent nature, and to creaturely beings in another way in accordance with their contingent natures."[49] The church fathers therefore were "able to relate the being and activity of the Son of God to bodily place (*topos*) when he entered into our human space (*hora*) and became man, without leaving God's 'place' and without leaving the universe empty of his presence and rule."[50] Space is regarded here within the context of the creative and redemptive activity of God in Christ; this is not the conception of space understood as infinite receptacle or as infinite substance. There emerges a concept of space in terms of the relations between God and the physical universe established in creation and incarnation: "Space in this formulation is a sort of differential concept that is essentially open-ended, for it is defined in accordance with the interaction between God and man."[51]

For Torrance, however, the emergence of the relational understanding of space was not without problems and difficulties. Torrance comments:

> The rise of these difficulties is particularly clear in the thought of John of Damascus, with whom the two poles in the Nicene concept of space began to draw apart. On the one hand, he appropriated fully the Aristotelian conception . . . which tended to give his notion of place or space a closed or rigid character;

48 Torrance, *Trinitarian Faith*, 52–3.

49 Ibid., 104.

50 Torrance, *Divine Meaning*, 371.

51 Ibid.

on the other hand, however, in order to balance this he had both to develop a concept of "mental place" and to carry his theology much further in an apophatic direction than Athanasius could go, even to claiming, like Basilides, that we cannot know what God is but only what he is not.[52]

One can see again that for Torrance the main issue here is epistemological, and the specific understanding of space entails a specific understanding of the nature of the relation between God and the world. In Torrance's view: "The Nicene conceptions of space and time have proved more fruitful and adaptable, and certainly have a much closer relation to more modern notions of space and time."[53]

For him the relational view of space adopted by the early Church anticipated the later emergence of the view of space expressed in the field theory introduced by James Clark Maxwell and in Albert Einstein's theory of relativity.[54]

The new scientific understanding of space-time has emerged as an alternative to Newtonian physics by providing a new ontological status of space-time. Newton made the successful hypothesis that space and time are fixed, structured background entities underlying material reality, which participate in governing the motion of physical objects. What Einstein discovered is that Newton had mistaken a physical field for a background entity.[55] The two entities hypostatized by Newton, space and time, could be actually considered as a particular local configuration of a physical entity – the gravitational field. Einstein's discovery was that Newtonian space and time and the gravitational field were the same entity. To emphasize the relational aspect of space-time one may express the meaning of Einstein's discovery in a radical way by saying that "there are no space and time: there are only dynamical objects. The world is made by dynamical fields. These do not live in, or on, space-time: they form and exhaust reality.[56]

Torrance was a great admirer of the scientific contributions of James Clark Maxwell and Albert Einstein. This fact is quite revealing

52   Ibid., 372–73.

53   Ibid.

54   Thomas F. Torrance, *Space, Time and Incarnation* (London: Oxford University Press, 1969), 57–9.

55   Carlo Rovelli, "The Disappearance of Space and Time," in *The Ontology of Spacetime*, Philosophy and Foundations of Physics Series, ed. Dennis Dieks and Miklos Redei (Amsterdam: Elsevier, 2006), 1:25–36.

56   Ibid.

since it illustrates Torrance's preferences for a relatively narrow spectrum of ideas within modern physics. However, according to John Polkinghorne, although Maxwell and Einstein are among the greatest scientists ever and definitely deserve their status as scientific heroes of Torrance, they are "the last of the ancients rather than the first of the moderns."[57] For Polkinghorne it is quite unfortunate that Torrance did not engage more seriously with the developments of quantum mechanics, which has developed a more subtle sense of reality. Torrance's appreciation of Einstein led him to stay on the same front with him in the debate concerning the possibility of a realist interpretation of quantum mechanics, a fact that evidently prevented Torrance from engaging in further dialogue with modern quantum physicists, especially with those who do not adhere to Einstein's interpretation.[58] For example, Torrance expressed multiple times his distrust of the Copenhagen interpretation of quantum mechanics and specifically of the epistemology of Niels Bohr. According to him, there were "difficulties which we still have with quantum theory, particularly as it stems from Bohr, Heisenberg, and Born, which may be traced, in part at least, to Kantian presuppositions."[59]

He also points out that there is a tension that arises between critical realism and the epistemological presuppositions latent in the Copenhagen interpretation of quantum theory.[60] According to Tapio Luoma, "the primary reason for Torrance's reluctance to the widely accepted Copenhagen interpretation of quantum physics lies precisely in his view of realism."[61] The particular feature in Torrance's thought that makes it incompatible with the Copenhagen interpretation of the behavior of elementary particles is associated with the problem concerning the real objective existence of the physical entities observed in quantum mechanical experiments. In Torrance's view the standard interpretation of quantum mechanics remains agnostic with regard to

---

57   John Polkinghorne, *Belief in God in an Age of Science* (New Haven: Yale University Press, 1998), 80.

58   Tapio Luoma, *Incarnation and Physics: Natural Science in the Theology of Thomas F. Torrance* (Oxford: Oxford University Press, 2002), 67.

59   Thomas F. Torrance, *Reality and Scientific Theology* (Edinburgh: Scottish Academic Press, 1985), 75.

60   Thomas F. Torrance, *Preaching Christ Today: The Gospel and Scientific Thinking* (Grand Rapids: Eerdmans, 1994), 41.

61   Luoma, *Incarnation and Physics*, 67–8.

the existence of an objective reality independently of the observer. This view is not unique to Torrance. For example, according to Fr. Stanley Jaki, a Roman Catholic priest and theologian whose ideas Torrance respected very much:[62]

> The possibility for Bohr consisted in restricting discourse to *aspects* of reality while barring questions about reality itself, and especially about its objective existence. In Bohr's case this was all the more laden with further problems because the *aspects* in question were more opposite, nay mutually exclusive, than merely distinct. He tried to hold them together by offering the idea of complementarity. These aspects could *really* complement one another only if they inhered in a deeper reality, about which Bohr could only be agnostic. A harmony of relations or aspects, complementing one another, such was Bohr's epistemological message, a message void of reference to the ontological reality of anything harmonious. About the entity which embodied the harmony of relations he was not permitted by his own premises to make any claim and he carefully avoided doing so.[63]

Unfortunately, the views of both Torrance and Jaki seem to be the result of a mere misunderstanding of Bohr's position. Bohr made a clear distinction between the unique identity of a quantum object and the specific complementary ways of its *energetic manifestation*. This distinction is crucial for Bohr in emphasizing the reality of the quantum world while at the same time accepting that it does not make sense to speak about its "being in a certain way" independent of the interaction with a specific experimental arrangement. Such a view does not conform to the classical understanding of realism; it adopts a more subtle way of looking at reality allowing for a self-subsisting object to manifest mutually exclusive (or complementary) types of natural properties depending on the specific circumstances of the interaction between the observer and the object.

How can we explain this misunderstanding of Bohr's ideas? One might point out two different reasons. The first one is the fact that both Torrance and Jaki formed their opinions before some of the most recent decisive experiments in quantum physics which proved the inconsistency

---

62   I am grateful to Fr. Prof. George Dragas from the Holy Cross Greek Orthodox School of Theology, Brookline, MA, who pointed out to me Torrance's admiration for the works and ideas of Fr. Stanley Jaki.

63   Stanley L. Jaki, "The Horns of Complementarity," in *The Road of Science and the Ways to God* (Chicago: Chicago University Press, 1978).

of their suspicions about Bohr's epistemological viewpoint.[64] The latest developments in quantum physics suggest that:

> we can no longer assume that the properties we measure necessarily reflect or represent the properties of the particles as they really are. As Heisenberg had argued, "we have to remember that what we observe is not nature in itself but nature exposed to our method of questioning." This does not mean that quantum particles are not real. What it does mean is that we can ascribe to them only an *empirical* reality.[65]

According to Christos Yannaras, in quantum physics it became evident that the result of the observation of the micro-world is connected with the specific type of instruments, and also with the specific method of observation and description.[66] The specific model that could be used to describe a physical system depends on the observer and the nature of the apparatus it is interacting with. Our perception of reality can change in accordance with our instruments or our method of observation; conversely, observed reality can be transformed by the fact of observing it. "What this means is that the nature of existing reality is not independent of human action, yet the answer nature gives us as the result of the individual measurement is random. The result is beyond our control, which indicates an independent physical reality."[67]

The second reason for Torrance's misunderstanding of Bohr's realist position is the lack of a proper understanding of the concept of hypostasis. It was already pointed out that Torrance had an unwarranted preoccupation with the danger of a potential disjunction between person/hypostasis and act/agency as if hypostatic acts and activity may exist independently of a specific hypostasis. This preoccupation seems to have been the source of Torrance's sense of dualism in relation to both the teaching on the distinction between essence and energies and

---

64   S. Groblacher, T. Paterek, R. Kaltenbaek, C. Brukner, M. Zukowski, M. Aspelmeyer, A. Zeilinger, "An Experimental Test of Non-Local Realism," *Nature* 446 (April 2007): 871.

65   Jim Baggott, *The Quantum Story: a History in 40 Moments* (Oxford: Oxford University Press, 2011), 356.

66   Christos Yannaras, *Postmodern Metaphysics*, trans. Norman Russell (Brookline, MA: Holy Cross Orthodox Press, 2004), 90–3.

67   Anton Zeilinger, "Quantum Physics: Ontology or Epistemology?," in *Trinity and an Entangled World: Relationality in Physical Science and Theology*, ed. John Polkinghorne (Grand Rapids: Eerdmans Publishing Company, 2010), 38–9.

Bohr's interpretation of quantum mechanics. It is true that Bohr did not use a well formed terminology allowing him to better articulate the inherent relationship between quantum entities and their specific natural manifestations. However, one may definitely see his struggle with the lack of such terminology. Just as an example, at one place he pointed out:

> Information regarding the behavior of an atomic object obtained under definite experimental conditions may . . . be adequately characterized as complementary to any information *about the same object* obtained by some other experimental arrangements excluding the fulfillment of the first conditions. Although such kinds of information cannot be combined into a single picture by means of ordinary concepts, they represent indeed equally essential aspects of any knowledge *of the object in question* which can be obtained in this domain.[68]

Here *"the same object"* and *"the object in question"* refer exactly to the quantum entity which triggers its specific natural manifestations during a specific quantum mechanical experiment. Werner Heisenberg noted several times that Bohr did not have a problem with language but was in the process of inventing a new one. In this process he "tried to keep the words and the pictures without keeping the meanings of the words and of the pictures, having been from his youth interested in the limitation of our way of expression, the limitation of words, the problem of talking about things when one knows that the words do not really get hold of the things."[69]

It is quite interesting that Torrance, who had developed a great sensitivity for the ways of using of language in theology and physics, did not show any empathy towards Bohr's efforts to develop a proper language in articulating the subtlety of quantum mechanical realism. On the other hand, the potential for a mutual terminological enrichment between theology and quantum mechanics has been already discussed within the context of Orthodox theology. For example, Christos Yannaras points out that when we speak of relations in quantum mechanics, we do not refer to predictable correlations, but rather "to a mode of correlation, referentiality, and coordination which has the character of the unpredictable, of the probable, of the possible, and which could be compared only with the

---

68 Niels Bohr, "Natural philosophy and human cultures," in *Essays 1932–1957 on Atomic Physics and Human Knowledge,* The Philosophical Writings of Niels Bohr (New York: Wiley, 1958), 2:23–31.

69 Folse, Henry J., *The Philosophy of Niels Bohr* (Elsevier Science Publishers B.V., Amsterdam, 1985), 111.

dynamic freedom of interpersonal human relations."[70] This is a key point suggesting that we may actually get closer to a better understanding of quantum phenomena if we describe quantum entities in terms of the theological terminology of essence, nature, hypostasis, and energy.[71] The basis for this claim is the fact that, by distinguishing essence or nature from person or hypostasis as well as the energies both from the nature and from the hypostasis, the theology of the Eastern Church has adopted a terminology that is very helpful in interpreting the reality of existence, the appearance, and disclosure of being.[72]

What is, however, even more interesting is that Yannaras provides a theological interpretation of space by using the concept of energy within the context of a relational understanding of person (*prosopon*): "we recognize space as the accommodation of personal reference, as a fact of relation."[73] The external view of personal relations objectifies space as the distance between the two terms of the relation and establishes distance as the basis for the measurement of space. The objectification of physical reality, however, does not negate the experience of space in terms of interpersonal relation. The ecstatic reference of the person is a fact that transcends the categories of measurable space. According to Yannaras, the second term of a personal relation may be here or elsewhere, present or absent, but is always referring to the same non-dimensional space of personal reference. "The power of personal relations negates the measurable dimensions of here and there, of nearer and farther, and points to both presence and absence as the experience of non-dimensional nearness."[74] The Byzantine theologians saw in personal energy the non-dimensional place both of the human person and of the Person of God. He refers specifically to John of Damascus (whose understanding of space Torrance considered as problematic), who defined the space of God's disclosure of his personal energy as the place of God: "What is

70   Christos Yannaras, *Postmodern Metaphysics*, trans. Norman Russell (Brookline, MA: Holy Cross Orthodox Press, 2004), 93.

71   Stoyan Tanev, "The Language of Orthodox Theology & Quantum Mechanics: St. Gregory Palamas and Niels Bohr" (Thessaloniki: n.p., forthcoming).

72   Christos Yannaras, *Elements of Faith: an Introduction to Orthodox Theology* (Edinburgh: T&T Clark, 1991), 43.

73   This section follows very closely the insights in: Christos Yannaras, *Person and Eros* (Brookline, Mass: Holy Cross Orthodox Press, 2007), 105.

74   Ibid., 107.

called the place of God is where his energy becomes manifest."[75] This is a statement that provides a link between the relational understanding of space in John of Damascus and modern physics where space and time are considered as a result of the presence of matter and energy. For Yannaras, God's personal energy becomes manifest primarily in the space of cosmic reality and the world is revealed to humanity as the non-dimensional place of divine personal energy. Cosmic space acquires its meaning only as a divine place. It is then not measured as conventional distance from humanity or as the interval between objects. The cosmos accommodates or gives space to the mutual relation between God and humanity. Humanity discovers the accessibility of God in the fact of the reality of the world, without this accessibility removing the *natural* distance of God from the world, the distance separating uncreated from created nature. The closeness of humanity to God within the context of the world is not natural but *personal* – a closeness defined by a relationship. In this sense, one could say that it is not the world that accommodates God or his personal energy, but the divine will and energy which accommodates or gives space to the world, a space outside God which is simultaneously God's place, the disclosure of the non-dimensional immediacy of his personal energy. The distinction between the nature and the energies of God, without denying the reality of the natural distance of God from the world, preserves the world as a space of the immediate personal nearness of God and manifests God as the place of the universe: "For God is not contained, but is himself the place of all."[76]

The theological understanding of space suggested by Christos Yannaras provides an example of an alternative approach to the encounter between theology and physics. Yannaras develops a comprehensive theological perspective of the world by borrowing ideas from both Albert Einstein (general relativity) and Niels Bohr (quantum mechanics) in combination with a genuinely personal understanding of divine-human communion which includes the distinction between divine essence and energies. The comparison of Yannaras' and Torrance's approaches provides an opportunity to demonstrate the correlation between their preoccupations with specific themes in modern physics and their specific theological insights. Thomas Torrance has clearly neglected the epistemological insights emerging from the advances of quantum

---

75 John of Damascus, *An Exact Exposition of the Orthodox Faith*, 1.13.

76 Theophilus of Antioch, *To Autolycus*, 2.3: What has become of the gods?

mechanics in the 20th century and has ended up with neglecting the value of the Orthodox teaching on the distinction between divine essence and energies. This neglect seems to be also associated with an underdeveloped understanding of person/*prosopon*/*hypostasis*. The overall result is the appearance of statements that contradict the apophatic character of the distinction between divine essence and energies and the subtlety of the apophatic realism of divine-human communion.

Conclusion

The purpose of this chapter was to review and discuss Thomas Torrance's interpretation of the Orthodox teaching on the distinction between divine essence and energies. As a way of conclusion one could make two final points:

First, some of Torrance's main concerns are associated with: (i) the danger of falling into dualistic divisions between what God is in himself and what he is towards us, and (ii) the danger of an understanding of the Trinitarian Monarchy on the basis of the Person of the Father as compared to a Monarchy of the Trinity based on the unity of the divine essence and agency. Torrance does not accept any ontological ordering within the Trinity starting with the Person of the Father and considers such teaching to be correlated with the distinction between essence and energies. This is one of the reasons for him to be suspicious in his interpretation of the teachings of St. Basil concerning the divine unity and the possibility to know God through the divine energies. There are two interesting "moments" in this approach. The first is that it goes directly against the theology of one of the major Orthodox theologians alive today – Metropolitan John Zizioulas.[77] What is even more interesting, however, is that Metropolitan John is himself also quite suspicious about the teaching on the distinction between essence and energies and its role in Orthodox theology in particular.[78] The discrepancy between the two theologians could be (schematically) expressed in terms of their different understanding of the ontological sources of divine energy or activity. If divine activity is grounded in the being and essence of God as tri-unity

77   See for example the relevant sections in John Zizioulas, *Communion and Otherness: Further Studies in Personhood and the Church*, ed. P. McPartlan (London: T&T Clark, 2006).

78   Ibid. See for example the theological context of all the references to St. Gregory Palamas.

(Torrance), the divine monarchy cannot be other but Trinitarian and *perichoretic*; on the other hand, if the divine activity, will and love are grounded in the person or hypostasis (Zizioulas), the divine monarchy requires a single hypostasis – the hypostasis of the Father, as a guarantee of the divine unity.

The second "moment" is that Torrance's approach has some interesting similarities with the theological synthesis of Fr. Dumitru Stăniloae, for whom the unity of the Trinity is both essential and personal. The essential unity is based on the common *ousia* which is not seen as a separate reality or in separation from the divine persons. The personal unity is based on the inter-subjectivity of the Persons in their coinherence or *perichoresis*. Interestingly, however, Fr. Dumitru is one of the few Orthodox theologians who have systematically employed the teaching on the distinction between divine essence and energies to provide probably the most comprehensive synthesis in Orthodox theology today. There have already been some good attempts at a systematic comparison of the theological approaches of Zizioulas and Stăniloae.[79] It would be quite relevant for future studies to concentrate on a more comprehensive comparison of the Trinitarian theologies of Torrance and Stăniloae.

Second, although Torrance has clearly vocalized his concerns with some key Orthodox theological teachings, his theology has been perceived quite sympathetically by contemporary Orthodox theologians. Without any doubt there will be more studies focusing on exploring his theological contributions. One of the subjects of such explorations should focus on Torrance's approach to the interplay between theology and science (see for example chapter 10 by Fr. Alexei Nesteruk). At the same time, the discussion of his specifically theological positions, including his critique of the distinction between divine essence and energies, should be considered as a fruitful resource in some of the ongoing Orthodox theological discussions.[80]

---

79 Calinic Berger, "Does the Eucharist Make the Church? An Eccesiological Comparison of Stăniloae and Zizioulas," St. Vladimir's Theological Quarterly 51 (2007): 23–70; Kevin Berger, "Towards a Theological Gnoseology: The Synthesis of Fr. Dumitru Stăniloae" (PhD diss., Washington: Catholic University of America, 2003); Tanev, "The Theology of the Divine Energies in 20th Century Orthodox Thought" – PhD thesis, University of Sofia, 2012 (in Bulgarian).

80 I would like to express my gratitude to Matthew Baker for the multiple fruitful discussions. His editorial suggestions to me were not only helpful but also insightfully encouraging.

Chapter 10

Universe, Incarnation, and Humanity: Thomas Torrance, Modern Cosmology, and Beyond

Alexei V. Nesteruk

Introduction

In 1969 Thomas Torrance published his seminal work, *Space, Time, and Incarnation*,[1] where he drew the attention of theologians, philosophers, and scientists to the fact that, if Christian theology is to have a real impact on the state of knowledge and mind of humanity, it should reconcile its teaching on the presence of God in the world through the Incarnation with the scientific views on the structure of the universe. One must admit that the impact of this book on modern studies in science and theology has been minimal. Apart from some generic references to this book and the complete ignoring of two associated papers,[2] one cannot find any serious development of the problems formulated there. It is sad that Torrance's frame of thought has not been fully understood nor accepted by modern participants in the dialogue between science and theology. It appears that Torrance's explicit theological commitment remains unpopular among scholars who follow the so-called "bottom-up" pattern of this dialogue. Interestingly enough, it is exactly because

1   Thomas F. Torrance, *Space, Time, and Incarnation* (London: Oxford University Press, 1969).

2   Thomas F. Torrance, "The Relation of the Incarnation to Space in Nicene Theology," in *The Ecumenical World of Orthodox Civilization, Russia and Orthodoxy*, vol. 3, *Essays in Honor of Georges Florovsky*, ed. A. Blane and T. E. Bird (The Hague: Mouton, 1974), 43–70 (reprinted as ch. 10 in Thomas F. Torrance, *Divine Meaning: Studies in Patristic Hermeneutics* (Edinburgh: T&T Clark, 1995), 343–73); "The Greek Conception of Space in the Background of Early Christian Theology," in *Divine Meaning*, 289–342.

of their explicit theological commitment that Torrance's ideas come very close to the heart of Eastern Orthodox thinkers working on the interface of science and theology. Thomas Torrance knew Greek Patristics well and in his personal contacts with the present author he clearly indicated that in his perception of Christianity he was an orthodox with a capital "O".

The most intriguing issue in Torrance's theology is the meaning of the Incarnation of the eternal Son as fully human as this relates not only to the interaction between God and humanity, but, in fact, to the interaction of God with the whole universe. In other words, Torrance posed a question concerning that which in modern theological thought can be termed "deep incarnation." According to the idea of "deep incarnation," "the incarnation of God in Christ can be understood as a radical or 'deep' incarnation, that is, incarnation into the very tissue of biological existence, and system of nature."[3] From this perspective the divine Logos has assumed not merely humanity, but the whole malleable matrix of materiality by uniting himself with the very basic stuff of creation. The flesh that was assumed in Jesus is not only that particularization of a physical human, but also the entire realm of humanity in its connection with all created matter, and ultimately with the cosmos, including its attributes which characterize this matter as existent. Jesus Christ was "not of this world" (John 17:17), i.e. the world in the state of human sin, but he conjoined fully with the material world in which he was "at home" (John 1:11).

It was Thomas Torrance who more than forty years ago anticipated a Christology along the lines similar to a "deep incarnation" idea, when he related the whole spatial structure of the universe (which, according to the modern anthropic cosmological inference is responsible for the necessary conditions of human existence and thus for the possibility of embodiment) to the Incarnation. Here Torrance went to the core of the created world by linking creation and Incarnation in a sophisticated dialectic of contingency and necessity, introducing into theological discourse a question of a double order in creation: on the one hand, its contingency, originating in *creatio ex nihilo* through the unconditional love of God with respect to the world, and, on the other hand, in its

---

3 The term "deep incarnation" was coined by Danish theologian Niels Gregersen in his paper "The Cross of Christ in an Evolutionary World," *Dialog: A Journal of Theology* 40 (2001): 192–207. See also his paper "Deep Incarnation: Why Evolutionary Continuity Matters in Christology," *Toronto Journal of Theology* 26 (2010): 173–87.

"necessary" divine order, following from the Incarnation of the Logos as foreseen before all ages, as a mechanism of the union between God and humanity. To assume all aspects of creation is to assume its expression in terms of space and time. Theologically, to assume space and time implies that creation needs to be healed. But this means that the assumption of space-time parameters of human existence in the Incarnation always presupposed that those properties of space and time that are due to the Fall can be redeemed and overcome in Christ himself.[4] Thus by being in space he was always beyond it in that "nowhere" from "where" the unity of "all in all" of the extended physical space has been preserved.

The assumption of spatio-temporal forms of the universe through the Incarnation of the Logos of God "in flesh" gives to all Christological discussions two dimensions. On the one hand here is the problem of the knowability of God: since the created world is permeated by the Incarnation which has been foreseen before the creation of the world, there must be signs of the divine in the world through the fact that the world was prepared to accommodate the coming of Christ.[5] Correspondingly, the relationship between the Father and the Son is implanted in the structure of the world and is recapitulated in the Incarnation of the Son in flesh. Thus to know God means to comprehend the fact of his existence

---

4 The idea that the perception of extended space and time of the physical universe corresponds to the postlapsarian state not only of humanity, but the universe itself, corresponds to the theologically understood loss of such a communion with God in which the whole universe was given to humanity as "all in all." In some studies it was suggested that the very expansion of the universe originating in the Big Bang, which is obviously associated with extensions of space, can be considered as the human perception of the event of the Fall projected onto a cosmic scale. See, for example, B. Rodzyanko, *Theory of the Universe's decay and Faith of the Fathers: Cappadocian Theology – The Key to Apologetics of Our Time* (Moscow: Palomnik, 2003, in Russian); S. Sokolov, *The Other World and the Time of the Universe: Time and Eternity* (Moscow: Kovcheg, 2008, in Russian).

5 St. Athanasius of Alexandria develops the thought that by becoming human, the Word of God "became visible through His works and revealed Himself as the Word of the Father, the Ruler and King of the whole creation," *De Incarnatione* 16 (Crestwood, NY.: St. Vladimir's Seminary Press, 1998), 45. However, despite the fact that the Father provided the works of creation as a means by which the maker might be known, this did not prevent humanity from wallowing in error, *De incarnatione* 12, 14, idem., 39, 42. Because of this, the Word of God descended to humans in order to "renew the same teaching." However one must admit in the vein of our argument that in order to send the Word for the renewal of God's teaching there must have been the conditions for the very possibility of the Incarnation related to the fact of existence of humanity.

through the world, but retaining in this comprehension a transcendent element not compromising God's otherness to the world. This is related to the "spatial" element in the Father-Son relationship. The physical forms of space and time which were assumed by the incarnate Logos do not manifest the actual relationship between God and the fully human Jesus, but those forms of comprehensibility of the divine which were set up by God in order to know him. Torrance speaks of the theological field of connections in and through Christ "who cannot be thought of simply as fitting into the patterns of space and time formed by other agencies, but as organising them round Himself and giving them transcendental references to God in and through Himself."[6] Torrance argued that the space-time forms of the world in their totality are relational upon the divine activity whose "axis" has, so to speak, a vertical dimension with respect to the horizontal dimension of the space-time of the world.[7] He implicitly employed an analogy with physics which claims that its immanent space-time forms are relational upon the material agents and their dynamics.

However it was clear that unlike physics, which predicts some definite geometrical shapes for the given dynamics of matter, theology, because of its open-ended character based in the ongoing revelation of the divine, cannot construct a causal dynamics between God's activity and the structure of space. This was the reason why Torrance did not attempt to propose a constructive interpretation of space-time of the universe as related to the dogma of the Incarnation, but rather discussed the possible methodology of such a theological science which, being informed of the natural scientific development, could lead to such a synthesis where the sense of space would be clarified not only physically, but theologically. Despite a generic theological conviction that the immanent forms of space and time must have their foundation in the otherness of the world, upon which the world is contingent, the dogma of the Incarnation implies an immanent paradox which relates the spatial milieu of Christian history to the whole universe, thus subordinating cosmic history to the history of salvation.[8]

---

6 Torrance, *Space, Time, and Incarnation*, 72.

7 Ibid., 75.

8 See a systematic exposition of this point of Orthodox cosmology in O. Clément, *Le Christ Terre des Vivants: Essais Théologiques*, Spiritualité Orientale 17, (Bégrolles-en- Mauges: Abbaye de Bellfontaine, 1976), 90–94.

Here a certain reversal with respect to the naturalistic view takes place: it is cosmic history which becomes an event of the history of salvation and thus it is cosmology which becomes, in a way, subordinated to Christian anthropology. The objective of this paper is to demonstrate that the paradox of the Incarnation, being intrinsically present in any articulation of the universe through the divine image in humanity, is, *de facto*, explicated in modern cosmology's portraying the universe as evolving from the idiosyncratic originary state of the Big Bang, whose idea, whatever this means, marks the ultimate limit in human understanding of the origin of the world mimicking the intuition of creation. We argue that the paradox of the Incarnation, asserting the *theological homogeneity* of the universe, is present in modern cosmology under the disguise of the cosmological principle of *spatial and material homogeneity* of the universe, which ultimately becomes a major epistemological requirement for the knowability of the universe as a whole.

The fact that the paradox of the Incarnation implies the principle of knowability of the universe leads us to another dimension of the dogma of the Incarnation, namely to its contribution to the theory of the *Imago Dei*, that is the divine image in human beings which makes knowledge of the universe possible in its totality. Thus the second objective of this paper is to link the paradox of the Incarnation to the perennial philosophical issue of the ambivalent position of humanity in the universe, being part of the universe and being the center of its disclosure and manifestation. We argue that the resolution of the paradox of human subjectivity in the universe depends upon the dogma of the Incarnation, which provides a pointer towards the divinely given capacity of embodied human beings to be commensurable with the infinite open-ended horizon of the divine manifestations in the world. And finally, in order to elucidate the sense of space in its relation to the divine, whose expression was attempted by Torrance, we employ some phenomenological ideas, borrowed from the discourse of space-constitution by human subjects.

Incarnation and its Space Paradox: A Cosmological Elucidation

It is worth taking a closer look at the space paradox which arises from the theology of the Incarnation as articulated by T. F. Torrance. On the one hand, Jesus Christ, being in his nature fully a man, lived in the world and was located in a body in a particular place and time in the earth's history. On the other hand, being fully God, he did not leave his "place" at the right hand of the Father; thus, being God, he was present not only in Palestine two thousand years ago, but was always present in all locations and ages of the universe created by him. We have here a non-trivial temporal and spatial relationship between the finite "track" of Jesus Christ in empirical space and time and the whole encapsulated history of the universe as the unity of "all in all" of spaces and times sustained by the Logos-Christ.

Historically it was Origen who first reflected on the extraordinary position of Christ, being man and God, in the universe conceived of in terms of space:

> Though the God of the whole universe descends in his own power with Jesus to live the life of men, and the Word which *"was in the beginning* with God and was himself God" comes to us; yet he does not leave his home and desert his state.[9]

Origen stresses here the point that God, who is the creator and governor of the whole universe, by becoming incarnate in the flesh in Jesus Christ did not cease to be, as God, the provider of existence and intelligibility for everything at every place in the universe. Being incarnate in the flesh, that is, being a man among humanity, Christ as God was still ruling the whole universe and holding together the entire creation. By creating the universe and giving it meaning so that it could receive his Son in the flesh, God has prepared a place for himself,[10] but in such a way, that while descending into the created world in a particular place and time he still holds the entire creation together (through *enhypostasizing* it), being hypostatically present in all possible "places" of the universe. Thus the Incarnation recapitulates not only human nature but the whole of creation in the totality of its spatial and temporal spans.

---

9   Origen, *Contra Celsum* 4 in *The Early Christian Fathers*, trans. and ed. H. Bettenson (Oxford: Oxford University Press 1969), 213, emphasis added.

10   Here it is appropriate to establish a linguistic parallel with G. Marcel's meditations on the sense of the term "receptivity." When we said above that God prepared a place for himself this must not be understood as "filling up some empty space with an alien presence, but of having the other person(s) [that is humanity] participate in a certain reality, in a certain plenitude." In this sense to receive humanity means "to admit someone from the outside to one's own home." To make space for God means to invite persons to participate in the Divine reality. G. Marcel, *Creative Fidelity* (New York: Fordham University Press, 2002), 90–91.

By being incarnate at one point of space and at the same time not leaving his "place" as transcendent Creator, and by holding together the wholeness of space, God demonstrates that his relationship to space is not a spatial relation. Origen asserts this explicitly:

> The power and divinity of God comes to dwell among men through the man whom God wills to choose and in whom he finds room without changing from one place to another or leaving his former place empty and filling another. Even supposing that we do say that he leaves one place and fills another, we would not mean this in any spatial sense.[11]

Athanasius of Alexandria expressed the unity of the divine and human in Christ appealing to the analogy of space in terms similar to those used by Origen:

> Then the incorporeal and incorruptible and immaterial Word of God entered our world. In one sense, indeed, he *was not far from it before*, for no part of creation had ever been without him who, while ever abiding in union with the Father, yet *fills all things that are*.[12]

Athanasius argues in this passage that in spite of the fact that the Son-Word of God descended to Earth in order to live with men, *he did not become closer to us* by doing so, for he *is always in everything* in the universe, which was made by him. "Space" is a predicate of the Word of God; it is determined by his agency and is to be understood according to his nature. This means that the "spatial relationship" between the Father and the Son is in no way analogous to the spatial relations among creaturely things. Human nature in Christ always operated within the reality of empirical space and historical time, whereas his divine nature was always beyond the empirical and intelligible aeons in the uncreated realm from where Christ the Logos of God coordinates the empirical space in which he dwelt in the body with the rest of the created universe. The Christ-event, being thus a manifestation of the spatio-temporal relationship between God and the physical universe expressed as an open-ended interaction between God and man, recapitulates the humankind-event in the universe, making the latter an expression of the interaction between humanity and God and of a contingent happening in the eternity of God.

11   Origen, *Contra Celsum* 1.277, trans. H. Chadwick (Cambridge: Cambridge University Press 1953), 187.

12   Athanasius, *De Incarnatione* 8, 33, emphasis added.

One can use a different analogy in order to illustrate this point. Indeed, extended space and time are perceived by human beings from *within* creation and can be treated as "internal" forms of the relation of the universe with the transcendent divine (the "extended" corresponds here to the old Patristic term *diastema*). The Greek term *diastema* meant in Classical Greek geometry the distance between two points, in music the interval between two notes. In the theological context the term *diastema* was used by Gregory of Nyssa in order to characterize the created world as extended in space and in time. He used this term in a negative sense in order to predicate about God by affirming that there is no *diastema* (that is, no extension of a spatio-temporal kind) in the being of God. It is more important for us to point out a different usage of the term *diastema*, which Gregory applied in order to describe the theological distinction between God and the world. This distinction contains an asymmetrical dialectic in the relationship between God and the world: on the one hand there is the *diastema* between God and the world, which is unbridgeable from within the world; on the other hand, God knows the world, which he created. The *diastema* in this case can be represented by an asymmetrical, one-way extension in relationship between God and the world: indeed, there is a basic *diastema* if one attempts to cross the gulf between the world and God from within the world; on the other hand, there is no extension, i.e. there is no *diastema*, in the divine hypostatic holding of the world.

Then the question arises as to how the extended internal space-time of the universe is maintained in relationship with the divine "environment" (that is, its non-extended "external" form) in which it is "embedded" (in the sense of being created). Here an analogy with the hypostatic union of the two natures in Christ can be used. Indeed, it is because of the hypostatic union between the divine and the human natures in Christ that one can argue by analogy that the interplay between the space and time of the universe (their internal form) and its uncreated ground (its external form) is also upheld hypostatically by God in the course of the "economy" of the Incarnation, when the link between the humanity of Christ (in the space of the created world) and his divinity as the Logos (who is beyond space and yet holds all space together) was established. This leads us to the assertion that the universe in its spatio-temporal extension manifests its Christologically evidenced hypostatic inherence in the Logos.

This theological understanding of the extended space-time structure of the universe as a manifestation of the relationship between God and the world, God and humanity, can cause discomfort among modern scientists who can easily conceive that space and time are relational upon the matter content of the universe (this is the main idea of General Relativity). To conceive of the whole spatial structure of the universe as expressing its relationality upon other- worldly divine agency would be very challenging for them. In particular, it would be difficult for them to conceive the meaning of the Patristic phrasing that the incarnate Word of God, that is the person of Jesus Christ, *was not far from the world before the incarnation*: for no part of the created universe had ever been without him who, while ever abiding in union with the Father, yet *fills all things* without leaving his *home* and deserting his state. It seems here that any logic is broken if Christ is approached only as an incarnate and corporeal being whose appearance in the universe took place at a very late stage of its evolution. However, that which is asserted in theology is not a physical statement but the assertion of that relationship between the universe and its otherworldly foundation which can be described by using the language of subsistence, or inherence, in the person of God. Inherence implies a different type of presence which escapes properties of spatial and temporal extension.

Interestingly enough, modern cosmology, in spite of the fact that it deals with the universe extended in space and time, characteristically implies, by its theory of the Big Bang, that whatever is physically seen as extended in space and time, in fact, evolved from an originary state beyond extended space and time. In this sense, all extended places in the universe that we observe in the sky point towards this original state with no space and time: thus we are, on this planet, in the same "place" as we would have been at the Big Bang. If now we explicate this simple mathematical fact theologically, one can realise that the words of Athanasius that Christ as the Logos *was not far from the world before the incarnation* can receive a literal interpretation.

If, for simplicity, we adopt a model of the evolution of the universe from the Big Bang, it can receive a pictorial representation through the following diagram:

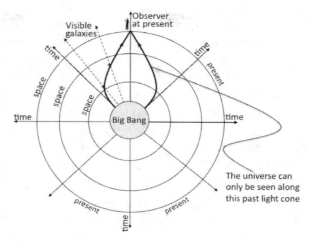

Fig. 1 The unity of the universe as generated from the Big Bang

This diagram attempts to express the unity of space and time as being generated from their non-originary origination "event" depicted by a circle of the Big Bang at the center of the diagram. The diagram consists of a series of expanding concentric circles which aim to represent spatial sections of space-time. The circles expand from the initial zero point that symbolizes the origin of the universe. The radii correspond to the world lines of particular objects (clusters of galaxies, for example) which originate at the singularity (corresponding to zero linear scale) and diverge in all directions. The fact that the spatial sections (that is, the concentric circles) in this diagram are compact must not be interpreted as an assumption of a topologically closed universe. If these imaginable circles are associated with some structural units of the universe (galaxies or their clusters), their expansion reflects only the process of the mutual recession of galaxies.

The major conceptual difficulty with the interpretation of this diagram is to conceive the meaning of the point of origin of the world lines. One must not treat this diagram as if it depicts the actual process of expansion in pre-existent space or time. Actually this origin is not *in* space and *in* time, so that its depiction as a point in the plane of the page is a metaphor. However, the diagram as a whole can be treated as representing the global structure of space and time within the context of natural human attitude, i.e. as if they existed objectively and independently of the human observer who appeared in the universe at its late stage. The distinction between past, present, and future has a purely symbolic nature (associated with the radius of a circle, or progression of the world line) as divisions in abstract "objective" time.

What is important in this diagram is that the spatial position of the human observer depicted at the top of the diagram is absolutely the same as if it would be at the very beginning of the universe in the Big Bang. It corresponds to a constant radius commencing at the Big Bang and going straight to the observer. The fact that the observer is situated exactly at the same place where the Big Bang took place is also confirmed by the curvilinear past light-cone (depicted as an onion shape), which has its origin in the Big Bang: indeed, whatever we observe in the sky is coming to us from the Big Bang. Why are these last two points important for our discussion of the Incarnation? The answer is simple: if we assume that the Big Bang is the point of origination of the universe as we see it and which we interpret as related to creation, then one can expect that the divine Logos was "present" at this point as the creator. But, as we have seen, this point of creation is now exactly where humanity is situated: thus the Logos was never "absent" from the "point" of creation and its extension in space, including our present location. Correspondingly, if the Incarnation happens at the same point of space where we are, then one can say that this is the same point where the Logos was present from the beginning. Then the phrasing of Athanasius that Christ as the Logos *was not far from the world,* i.e. the human world on this planet, *before the incarnation* indeed receives a literal interpretation: the Incarnation has happened at the same location in space where the Logos was "present" from the beginning of the world.

Thus cosmology involuntarily reproduces in a geometrical language a simple theological truth that the universe, as being created, is related through all its ages and locations to the Logos-Creator who became incarnate at the same location where he was present from the beginning. Interestingly enough, the issue of the contingency of the event of the Incarnation in space loses in this picture any sense: the Incarnation happens in such a location in the universe, which remains the centre of its expansion and is geometrically and physically equivalent to all other points of the universe (the universe is theologically homogeneous).

Since the universe was created by the Logos and through the Logos, one can say that it is subsistent (inherent) in the Logos, not on the level of physical substance, but hypostatically, that is, in his person (the universe does not have its own hypostasis and thus, as it was said in Patristic times, is *enhypostasized*).[13] This entails that the Logos is hypostatically present everywhere in the universe. However, the Incarnation makes a further reification to this saying. Since Christ receives human flesh, he turns out to be in a double position: as the person-Logos he is present everywhere; however, as being fully human Jesus is subjected to physical causality. This means that he has access to that part of the universe which contains the physical conditions for corporeality and is subject to restrictions on the knowability of the universe following it. Christ's presence everywhere manifests the lack of *diastema* in the God–world direction, whereas his subjection to the worldly causality manifests exactly the opposite, namely the *diastema* between humanity and God in terms of extended space. Theologically, the *diastatic* perception of space which pertains to humanity corresponds to the state after the Fall. Correspondingly, the extended universe perceived by humanity can be treated as originating in the human incapacity to actualise the archetypical vision of the universe as "all in all" (which is discursively disguised under the name of the Big Bang).

Christ, being human, but devoid of any affections by the Fall, experiences the universe in the conditions of space-time extension, but this extension, having nothing to do with human sin, is not in any tension with his hypostatic perception of the universe as a whole. If in Christ the overcoming of the tension between the perception of the universe as extended and instant has an ontological character, because of the hypostatic union of his two natures, then in human beings, who have the archetype of Christ, this happens only epistemologically. This means the following: since humanity is physically prevented from communion with the whole universe, it develops its intelligible image whose possibility proceeds from the divine image in humanity itself. If in Jesus Christ the intelligible image of the universe does not share the phenomenality of objects, because this universe is inseparable from the Logos-Christ consciousness, then in human beings the intelligible image of the universe does appear in the phenomenality of the already created objects. Human beings can *enhypostasize* the universe, that is, articulate it, on a different level through knowledge, but still the universe will remain

13 The Greek words *enhypostatic* or *enhypostasis* were introduced into theology by Leontius in the context of Christological discussions of the sixth and seventh centuries AD. Their meaning, according to *A Patristic Greek Lexicon* – ed. G. W. H. Lampe (Oxford: Clarendon Press, 1961), 485 – can be described as: "being, existing in an hypostasis or Person," "subsistent in, inherent." *Enhypostasis* points towards something which is not self-contingent, but has its being in the other and is not contemplated as it is in itself. *Enhypostasis* is the reality in the other hypostasis.

an object of humanity's intentions for finding its accomplished mental representation. This point can be illustrated as a mental transition from the ontological principle of *theological homogeneity* of the universe (which is effected by the Logos) to the epistemological principle of the *spatial and material uniformity* of the universe, i.e. the cosmological principle, which justifies all speculations about the universe as a whole in physical terms. In a way, this cosmological principle acts as a principle of explication of the universe which has some *teleological* overtones: for the universe to be known by human beings it must be uniform, and this uniformity proceeds from its theological uniformity confirmed by the Incarnation.

The split in human comprehension of the universe as extended physical reality, which contains human beings corporeally, and as an integrated intelligible image of the universe as a whole, which stands in front of humanity in its articulated form, creates a paradox in the human condition similar to the paradox of the Incarnation.

The Paradox of Human Subjectivity and the Paradox of the Incarnation

We now focus on the paradox associated with the ambivalence of the human position in the universe. If one tries to articulate the grandeur of the world in terms of typical sizes, putting atoms, molecules, DNAs, etc. together with mega-objects like planets, stars, galaxies, clusters of galaxies, and even the whole universe, then human beings find themselves in a somewhat strange situation because the inhabited planet Earth occupies a tiny portion of the space of the volume of the visible universe. Also, the spatial scale of the human body is negligible as compared to the size of the visible universe. In a similar way, it is not difficult to realize that the phenomenon of humanity came into existence at a very late stage in the history of the universe, so that the universe was devoid of human life and hence devoid of its self-expression during most of its "history." If human presence in the universe is judged from the point of view of its spatial and temporal dimension, human beings turn out to be a contingent and *insignificant* part of the universe.

The paradox which is present here arises when one realizes that the very representation of the universe as a whole, and all particular objects in the universe organized against a spatial grid, are the products of human intellectual activity. The paradox is obvious: the finite, even insignificant embodied human agencies in the vast universe articulate the entire universe from a point-like position in space and time. Humanity actualizes in knowledge the totality of the universe as its intentional correlate and this manifests a fundamentally non-local essence of the human presence, being a quality and a mode of being which transcends the finitude of its corporeality, as well as all particular objects and laws associated with it. In this sense the famous characteristic of humanity as "microcosm" (based simply on the observation of the consubstantiality of human bodies and the universe)[14] is fundamentally inadequate.[15] There is a mystery of the articulating consciousness which cannot be accounted for through any references to consubstantiality. The natural attitude of consciousness, which effectively attempts to explain the origin of this consciousness as the epiphenomenon of the physical and

14   The so-called "anthropic inference" in cosmology refines assertions about humanity's position in the universe, asserting consubstantiality of the universe and humanity in quantitative terms pertaining to a specific embodiment. Anthropic inference deals with the so-called "fine-tuning," establishing a balance between the physical constants responsible for the large-scale structure of the universe and conditions of biological existence. The literature on it is vast, so that we refer only to the classical monograph by J. D. Barrow and F. J. Tipler, *The Cosmological Anthropic Principle* (Oxford: Oxford University Press, 1986); see also J. Barrow, S. Morris, S. Freeland, Ch. Harper, ed., *Fitness of the Cosmos for Life: Biochemistry and Fine-Tuning* (Cambridge: Cambridge University Press, 2008). The anthropic inference deals with the necessary conditions for physical and biological existence of humanity and does not cover the realm of its sufficient conditions, related to humanity's intellectual capacity. The sufficient conditions become actual in the present state of technology when humanity effectively can control the factors of life's existence on the planet Earth from the side of, so to speak, "negative conditions": indeed, humanity is capable of exterminating life on Earth so that the future continuation of life depends not only on the natural conditions and possible disasters which can terminate this life, but also on a conscious desire to have this life. This desire, however, belongs to the sphere of human morality and humanity's vision of its own destiny; that is why it is not entirely controlled by the physical factors. In this sense the sufficient conditions of the existence of humanity in the universe depend on humanity's own vision of its place in the universe, its importance or non-importance for the fate of the universe itself. See discussion in A. Nesteruk, *Light from the East* (Minneapolis: Fortress Press, 2003), 195–208.

15   Being popular in classical Greek philosophy, the idea of microcosm was strongly criticized in Christian literature because it did not take into account those dimensions of human existence which endow it with intellectual abilities to disclose the sense of the universe. Consubstantiality is triviality and, according to Gregory of Nyssa, "there is nothing remarkable in Man's being the image and likeness of the universe, for earth passes away and the heavens change . . . in thinking we exalt human nature by this grandiose name (microcosm, synthesis of the universe) we forget that we are thus favoring it with the qualities of gnats and mice." Quoted in O. Clément, *On Human Being: A Spiritual Anthropology* (London: New City Press, 2000), 34.

biological, fails to recognise that it attempts to explain itself from itself.[16] It is because science cannot accommodate the dimension of personhood that it has to abandon the reference to hypostatic embodiment in totality and to treat consciousness as a medium of access which is hypostatically uniform (and thus non-observable), so that the human presence becomes irrelevant to the universe, so that sciences themselves become obscure.[17] In a similar vein, Merleau-Ponty writes:

> Scientific points of view, according to which my existence is a moment of the world's, are always both naïve and at the same time dishonest, because they take for granted, without explicitly mentioning it, the other point of view, namely that of consciousness, through which from the outset a world forms itself round me and begins to exist for me.[18]

The ambivalence in assessing humanity's position and role in the universe can be expressed in terms of a famous philosophical *paradox* asserting that while being *in* the universe, humanity is not *of* the universe; i.e. in a certain sense, it transcends the universe by "holding" it through humanity's grasp. Any cosmological discourse has to reconcile the locality and contingency of the cosmic position of humanity with its abilities to transcend this locality and encompass in theory the universe as a whole. Consciousness manifests its "irreducible ambiguity," which follows from the fact that this consciousness is *in* the world, as well as *of* the world insofar as it is consciousness of the world.[19] Any naturalistic attempt to suppress or subvert the essential ambiguity of consciousness distorts the sense of the created universe.

---

16   On accentuating the personal dimension of embodied consciousness, A. Gurwitsch comments: "what is decisive and of crucial importance is not whether the existence of consciousness is conceded or denied but rather that, even if this existence is conceded, consciousness and whatever pertains to it are considered as 'private' and thus not on principle subject to scientific investigation." A. Gurwitsch, *Phenomenology and the Theory of Science* (Evanston: Northwestern University Press, 1974), 133.

17   Ibid., 399–400.

18   M. Merleau-Ponty, *Phenomenology of Perception* (London: Routledge, 1962), ix. Apart from an inadequacy in comprehension of the foundations of science, the whole stream of thought can be supplemented by a spiritual sentiment, namely that separating the world and the universe from the conditions of the functioning of human subjectivity, science based on the natural attitude – using the words of the Russian philosopher S. Bulgakov – "acquires lifeless intentionality and orientates us in the kingdom of dead things." S. Bulgakov, *Philosophy of Economy* (Moscow: Nauka, 1993), 207, in Russian.

19   A. Gurwitsch, *The Field of Consciousness* (Dordrecht: Springer, 2010), 160.

The above-mentioned paradox was coined by E. Husserl as "the paradox of human subjectivity being a subject for the world and at the same time being an object in the world." [20] However, the paradox has been known since ancient times, and Kant, for example, expressed it in his *Critique of Practical Reason* as the difference in appreciation of "the starry heavens above and the moral law within."[21]The paradox received numerous formulations and interpretations[22] and we would like to make a few generalizing and clarifying references. E. Fromm gave to this paradox a status of "existential dichotomy," arising from the fact that humanity emerged in being as an "anomaly" and "the freak" of the universe, whose being exists in a state of constant and unavoidable disequilibrium, anxiety, dissatisfaction, and restlessness, which follow from being part of nature and transcending it.[23] Similarly to Fromm, R. Ingarden describes the existential dichotomy as a very special and doubly-complexioned perception of being: on the one hand, each person is quite alien to everything that happens in nature independently of them, so that he sees himself deprived by it of any kindly help and almost loses trust in fate; on the other hand, "in his pure and autonomous essence he feels himself to be something that stands out above nature, something that is so much more dignified than purely physical processes or what transpires in animals, that he cannot feel in solidarity with nature and live fully happily by being united with it in its domain."[24] According to Fromm and Ingarden's insights, humanity, when it narrows its perception of the place in the universe to the status of a thing among other things, dooms itself to depression and anxiety over its own insignificance in the vast cosmos, because life is enslaved and controlled by it. Contrary to this, the cosmos acquires some inward meaning if humanity sees itself as the centre of its disclosure and manifestation. Then the universe receives intrinsic human qualities, thus being united to humanity: the question then is not of being positioned in the universe, but that of living here and now in communion with the universe. But this communion means that a human

20   E. Husserl, *The Crisis of European Sciences and Transcendental Phenomenology* (Evanston: Northwestern University Press, 1970), 179.

21   I. Kant, *Critique of Practical Reason*, trans. and ed. T. K. Abbott (London: Longmans, 1959), 260.

22   See D. Carr, *Paradox of Subjectivity* (Oxford: Oxford University Press, 1999).

23   E. Fromm, *Man for Himself* (London: Routledge and Kegan Paul, 1967), 40.

24   R. Ingarden, *Man and Value* (Washington, D.C.: Catholic University of America Press, 1983), 17–18.

being can "transcend" the universe while retaining its immanence with the universe. As was asserted by M. Scheler:

> Only man, because he is a person, can rise *above himself* as a living being and make all to be its subject of knowledge, including himself, as if he would be a single centre on *the other side* of the space-time world. But this centre of human acts appropriating the world, its own body and its psyche cannot be itself a "part" of this world, that is, it cannot have any definite "where" and "when"; it can only be in the highest foundation of being. Thus man is a being which is above himself and the world.[25]

The paradox of human subjectivity was understood long before by Patristic theologians as well as by recent Christian thinkers.[26] Here is a passage from St. Gregory the Theologian (Nazianzus) with a characteristic formulation of the paradox:

> the Logos created man as a single living creature from both elements. On the one hand He took the body from already pre-existing matter, on the other He endowed it with breath from Himself, which Scripture terms the intelligent soul and the image of God (Gen. 1:27; 2:7). He sat man upon the earth as a second world, a great world in a little one . . . both earthly and heavenly, both transient and immortal, both visible and invisible . . . situated between greatness and lowliness, at the same time both spirit and flesh.[27]

In Maximus the Confessor the paradox was interpreted in the context of faith in God who created man in his own image and likeness, so that initially man was "like" God, that is, he was "all in all" (cf. Col. 3:11). For example, Maximus the Confessor described this presence of humanity in all things in terms of a potential unity of all creation, which was to be realized by human persons as originally created: "man was introduced last among existent things, as the natural bond mediating between the extremes of the whole through his own parts, and bringing into unity in his own person those things which are by nature far distant from each other."[28]

25 M. Scheler, *Die Stellung Des Menschen im Kosmos* (Moscow: Gnosis, 1994), 160.

26 The detailed discussion of the paradox of human subjectivity in a theological context can be found in my *The Universe as Communion: Towards a Neo-Patristic Synthesis of Theology and Science* (London: T&T Clark, 2008), 175–84.

27 Gregory Nazianzus, *Oration 45, On Easter 7* in Panayiotis Nellas, *Deification in Christ*, (Crestwood: St. Vladimir's Seminary Press, 1997)), 203.

28 Maximus, *Ambigua 41* (*PG* 91:1304-1312B) in *Deification in Christ*, 212.

Humanity was created in order to mediate between all divisions in creation, for example between the sensible (visible) and intelligible (invisible): "As a compound of soul and body he [man] is limited essentially by intelligible and sensible realities, while at the same time he himself defines [articulates] these realities through his capacity to apprehend intellectually and perceive with his senses."[29]

Some Russian Orthodox thinkers of the 20th century also contributed to the recapitulation of a theological sense of the paradox. According to N. Berdyaev, "Man as personality is not part of nature, he has within him the image of God. There is nature in man, but he is not nature."[30] The human is not only an object in this world, first of all she is a subject which cannot be deduced from an object. Taken with this, the relation of the human to the cosmos is defined by her being a microcosm in a non-trivial sense: she enfolds cosmic history from within human, God-driven history. Humanity cannot be a part of something, it is the whole. Through the spiritual in it, humanity is not subordinated to nature and independent of it – although natural forces can kill it.[31] If humanity would be just a natural and finite being, its death would not be so tragic: what is tragic is the death of an immortal being who aspires to infinity. Only from an object-perspective is the human part of nature; from the perspective of man's spiritual interior, nature is in him. Humanity is both a slave of nature and its lord.[32] A famous Russian scientist and priest, P. Florensky, wrote in the same vein:

> Nature and man are both infinite. And it is because of being infinite, that they are commensurable and can be parts of each other . . . Man is in the world, but man is complex to the same extent as the world. The world is in man, but the world is also complex as man.[33]

29   *Ambigua* 10:26 (*PG* 91:1153B) in "Various Texts on Theology, the Divine Economy, and Virtue and Vice, Fifth Century" 71 in *Philokalia*, ed. G. E. H. Palmer, P. Sherrard, and K. Ware (London: Faber, 1981), 2:277.

30   N. Berdyaev, *Slavery and Freedom* (London: Centenary, 1944), 94–95.

31   Cf. B. Pascal, *Pensées: Selections*, trans. and ed. Martin Jarret-Kerr (London: SCM Press, 1959), 78.

32   N. Berdyaev, "The Kingdom of Spirit and the Kingdom of Caesar," in *Spirit and Reality* (Moscow: AST, 2003), 565–671, in Russian.

33   P. Florensky, "Macrocosm and microcosm," in *Apology of the Cosmos* (St. Petersburg: Russian Christian Humanitarian Institute, 1994), 186, in Russian.

And further, "Man is the recapitulation of the world, its summary; the world is the disclosure of man, its projection."[34] S. Bulgakov contributed to the same stream of thought: "On the one hand, man is potentially all, the potential centre of the anthropo-cosmos, which, although, not yet realised but is being realised, on the other hand man is the product of this world, of the empirical."[35]

If the paradox of human subjectivity reflects the intrinsic feature of the human condition in general, then, according to the Chalcedonian Definition, Christ himself, by being fully human, i.e. through his belonging to the created world, must have experienced and exhibited the presence of the above paradox. By his human nature Christ was contained in the universe, while because of his divine nature it was him who contained the universe in his divine hypostasis. The two natures were united in the hypostasis of the Logos, thus manifesting the mutual co-inherence of two different senses of space – as containing Jesus and as being contained by Christ. The power of upholding the entire universe by the Logos-Christ while being on this planet (which can be seen as the explication of co-inherence between the geography of the holy history and the entire universe) can be interpreted as an anticipatory sign (type) of what humanity, made in the image of God, is endowed with. By the power of comprehension, human beings can hold the entire universe in the integrity of their intersubjectivity, suspending its apparent spatial extension and differentiation, thus relating the universe to its transcendent Creator. The Incarnation of the Logos in Jesus Christ thus revealed to human beings that the mystery of their paradoxical existence in the world is rooted in their special origin in God, who himself, through his Incarnation, provides humanity with the only possible reference for spiritually comprehending and ascetically overcoming this paradox.

In the same way as the presence of Christ in a particular location in space and time in the universe did not prevent him, as the Logos, from being hypostatically present everywhere in the universe, the physical presence of humanity in a particular location in the universe does not preclude it from being "present" everywhere through articulating the entire universe by exercising its divine image, i.e. the archetype of Christ himself.[36] One should understand, however, that the universe as an

---

34   Ibid., 187.

35   Bulgakov, *Philosophy of Economy*, 160, in Russian.

36   Here an implicit transition from the perceived *theological uniformity* of the universe to its *cosmographic uniformity* takes place.

intentional correlate of human subjectivity is not an "ontological" mode of being in the same sense as the hypostatic inherence of the universe in the Person of the Logos. The universe is created by the Logos and that is why it is ontologically contingent upon and derivative from the Logos. Whereas humanity discloses in language and thought what it means that the universe in its entirety is created in such a shape and with such content that the Incarnation of the Logos became possible.

The Incarnation of the Logos in human flesh at one particular point of the universe, and his simultaneous presence everywhere in the universe, provides us with the archetype of how the all-penetrating human subjectivity can claim its "presence in absence" in the entire universe while remaining corporeally at a particular location in the cosmos, i.e. on the planet Earth. It is through our inherence in the Logos who assumed the humanity that human beings share an ability to articulate the world as inherent in the Logos. T. F. Torrance called this inherence in the Logos a "vertical relation to God." According to him, without this relation "man has no authentic place on the earth, no meaning and no purpose, but with this vertical relation to God his place is given meaning and purpose."[37]

Space as the Explication of Personal Relatedness to God

Finally, we would like to explicate Torrance's intuitions about the sense of space as the form of comprehensibility and communion with God in phenomenological terms, taking into account methods of constitution of space by human subjects. The paradox of human subjectivity can be formulated in terms of space, i.e. in terms of humanity's topological position in the universe. The formulation in terms of space is achieved through a metaphor of the container and of the contained: on the one hand, by its physical and biological parameters, humanity is contained in the universe, on the other hand the universe itself is "contained" by human hypostatic subjectivity as its intentional correlate. In this formulation the ontological centrality of humanity is contraposed to its cosmographic mediocrity (cosmological principle). The distinction between two worlds is accentuated here: the world which is affirmed by cosmology as existing whole and scientifically thematized in terms of elements and essences, and another world, associated with the immediate life of consciousness, the so called "life-world," the medium of indwelling into which every

---

37   Torrance, *Space, Time, and Incarnation*, 75.

human being is brought into existence. This life-world, being "here and now" for every particular being, is linked to the planet Earth and is thus geocentric. Earth is ontologically central in a spiritual sense:[38] that is, in the sense of the "where" from whence manifestations and disclosures of the universe originate. In spite of the fact that astronomy and cosmology deal with Earth as an object and ascribe to it a movement in space, both cosmology and astronomy were produced by human beings on Earth, and it was here, on this planet, that scientific thought developed the definitions of motion, rest, and space understood in a general, objective sense. Cosmologists' statements concerning the indifferent position of Earth in cosmic space (cosmological principle) receive their meaning from experiences acquired here, on the planet Earth. The *here* which is the place of this initial experience *is not* therefore a place in space, since it is itself a place of origin of a notion of space.[39] In this sense the cosmological principle, as a philosophical hypothesis, enters into contradiction with the singular and unique "here" which is radically incomparable with any "there," thus predetermining the non-homogeneous topology of any ideation about space at large.

A phenomenological stance on space is different: phenomenology treats space not as the pre-existent objective "out there" (articulated through a subject's passive contemplation of it), but in terms of subject's comportment "in" it. This so-called "attuned space" becomes an initial instant and a medium of disclosure of that "objective" space through relation to which this subject is constituted as corporeal existence in space. However, this relationship manifests a paradox similar to that of the container and of the contained, put in an interrogative form: how can one grasp the relationship of a particular being (subject) as if it is "in" space when this being is essentially constituted by being "over against," and hence beyond space?[40] It is interesting that this question

38 This point was clearly articulated by V. Lossky: "the mysteries of the divine economy are thus unfurled on earth, and that is why the Bible wants to bind us to the earth . . . it forbids us to lose ourselves in cosmic immensities (which our fallen nature cannot grasp anyway, except in their aspect of disintegration) . . . it wants to win us from usurpation of fallen angels and bind us to God alone . . . In our fallenness we cannot even place our world amidst these spiritual immensities." V. Lossky, *Orthodox Theology* (Crestwood: St. Vladimir's Seminary Press, 1997), 64.

39 This point has its theological reference in Christ the Logos as the source of all space by himself not being in space.

40 E. Ströker, *Investigations in Philosophy of Space* (Columbus: Ohio University Press, 1965), 15. This reminds me of a Kantian stance on human being as being

can be easily elucidated in the context of the Incarnation: how can one grasp the relationship of the fully human Jesus Christ as if he is "in" space, when Jesus Christ as the Son of God is essentially constituted by being "over against," and hence beyond space. This is related not only to the place of physical embodiment, but also to the "place" of the whole universe. Place (as space-time extension of the universe) is a predicate of the Occupant in the sense that it is predetermined by his agency. This theological thought has connections with General Relativity's stance on the space-time structure of the universe as being relational, namely being a predicate of its "occupant," that is, the material content. This analogy between theology and physics has a very limited value for the relationality of physical space-time, which has a strictly created nature; whereas when the space-time of the whole universe is predicated in terms of the divine activity, it has, so to speak, a transcendent meaning where the generation of space as relational upon divine activity and nature has the sense of creation of this space out of nothing in view of the forthcoming Incarnation of the Son-Logos of God in Jesus Christ. What is obvious, however, is that the constitution of space, first of all of the attuned space, is intertwined with and not detachable from the fundamental aspect of human embodiment or corporeity, where embodiment or corporeity manifests itself neither as a system of some biological processes, nor as simply a body animated by the soul, nor even as a simple unity of both of them. It is a living being in relation to other beings and to the world, in whom this relation is announced and articulated in a way of its sense-reaction and its comportment, or its action in situation. In this sense, the constitution of space in all its varieties (from attuned space of immediate indwelling to mathematical space of the universe) represents the modes of explication of embodiment or corporeity through which human beings interact with the world. Thus the lived body entails a sort of lived space which bears the character of self-givenness "in the flesh." In other words, the stance on the initial point of any discourse in corporeity and associated spatiality implies a kind of knowledge as presence "in person" or "in the flesh" as a mode of givenness of an object in its standing in front of the functioning corporeity. Correspondingly, when one speaks of the Incarnation, Jesus Christ represents the lived space which bears the

---

simultaneously phenomenal and noumenal: on the one hand, space is an *a priori* form of sensibility which allows a subject to order experience; on the other hand, this form of sensibility is unfolded not from within that space which is depicted by it, that is it comes from beyond any possible spatial presentation of experience.

character of self-givenness in his human flesh, but also the foundation of this lived space in the space of the whole universe which bears the character of self-givenness in his divine Hypostasis.

In cosmology, by articulating the entirety of the universe human beings remain corporeal, so that their corporeity as relationship to all things contains in its facticity the very premise of being physically and spatially *incommensurable* and at the same time hypostatically *commensurable* to the totality of the universe (as constituted by human agency) which humanity attempts to reveal. The attitude to this totality is two-fold: on the one hand humanity attunes to it through belonging to it; on the other hand, humanity positions itself as if it were beyond the universe, as if it "looked" at this universe as an object and depicted the latter as something being present over against "the flesh" and in person. However, since humanity cannot abandon its position of corporeal existence *in situ* on the planet Earth, all cosmological models contain the traces of embodiment even in those cases when they predicate the universe in trans-human or even non-human (the early universe) terms. In other words, the commensurability with the universe is not *of* space, but originates *in* space.[41]

One may now, in order to articulate the sense of the paradox of space in the Incarnation, suspend the natural attitude with respect to space and consider a genesis of spatiality as a certain form of relation to the world formulated from within the developing subjectivity. For example, if one looks at a child's entrance into this world in the act of birth, from the external point of view his life depends on the world's conditions and in this sense is open to the world's invitation to exist. The main existential factor in this initial mysterious unseparatedness between a child and the world is the early sensual consciousness of the other – the mother who through love inaugurates in a child the sense of space. Space appears as a mode of relationship, in which, on the one hand, a loving human being manifests itself as a pre-conscious ecstatic reference; whereas on the other hand, the same human person is caught in consciousness as the other, supplemented by the spatial attributes of this otherness expressed

41 For human beings to achieve the sense of commensurability with the universe, one must be in space as a delimiter of their embodiment. Interestingly, this conclusion is similar to a Christian theological stance on space in the context of knowledge of God. It is because the incarnation of the Logos of God took place in rubrics of space and time that no knowledge of God is possible outside the ways of Christ in space and time. This was a point of T. F. Torrance in his *Space, Time and Incarnation*.

in terms of extended (and measurable) space. This dialectical "standing in front of" and "standing apart from" in personal relation is an existential fact which cannot receive any further foundational justification. Its contingent facticity is a historical event which cannot be repeated and reproduced in experiments. This is an event of emergence of personhood through relationship and thus through "standing apart from" (expressed through local distance and other measurements) that creates a spatial dimension of this relationship.

Knowledge of other persons is possible through this "standing in front of" or "standing apart from" and implies the intuition of space either as inseparable presence or absence. This is related not only to other human beings, but also to knowledge of nature as the reality of the other. One can admire the grandeur of the visible universe by experiencing it either through the personal "opposite" of ecstatic reference (that is, as presence) or as the opposite measured through spatial dimensions (that is, as absence; remote objects). In this dichotomy, the presence of the personal ecstatic reference to the other, its fundamental irreducibility from sensual experience and personal consciousness, predetermines the intuition of space as a definite form of experience and subjectivity. Here the "I" that cannot give an account for the facticity of its personal ecstatic reference to the world is formed by this reference which is projected in consciousness as a form of "standing apart," that is, of space. Thus the perception of space can be considered as an apophatic mode of expression of the initial inseparability in relationship between humanity and the world, which follows not only from consubstantiality, but also from the implanted divine image sense of "all in all." Space becomes a vehicle of human involvement in the world through hypostatic differentiated embodiment, which makes possible the relationship with the world's objects as well as other persons.

The language of ecstatic reference to (communion with) the world and other persons implies in a way a phenomenological attitude because the space of personal relationship is unfolded from within events of life. In this attitude the very notion of the outer world originates from within the boundaries of the same personal relationship; thus the making of the world an abstract and independently existing object can originate only from within the condition when the very personal relationship to the world receives a status that is similar to the status of all other objects. The world as a personal "opposite" of ecstatic reference is perceived in the dialogue between humanity and the world as some other "I" hypostatically subsistent in my "I." The representation of the personal relationship with the world in the phenomenality of objects consists in the world becoming a passive object of observation and study, from which feelings and the Eros of consubstantial communion is removed. The very consubstantiality with the world becomes an abstract notion, which is not experienced through communion. The world becomes an object and the personal space of "standing in front of" the world transforms into a sheer "standing apart from" the world in space as measurable and controlled extent. Space is presented in the phenomenality of objects when the relationship with the world is transferred into the sphere of pure thought which thinks this relationship but does not experience it. It is in the conditions of this breakdown of the unity between subject and object that the representation of space acquires a more and more geometrical, measurable character associated with the boundaries of things (as objects) that fill in the universe.

It is exactly this way that cosmology thinks of space, where the measure of this space is determined by its capacity to contain astronomical objects, i.e. by the "density" of these objects as the measure of their standing apart from each other. This measure is determined by the number of light years required to "join" these extended objects in one united cosmic whole. Despite such a vision of the universe in the phenomenality of objects, the experience of *placelessness* in the universe – the experience of the universe through an ecstatic inarticulate personal reference – remains irreducible and unavoidable. This "standing in front of" the universe as the personal "opposite" is free from any physical references and its actual, physically infinite extent, and thus remains indeterminate in the limits of scientific thinking rooted in the category of quantity and mundane geometrical intuitions of spatial hierarchy in terms of "closer" and "far," "here" and "elsewhere," "right" and "left," etc. In this sense the universe as a term of personal relationship manifests its sheer presence, but such a presence that cannot be described in terms of place.

Here we find a delicate form of *presence in absence*. It is indicative that the experience of the universe as absent in terms of space and its undisclosed content turns out to be more impressively and apophatically manifesting the whole majesty of the personal ecstatic reference to the universe in comparison with any specific aspect of the universe's presence in details of spatial objects. In both cases – either through the experience of belonging to the universe through consubstantiality with it, or through experience of its absence because of the impossibility to circumscribe the universe in forms of thought – this experience determines the space of personal relationship as a certain indeterminacy of "standing in front" of the universe (as non-extended and non-measurable). Space as relationship thus signifies the modality of life, a certain existential aspiration and interest which cannot be dissected into motivating components. Space expresses existential events of movement towards the other as manifestations of the very basic foundations of human being. However, this movement towards the other is not self-evident and indistinguishable in itself. Its revelation is possible and is taking place only in the conditions of awareness of space as a potential threat of "standing apart," that is separation, if that movement towards the other and "standing in front" of the universe cease to function as elements of life. Here is a dialectics of space: it is always capable of being transformed from the condition of personal relationship into a soul-less form of separation and quantitative measurement if the life of a hypostatic, embodied subject starts to be treated as determinative of biological survival, and the universe, instead of being a participant of the relationship, becomes an impersonified background of existing whose contingency not only cannot be comprehended, but, in fact, cannot be even detected.

Modern cosmology can hardly comprehend the sense of non-extended space of personal relationship with the universe, not only because one cannot physically transcend the universe and "look" at it as a single whole from outside, but because it does not dare to consider the unity of the universe as originating in its subsistence in the Person of the Logos. It cannot deal with the representation of the universe from the God's eye view as a non-extended whole. Cosmology treats the universe in terms of its "elementary" constituents, such as galaxies and their clusters, and they are treated as present in physical space as if consciousness could shift itself from its home place on Earth and treat these objects in the same phenomenality which pertains to the objects on Earth. Presence here implies "standing apart," as experience of substitution of the home place. Then the very space of the universe is objectified as extension.[42] However, the intuition of the universe as the created wholeness always functions as that invisible background (present in absence) for the natural attitude, which implies such a relationship of

42 Torrance, *Space, Time, and Incarnation*, 134–35.

"standing before" when all extensional plurality of experience is reduced to null in the event of ecstatic relationship and kenotic aspiration towards the universe's creator.[43] There is a double meaning hidden in this event: the ecstatic personal relationship with respect to God precedes any consciousness either of his presence or absence in the universe and thus of consciousness of presence or absence of the universe as created totality. Said formally, there is no automatic assurance based in understanding, not only in objective expression of God's presence in the universe, but also in an objective existence of the universe as a whole. The existential reality of God and the world, created by him, are defined through the immediate proximity of the relationship, so that the very person and its subjectivity, not being able to verbalise and objectivise this relationship, are constituted by this relationship in "non-objectivised space."

It is this non-extended and non-measurable intimate "opposite" of the personal relationship that constitutes space as relation. The universe as "noema" of the divine intention "stands before" God without any extension; however this "standing before," as relation, has a tendency of being expressed, in the human perception of God, as extended space.[44] On the one hand there is no space between God and the world (God abides in the human heart without any spatial connotation); on the other hand, being an embodied creature in the extended universe, human beings experience their relationship with God and his creation in the modality of space. On the one hand man manifests himself in the placeless totality of its own articulating hypostasis: the world is present in absence through the imitation of the Logos-given capacity; on the other hand, as functioning corporeity (i.e. as embodied being), he feels himself isolated in the world of dividing-but-*present-in-presence* extension.

It is because humanity, being embodied creation, exists in the world in the conditions of the paradox of its own physical finitude and theological infinity, it transfers this paradoxical situation to the event of the Incarnation of the Word- Logos of God in Jesus Christ. Since in Christ's Incarnation human nature is conjoined to the divine nature through his person, Christ, being fully human, does not experience the duality which is explicated in the paradox of subjectivity. The hypostasis

43 As an example of this, one can point to the Anaphora in the Divine Liturgy, or to the prayer for the whole world of monks living in reclusion and "beyond" the world, contemplating the whole being from the cell of their solitude.

44 This is typical for all sorts of mythologies which develop a theme of a gradual and spatial relation between gods and the world.

of the Logos controls the conditions of its own Incarnation and the Christ-man does not experience any ambivalence of his placeless being in the plenitude of God and, at "the same time," of his existence in the conditions of the spatial extension of "standing apart from" God in his creation. Since the Logos in the Incarnation does not leave his place at the right hand of the Father, the placeless presence of God in the Christ-man means his omnipresence in the conditions of extended space.

The refusal of the natural attitude in contemplation of space, when the extension, as a physical property, becomes a non-extended "object" of an intentional gaze in the phenomenological attitude, could be paralleled with consciousness of God himself, for whom the whole world is an event-relationship. Transcendence as the overcoming of extended space and division of the objects of the world is related not to getting beyond its external cosmological limits, but to the bringing of space inside the intentional consciousness; thus reducing the problem of space to the problem of the foundation of its contingent facticity in this consciousness. Space remains an inherent element of every perception and thought in the natural attitude, being a mode of the extended world subsistent in the Logos as the unity of "all in all." It is the pole of the all-unity of space, when the extension is subjected to bracketing and suspension, that remains an inerasable trace of non-spatial spatiality.[45]

The issue of the facticity of space leads inevitably to the problem of the facticity of consciousness itself. The facticity of human embodied consciousness is exactly accompanied by the paradox which has so long been discussed. Any attempt of overcoming this paradox would correspond to transcendence of the boundaries of the very factual givenness of this paradox and this would entail either an exit beyond the embodied consciousness or an exit out of the world order. Since this is not an option for human beings – the paradox is unavoidable in the post-lapsarian condition – what is left to humanity is to find

----

45   It is worth quoting Gregory of Nyssa who wrote in the context of the unknowability of God that "no created being can go out of itself by rational contemplation. Whatever it sees, it must see itself; and even if it thinks it is seeing beyond itself, it does not in fact possess a nature which can achieve this. And thus in its contemplation of Being it tries to force itself to transcend a spatial representation, but it never achieves it. *For in every possible thought, the mind is surely aware of the spatial element which it perceives in addition to the thought content*; and the spatial element is, of course, created." Gregory of Nyssa, *Commentary on Ecclesiastes*, sermon 7 (*PG* 44:730A) in *From Glory to Glory: Texts from Gregory of Nyssa's Mystical Writings*. ed. J. Daniélou (New York: St. Vladimir's Seminary Press, 1981), 127.

its ultimate archetype in which the "standing before" and "standing apart" in the relationship between the world and God is overcome by the divine humanity of Jesus Christ. This archetype confirms, in words of T. F. Torrance, that "the transcendent God is present and immanent within this world in such a way that we encounter His transcendence in this worldly form in Jesus Christ, and yet in such a way that we are aware of a majesty of transcendence in Him that reaches out infinitely beyond the whole created order."[46] By rephrasing this one can say that the transcendent foundation of the extended space and time of the universe is present and immanent within this world in such a way that we encounter its transcendence through the incarnate Christ who, while being in this world, manifests its majesty and transcendence as the Logos who reaches out infinitely beyond the whole created world. To acquire the sense of the unity of all extended space as an instant of the divine love, one must exert a synthesis of mediation between divisions in creation and then between the world and God. The Orthodox tradition calls this way of spiritual ascent *deification*. To grasp the sense of the universe as a whole, including all of space and time, one needs to "acquire" the mind of Christ, that is to believe and love him in such a way that by being loved by him, and hence being known by him, one comes to truly know the things of the universe and the sense of its space.

---

46   Torrance, *Space, Time, and Incarnation*, 79.

Chapter 11

The Rationality of the Cosmos: A Study of T. F. Torrance and Dumitru Stăniloae

Taylor Carr

Despite his extensive contacts with Orthodox theologians during his long and distinguished career as a theologian, professor, and ecumenist, there is no reference in T. F. Torrance's published writings to the Romanian Orthodox theologian Fr. Dumitru Stăniloae (1903–1993). This is perhaps surprising, since Stăniloae is generally considered to be one of the greatest Orthodox theologians of the last century.[1] However, Stăniloae lived, taught, and wrote for most of his life under one of the most repressive regimes of Communist Europe, which drastically restricted his freedom of movement and communication.[2] He also wrote in Romanian, which further reduced his potential readership. These facts likely explain why, although Stăniloae refers to Torrance in two of his key essays, Torrance seems to have been completely unaware of his work.[3] Only now is Stăniloae beginning to receive a portion of the attention he deserves, as his *Orthodox Dogmatic Theology* is being translated into Western tongues[4] and academic studies are bringing him

1 Kallistos Ware, Foreword to *The Experience of God* (Brookline, MA: Holy Cross Orthodox Press, 1994), 1:ix.

2 Like many Orthodox churchmen in Romania, he was actually imprisoned by the Communist authorities for several years (1958–1963).

3 These references to Torrance's essay "Spiritus Creator: A Consideration of the Teaching of St. Athanasius and St. Basil," can be found in Chapters 1 and 3 of *Theology and the Church* (Crestwood, NY: St Vladimir's Seminary Press, 1980).

4 *Teologia Dogmatica Ortodoxa*, 3 vols. (Bucharest: Editura IBM al Bor, 1978), has been partially translated into French: *Le génie de l'Orthodoxie* (Paris: Desclée de Brouwer, 1985); and completely translated into German: *Orthodox Dogmatik*, 3 vols. (Zurich: Gerd Mohn, 1985). In the English edition, the editors have split each Romanian volume in two, creating six volumes. They have been published under the title *The Experience of God* (Brookline, MA: Holy Cross Orthodox Press, 1994, 2000, 2011, 2012, 2013). A detailed table of contents, translated from the Romanian

to the attention of academic theologians in the West.[5] However, much work remains to be done both in translation and elucidation of this great theologian, who has so much to say to the contemporary world.[6]

A major task of Orthodox theology today is thus to bring the enormous riches of Stăniloae's theology into dialogue with those whom, because of linguistic and political barriers, he did not interact with in life. An important figure among these potential interlocutors is the Scottish Reformed theologian T. F. Torrance. Although they approach the topic from different directions, both Torrance and Stăniloae are deeply concerned about the place of the created, material world in Christian life and thought. This is evinced in Torrance primarily by his dialogue with scientific thinking: regarding the fact that God reveals himself within the "creaturely objectivities" of this world, he writes, "Thus arising out of the heart of theology there is an unquenchable interest in the scientific understanding of creaturely being, and for the whole fabric of worldly existence as the medium in which God has placed man."[7] The same concern is shown in Stăniloae by his thoroughly anthropocentric and teleological understanding of the cosmos: "Salvation and deification undoubtedly have humanity directly as their aim, but not a humanity separated from nature, rather one that is ontologically united with it. For nature depends on man and makes him whole, and man cannot reach perfection if he does not reflect nature and is not at work upon it."[8] Both theologians are rooted in the fathers, and both clearly see in Christian dogmatics the potential for a theologically informed "basic outlook" on the world that brings the wisdom of Christian tradition to bear upon the besetting dualisms of modern culture, such as those between person and nature in anthropology and cosmology, and God and creation in science and theology.

edition, can be found in Charles Miller, *The Gift of the World: An Introduction to the Theology of Dumitru Stăniloae* (Edinburgh: T&T Clark, 2000), 105–15.

5   The most recent major study is Radu Bordeianu, *Dumitru Stăniloae: An Ecumenical Ecclesiology* (Edinburgh: T&T Clark, 2013).

6   Stăniloae's bibliography rivals Torrance's in terms of output: for a complete listing up to its date of publication, see the festschrift *Persoana si Communiune* (Sibiu: Editura si tiparul Arrhiepiscopiei ortodoxe Sibiu, 1993), 16-67 (available online).

7   Thomas F. Torrance, *Theological Science* (Edinburgh: T&T Clark, 1996), 57.

8   Stăniloae, *The Experience of God*, 2:1. Ultimately and precisely, Stăniloae's cosmology is *Christocentric*; however, relative to some contemporary strains of thought regarding theology and ecology what stands out in Stăniloae is his profound concern for man as the center and goal of the created order.

The World: Its Objective Rationality

Torrance's interest in what he calls "fundamental attitude" or "basic outlook" (drawing primarily on the German *Weltbild*) goes back almost to the beginning of his career. In one of his key early essays, he writes, "even the conclusions of our abstract thinking do not really arise from the logical basis on which they seem to repose. They come from something much deeper, a certain habit or set of mind which gives these arguments their real force." Even scientists and metaphysicians do not reason without an "elemental orientation of mind" chosen prior to positive knowledge and analysis.[9] Torrance's interest in this aspect of thought persists throughout his later work, and is a hallmark of his writings on the dialogue between science and theology. Probing deeper into the history of ideas and modern scientific thinking, Torrance realized that a distinctive element of contemporary physics was that it forced scientists to reckon with the fact that they can no longer see themselves as neutral with regard to the basic design of the cosmos, a key aspect of *Weltbild*: "Hence we are forced to grapple with cosmological questions and to adopt a fundamental attitude to the universe as a whole."[10] This brings science into conversation with theology, for theology is also concerned with seeing the world in a particular way, a way that allows for the reality of divine revelation in space and time.

Common to both scientists and theologians in their fundamental outlook on the world, Torrance tells us, is a commitment to the objective rationality of the universe and man's ability to apprehend it. Both claim to have knowledge about reality and not merely about their own subjective states. In regard to scientific knowing, in our inquiry into something we seek to align our minds with the *nature* of that thing: "knowledge in any field is governed by the nature of its object as it is progressively disclosed to us."[11] Our ultimate aim is to allow our minds to be passively receptive of the objective structure of the reality under consideration; thus, science is in service of the "material logic" or "inner logic" in things manifested in their real interconnections and

9 Thomas F. Torrance, "Faith and Philosophy," *Hibbert Journal* 45 (1948–9): 237. Torrance is paraphrasing an insight from Dilthey.

10 Thomas F. Torrance, *Ground and Grammar of Theology* (Charlottesville, VA: University Press of Virginia, 1980), 45.

11 Torrance, *Theological Science*, xix.

relations.[12] To get to this state of passivity, however, requires a lot of active work. To begin with, one must ask questions in the right kind of way: "This means that as we seek to penetrate into the rationality of something, our inquiry must also cut back into ourselves and into our presuppositions;"[13] in other words, "man with his questions must be questioned down to the roots of his existence before the object."[14] Thus, concepts formed in the process of inquiry must not be thought of naively as simple reflection of objective reality; rather, they are "disclosure models," heuristic instruments through which we inquire into the reality under consideration. The formation of these models requires human ingenuity: "he [the scientist] must act with imagination and insight in detecting and developing the right clues and act creatively in constructing forms of thought and knowledge through which he can discern the basic rationality" of the thing.[15] There is thus a movement between activity and passivity in the cognition of an object:

> The reason is actively at work in constructing the model or developing the analogue as it puts its questions to nature and elicits its answers, but throughout the reason submits itself to the objective realities and seeks to cognize them passively through its theoretic constructions.[16]

Throughout this whole process the inquirer must assume that what he is seeking to know is in fact intelligible: "The scientist does not doubt the object of his inquiry, for he is committed to a profound belief in its intelligibility, otherwise he would not be involved in its investigation."[17]

This commitment implies both critical detachment and intense, personal attachment. The scientist must be dedicated to pursuing knowledge of his object: his passionate attachment must be so great that he is willing to be detached from his own preconceptions about the object.[18] This latter requires a purification not an elimination, of subjectivity, in which the scientist continually rids himself of false

---

12   Ibid., 262; cf. 269.

13   Ibid., xi.

14   Ibid., 120.

15   Ibid., 318.

16   Ibid., 288.

17   Thomas F. Torrance, *God and Rationality* (Edinburgh: T & T Clark, 1997), 8.

18   Cf. Torrance, *Theological Science*, 135.

preconceptions in the process of further inquiry.[19] The primary requirement here is intense self-criticism: "It is not normally the object that is responsible for our failure to observe or cognize it aright but we ourselves;" "true questions are a form of self-criticism."[20] Self-criticism is coupled with social criticism; for, also inhibiting the scientist's grasp of the object is the social "baggage" embodied in his language and culture, which often contain metaphysical beliefs that have to be brought to light, examined, and often reconstructed before new concepts more closely aligned with reality can be formed.[21] Torrance does not flinch from speaking of this self-criticism, in science as well as theology, as a kind of *repentance* in the face of reality: "Objectivity in theological science, like objectivity in every true science, is achieved through rigorous correlation of thought with its proper object and the self-renunciation, repentance and change of mind that it involves."[22]

In fulfilling this task, man brings "mute" creation to articulate speech, serving a special role before God: "Man as scientist can be spoken of as the priest of creation, whose office it is to interpret the books of nature written by the finger of God." By communicating the wonders of creation, the scientist, knowingly or not, serves the creator: he "bring[s] it all into orderly articulation in such a way that it fulfills its proper end as the vast theater of glory in which the Creator is worshipped and hymned and praised by his creatures."[23]

While Torrance sees the objective rationality of the world as an article of faith in science and theology,[24] being primarily concerned with the actual act of knowing, Stăniloae is interested in the larger theological framework within which Christian thought is committed to

---

19   Ibid., 93. Torrance here is drawing on the thought of Michael Polanyi.

20   Ibid., 121; cf. 125.

21   Ibid., 221; cf. 266.

22   Torrance, *God and Rationality*, 10. One notes a similarity here between Torrance's epistemology and Stăniloae's presentation of the knowledge of God in creation in *Orthodox Spirituality* (South Canaan, PA: St Tikhon's Seminary Press, 2002), 203–223. Torrance is pointing to the ascetic dimension of thought that is so prominent in the Orthodox tradition.

23   Torrance, *Ground and Grammar of Theology*, 6.

24   A major aspect of Torrance's work on the boundary between science and theology is his teaching, drawn from Polanyi, that *faith* is a necessary part of any rational undertaking, not something opposed to reason: see his essay in *Belief in Science and Christian Life: The Relevance of Michael Polanyi's Thought for Christian Faith and Life*, ed. Thomas. F. Torrance (Edinburgh: Handsel Press, 1980), 1–27.

the objective rationality of the cosmos. This, he tells us, is grounded in the doctrine of creation:

> The cosmos is organized in a way that corresponds to our capacity for knowing. The cosmos – and human nature as intimately connected with the cosmos – are stamped with rationality, while man (God's creature) is further endowed with reason capable of knowing consciously the rationality of the cosmos and of his own nature.[25]

Stăniloae, steeped in the theology of St. Maximus the Confessor, ties the rationality of the world to Maximus' doctrine of the "*logoi* of beings," that is, the divine thoughts or reasons about creation that are manifested in actual created things. Stăniloae writes, "Created things are the created images of the divine reasons given material form."[26] According to Maximus, the *logoi* are the eternal plans and purposes God has for the whole hierarchy of created being, from the lowliest plant to the most exalted angel: "For having the *logoi* of beings, pre-established before the ages, in his good will God founded the visible and invisible creation according to them, by his Word and Wisdom making all things at the proper time, both what is universal and what is particular."[27] While not identified with created beings, the *logoi* are reflected in actual created beings, and, through man's use of his own God-given faculty of rationality, purified from the passions, he can discover the *logoi* in creation. Maximus is primarily interested in what the *logoi* tell us about God and about the origin and end of man within the whole economy of creation.[28] Stăniloae, while basing himself on

---

25   Stăniloae, *The Experience of God*, 1:2.

26   Stăniloae, *The Experience of God*, 3:1.

27   PG 91:1080A. For the central text on the *logoi*, see the whole of *Ambiguum* 7 (PG 91:1068D–1101C). English translation and critical edition by Monk Maximos of Simonopetra, *The Ambigua to Thomas and the Ambigua to John* (Washington, DC: Dumbarton Oaks Medieval Library, forthcoming). The translation here is my own, though heavily indebted to the work of Nicholas Constas.

28   Maximus' doctrine of the *logoi* has many dimensions. Here I only touch on their importance to his cosmology. An English translation and improved Greek text can be found in Nicholas Constas, "On Difficulties in the Church Fathers", *The Ambigua* Vol. 1, Dumbarton Oaks Medieval Library 28 (Cambridge, MA: Harvard University Press, 2014). Stăniloae did his own translation and commentary of *The Ambigua*. A French translation of the footnotes from this edition can be found in *Sainte Maxime le Confesseur, Ambigua*, trans. Emmanuel Ponsoye (Paris: Éditions de l'Ancre, 1994), 375–540.

Maximus, uses the doctrine of the *logoi* to shed light on the meaning and purpose of rationality in non-human creation.[29]

The key to Stăniloae's insight into the rationality of the created order is found in the personalist dimension of his thought, particularly in the dictum that rationality implies and is constitutive of *relationality*: "Everything which is an object of reason can only be the means for an interpersonal dialogue."[30] Like many Roman Catholic and Orthodox theologians of his day, Stăniloae was deeply influenced by personalist philosophy and the notion that man's being is constituted by dialogue, both with God and with his fellow humans. Stăniloae also emphasizes the importance of *nature* in this dialogue, teaching that the rationality of the natural order invites, and provides the basis for, divine-human communion. In critiquing a form of extreme personalism that would overlook the world, he writes,

> Nor do we contest the fact that the human person cannot experience himself fully except in relation with another human person or that this experience is most marked in loving relationship with the other. But over and above this we add: the human being cannot exist apart from his relationship with nature. The three together make up an inseparable whole: I–Thou–Nature.[31]

Rationality implies speech and invites conversation, and it is the rationality of the natural world that forms the primary content of this conversation. The initiator of this conversation is God. If it were not so, if the world had no external *personal* referent in a rational creator, the rationality in the world would be a kind of "absurd rationality," closed in on itself and leading to despair rather than dialogue.[32]

The rationality of the world, for Stăniloae, is a form of speech that God has directed to man through the medium of created things.

29   Like Maximus, Stăniloae has a complex understanding of the logoi. While he shares much in common with Maximus, what stands out in Stăniloae's thought in relation to his predecessor is the amount of attention he gives to non-human creation, particularly in the second English volume of his *Dogmatics*.

30   Stăniloae, *The Experience of God*, 1:11.

31   Stăniloae, *The Experience of God*, 2:198. One is reminded here of Torrance's statement that "In theological science . . . we are concerned . . . not just with God/man relations, but with God/man/world or God/world/man relations, so that an understanding of the *world* enters into the coefficients of theological concepts and statements," *Ground and Grammar of Theology*, 45.

32   Ibid., 98. This is Stăniloae's diagnosis of modern thought (cf. Ibid., 11).

The most salient example of this is Adam's naming of the animals: commenting on Genesis 2:19-20, he writes, "Thus God himself has asked man to speak inasmuch as he urged him or put within his nature the need to discover the words that God himself communicated to man through created things, that is, the meanings given things by God." This was not simply an exercise in rationality, but an invitation calling for man's response: "God bound the human person to make response through the created things he placed before him"; "Through the giving of names to things, our being began to bring itself into . . . act and to develop itself as partner in the dialogue with God."[33]

The created world is rich in both meaning and purpose for Stăniloae. Working from this robust theological understanding of created rationality, Stăniloae ends up with a *realist* epistemology, in which man does not construct his knowledge of the world but discovers it.[34] The process of knowing can be arduous – as Stăniloae tells us, this is because God is soliciting our continued response to his invitation to dialogue through created things.[35] However, once we discover the rationality in things it compels our assent: in a passage reminiscent of Torrance, he writes, "The order of meanings is not the product of the human psyche . . . For this order imposes itself on us without our willing it and, through the aspirations it instills within us, surpasses our own psychic possibilities."[36] It is the personal dimension of reason, however, which forms the basis of Stăniloae's rejection of constructivist and skeptical epistemologies. The root of the problem of much of modern thought, he maintains, is "depersonalized reason," which denudes the

---

33 Stăniloae, *The Experience of God*, 2:36. In Stăniloae's understanding of the *logoi*, he distinguishes a hierarchy of levels. There are created "reasons," reflective of uncreated reasons or *logoi*; and there are also "meanings" – the higher, more comprehensive aspects of things grasped in their interconnections with other things or in terms of the whole. Like Torrance, Stăniloae believes that it is the synthetic power of *intuition* and not the analytical reason alone that grasps things in their meanings, that is, in their complex inter-relations. Cf. Stăniloae, Ibid., 29; Torrance, *Ground and Grammar*, 30; and *Transformation and Convergence in the Frame of Knowledge* (Grand Rapids: Eerdmans, 1984), 78.

34 Stăniloae does not use the term "realist" to describe his epistemology, though in his insistence that we have genuine knowledge of reality above and beyond our own subjective states, he is clearly operating within a realist framework.

35 Stăniloae, *The Experience of God*, 2:37.

36 Ibid., 1:8.

cosmos of the divine presence.[37] It is only this personal referent that makes thought possible in the first place: "human thinking would have no content at all had God not first created the things conceived by him at the level of human understanding, or had the created things themselves not possessed a spoken content already given."[38]

The Contingence of Creation

In reading this exegesis of Stăniloae's work on the doctrine of creation, students of Torrance's thought will likely find that a key element seems to be missing: contingence.[39] Contingence is a concept that holds an important place in several areas of Torrance's thought: not only in his cosmology proper, but also in his understanding of the relationship between science and theology, the history of theology, the history of thought in general, and in his critique and reconstruction of traditional natural theology. Without hoping to cover this topic in the depth that it deserves, we will attempt to isolate a few points of importance. Regarding contingence Torrance tells us, "The contingence of the universe means that it might not have been, or might well have been other than it is, so that we must ask our questions of the universe itself if we are to understand it."[40] That the universe is contingent means that its existence is not necessary – neither to God nor to itself. Yet, contingence is not to be conceived merely in opposition to what is necessary or determined: such a view would flatten contingence into randomness.[41] For Torrance, contingence means something like "open structured order," that is, order that is open to influence from outside itself: "By contingence is meant, then, that as created out of nothing the

---

37   Ibid., 3:23.

38   Ibid., 2:34.

39   Stăniloae does in fact discuss contingence, both in reference to human use of the world (as I discuss below) and in reference to the world's creation *ex nihilo*: cf. Ibid., 43. However, from Torrance's point of view any doctrine of "eternal reasons" such as Stăniloae's use of the *logoi* would undermine the utter contingence of the world. As I argue below, I believe that Stăniloae and his patristic sources are actually working with a very deep notion of contingence, founded in the doctrine of creation, which ultimately complements Torrance's own interests and concerns.

40   Torrance, *Ground and Grammar of Theology*, 56.

41   Thomas F. Torrance, *Divine and Contingent Order* (Oxford: Oxford University Press, 1981), 43.

universe has no self-subsistence and no ultimate stability of its own, but that it is nevertheless endowed with an authentic reality and integrity of its own which must be respected."[42] Contingence has a double aspect: "Contingence has at once an orientation toward God in dependence on him, and an orientation away from God in relative independence of him."[43]

Contingence is a concept very important to modern physics; however, it is an idea that is not produced by science itself. Rather, it is a concept that can only come from theology and the doctrine of creation *ex nihilo*. In this sense, modern scientific thinking depends heavily on a notion that was introduced to the "basic stock of ideas in our understanding of nature" in Western thought by early Christian theology.[44] According to Torrance, three masterful ideas originated in early patristic theology have been determinative for the subsequent development of scientific thinking: one is the rational unity of the cosmos (united in its character as created by God); and the other two have to do with contingence: the *contingent rationality* and the *contingent freedom* of the universe.[45] These ideas were cemented and enshrined in Christian theology by the fathers immediately before and after Nicaea because the doctrine of creation *ex nihilo* and the corresponding distinction between the uncreated Son and the created world were key to Nicene thought.[46] However, in Torrance's interpretation of the history of theology, these notions, so central to Greek patristic theology, were overcome by the influence of Neoplatonic thought, resurfacing again only in the Reformation.[47]

It is medieval, not late patristic theology, however, that receives the brunt of Torrance's criticism. Medieval thought, with its view of the

---

42   Ibid., vii.

43   Ibid., 110.

44   Ibid., viii.

45   Torrance, *Ground and Grammar of Theology*, 55.

46   Expressed formally in the creedal phrase, "begotten, not made." Lying behind this is the theology of Athanasius *Contra Arianos* 3.59-67, where he teaches that the Son is according to God's *nature* while the created world is a product of the divine *will* (and thus contingent).

47   Two key figures here for Torrance are Dionysius and John Damascene. Cf. Torrance, *Ground and Grammar of Theology*, 78. Torrance saw an alternative tradition in the Alexandrian theology of Athanasius, Cyril, and John Philoponos, a tradition that was crushed finally in the person of Philoponos by the reaction to non-Chalcedonian theology (cf. ibid., 127).

world as "impregnated with final causes" led to a "sacralization of the universe": "This passage of thought [to what was universal rather than particular] took place through a sort of reduction upwards of accidental or contingent phenomena and events to a realm of necessary forms and unchanging essences." This had the effect of inhibiting empirical scientific activity, focusing instead on an exclusively teleological understanding of the universe.[48] Torrance singles out for particular criticism the notion that the universe exists eternally in the divine intellect. He tells us that Athanasius rejected the idea "that creation exists eternally in the mind of God" along with its correlate, the actual eternity of creation.[49] He tells us that this idea, in its Augustinian-Thomist form, "smothered" "the all-important concept of the objective contingent rational order of nature."[50] It implied the necessity and even eternity of the world, depending as it did on the notion that God is "First Cause" of the universe in an Aristotelian sense.[51] The result of all this, Torrance writes, is "the *loss of contingence*."[52] This was only remedied in the Reformation, with its emphasis on God's relation to the world as an active one – *actively* bestowing grace and redemption, which "preserves its [the world's] utter contingency and obstructs its divinisation."[53]

Torrance's rather sweeping appraisals of the history of theological thinking about the relation between God and the world have all of the benefits and problems that such generalizations usually have. Without debating the details of Torrance's interpretation of history, we will discuss a few points of importance. Torrance emphasizes the contingence of creation, its non-necessary and non-eternal character.

---

48 Ibid., 82.

49 Torrance, *Ground and Grammar of Theology*, 66. I do not believe that Torrance is correct here in the first part of his assertion about Athanasius. He does indeed reject the eternity of the world (a doctrine which would have been known as Origenist), but to my knowledge he does not discuss the eternity of the divine plan for creation. As I argue below, I think this doctrine is supported by the doctrine of divine providence, which Athanasius defends against the Epicureans (*De Incarnatione*, 2).

50 Torrance, *Transformation and Convergence in the Frame of Knowledge*, 3.

51 Torrance, *Divine and Contingent Order*, 6. Torrance is more careful regarding this point than he seems at first. His criticism is not directed at the doctrine of the eternity of the world in the divine intellect *in itself* so much as the implications that are easily (and perhaps falsely) drawn from it.

52 Torrance, *Ground and Grammar of Theology*, 64 (emphasis original).

53 Torrance, *God and Rationality*, 82.

Yet, there is a corresponding problem that he does not address: does God *change*? Is creation really something "new" for God in an absolute sense, as Torrance seems to tell us?[54] If so, what would that do to our understanding of divine *providence*, which (in both its Latin and Greek forms) teaches that God *foresees* and *foreknows* the course of time from eternity, and that from eternity his plans and will for creation are known to him alone?[55] Such a doctrine seems to justify the notion of Maximus and Stăniloae's eternal *logoi* of beings. In Torrance's defense, however, there is actually some divergence on this topic between the Greek fathers (primarily Dionysius the Areopagite, Maximus the Confessor, and John Damascene) and Thomas Aquinas; and a brief inquiry into this may allow us to preserve some of Torrance's concerns while also exonerating the Greek patristic tradition from charges of submitting wholesale to Neoplatonic influence.

As Fr. Georges Florovsky points out, the Greek patristic tradition finds its lodestar in the Nicene distinction between uncreated and created, the Son and the world, the divine essence and the divine will.[56] Key to this distinction is the notion that the world is due to a *voluntary* act of God – it is not a generation from the divine essence (as the Arians held, confusing generation and creation); or an involuntary emanation, as the Platonists held. Because the world is due to a voluntary and decisive act of God, it is utterly contingent. However, the divine will is not bound to what happens in time: its decisions are everlasting. Florovsky addresses this apparent conundrum by positing a kind of "second-order eternity" in God which preserves both the non-necessary character of creation as well as eternal existence of the divine will for creation: "The idea of the world, God's design and will concerning the world, is obviously *eternal*, but in some sense *not co-eternal*, and *not conjointly everlasting* with Him, because 'distinct and separated,' as it were, from His 'essence' by His *volition*."[57] This same

---

54   Torrance, *Ground and Grammar of Theology*, 66.

55   Clearly Torrance believes in providence: see, for example, *God and Rationality*, 89.

56   George Florovsky, "Saint Gregory Palamas and the Tradition of the Fathers," *Greek Orthodox Theological Review* 5:2 (Winter 1959–1960): 129. Florovsky, like Torrance, was deeply concerned with contingence. Torrance recognized this, dedicating *Divine and Contingent Order* to him along with E. L. Mascall and Stanley Jaki, calling them "champions of contingence" (the dedication is only found in the original edition, not in subsequent reprints).

57   "Creation and Creaturehood," *Creation and Redemption. The Collected*

concern is evident in the Greek fathers, who actually never use the term "divine ideas," which derives instead from Thomas by way of Augustine. Dionysius speaks of *logoi* or of "predeterminations" and "divine willings." Maximus, as we have seen, prefers the term *logoi*; and John Damascene writes of "volitional thoughts."[58] Aside from *logoi* (which emphasizes creation's derivation from the divine Logos), all of these terms emphasize creation's contingency, its origin in the divine will. Thomas Aquinas, however, compromises this emphasis on two counts in his discussion of the topic in the *Summa*.[59] First, he speaks of divine *ideas*, drawing on Plato through Augustine, which implies their self-subsistent character; or, at the very least, suggests their isolation from the divine will in the divine intellect, which in turn suggests their static necessity rather than contingence. Secondly, Thomas posits ideas in God for things which are never created – that is, things that, while conceived by the divine intellect, are never chosen by God to create in time. This, too, suggests that thoughts in the divine intellect have a kind of absolute or necessary character, existing in isolation from the divine will.[60] The Greek fathers, working within the fundamental Nicene distinction between essence and will, however, do not expose themselves to these potential problems, and, I would argue, share the same concern as Torrance for contingency.

Torrance, while praising the Reformation emphasis on the contingency and independence of creation, also recognizes its dangers: if the tendency for medieval thought was toward a "sacralization of the universe," the temptation of Reformation thought (embodied in its natural theology) was toward the secularization of culture. Although this

---

Works of Georges Florovsky (Belmont, Mass: Nordland, 1976), 3:56. Florovsky may be drawing here on St Maximus' statement in *Ambiguum* 7, "For he [God] is Creator eternally according to his activity, but things exist *in potentia*, not yet in act" (Ἐπειδὴ ὁ μὲν ἀεὶ κατ' ἐνέργιάν ἐστι Δημιοθργός, τὰ δὲ δυνάμει μέν ἐστιν, ἐνεργείᾳ δὲ οὐκ ἔτι) (PG 91:1081A).

58   Dionysius *Divine Names* 5.8; John Damascene *De Fide Orthodoxa* 2.2.

59   *Summa Theologiae* 1.15. Though I would argue, contra Torrance, that even here contingency is not totally lost. For an account of Thomas' doctrine as well as an extensive look at his influences, see Vivian Boland, OP, *Ideas in God According to Saint Thomas Aquinas: Sources and Synthesis* (Leiden: Brill, 1996).

60   *Summa Theologiae* 1.15.3.2. The distinction is between God's practical and speculative knowledge. For Thomas, there is likely also some connection here to the troublesome distinction between God's absolute and ordained power, *potentia absoluta* and *potentia ordinata*.

made possible the advance of science, it also created a deistic disjunction between God and the world; and, after advances in knowledge made a "god of the gaps" unnecessary, materialism: "scientific concentration upon understanding the universe out of itself had the effect of shutting it up within itself, with consequent widespread loss of meaning in any semantic reference beyond the world."[61] Modern physics has remedied this: "with the end of determinism, and the discovery that the universe is, not a closed, but an open or nonequilibrium system, a genuine contingency is massively restored."[62] However, powerful forces in Western culture continue to maintain a mechanistic, instrumentalized view of the cosmos – in effect, retaining the degenerate post-Reformation understanding of contingence while refusing to recognize that its roots lie in the Christian doctrine of creation *ex nihilo*. This is particularly evident in the exclusively technological understanding of science, maintained by many today, and its fruit, ecological chaos.[63] While Torrance does not spend much space in his writings discussing Christian ethics, he does recognize that *here* there is a moral dimension to the understanding of contingence. Torrance points toward this in a passage on Christian service, easily overlooked, where he tells us that Christian respect and honor for the world as God's creation is the remedy for man's disordered misuse of the world:

> if we are to engage in scientific exploration of the universe, in response to the Word of God incarnate in Jesus Christ by whom it was made, we must learn to respect the nature of all created things, using pure science to bring their mute rationality into such articulation that the praises of the Creator may resound throughout the whole universe, without falling into the temptation to exploit nature through an instrumentalist science in the interest of our own self-aggrandizement and lust for power, for then also we would contract out of Christian service as *service* and sin against the hiddenness of Jesus in the world.[64]

In other words, while we must not "sacralize" the universe, we must not fall into the opposite error of denigrating its goodness. From this remarkable passage it is clear that only a Christian outlook on the world,

61 Torrance, *Ground and Grammar of Theology*, 85.

62 Ibid., 72.

63 Torrance, *Transformation and Convergence in the Frame of Knowledge*, 71.

64 Torrance, *God and Rationality*, 164.

accepting both contingence and God as the source of contingence, is capable of overcoming the ecological chaos in which we find ourselves, in which both man and nature is abused. What is needed is a *Weltbild* that clarifies Christian responsibility in the world that makes room for a robust Christian understanding of contingence as founded in the fact of creation. Though left unsaid by Torrance, key to this *Weltbild* is *teleology*.

The formation of such a *Weltbild* is a major aspect of Stăniloae's theological vision; while Torrance points toward the ethical dimensions of man's place in creation without developing this theme, this comprises a major theme of Staniloae's thought. Christian responsibility in and to the world, for Stăniloae, stems from the fact that creation is a *gift* of God to man. *Gift* names both creation's origin and its *telos*. It is precisely because he has lost the understanding of the world as gift that man has lost his sense of Christian service in the world, detaching science from ethical responsibility:

> Left with a narrowly rational knowledge of nature and of his fellow humans, the human being has detached knowledge from the understanding of creation as the gift of God and from the love of God as the one who is continuously bestowing creation as gift, providing the human being with his neighbors as partners in a dialogue of love.[65]

It is here that Stăniloae introduces his own concept of contingence: while Torrance focuses on the contingence of the created world vis-à-vis God, Stăniloae emphasizes its contingence vis-à-vis man. While even man, as created, is contingent toward God, toward non-human creation man takes the role of an "active contingency," molding and transforming the world, which toward man takes the role of a "passive contingency," serving man's needs in a practical way: "God created the world entirely contingent with respect to himself, while in relation to the human person he created the world as something passively malleable to human hands." The world has this character "so that the human person might be able to exercise his own free and active malleability in relationship to it."[66] Stăniloae's writes of how human rationality interacts with the rationality in things – by taking it up and making it serve human concerns and goals – not simply as use

65 Stăniloae, *The Experience of God*, 2:175.
66 Ibid., 44.

put as transformation: "Every man, depending on his own conscience and freedom, makes use of the different levels inferior to himself. And in order to make use of them, man organizes and transforms by his labor the data of the world, imprinting on them his own stamp."[67] Only through this transformation does the rationality of the world become meaningful in an absolute, rather than merely self-referential, sense.

The world, when man sees it as it truly is – as a gift from God meant to be given back to God and to his neighbor – becomes transparent, manifesting its true purpose: "Man is called to grow by exercising spiritual rule over the world, by transfiguring it, by exercising his capacity to see the world and make of it a medium transparent of the spiritual order that radiates from the person of the Word."[68] Man's constant temptation is to deny the world's character as gift, seeing it rather as the final reality, an end in itself meant to serve his egotistic passions. He is therefore called, in some cases, to renunciation of the world; "Through the gift of the world, God wishes to make himself known to the human person in his love. Therefore the human person, too, must rise above the gifts he has received and come to God himself who gave them."[69] This does not mean that the world has no value: rather, "to rise above the things of this world does not mean that these disappear; it means, through them, to rise beyond them."[70] The profound teleological orientation of human nature in Stăniloae's theology may owe something to the massive shift in Roman Catholic thought initiated by Henri de Lubac and his famous defense of "the natural desire for the supernatural."[71] However, while de Lubac locates the element of transcendence in the human *spirit*,

67   Stăniloae, *The Experience of God*, 1:5.

68   Ibid., 102.

69   Ibid., 24.

70   Ibid., 99. Here we see the ascetic dimension, so important to Orthodox theology.

71   See *The Mystery of the Supernatural* (New York: Herder and Herder, 1967). Torrance, in his recognition of "the end of determinism" in scientific thinking, is also at the forefront of theology in this regard, overturning the closed, Newtonian view of the world (a view similar in its effect to the neo-scholastic "natura pura") to which much of modern theology was captive. Some recent postmodern theology has also attempted to come to grips with the new view of the world presented by science (such as Catherine Keller, *Face of the Deep: A Theology of Becoming* (London: Routledge, 2003)). However, with his deeper grounding in modern science, Torrance surpasses even this recent work. Compare, for example, Keller's treatment of chaos and indeterminacy with Torrance's masterful exposition in the last chapter of *Divine and Contingent Order*, 84–142.

Stăniloae sees the locus of freedom and transcendence in *rationality*. Building on a robust theology of creation, Stăniloae also sees a place for the world in man's transcendent goal: thus, the entire created order, not simply the human spirit, is ordered toward God through the agency of man, who is able to order and direct it in service to God.[72] Far from resulting in a "divinisation of the universe," which Torrance accused medieval theology of fostering, Stăniloae's teleological vision allows the world to be seen within the larger economy of creation and redemption as an irreducible, though relative, component of human salvation.

Conclusion: A Complete Vision

These two theologians, while working with very different areas of focal awareness, are, I believe, deeply complementary. In his dialogue with scientific thinking, and particularly in his concern for the fundamental beliefs forming a *Weltbild* common to science and theology, Torrance provides a deeper theological connection with this key area of human rationality than perhaps any other figure of the modern era. Stăniloae, while showing appreciation for scientific rationality, does not really give this topic the attention it deserves.[73] On the other hand, Torrance focuses perhaps too exclusively on scientific *knowledge* as the mode of interaction between man and the world. As Stăniloae's thought reveals in contrast, only when we see rational scientific knowledge within a larger, teleological vision of the world do its ethical dimensions come into relief. While we surely cannot take God into account in scientific inquiry, as though he could be numbered among the efficient causes in the world,[74] allowing the objects of rational inquiry to be seen within the larger plans, goals, and purposes that God has for creation does not

72   Interestingly, Stăniloae speaks of nature apart from human rationality as "mechanistic," captive to "automatism" and "repetition" (see, for example, *The Experience of God*, 2:60). Man, as the element within the material world possessing freedom, brings nature out of its captivity to mechanism, ordering it towards himself and his neighbor and, through this service, to God. This vision is probably too anthropocentric for scientific thinking to know what to do with; however, in terms of a fundamental *Weltbild* it radically unites being, knowing, and doing; anthropology and epistemology with ethics in a way that is particularly crucial for our time.

73   See, for example, Stăniloae, *The Experience of God*, 2:102.

74   Torrance speaks of this as a "methodological bracketing off of God," in *God and Rationality*, 96–97.

transgress science's self-limited aims; rather, it opens science up to the larger questions of human existence and purpose.[75]

Teleology, in fact, has in recent years become a very important concept in scientific thinking, particularly in biology. Torrance notes in several passages biology's mid-century captivity to mechanistic thinking, writing that:

> Biology . . . has not yet found its Einstein or perhaps even its Maxwell . . . biology is still largely stuck in the attempt to interpret the field of living structures in mechanistic terms, and therefore in such a way that the distinctive kind of connection manifested in organisms is suppressed or reduced through explanation in terms of molecules alone, in accordance with the laws of physics and chemistry, to the kind of connection that obtains in some physical field (nuclear or perhaps electromagnetic).[76]

The importance of such concepts as "emergence," "information," and "complexity" in recent scientific thinking indicates that the insights of thinkers such as Torrance and his teacher in this regard, Michael Polanyi, have finally come to fruition.[77] The burgeoning field of epigenetics is a key example among the special sciences. Early thinking about human genetics proclaimed that the discovery of the genome would provide the means to understand not only human illness but every aspect of human behavior.[78] This hope, however, was built upon a mechanistic understanding of the human organism: one that saw the human as merely a sum of its component parts and completely

---

75 Torrance points towards this conclusion, particularly in his critique of the tendency toward secularism within post-Reformation thought. However, while he points toward a complete vision he does not, finally, provide it. One looks in vain for a full theological doctrine of creation in his works (though he hints at such the principles of such a doctrine in various places; cf. *Scientific Theology*, 301). Perhaps this lack is due to his insistence that theology and science have totally distinct material content (Cf. ibid., xx), which, of course, cannot be said in a really final sense from a theological point of view.

76 Torrance, *God and Rationality*, 14–15.

77 Polanyi must be particularly credited with seeing the importance of "emergence" as a concept and a potential new paradigm in evolutionary biology. See his *The Tacit Dimension* (1966; repr., Chicago: University of Chicago Press, 2009). John Haught notes the importance of Polanyi's thinking in his volume *God After Darwin*, 2nd ed. (Boulder, CO: Westview Press, 2009).

78 Hence Richard Dawkins' "God gene" and other similarly speculative hypotheses.

determined by its genetic code. More thorough research has shown that genes, far from predetermining the human physical makeup and behavior, in fact express or hold back their content in response to a wide range of factors, some of which are in control of the complete human organism.[79] This demands a more teleological way of thinking about genetics, one which sees genes within a stratified, hierarchical vision of the organism as a whole. It demands, in Torrance's phrase, thinking in terms of "organismic order" rather than mechanistic determinism.[80] These demands affect not only scientists but also theologians – and particularly those followers of Torrance and Stăniloae who wish to think from within a unified frame of knowledge.

Both of these profound thinkers, while working from different directions, point towards the need for a unified outlook (or *Weltbild*) regarding the world and man's place within it, one that takes account of the fundamental goodness of the material world, its objective rationality and contingence, while also seeing it in the light of its ultimate destiny within the dialogical relation between God and man. What is at stake, Stăniloae tells us, is not only man's physical survival but his spiritual development as well: "when nature is . . . made use of in conformity with itself, it proves itself a means through which man grows spiritually . . . but when man sterilizes, poisons, and abuses nature on a monstrous scale, he hampers his own spiritual growth and that of others."[81] If we shrink from the imperative of seeing the moral teleology embedded in the world, Torrance tells us, "we sin against the hiddenness of Jesus." This is surely correct, for the reasons of the world are not bound by self-referentiality; rather, they find their ultimate meaning in a reference beyond themselves to the Divine Logos, the source and goal of all created rationality. As Torrance writes elsewhere, "Truth as we know it consists in the conformity of things to their reason in the eternal Word of God, so that the truth of every created thing is evident only in the light of God Himself."[82] To abuse the creation is thus to do violence

---

79   Other influences may be due to the environment. "Epi-genetics" literally refers to any aspect "above" the DNA that exercises control over the genome. For more information, see the materials on the website of the Genetic Science Learning Center, University of Utah, http://learn.genetics.utah.edu/content/epigenetics/.

80   Torrance, *Divine and Contingent Order*, 19.

81   Stăniloae, *The Experience of God*, 2:3.

82   Torrance, *Theological Science*, 142.

to the rationality of the world, sinning against its source, the Divine Reason, who not only created the world but became Incarnate within it.

To see creation in this light, then, does not elide the contingency of created rationality but firmly establishes it, opening it up the redemptive and restorative activity of its Creator. Man, as the center of creation, has a clear responsibility in this: as Staniloae tells us, speaking of the creation of Adam, "creation does not reach its completion until, in humanity, God has revealed to it its meaning. Man appears at the end because he has need of all the things that have gone before him, while all that has gone before man only finds its meaning in him."[83] As both Torrance and Stăniloae affirm, only when man does what he was created to do, uncovering the rationality of the world and offering it up to God as Priest of Creation, does the world find its true purpose. Only here are the besetting dualisms of the modern world finally overcome.

83   Stăniloae, *The Experience of God,* 2:12.

Chapter 12

T. F. Torrance and the Christological Realism of the Coptic Orthodox Church of Alexandria

Emmanuel Gergis

"I can foresee the day when there will be only one Orthodox Church serving Greeks, Ethiopians and Copts, and Reformed, within the ancient bastion of Christianity"[1]

Introduction

For hundreds of years, Coptic Orthodox youth and Greek Orthodox youth would meet on Sunday afternoons to play soccer in the streets of Alexandria. Ironically, both groups could agree on soccer rules but not on the rules circumscribing Christology. Meeting directly after their Sunday liturgical services, both groups would share what they heard in the sermon of the day delivered by their respective priests and immediately recognize a shared spiritual experience. They aspired to share in celebrating the liturgy as they shared their neighborhood, school and other activities; yet each of them was aware that their churches were still not reconciled. The Coptic youth would insist that Christ has one nature, while the Greek youth would profess two natures. Both would resort to a long lineage of Christian martyrs to justify their two seemingly opposed views. After lengthy historical and philosophical debates, they would turn back to their soccer match, always recognizing that despite their differences, they could not ignore the reality of their Christian brotherly love.

---

1   An excerpt of a letter by Thomas F. Torrance to Fr. Georges Florovsky in Matthew Baker, "The Correspondence Between T. F. Torrance and Georges Florovsky (1950-1973)," see 319 in this book.

The ethos of both of the two groups in the city of Alexandria resembled that of T. F. Torrance: a Christocentric ethos. This chapter will examine Torrance's Christology from a Coptic Orthodox perspective and in doing so will also assess the writings of John Philoponos, the liturgical texts of the Coptic Orthodox Church, and two contemporary Coptic theologians, Bishop Gregorios[2] and Fr. Matthew the Poor.[3]

T. F. Torrance has been instrumental, indeed a pioneer, in suggesting paths beyond the age-old Christological dilemma through his Christocentric synthesis of Patristic theology. This is largely due to the fact that Torrance, following in the footsteps of the Alexandrian Fathers, communicated the Christian faith and theology through his understanding of the apostolic and Patristic tradition in light of philosophy and science. The Alexandrian view of the Patristic tradition itself often depended on contemporaneous scientific and philosophical definitions in the attempt to articulate divine truth. In doing so, however, the Fathers, like Torrance, never reduce the totality of the divine truth to mere scientific or philosophical equations.

For example, in trying to apprehend the mystery of God, the Fathers employ scientific terms such as οὐσία and φύσις, yet all the while they maintain that the totality of God can never be understood in these terms but can only be apprehended mystically through *apophatic* language. Therefore, it is pivotal that theologians strive to update the philosophical and scientific language used to articulate divine truths while admitting its inherent inadequacy. At the heart of the Chalcedonian dilemma, we face a lack in this essential scientific and philosophical terminology that would have been necessary to describe adequately the Christological reality. Even if that terminology is ultimately inadequate to understanding the

---

2   Bishop Gregorios (1919–2001), by birth Waheeb Atalla Girgis, was the Coptic Orthodox Bishop of Theological Studies, Coptic Culture and Scientific Research. He obtained his Ph.D. in Coptic Studies from the University of Manchester and later became a monk at Al-Muharraq Monastery. He was ordained Bishop by the late Pope Kyrillos VI. He played an important role alongside Fr. George Florovsky and Fr. John Romanides in the ecumenical dialogues between the Oriental Orthodox and the Eastern Orthodox churches.

3   Fr. Matthew the Poor, or Mattá al-Miskīn (1919–2006), by birth Youssef Iskander, was a Coptic Orthodox monk at the Monastery of St. Macarius in the Egyptian Scetis. He was nominated twice for the Coptic Papal office and was an instrumental figure in the revival of theological scholarship and the spiritual formation of the Monastery of St. Macarius. He was the author of hundreds of spiritual books and scholarly articles.

fullness of God, it is necessary to understanding each other as members of the one body of Christ.

This chapter will outline the way in which the (non-Chalcedonian or "Oriental" Orthodox) Coptic Church understands the unity of Christ by maintaining the sort of theological realism that was founded by Sts. Athanasius and Cyril of Alexandria and preserved in the Coptic liturgical tradition. The same Christological realism was scientifically and theologically illustrated by T. F. Torrance who revived the unitary *miaphysite* Christology as taught by John Philoponos, and is alive today in contemporary Coptic writings, including those of Bishop Gregorios and Fr. Matthew the Poor.

As eloquently articulated by Fr. Matthew the Poor, "in the life of Christ, God is revealed – or the divinity is revealed – as a perfectly complete and visible truth, exerted in amazing love and purity and impeccable of any weakness, and in transcendent spiritual holiness, all of which is directed toward humanity."[4] Despite Fr. Matthew's claim that the revelation of God is a perfect visible truth, he also asserts that the human intellect is limited in its understanding of this visible truth without the divine illumination given by Christ: "all principles held rationally by humanity regarding the divinity of Christ remain under a dense intellectual darkness until Christ himself enters to the heart and illumines it, only then will the darkness be dissipated and the truth is revealed."[5] Therefore, one must pray and wait for divine illumination to properly undertake such a serious task of discussing Christology. Unworthy of undertaking such a task, I must, therefore, quote here with utmost admiration the astute sixth century Alexandrian theologian and philosopher John Philoponos when he writes "if anything has slipped from our judgment or examination, may they grant us forgiveness for our slip."[6]

Before engaging critically with the Christology of T. F. Torrance and that of the Coptic Church, we must define the cosmological models that will circumscribe this assessment. As described by Torrance,

---

4   Mattá al-Miskīn, *The Faith in Christ*, 8th ed. (Cairo: The Monastery of St. Macarius, 2013), 9. All excerpts included in this chapter from the works of Fr. Matthew the Poor are my own translation directly from the Arabic language.

5   Ibid., 20–21.

6   Valter Lang, *John Philoponus and the Controversies over Chalcedon in the Sixth Century: A Study and Translation of the Arbiter* (Sterling, Va: Peeters Publishers, 2002), 217.

the Ptolemaic, Newtonian, and Einsteinian cosmological models are the underpinnings of the entirety of Western cosmological thought, and have, to a great extent, repeatedly changed and shaped Christian dogma.[7] Ptolemaic cosmology consists of a sharp dualism where there is disjunction between terrestrial mechanics and celestial mechanics. This cosmological model seeks to escape the terrestrial material reality into the celestial ethereal reality,[8] lending to a gnostic worldview that despised material as a lower state of being and sought to ascend to the heights of celestial ethereal existence.[9] This Ptolemaic model was also used by Augustine as the basis of his theology of the intelligible versus sensible,[10] upon which the totality of Roman Catholic and later Protestant dualistic theology stands.[11] This, in turn, paved the way for Augustine's student, Pope Leo, in his seemingly dualist understanding of Christology at the Council of Chalcedon.[12]

Torrance writes:

> The tragedy of the Chalcedonian formula in the history of thought is that it soon became caught in the rising tide of Byzantine and Augustinian dualism, already evident in the teaching of Leo the Great; and it was from that dualist interpretation of Chalcedonian Christology that John Philoponos, whose Christological writings will be of great importance to our discussion, was castigated as "monophysite." But the ancient Chalcedonian formula can be resurrected today and re-interpreted in a non-dualist framework of thought.[13]

Later, after Newton established a distinction between the absolute and the relative, we also find the same kind of dualism entering Christian theology.[14] For example, Newton discussed the concept of inertia which further shaped the already dualist western mind to think that the world

---

7   Thomas F. Torrance, *The Ground and Grammar of Theology* (Charlottesville, VA: University Press of Virginia, 1980), 72.

8   Ibid., 21.

9   Ibid., 38.

10   Augustine of Hippo, *De Libero Arbitrio* II.7 and *Confessions* XI.xxxix.39.

11   Torrance, *The Ground and Grammar of Theology*, 61.

12   Ibid. See also Bernard Green, *The Soteriology of Leo the Great* (Oxford: Oxford University Press, 2008), 120.

13   Torrance, *The Ground and Grammar of Theology*, 127.

14   Ibid., 23.

is not contained in God and thus God would have to act inertially upon the universe by imposing rationality from the outside.[15]

The last cosmological model discussed by Torrance is the non-dualist Einsteinian model which Einstein established on the epistemological interactionist assimilation of ontological and theoretical knowledge.[16] Torrance notes that this model "operates with the very basic ideas that classical Christian theology produced" at the hands of the church Fathers.[17] It is through this lens that Torrance reads and interprets various church fathers like Athanasius and Cyril of Alexandria. Additionally, he also uses this model to evaluate the Christological statements of John Philoponos, noting that "to study the thought of John Philoponos along with that of Athanasius, Cyril of Alexandria and Severus of Antioch will be an immense boon for the rebuilding of a distinctively Christian outlook upon the world today."[18]

A Dubious and Dualistic *Interpretation* of Chalcedon

Torrance's engagement with the three cosmological models and the writings of Athanasius and Cyril enabled him to see the Christological equation in a unique light. As mentioned earlier, Torrance emphasized the tragedy of the Chalcedonian formula as it became caught in the rising tide of Byzantine and Augustinian dualism as evident in the teaching of Leo the Great.[19] Ultimately, therefore, it is necessary to note and emphasize that there are multiple ways in which Chalcedon can be interpreted. Namely, there is a dualist Latin-Antiochene interpretation and a unitary Byzantine-Alexandrine-Semitic interpretation which is based on Athanasian and Cyrillian theology. Torrance emphasized his refutation of the former: "When this dualist outlook infected the thinking of people within the Christian Church, it was found that they inevitably cut Christ into two, into a divine aspect and a human aspect. Then in formulating a doctrine of Christ they inevitably started either from his humanity and tried to get across to his divinity or started from

---

15 Ibid., 147.

16 Ibid., 72.

17 Ibid.

18 Thomas F. Torrance, *Theological and Natural Science* (Eugene, OR.: Wipf & Stock, 2005), 99.

19 Torrance, *The Ground and Grammar of Theology*, 127.

his divinity and tried to get across to his humanity."[20] It is this dualistic foundation, as discussed later, that broke the unitary and more holistic understanding of personhood and created unnecessary tension in the notion of a single reality, causing both *hypostasis* and *physis* to lose their original meaning.

This dubious and dualistic reading of Chalcedon, which creates a confusion of definitions, was recently reflected in the work of Oliver Crisp, who criticizes Chalcedonian Christology on the basis of its lack of definitions. Crisp states that "we are told that Christ is one person subsisting in two distinct, unconfused natures (human and divine). But we are not told what a nature is, or what a person is in this instance."[21] Ultimately, the questions raised by Crisp must inevitably be on the mind of many modern theologians, especially in the West.

Attempting to further define Chalcedonian theological language, Constantinople II (553 AD) used the idea of the *an/en-hypostatic* distinction to "claim that his [Christ's] human nature is 'personalized' in the life of the second person of the Trinity ... [and] has no existence independent of that second person."[22] Even then, however, the terminology was still unclear. Perhaps the first signs of confusion regarding the meanings of these terms started with the way in which they were defined by John of Damascus. For example, regarding the notion of *anhypostatic* he writes: "The term anhypostaton is also used in two senses. Thus, it sometimes means that which has no existence whatsoever, that is to say, the non-existent. But it sometimes means that which does not have its being in itself but exists in another, that is to say, the accident."[23] He further defines *enhypostatic* as follows: "In its proper sense, however, the enhypostaton is either that which does not subsist in itself but is considered in hypostases ... Or it is that which is compound with another thing differing in substance to make up one particular whole and constitute one compound hypostasis."[24] There is some overlap

---

20   Thomas F. Torrance, *The Mediation of Christ* (Colorado Springs, CO: Helmers & Howard, 1992), 53.

21   Oliver D. Crisp, et al., *Christology, Ancient and Modern: Explorations in Constructive Dogmatics* (Grand Rapids: Zondervan, 2013), 27.

22   Ibid., 35.

23   John of Damascus, *Writings*, trans. Frederic H. Chase. The Fathers of the Church: A New Translation 37 (Washington, DC: Catholic University of America Press, 1958), 69.

24   Ibid., 68.

in his definition of these two terms: namely, both *anhypostaton* and *enhypostaton* define "that which does not subsist in itself."

Crisp expresses a certain reluctance to use this *an/en-hypostatic* distinction.[25] His averseness appears to be based on an earlier statement made by Jürgen Moltmann:

> If the eternal Logos assumed a non-personal human nature, he cannot then be viewed as a historical person, and we cannot talk about "Jesus of Nazareth." The human nature that was assumed should then seem to be like the human garment of the eternal Son – something which he put on when he walked on earth. It becomes difficult to find an identity here between his human nature and our own. Or has the eternal Son of God taken on "human nature without personhood" in the modern sense, so that he has assumed the human being who is really a "non-person"? . . . Or is the "true" human nature itself anhypostatically enhypostasized in the divine person? . . . But then "real," actual human personhood would in itself already have to be termed the sin of egocentrism.[26]

Following Moltmann's thought to its logical conclusion, Crisp states:

> The an-enhypostatic distinction implies that Christ's humanity is somewhat unreal, that it would be "like the human garment of the eternal Son" – something he puts on and can take off again. Second, he [Moltmann] thinks this tells against Christ being a truly historical person. For what sort of concrete, real person has a nonpersonal human nature? Finally, [Moltmann] worries that this an-enhypostatic distinction means "the eternal Son of God" has "taken on 'human nature without personhood'" and that this has implications for how we should think of human personhood since Christ does not need to be a human person to be fully human.[27]

Nonetheless, contrary to Crisp's statement, the key to defining the Chalcedonian terminology is in the way the Alexandrian Fathers initially used it. The Alexandrian Fathers were meticulous in their choice of words to ensure a proper understanding, and did not use them arbitrarily or haphazardly.

25   Crisp, *Christology, Ancient and Modern*, 36.

26   Ibid., 30.

27   Ibid., 36. It should be noted that both Crisp and Moltmann pay no attention to the development of Eastern Christian theology in discussing these issues, whether Byzantine or Oriental, as they misunderstand the real implications of the an/en-hypostatic distinction as discussed further below.

The Alexandrian Miaphysite Unitary Reality

Athanasius and Cyril

Torrance eloquently states that "it became clear to great patristic theologians that a very different unitary approach to the doctrine of Christ was needed, one in which they understood him right from the start in his wholeness and integrity as one Person who is both God and man."[28] This unitary approach is evident in both Athanasius and Cyril of Alexandria's understanding of the meaning of *physis,* which is fundamentally different from the understanding of *physis* as the Latin *natura.*

Athanasius and Cyril understood φύσις as one reality with reference to Christ. Hans Van Loon notes that "Cyril emphasizes that the incarnate Word is not two persons, not two SEPARATE REALITIES, but that he is one REALITY, that is, one ὑπόστασις or one φύσις."[29] In other words, Cyril understood μία φύσις to mean the reality of the union of the divine with the human in the one person of Christ. Therefore, as Van Loon clarifies:

> In Cyril's own Christological language, then, the words φύσις, ὑπόστασις, and πρόσωπον are always synonymous, and they designate an individual being, subsisting separately from other beings. Therefore, Cyril could never accept dyophysite language, since "two natures" for him implied two separate persons.[30]

Torrance adds that "*nature* meant 'reality,'" so that for him to think of Christ as 'one nature' meant that he was 'one reality,' and not a schizoid being."[31]

This understanding was not unique to Cyril. Athanasius before him also understood it in the same way. Torrance argues that "Athanasius used *physis* more or less as the equivalent or as the synonym of reality (ἀλήθεια or οὐσία), as we see in the very frequent use of the expression 'in accordance with nature' (κατά φύσιν) where to think in accordance with the nature of things is to think truly (ἀληθῶς) of them."[32] As summarized by Torrance:

28　Torrance, *The Mediation of Christ,* 53.

29　Hans Van Loon, *The Dyophysite Christology of Cyril of Alexandria* (Leiden: Brill, 2009), 232.

30　Ibid., 16.

31　Torrance, *The Ground and Grammar of Theology,* 61.

32　Thomas F. Torrance, *Divine Meaning: Studies in Patristic Hermeneutics* (Edinburgh: T&T Clark, 1995), 211.

> To know and understand something involves a way of thinking
> strictly in accordance with what it actually is, that is, in
> accordance with its nature (κατά φύσιν) as it becomes disclosed
> in the course of inquiry, and thus in accordance with what it
> really is, or in accordance with its reality (κατ' ἀλήθειαν), and
> allow its nature (φύσις) or reality (ἀλήθεια) to determine for us
> how we are to think and speak appropriately of it.[33]

In the integration of the divine and the human, there is no gap between
the realm of truth and the realm of event.[34] Divine acts and human acts
"are *both acts of one and the same person*,"[35] therefore it would be difficult
if not impossible to speak of the two natures after the union, because in
reality they have indeed already been united. Athanasius and Cyril of
Alexandria were not the first to define or understand *physis* in this way.
Clement of Alexandria, a few centuries before them, defined it as φύσις
ἐστὶν ἡ τῶν πραγμάτων ἀλήθεια.[36] It is therefore evident the Alexandrian
tradition always understood *physis* to mean "true reality."[37]

Torrance synthesizes the distinctions in the use of terminology and
its contribution to the Christological differences between "monophysites"
and "dyophysites" in this way:

> There is, however, still another way of using *physis* found among
> the fathers, mostly of the Greek Antiochene sort. This derives from
> a more Aristotelian, biological or vitalist approach, in which the
> stress is on the relation of *physis* (=nature) to *phuo* (to produce or
> grow). It is this naturalistic sense of the word *physis*, corresponding
> to the Aristotelian "second substance," that is properly translated
> by the Latin *natura*. Serious difficulties and misunderstandings
> arose among the fathers when this vitalistic or naturalistic sense of
> *physis* was employed of the divine and the human *physeis* in the one
> Person of Christ, as though it were the equivalent of the word physis
> in its other meaning as reality. Problems such as these are found in
> the differences between the so-called Eastern "monophysites" and
> the "Chalcedonians" who, as far as I can see, basically intend the

33 Torrance, *Theological and Natural Science*, 100.

34 Thomas F. Torrance, *Incarnation: The Person and Life of Christ* (Downers
Grove, IL: InterVarsity Press, 2008), 107.

35 Ibid., 190.

36 *Sancti Maximi Confessoris Opuscula Theologica Et Polemica* (PG 91:264C).

37 It is noteworthy to mention that the Lampe Patristic Greek Lexicon also
defines "*physis*" as "reality." See G. W. H. Lampe, *A Patristic Greek Lexicon* (Oxford
University Press, 1969), 1498.

same thing! Indeed more actual monophysitism may be found in the West than in those who today are usually called "monophysite".[38]

John Philoponos

Following shortly after Athanasius and Cyril, John Philoponos, whose reading of the Alexandrian Fathers was validated by Torrance through his Einsteinian lens, further develops this unitary model. Philoponos was centuries ahead of his peers in his understanding of Christology due to his ability to efficiently synthesize theology, philosophy, and science. In the Christological expositions in his work the *Arbiter*, Philoponos ascertains that "the union of divinity and humanity is not a mere name, but a reality (οὐκ ἄρα ψιλόν ὄνομα τοῦτο ἐστίν, ἀλλά πράγμα)[39] which is united by substance, not by any accompanying accidents . . . If what results from the union is a substance viz. nature (both terms are used synonymously), it is right to assert one nature of Christ after the union, albeit not simple but composite."[40] He adds:

> The divine nature of the Logos and the human [nature] having been united, a single Christ has resulted from the two; not merely a simple union of natures has resulted, as it may be said that God has been united with a man, or a man with a man, while their natures are divided and no single entity has been constituted by each of them, such as, for example, a single man or a single living being . . . a relation of such kind, in the case of our Lord Christ, belongs to the whole human entelechy.[41]

Philoponos is keen on explaining that the unity of the divine and human in the one person of Christ is not just an eventuality but an ontological truth. Philoponos continues to argue in his exposition that the unity of the divine and the human results in a single entity which is "not a mere name, but a reality."[42] He also underscores that if "Christ is truly one in name and in reality [then] one cannot speak in any way at all of 'two Christs' in regard to the Lord's incarnation."[43] Philoponos concludes his rebuttal saying:

38   Torrance, *Divine Meaning*, 212.

39   PG 140:56A

40   Lang, *John Philoponus and the Controversies over Chalcedon in the Sixth Century A Study and Translation of the Arbiter*, 48.

41   Ibid., 175.

42   Ibid., 179.

43   Ibid., 183.

> If, therefore, we profess in common an indivisible union, and the indivisible cannot be divided, for whatever reason this is not possible, then the union, i.e. the end-product of the union cannot be divided. If this is so, and duality . . . is nothing else than a parting and a first division of the monad, then the end-product of the union cannot receive the reality or the name of duality. The end-product of the union, however, is Christ. For this reason, if the union is preserved, we cannot call Christ "two natures", unless someone understands by the word ["union"] a difference between the united [elements].[44]

Torrance endorses the Christological understanding of Philoponos to be in line with both Athanasius and Cyril:

> In that context the Athanasian and Cyrilian expression μία φύσις σεσαρκωμένη, used by Philoponos, referred to "one incarnate reality", indeed one undivided Being or Person (one *ousia* or *hypostasis*, and in that sense also as one *physis*) without any rejection of the truth that Jesus Christ is God and Man in one Person, one incarnate reality both perfectly divine and perfectly human. The *mia physis* was just as important for Philoponos, as it had been for Athanasius and Cyril for whom it affirmed the oneness of the incarnate Word of God (μία φύσις τοῦ θεοῦ λόγου σεσαρκωμένη). That is to say, like Athanasius and Cyril, John Philoponos would have nothing to do with a schizoid understanding of Christ for in him God and Man were one Reality and Person, but that does not mean that Philoponos was a "monophysite" in the heretical sense, any more than was Athanasius or Cyril.[45]

Philoponos' balanced understanding of Alexandrian Christology prompted Torrance to call for and encourage the Greek Orthodox Church to lift the anathemas issued against him.[46] The invitation was met with enthusiasm and support by members of the Greek Orthodox Church including Fr. George Dragas and Archbishop Methodios Fouyias of Thyateira and Great Britain.[47]

---

44 Ibid., 200.

45 Torrance, *Theological and Natural Science*, 111.

46 See "John Philoponos of Alexandria – Theologian & Physicist" by Thomas F. Torrance, *KANON XV, Yearbook of the Society for the Law of the Eastern Churches* (Roman Kovar, Eichenau, 1999), 315–330.

47 I would like to renew T. F. Torrance's initiative and Fr. George Dragas' enthusiasm by re-inviting the Greek Orthodox Church and my own Coptic Orthodox

Christological Realism in the Coptic Church

From its inception, the Coptic Orthodox Church of Alexandria has been an educator of theological realism. Clement of Alexandria "spoke of faith as a 'willing assent' of the mind to reality, an act in which the truth of things seizes hold of us and brings us to assent to it in accordance with its own self-evidence."[48] Centuries later, Athanasius and Cyril taught the same doctrine, as discussed earlier. To illustrate how this manner of thinking has been carried through to modern times, we must examine the writings of contemporary Coptic theologians, including Bishop Gregorios and Fr. Matthew the Poor.

Bishop Gregorios has been an instrumental figure in various ecumenical discussions. He bases his expositions of Christology on the notion that theologians often need to update their philosophical language to express theological concepts. He writes: "If philosophical expressions are not fit to express all that philosophers mean to say, new terms are often created."[49] The Bishop ascertains that while it is important to update philosophical expressions, theological meanings are not merely developed philosophically but are rather mystically revealed through a life of prayer.[50] He further explains:

> The Godhead and the Manhood are united in Him in a complete union, i.e. in essence, hypostasis and nature. There is no separation or division between the Godhood and the Manhood of our Lord . . . In other words we may speak of two natures before the union took place, but after the union there is but ONE nature, ONE nature having the properties of the two natures.[51]

Church to reintegrate the writings of John Philoponos into our theology and base our ecumenical dialogues on his writings. This indeed would be a tremendous task as we would for the first time since Chalcedon develop our theological discussions based on someone who is agreed upon by both families beyond Cyril of Alexandria.

48   Thomas F. Torrance, *Transformation and Convergence in the Frame of Knowledge: Explorations in the Interrelations of Scientific and Theological Enterprise* (Eugene, OR: Wipf and Stock Publishers, 1998), 197.

49   Waheeb Atalla Girgis, *The Christological Teaching of the Non-Chalcedonian Churches* (Ramses: Coptic Orthodox Theological University College, 1951), 4.

50   Ibid., 5.

51   Ibid., 6.

Gregorios also states that "the Godhead and the Manhood are united not in the sense of a mere combination (συναφεια) or connection or junction, but they are united in the real sense of the word union . . . this union is a real union."[52] He is quick to discern that "there is no duality here between the natures . . . This is a real proof of the Union in the sense in which the non-Chalcedonian Orthodox Churches profess it."[53] According to him, this dualistic view of the one reality creates "a dangerous expression against our salvation. If there were two natures in Christ after the union, then the redemption of Christ was an act of His humanity, for it is the flesh that was crucified."[54]

As mentioned earlier, no matter how hard theologians try to articulate the *hypostatic* union, it remains transcendent to our rational categories, a great divine mystery. Torrance states that

> the doctrine of Christ is the doctrine of *the mystery of the true divine nature and the true human nature in one person* . . . In Christ something has taken place which is so new that it is related to our ordinary knowledge only at its extreme edges; if it is apprehended by us it must be apprehended from outside the limits of our ordinary human experience and thought. It is a new and unique reality which has certainly invaded our human life but which we can know only by refusing to categorise it in the sphere of what we already know.[55]

Therefore, talk of the *hypostatic* union has to be guarded by *apophatic* language, as it is a personal union of a singularly unique kind. Torrance refers to it as "*sui generis.*"[56] He emphasizes that the hypostatic union is a matter of mystery. Hence, the four *apophatic* terms describe the one reality of Christ: the union of divinity and humanity is without confusion, without division, without change, and without separation.[57]

It is rather fascinating to see that despite their apparent differences, both Chalcedonian and non-Chalcedonian Christians employ the same *apophatic* terms to refer to the union. As this Chalcedonian *apophatic*

52   Ibid., 7.
53   Ibid., 11.
54   Ibid.
55   Torrance, *Incarnation*, 83.
56   Ibid., 207.
57   Ibid., 83.

formula is celebrated in the Eastern Orthodox tradition, it is also clearly celebrated in the Coptic tradition. Bishop Gregorios states:

> contrary to Eutyches, the non-Chalcedonian Orthodox Churches profess that Christ is ONE nature in which are completely preserved all the human properties as well as all the divine properties, without confusion, without mixture, and without alteration, a profession which the Coptic celebrant priest cries out in the liturgy, holding up the paten with his hands.[58]

Indeed, in the Coptic Orthodox liturgy, the priest declares in a loud voice:

> I believe and confess to the last breath that this is the life-giving Flesh that Your only-begotten Son, our Lord, God, and Savior Jesus Christ, took from our Lady, the Lady of us all, the holy Theotokos, Saint Mary. He made It one with His divinity without mingling, without confusion, and without alteration.[59]

Additionally, the Coptic Bright Saturday liturgical rite states: "you became man like us, O only-begotten God, without alteration or change."[60] Furthermore, in the Coptic Psalmody we say "the true God, of the true God, who was incarnate, of you without change,"[61] and more succinctly, "Jesus Christ the Word, who was incarnate without alteration, became a perfect man. Without alteration of His being, or mingling or separation of any kind after the unity. For of one nature, one hypostasis, and one person, is the Word of God."[62]

The writings of Fr. Matthew the Poor, who was pivotal to the revival of the development of doctrinal theology in the Coptic Church and the Orthodox tradition at large, always reflect a deep spirituality and Christocentric life through which he gained the illumination to understand divine revelation and the mysteries of faith. Although Fr.

---

58   Girgis, *The Christological Teaching of the Non-Chalcedonian Churches*, 7.

59   Basil, Gregory, and Cyril, *The Divine Liturgy: The Anaphoras of Saints Basil, Gregory, and Cyril*, 2nd ed. (n.p.: Coptic Orthodox Diocese of the Southern United States, 2007), 233.

60   See Psali Watos of Bright Saturday in *Coptic Orthodox Rite of The Holy Pascha*, n.d., 553.

61   See the Sunday Theotokia, part 5 in *The Holy Psalmody* (Ridgewood, NY: Saint Mary and Saint Antonios Coptic Orthodox Church, n.d.), 95.

62   See the Monday Theotokia, part 6 in *Holy Psalmody of Kiahk: According to the Orders of the Coptic Orthodox Church*, 1st ed. (Pierrefonds, QC, Canada: Saint George and Saint Joseph Coptic Orthodox Church, 2008), 55.

Matthew does not directly address the nature(s) of Christ as a main topic in any of his works, he explains his Christological viewpoint from the faith he received throughout his life from the church fathers and the Coptic liturgical tradition in his various commentaries on the gospels and Pauline epistles. He states that "the faith of the Church that the nature of Christ who is born in Bethlehem is one nature of the incarnate Word – the Son of God – is a faith which places us now and today in front of a realistic truth which is that God is fully and perfectly encountering us in the person of Christ."[63] He further explains that the one nature of Christ as a "realistic truth" is an ontological expression where:

> the word "truth" here is ἀληθινόν, as a characteristic of light, means perfect truth which is self-illumined with an invincible power. Truth which is not limited by time or space and is not affected by any condition, one which does not only reveal the visible, but the hidden things of the heart and the conscience and which also shines in darkness, and the darkness did not comprehend it.[64]

He also says that "the word 'true' or αληθινή means that which is rooted in the essence of facts and their origin. The 'truth' in Christ is not an image, likeness, or symbol, but the essence and the radix which is immutable, incorruptible, and infinite."[65] Therefore, although he uses terms like "nature," his use of the word is rooted in an ontological sense, where reality is the root of faith. Additionally, he writes:

> Truth or "ἀλήθεια" in the New Testament is a realist expression which is heavily and powerfully repeated as an indication that Old Testament symbols, names, and characteristics were metaphors, images, and shadows of the truth . . . The word "truth" accompanies Christ in all his characteristics. He is "the true light", "the true bread", "the true vine", "truly you are the Son of God", "truly risen", "this is truly the Christ, the savior of the world", "this is truly the Prophet who is to come into the world", and "you have sent to John, and he has borne witness to the truth". In all these instances, the word "ἀλήθεια" which is truth or true, means the perfect act or the seamlessly immutable state which is beyond

63 Mattá al-Miskīn, *The Feasts of Theophany*, 4th ed., vol. 1 (Cairo: The Monastery of St. Macarius, 2011), 180.

64 al-Miskīn, *The Faith in Christ*, 87.

65 Ibid., 130.

any doubt because it has been revealed fully and both visible materially and spiritually. It is also continuous realist ontology or a perfect constant essence. The word also denotes sensing the truth and comprehending it at the same time.[66]

In this excerpt, Fr. Matthew rejects Aristotelian dualism by affirming that the reality of divine "truth" has been revealed both materially and spiritually. His theological realism and understanding of the unitary model is evident from his discussion of the notion of truth. In doing so, Fr. Matthew upholds his Alexandrian roots as founded by Athanasius and Cyril.

Implications of the Unitary Alexandrian Model for Christology and Human Personhood

In light of this appropriate historical patristic understanding of *physis* and *hypostasis* we must examine whether or not humanity can be adequately described as having personhood. Furthermore, these definitions may affect our understanding of the an/en-hypostatic distinction, and precisely what it means when Christ is described as having a "full humanity." John Zizioulas describes a person, as distinct from an individual, as such:

Being a person is basically different from being an individual or "personality" in that the person cannot be conceived in itself as a static entity, but only as it relates to. Thus personhood implies the "openness of being", and even more than that, the ek-stasis of being, i.e. a movement towards communion which leads to a transcendence of the boundaries of the "self" and thus to freedom. At the same time, and in contrast to the partiality of the individual which is subject to addition and combination, the person in its ecstatic character reveals its being in a catholic, i.e. integral and undivided, way, and thus in its being ecstatic it becomes hypostatic, i.e. the bearer of its nature in its totality.[67]

This understanding of personhood generally leads us to question the colloquial way in which we refer to human entities as persons and how

---

66   Ibid., 172–173.

67   J. D. Zizioulas, "Human Capacity and Human Incapacity: A Theological Exploration of Personhood," *Scottish Journal of Theology* 28, no. 5 (1975): 408.

our personhood relates to the personhood of Christ. Is person an accurate description of our fallen state? Or is personhood falsely attributed to our distorted nature?

The question then becomes: are we as human beings the bearers of our reality in its totality? Do we possess the totality of what it means to be human? Based on an Alexandrian perspective, I would argue that we are the bearers of our fallen reality, a reality of servitude to sin and not the totality of our reality, i.e. eschatological life. Torrance clarifies this notion based on his Athanasian understanding: "the Chalcedonian statement does not say that this human nature of Christ was human nature 'under the servitude to sin' as Athanasius insisted; it does not say that it was corrupt human nature taken from our fallen creation, where human nature is determined and perverted by sin."[68] The "diseased humanity" therefore is not the perfect humanity; it is not the real humanity that was created at the beginning. The true humanity is that of Jesus Christ and "far from measuring its truth and fullness by our human nature, we must judge the poverty of our human nature by the perfection and the fullness of his human nature."[69] That is not to say that Christ had a human nature which is different than ours, but as Torrance stated, he is like us and he is unlike us. He is like us "in our frail, feeble and corrupt and temptable humanity, yet without being himself a sinner."[70]

This understanding impacts how we comprehend the an/en-hypostatic distinction and additionally the concept of human personhood in the current fallen state. The an/en-hypostatic distinction does not mean – as Crisp suggested[71] – that "Christ's humanity is somewhat unreal." On the contrary, it implies that *our* humanity is somewhat unreal, or incomplete. Therefore, Crisp's phrase "the human garment of the eternal Son" is somewhat misleading. It is Christ – who is eternally the perfect and most real human – who has "in history" put on the "distorted human shirt" until his resurrection. But then after the resurrection, we humans put on the perfect and most real humanity. In other words, employing Athanasius' notion of the "exchange," one could argue that Christ has put on the humanity that was in servitude to sin, so that we may put on the humanity that is in the true and real image and likeness of God; more

---

68 Torrance, *Incarnation*, 201.

69 Ibid., 204.

70 Ibid., 205.

71 See references on 272-73 of this chapter.

precisely, so that we may become the "bearers of its totality." Perhaps this is how Moltmann's statement would be correct that "the eternal son has taken human nature without personhood." It is in this manner that the Alexandrian fathers interchange their use of the terms *physis* and *hypostasis*, because what is "real" is what "bears its own totality."

Furthermore, the Alexandrian Fathers' notion of the hypostatic union is about the unity between the hypostatic and the anhypostatic, where the hypostatic is the "one who gives . . . reality."[72] This is precisely what St. Athanasius meant when he wrote "'God had special pity for the human race, seeing that by its nature it would not be able to persist forever', that is, the human race might, as a result of transgression, return to its original nature, to non-existence."[73] The distorted humanity is incapable of persisting forever, as it lost its concrete reality when it declared itself independently divine. The en/an-hypostatic distinction therefore should be applied to the fallen human nature, and not to Christ in himself. On this reading, anhypostatic would mean "that human nature is not a person independent of Christ."[74] Enhypostatic would mean that the distorted human nature is assumed and healed by the person of the Son and given existence in the existence of God – as opposed to going back to non-existence as Athanasius mentioned – and therefore co-exists in the divine hypostasis of the Son. In this manner, the "shirt" is not humanity *par excellence*, it is rather, the fallen humanity. It would only appear logical that in his resurrected form, Christ has divested himself from the feeble and fallen human *natura* which is characterized by its servitude to sin, because it is not how humanity was initially created. Therefore, in wearing Christ through baptism, we enter into his concrete reality and we unite personally, that is hypostatically with him, and only then do we too become "the brightness of his glory, and the express image of his person."[75]

Conclusion

T. F. Torrance spent a great deal of his life studying the Alexandrian Fathers and came to realize the true meaning of their expressions. His

---

72 Lampe, *A Patristic Greek Lexicon*, 1461.

73 Athanasius of Alexandria, *On the Incarnation* (PG 25.101A, 104BC).

74 Torrance, *Incarnation*, 105.

75 Hebrews 1:3.

ability to master the Alexandrian tradition, particularly through the writings of Clement, Athanasius and Cyril, opened his eyes to the erroneous ways in which the Coptic Christology has been interpreted through the centuries. In his attempt to clarify the miaphysite non-Chalcedonian position, he reintroduced the writings of John Philoponos and, along with it, the Alexandrian understanding that "*physis* describes actual reality which confronts us in its own independent being, and which is known in accordance with its own inherent force or natural force in virtue of which it continues to be what it actually and properly is."[76] Therefore, for Torrance, as well as for the Copts, "the terms φύσις and ἀλήθεια, nature and reality, were more or less synonymous in their use."[77] In this context, Torrance further insisted that "we cannot understand *physis* by reading *natura* into it."[78] This understanding properly reflected the non-Chalcedonian position (and the correct unitary Chalcedonian interpretation) that Jesus Christ "is not two realities, a divine and a human, joined or combined together, but one Reality who confronts us as he who is both God and man."[79] This is also clear from the sampled writings of modern Coptic theologians like Fr. Matthew the Poor, Bishop Gregorios, as well as the historic and daily celebrated Coptic liturgical texts. The works of Torrance have opened a new horizon for the dialogue between the non-Chalcedonian and Chalcedonian families, and have shown the Copts' continuous correct reading of their own theology and history.[80]

---

76 Torrance, *Divine Meaning*, 211.

77 Torrance, *Theological and Natural Science*, 100.

78 Ibid., 101.

79 Torrance, *The Mediation of Christ*, 56.

80 It is pivotal for both families to follow in the footsteps of the Alexandrian Fathers, John Philoponos, and T. F. Torrance in developing the theological language that best represents our contemporary scientific and philosophical outlooks. For example, this can be achieved by closely studying the ideas and methodologies employed by Torrance in his utilization of James Clark Maxwell's "knots of energy" to develop his onto-relational concept of personhood. See Torrance, *The Mediation of Christ*, 48.

Part III

Primary Sources

Chapter 13

The Correspondence between T. F. Torrance and Georges Florovsky (1950–1973)

Matthew Baker

The intellectual friendship between Thomas F. Torrance, sometimes regarded as the major British theologian of the 20th century, and Georges Florovsky, often called the leading Orthodox theologian of the same period, is of interest both for an understanding of the respective work of both theologians as well as for the glimpse it provides into the ecumenical dialogue between Orthodoxy and Protestant theology, particularly of the so-called "Barthian" or "neo-orthodox" variety, in the last century. The present publication introduces fifteen letters between Torrance and Florovsky written between the years 1950 to 1973, plus a letter of Florovsky to Oliver Tomkins and an appended commentary by Florovsky relating to an ecumenical proposal of Torrance.

It is uncertain when exactly Georges Florovsky and Thomas Torrance first met. The correspondence here begins in January 1950, but seems to indicate a friendship already well-established beforehand. Father Georges Florovsky was at this time Dean of St. Vladimir's Seminary in New York and already an international name, both in Orthodox theology and in the ecumenical movement.

T. F. Torrance, then thirty-six years old and twenty years Florovsky's junior, was at this time still a relatively unknown parish minister, but one who had already behind him a period of study with Karl Barth, experience as a chaplain during World War II, as well as two published books, and was about to take up a post as professor of Church History at New College, Edinburgh.

The letters give a window into the dominant concerns of both theologians during this period, in particular as relating to their dialogue within Faith and Order. At the heart of this discussion was ecclesiology and communion, particularly in light of Christian disunity and the ecumenical imperative. Torrance's first letters to Florovsky reflect the focus on eschatology, particularly in relation to the doctrine of the Church, found also in his publications of this period: his parish homilies on the book of Revelation, later published as *The Apocalypse Today* (1959), his book on the eschatology of the Reformers, *Kingdom and Church* (1956), and his volume of sermons, *When Christ Comes and Comes Again* (1957).[1] In fact, the apocalyptic note, while less evident in Torrance's later work, was somewhat characteristic of theology in general within Faith and Order in this period.

A certain eschatological emphasis and, at times, an apocalyptic tone can be found in Florovsky's lectures of this time as well.[2] In an article on the preparatory documents for the Amsterdam Assembly, published in 1949, Torrance had himself praised Florovsky's "eschatological conception of the Church."[3] Florovsky and Torrance concur strongly in understanding

---

1 For a study of Torrance's eschatology of this period, see Stanley S. MacLean, *Resurrection, Apocalypse, and the Kingdom of Christ: The Eschatology of Thomas F. Torrance* (Eugene, OR: Pickwick Publications, 2012).

2 See, for instance, Florovsky's Amsterdam speech, "Determinations and Distinctions: Ecumenical Aims and Doubts," *Sobornost*, 4, series 3 (Winter 1948): 126–32, and his sermon, "Consider Your Ways (Haggai 1:4–7): An Orthodox Sermon on the Evanston Theme," *The Pulpit* 25, no. 6 (June 1954): 5–7. It is unfortunate that Florovsky never produced the article on history and eschatology that Torrance repeatedly requested from him in the letters below for *Scottish Journal of Theology*; a fine example of his thinking on eschatology can be found in his essay (originally written for a *Festschrift* for Emil Brunner) "The Last Things and the Last Events," in Florovsky, *Creation and Redemption* (Belmont, MA.: Nordland Press, 1976), 243–65.

3 Thomas F. Torrance, "Concerning Amsterdam. I. The Nature and Mission of the Church; A Discussion of Volumes I and II of the Preparatory Studies," *Scottish Journal of Theology* 2 (1949): 241–70, reprinted in Thomas F. Torrance, *Conflict and Agreement in the Church*, vol. 1, *Order and Disorder* (Eugene, OR.: Wipf & Stock, 1996), 195–225.

the Church as the Body of Christ, understood in Eucharistic and eschatological terms. Both, too, agree in identifying Jesus Christ as the "sole priest" of all sacramental action in the Church. Yet – to strike a note often sounded by Florovsky as well as by Barth in their ecumenical *dicta* – it is precisely through this agreement that serious *disagreements* between Florovsky and Torrance become manifest.

These disagreements concerned particularly the respective understanding of eschatology and its relationship to the Church in history. Torrance, while affirming Church order – even episcopate – as of the *esse* (not just *bene esse*) of the Church as Body of Christ, understood the relationship between eschatology and historic church order largely in terms of a *negative dialectic*.[4] The kingdom of God pronounces a judgment on all claims of history, including those of historic priestly succession. Given that the Eucharist itself is an in-breaking and a foretaste of this coming kingdom, the Lord's Supper thus relativizes all historical claims to apostolic succession as constitutive of the Church and a litmus test for ecclesial communion.

In contrast, Florovsky understood the Church *in via* as being herself a "proleptic eschatology" constituted in the sacraments. In Florovsky's emphasis, history and eschatology should never be simply opposed in negative dialectic. The history of the Church *zwischen den Zeiten* is no mere waiting room. Something is being built up which, though presently veiled, is a real and positive anticipation of the kingdom to come, and which will perdure beyond its threshold. Through the historic episcopate, each local church is inserted into the eschatological community of the Twelve

---

4   For evidence of this, see especially the appendix of lectures dealing with eschatology in Thomas F. Torrance, *Incarnation: The Person and Life of Christ*, ed. Robert T. Walker (Downers Grove: IVP/Milton Keynes: Paternoster, 2008). Torrance's early views on Church order can be found especially in the volumes *Royal Priesthood*. Scottish Journal of Theology Occasional Papers, No. 3 (Edinburgh: Oliver and Boyd, 1955) and *Conflict and Agreement in the Church*, vol. 1, *Order and Disorder* (London: Lutterworth Press, 1959); *Conflict and Agreement in the Church*, vol. 2, *The Ministry and the Sacraments of the Gospel* (London: Lutterworth Press, 1960) (republished by Wipf and Stock in 2 volumes in 1996), and in the essays collected in Jock Stein, ed., *Gospel, Church and Ministry* (Eugene, OR.: Pickwick Publications, 2012). In his later work, what I have called the "negative dialectic" of relationship between eschatology and historic Church order fades considerably, and is displaced by a new emphasis – drawn in great part from Torrance's reading of Irenaeus – on the "embodied" character of the Gospel in the apostolic order of the Church: see, for instance, "The Trinitarian Foundation and Character of Faith and Authority in the Church," in Thomas F. Torrance, ed., *Theological Dialogue Between Orthodox and Reformed Churches* (Edinburgh: Scottish Academic Press, 1985), 79–120.

and the Jerusalem Church, the reconstituted Israel. "Eschatological" here means primarily "permanent," "once and for all," and can in no wise be set in opposition to the "historical." Apostolic succession and church order are therefore no "merely" historical principle, but a charismatic reality, a continuation of Pentecost and an anticipation of the last things.[5] *Some* kind of objective unity still exists among Christians ecclesially divided – an objective unity, uniting all who confess Christ as God and Savior. Yet no "intercommunion" is possible between divided bodies. Communion is possible only on two conditions: full agreement in the complete faith of the Ecumenical Councils and a sharing in the historic apostolic and catholic Church order. For Protestantism, this requires an act of reintegration and restoration, as the Reformation marked a definite departure from historic priesthood.[6]

Together with Anders Nygren and Edmund Schlink, Torrance and Florovsky were instrumental in persuading the Faith and Order assembly at Lund in 1952 to establish a special theological commission on Christ and his Church.[7] Three items from Florovsky published below (numbers 12, 13, and 14) concern the draft of a paper that Torrance was asked to write for a sub-committee of this commission. Florovsky was asked to write a critique of Torrance's draft and Oliver Tomkins was to revise

---

5 Florovsky's criticisms of Torrance's eschatology and its impact on ecclesiology in this period would have likely been similar to his criticisms of Barth, with whom a crucial disagreement (as acknowledged on both sides) concerned eschatology; for discussion of this, see my "'*Offenbarung, Philosophie, und Theologie*': Karl Barth and Georges Florovsky in Dialogue," in *Karl Barth in Dialogue: Encounters with Major Figures*, ed. George Hunsinger (Eerdmans, forthcoming).

6 For a summary of Florovsky's ecumenical views, see Matthew Baker and Seraphim Danckaert, "Georges Florovsky," in *Orthodox Handbook on Ecumenism: Resources for Christian Education*, ed. P. Kalaitzidis, T. FitzGerald, C. Hovorun, Aik. Pekridou, N. Asproulis, G. Liagre, D. Werner (Volos: Volos Publications in partnership with Regnum, 2013), 209–213. A historical overview of Florovsky's ecumenical activities can be found in Andrew Blane, ed., *Georges Florovsky: Russian Intellectual, Orthodox Churchman* (Crestwood, NY.: St. Vladimir's Seminary Press, 1993); readers interested in Florovsky's ecclesiology should refer to the bibliography found in the back of that volume. For a study of Florovsky against his Russian background, see Paul Gavrilyuk, *Georges Florovsky and the Russian Religious Renaissance* (Oxford: Oxford University Press, 2014). A full bibliography of literature on Florovsky can be found in Matthew Baker, "Bibliography of Literature on the Life and Thought of Father Georges Florovsky," *Transactions of the Association of Russian-American Scholars in the U.S.A*, 37 (2011–2012), 473–546.

7 Alister E. McGrath, *T. F. Torrance: An Intellectual Biography* (Edinburgh: T&T Clark, 1999), 97.

and reduce it, in order that the paper might then be used as the working paper for the Faith and Order section at the 1954 Evanston Assembly. Torrance later published the paper in his volume *Conflict and Agreement in the Church*, vol. 1, *Order and Disorder* as "Our Oneness in Christ and Our Disunity as Churches."[8] In his response, Florovsky is concerned to underscore the reality of Christian divisions as rooted, not simply in a loss of charity, but in real disagreements about the truth – disagreements maintained in good faith, and for which no "repentance" alone will suffice in healing. Not least among these disagreements is the conflict concerning the very significance of historic Church structures. Florovsky opposes Torrance's call for theological latitude regarding Eucharistic doctrine, as well as Torrance's tendency to negate historic claims by reference to "eschatology." Stating his own characteristic emphasis, Florovsky underscores that "'Eschatology' in the Church is mediated through History and her 'structures.'" The ecumenical task and the cause of truth could not be helped in the long run by hasty common measures that paper over what are in reality serious and unresolved disagreements regarding the very nature of the Church as founded in the will of her Head and Lord.

As is evident from his response to Torrance's ecumenical draft, a great part of the thrust of Florovsky's ecumenical work during this period lay simply in his attempt to convince his Protestant interlocutors to take seriously the importance of the historic doctrinal disagreements that stood behind Christian divisions. It was typical of Florovsky to stress the need for "ecumenical patience," and for greater "molecular work" in common theological study. It is interesting that in attempting to illustrate the difficulty of this ecumenical task in which every apparent agreement even in basic matters only reveals a hidden disagreement (thus making the approach of doctrinal minimalism futile), Florovsky named his relations with Torrance as an example. Speaking of the doctrinal minimalism and historical relativism of the ecumenical proposals of his Russian colleague Lev Zander's *Vision and Action* in an unpublished talk from 1955, Florovsky said:

> here begins probably a very terrible experience. You may say sometimes it is a confusing embarrassing experience. You do everything that Professor Zander wants you to. You discover

---

8   See Thomas F. Torrance, *Conflict and Agreement in the Church*, vol. 1, *Order and Disorder* (Eugene, OR.: Wipf & Stock, 1996), 263–83.

– excuse me for using just the name – Tom Torrance is an awfully nice fellow, but unfortunately he is a Calvinist. I might love him as a man, and then we have a terrible row. He is a very close friend of mine, but twenty years younger, and an excellent theologian. We know each other as brothers and yet we disagree; this is a real experience. We agree at a certain point, well then we cannot agree. The point is, one may say, that because I was educated in Russia and he was educated in Scotland . . . this would be fatalism and probably all the circumstances had some importance, but there is something else.[9]

Florovsky's disagreements with Torrance were not limited to matters of eschatology and Church order. At a Faith and Order Commission meeting at Davos, Switzerland in July 1955, Florovsky challenged Torrance's teaching regarding Christ's assumption of "fallen human nature."[10] Indeed, it may have been precisely this disagreement that Florovsky had in mind in his above comments referencing Torrance's "Calvinism." The two found reason to agree emphatically, however, on the need for a Christocentric doctrine of the Church and pneumatology, and on the need to guard against the modern tendency to "de-christologize" ecclesiology, as manifested especially in various Romantic, Slavophile, and Neo-Protestant theologies taking their starting point in a pneumatology rooted in notions of religious self-consciousness or "community."[11] Apparently, no correspondence between Florovsky and Torrance from the 1960s now survives. It is certain, however, that the two were in contact at least during the beginning of that decade. The Special Commission on Christ and his Church appointed at Lund in 1952 lasted ten years. And with Florovsky's interventions, a Faith and Order patristics study group was established, choosing the *Ad Serapionem* of St. Athanasius and the *De Spiritu Sancto* of St. Basil as its study texts.[12] This group met in

9 Typescript of an audio lecture, "The Vision of Unity," p. 24, Carton 3, folder 1, 1955, Princeton University Firestone Library Rare Books and Archives.

10 *Commission on Faith and Order. Minutes of the Working Committee, July 1955, Davos Switzerland* (WCC). For my comments on this debate, see Matthew Baker, "The Place of St. Irenaeus of Lyons in Historical and Dogmatic Theology According to T. F. Torrance," *Participatio: The Journal of the Thomas F. Torrance Theological Fellowship* 2 (2010): 5–43.

11 *Commission on Faith and Order: Minutes, Commission and Working Committee*, no. 17 (1955), 18. For discussion, see Matthew Baker, "The Eternal 'Spirit of the Son': Barth, Florovsky and Torrance on the *Filioque*," *International Journal of Systematic Theology* 12 (Oct 2010): 382–403.

12 A note found in the Florovsky archive at St. Vladimir's Seminary seems to

Paris in March 1962.[13] It seems that Torrance's important paper, "Spiritus Creator: A Consideration of the Teaching of St. Athanasius and St. Basil," grew out of this study.[14]

While there is little to gauge the possible influence of Torrance's thinking over Florovsky, whose basic thinking was already well established before the two met, there is plenty to suggest that Florovsky's influence and example were important for Torrance. Torrance's student, longstanding friend, and collaborator Father George Dragas has recalled how Torrance once remarked to him that Florovsky was one of the few who could force him to reconsider his position on a given theological point.[15] Such a change of mind is certainly evident in Torrance's view of the Greek patristic teaching on *theosis*. In the first letter of Torrance reproduced below, written in Jan. 1950, Torrance registers his rejection of the doctrine of *theosis* as "un-Hebraic and un-biblical."[16] By 1964, however, he would address the World Alliance of Reformed Churches with a plea "for a reconsideration by the Reformed Church of what the Greek Fathers called *theosis*."[17] In his 1970 lecture "The Relevance of Orthodoxy," Torrance described *theosis* as the experience of "our participation in the Holy Spirit, in which we come under the direct impact of God's uncreated energies in all their holiness and majesty, and are sanctified and renewed by them . . . God Himself acting upon us personally and creatively."[18] It was surely no coincidence that in this same published sermon, when remarking on how ecumenical dialogue with the Orthodox had often led him to reconsider his Reformed presuppositions in his reading of the

suggest that it was Florovsky who determined this choice of texts.

13   See *The Ecumenical Advance: A History of the Ecumenical Movement*, vol. 2, 1948–1968, ed. Harold E. Fey (London: SPCK, 1970), 160.

14   Published in Thomas F. Torrance, *Theology in Reconstruction* (London: SCM Press, 1965), 209–28. Again, see my "Eternal Spirit of the Son."

15   Remarkably, Dragas recounts also how, when he first met Florovsky in Princeton in 1971, Florovsky said a similar thing about Torrance.

16   Torrance echoes here the Harnackian view of theosis put forward in his dissertation, *The Doctrine of Grace in the Apostolic Fathers* (1948 reprint: Eugene, OR.: Wipf & Stock, 1996), 140n3: "The idea of deification was taken up even by such good theologians as Irenaeus and Athanasius. Nothing could be more characteristically Hellenistic."

17   Thomas F. Torrance, *Theology in Reconstruction* (Eerdmans, 1975), 243; cf. 214.

18   Thomas F. Torrance, *The Relevance of Orthodoxy*, edited with Introduction by John B. Logan (Stirling: The Drummond Press, for The Fellowship of St. Andrew, 1970).

Bible, Torrance stressed the crucial influence of Florovsky in particular.[19] He would later cite Florovsky's essay on "St Gregory Palamas and the Tradition of the Fathers" approvingly for its understanding of *theosis* in terms of "personal encounter."[20]

Although increasingly critical of the direction of the WCC from the late 1950s onward, Florovsky continued to be involved directly all through the 60s, his last participation being at the 1971 Louvain Assembly of Faith and Order. Torrance, however, had little such direct involvement after the early 1960s in official events of Faith and Order or the World Council of Churches, where he would have been afforded contact with Florovsky. In 1964, Florovsky moved to Princeton, where he would spend the remainder of his life researching and teaching at both Princeton University and Princeton Theological Seminary. In 1971, Torrance spent his sabbatical in Princeton. It seems that it was during this time that the two theologians renewed their old friendship.[21]

The last three letters reproduced below, dating from shortly afterward in 1973, reflect a very different set of interests than those of the 1950s. The conversation has shifted from ecclesiology, communion, and the Eucharist, to created contingency, space and time, and the relationship between *theologia* and *oikonomia,* with a more obvious stress in Torrance on the foundational importance of Greek patristic theology. Florovsky's October 21, 1973 letter dealing with the theology of time is a small gem of concise theological reflection, and provides crucial clues into Florovsky's views on the theology of Karl Barth[22] as well the concerns driving his objections to the sophiology of Fr. Sergii Bulgakov – the controversy over which had long before been a major determining force in Florovsky's development as a theologian and churchman.

One sees from these last letters, too, that it was not only his reading of Florovsky's essays,[23] but also personal exchanges that led Torrance to

19   Ibid., see 332 of this volume for a reprinting of this valuable sermon.

20   Thomas F. Torrance, *The Christian Doctrine of God: One Being, Three Persons* (Edinburgh: T&T Clark, 1996), 96.

21   This friendship continued to the last year of Florovsky's life. In a letter found in Florovsky's Princeton archive, dated October 27, 1978 – less than a year before Florovsky's death in August 1979 – James McCord, President of Princeton Theological Seminary, wrote to Florovsky: "I very much enjoyed being with you when Tom Torrance was in town last week. He was particularly eager to see you, and I am happy that he found you at home when he called on Sunday afternoon."

22   See the discussion and references in the footnotes appended to letter 16 below.

23   Torrance refers repeatedly in his later works to Florovsky's essays "Creation

credit Florovsky particularly for his insight into created contingency.[24] It is telling that Torrance dedicated his 1981 book *Divine and Contingent Order* to Florovsky along with Eric Mascall and Stanley Jaki, calling them "champions of contingence."[25] Torrance brought his own characteristic notes here: where Florovsky tended to stress indeterminism and divine and human freedom, Torrance highlights contingent *order* or *rationality*.[26] Yet Torrance's later thought builds heavily on Florovsky's interpretation of how "the idea held by Origen that God's relation to the universe is necessary to his own Being was comprehensively destroyed by Athanasius."[27] This insight had broad implications, and was perhaps crucial in helping to lead Torrance away from the charge of "Hellenization" against patristic thought found in his earliest work (e.g., his dissertation on *The Doctrine of Grace in the Apostolic Fathers*) increasingly toward something like Florovsky's affirmation of the "Christian Hellenism" of the Fathers: "far from a radical Hellenization having taken place [in

and Creaturehood" (1928), "The Idea of Creation in Christian Philosophy" (1951), "St. Athanasius' Concept of Creation" (1962), confessing a special indebtedness to the last.

24   In his book *The Christian Frame of Mind: Reason, Order and Openness in Theology and Natural Science* (Colorado Springs: Helmers & Howard, 1989), 2, Torrance writes: "As the late Professor Georges Florovsky used to point out, this idea of the radical contingency of the universe and its inherent rational order was utterly alien to and indeed quite unintelligible to the Greek mind. For classical Greek thought the universe was necessary and self-explanatory, eternally co-existing with God. The rational forms immanent in the universe which gave it its beautiful geometrical order were held to be divine, so that to speak of the universe as created in form and being out of nothing was regarded as an act of impious atheism."

25   I owe this observation to Taylor Carr. The dedication is only found in the original edition, not in subsequent reprints of the book. For succinct summary of Florovsky's thinking on creation, see Matthew Baker, "Georges Florovsky (1893–1979): *Agon* of Divine and Human Freedom," in Ernst Conradie, ed., *Creation and Salvation: A Medley of Recent Theological Movements* (Berlin: LIT Verlag, 2012), 29–35.

26   In Torrance's definition, "By contingent order is meant that the orderly universe is not self-sufficient or ultimately self-explaining but is given a rationality and reliability in its orderliness which depend on and reflect God's own eternal rationality and reliability," *Divine and Contingent Order* (Oxford and New York: Oxford University Press, 1981), viii. For further discussion, see Matthew Baker, "Cosmological Contingency and Logical Necessity According to G. Florovsky and T. Torrance," in *Orthodox Theology and the Sciences*, ed. Stoyan Tanev, Pavel Pavlov, and George Dragas (Columbia, MO.: New Rome Press, 2013).

27   Torrance, *The Christian Doctrine of God*, 4.

patristic thought]," says Torrance, "in making use of Greek thought-forms Christianity radically transformed them."[28]

In his introduction to the first volume of papers from the official Orthodox-Reformed dialogue initiated in 1977, Torrance noted that serious theological dialogue between Orthodox and Reformed Christians really began at Amsterdam (1948) and Lund (1952), and was continued especially through the special ten-year Commission on Christ and his Church appointed at Lund. Torrance took occasion here to note the crucial importance of Florovsky for this dialogue: "Particular mention must be made of the late Very Rev. Professor Georges Florovsky, whose profound theological instinct, at once catholic and evangelical, and whose Christocentric and Trinitarian interpretation of Greek Patristic Theology won the admiration and inspired the lasting confidence of his Reformed colleagues."[29]

While granting us only a tantalizing glimpse into the historical dialogue between these two important figures, the present publication of the correspondence between Florovsky and Torrance should be an encouragement to devoted students of each theologian to read the other, and to learn from both their labors. To know that Florovsky read Torrance's work on the relationship of the incarnation to space in Nicene patristic theology "with great interest and satisfaction" and regarded it as "a magnificent piece of work, and very convincing" suggests that Florovsky would not have disapproved of a further extension of the neopatristic program into the realm of theology/science dialogue, such as Torrance opened up, as an item on the agenda of Orthodox theology today – and also that, clearly, Orthodox theologians have hardly yet to learn from all that Torrance's work has to offer. Conversely, to read from Torrance that it was Florovsky's "agreement and support" that encouraged him "above all others," and that it was the Greek Fathers that remained his "main love," to which he repaired all the time, learning from them "more than from any other period or set of theologians in Church history," suggests an apt program of study for his contemporary devotees – from Torrance "back to the Fathers." The dialogue begun by these two Christian thinkers over a half century ago has yet to reach its full fruition.

* * *

28 See Thomas F. Torrance, *The Trinitarian Faith* (Edinburgh: T&T Clark, 1988), 68.

29 Torrance, ed., *Theological Dialogue Between Orthodox and Reformed Churches*, ix.

Several of the originals of the letters below lack a date for the year; these have been dated here based on internal evidence – this is indicated where the year is placed in brackets. Underlinings in the original have been retained, but foreign words and book and journal titles have been placed in italics. Except where indicated otherwise by footnote, the originals of the letters are to be found in the Florovsky archive at the Firestone Library of Princeton University. Thanks are offered to the Firestone Library of Princeton University, Department of Rare Books and Archives, and to the libraries of St. Vladimir's Seminary and Princeton Theological Seminary for allowing the publication of these letters from their archives. A debt is owed to the Very Rev. Prof. George Dragas for many conversations in which he shared his personal reminiscences of T. F. Torrance as well as of Georges Florovsky – an invaluable source of historical insight. Finally, we wish to express our warm gratitude to Benjamin Taylor for his labor of love in transcribing these letters in preparation for their annotation and publication.

1.   Beechgrove Manse, 39 Forest Road, Aberdeen.

          Jan. 25, 1950

My dear Professor Florovsky,

          I have to thank you for your kind thought in sending me a Christmas card which was very much appreciated; and also for several contributions from your pen which I have read with the greatest interest. I like the best the one on 'the Lamb of God'[30] – there being, I suppose, least to disagree with in it! I would like one day to examine carefully this notion of *theiosis* [*sic*] which is extremely un-Hebraic and un-biblical.[31] The most the Bible will say is that we are made partakers of the divine nature in Christ.[32] But to go a hair's breadth beyond that is the most dangerous speculation! Besides what more could mortal man want! But I enjoyed that article

---

30   Torrance refers here to Florovsky's essay, "The Lamb of God," in *Lovet være du Jesus Krist. Inkarnationen. Seks Forelæsninger,* ed. Louise Berner Schilden-Holsten (Bringstrup: Theologisk oratoriums forlag, 1949), 66–83.

31   For discussion of how Torrance's views changed on this later, see the introduction to these letters above; for further systematic discussion, see the studies by Myk Habets, *Theosis in the Theology of Thomas F. Torrance* (Farnham: Ashgate, 2009) and Øyvind Rise, *"Sharing in the Life of God": A Study and Discussion of the Theme of Participation in Divine Life* (Stavanger: Misjonshøgskolens Forlag, 2012).

32   2 Peter 1:4.

enormously and have marked down passages for close study when I am working on that subject.

At the moment I am working on a paper for the Intercommunion Conference.[33] I declined to do one for the Student World in which you have one[34] as I really could not have found the time, and besides it would have been duplicating to a large extent what I shall say elsewhere. This is however the crucial point.

I understand your Orthodox teaching about the Church and its plenitude and subscribe to it pretty fully; and I believe too that orders belong to the articles of faith – this has always been a Calvinist doctrine. But I believe firmly that the Eucharist is made for man and not man for the Eucharist and that the Son of man (*Eschatos*)[35] is Lord also of the Eucharist. This means we cannot lord it over the Eucharist, but receive from the Eucharist our orders. In every Eucharist there comes the moment when we are confronted with the *Eschatos* and we are carried beyond the Eucharist into the Marriage-Supper of the Lamb, and so at every Eucharist there comes a point where we must surrender our earthly and ecclesiastical authority to the final Authority of the Judge: the Lamb of God.

That is the point where in every true Eucharist "The Spirit and the Bride will say, 'Come.' And let him that heareth say, 'Come.' And let him that is athirst come. And WHOSOVER WILL, let him take of the water of life freely".[36] Who is the Orthodox Church therefore, or the Roman Church or the Reformed Church or the Anglican Church so to lord it over the Eucharist as to repel and prevent sinners from coming to the table of

33 The conference to which Torrance refers was a meeting of the 3rd Theological Commission appointed by the "Continuation Committee" of Faith and Order, charged with theological work between major conferences; its proceedings were published in the volume edited by Donald Baillie and John Marsh, *Intercommunion* (New York: Harper and Brothers, 1952). Torrance's paper, included in the volume, was entitled "Eschatology and the Eucharist" – a connection that occupies him also in this letter; Florovsky published two essays in this volume: "Terms of Communion in the Undivided Church," and "Confessional loyalty in the Ecumenical Movement."

34 Florovsky, "Confessional Loyalty in the Ecumenical Movement," *The Student World* 43 no. 1 (1950): 57–70; cf. also, Florovsky, "Intercommunion: An Inter-Catholic Discussion," *The Student World* 43 no. 2 (1950), 169–171.

35 Torrance likely has in mind here Rev. 22:13: "I am the Alpha and the Omega, the first and the last [*ho protos kai ho eschatos*], the beginning and the end." See also 1 Cor. 15:45: "The first man Adam was made a living soul; the last Adam [*ho eschatos Adam*] was made a quickening spirit."

36 Revelation 22:17.

the Lord? Will not the *Eschatos* ask questions of us in that day and say in judgment that will surprise the Churches, or the Church as you would have it, at any rate every one of the seven branches of the Church as we have it in the Apocalypse:[37] "I was an hungred, and ye gave me no meat; I was thirsty and ye gave me no drink."[38] That parable has been spoken to us, I feel convinced, to teach us the meaning of intercommunion.[39] I pray and am fearful for those who would turn the *Kuriakon deipnon* into their *idion deipnon*[40] thus introducing, as Paul says so plainly, *schismata* into the Church.[41]

I am ready to understand the theological significance of defection from a united Eucharist, behind which there is a certain theological earnestness and sincerity so often lacking in those who are not very pained at our divisions; but ultimately refusal of intercommunion can only mean for me a lack of trust in the opus Dei in the Eucharist and a fear that it is not so powerful as to overcome our mistakes and heal our divisions, and bring medicine to our mortal strifes. If the real presence of the Lord, the Son of Man, the *Eschatos*, the Lamb of God, is with us in the Eucharist, as I most firmly believe it is, then I am ready to put the Lord and Head of the Church before Church Order, before Doctrine, before Tradition. All our Church Order and Doctrine come as the result of the *charismata* given us by the Lord of the Church in his Ascension-gifts; but, says Paul, even these *charismata* will pass away, though faith, hope, and love will remain. Even the Ämter[42] of the Church, as Eugen Walter of Freiburg says in a recent powerful book (*Das Kommen des Herrn* – R.C.!)[43], will pass away before the apocalypse of the New Creation which

37   Revelation, chapters 2–3.

38   Matthew 25:42.

39   The parable of the sheep and the goats in Matthew 25:31–46 (a rarely cited text in Torrance).

40   1 Cor. 11:20–21: "When ye come together therefore into one place, this is not to eat the Lord's supper [*kuriakon deipnon*]. For in eating every one taketh before other his own supper [*idion deipnon*]: and one is hungry, and another is drunken."

41   Torrance has in mind Paul's reference to divisions (*schismata*) in the context of discussing the Eucharist in 1 Cor. 11:18. Torrance does not note, however, the fact that here (see verse 19) as well as elsewhere (Rom. 16:17 and 1 Cor. 1:10), Paul associates these *schismata* precisely with heresy and disagreement in faith.

42   German: "offices," "orders."

43   "R.C.": Roman Catholic Walter's study *Das Kommen des Herrn* (Freiburg im Breisgau: Herder, 1948–1950) was published in two volumes: *Die endzeitgemässe Haltung des Christen nach den Briefen der heiligen Apostel Paulus und Petrus*

is absolutely one with the risen Body of the Saviour.[44] This is the notion that the Reformed Church takes seriously, the Lordship of the Real Presence in the Church, and not the domestication of the Real presence to be the manipulable tool of Church history and ecclesiastical orders that are necessarily fraught with the misunderstandings of this passing world. The Reformation stands for a Christological correction of the doctrine of the Church and sacraments in accordance with the principles of Nicaea and Chalcedon, which was NEVER carried out anywhere until a beginning was made at the Reformation. This is what it means to put on the wedding garment for the Marriage Supper of the Lamb – "not being conformed to this world but being transformed by the renewing of the mind . . . Let this mind be in you which was also in Christ Jesus," etc.[45] But there is no need to say all this to you, for as a Biblical theologian you will agree with it.[46] Our divisions come however where we arrest some particular doctrine and freeze it a special point, and refuse for pride or prejudice or history to carry this doctrine critically through the whole pleroma of our Church life and thought and practice. This may be painful to you, but I submit that as we look over at the Catholic sections of the Church, conscious though we may be that <u>we have yet to reform ourselves anew</u> in areas where we became deficient through defection at the Reformation, there are areas in the Catholic Churches where a refusal to submit to self-correction in terms of the great Christological Councils is the greatest stumbling block to reunion.[47]

(1948); II. *Die eschatologische Situation nach den synoptischen Evangelien* (1947).

44 Torrance notably does not address here the apostolic thrones still to be found in the kingdom of God (Matt. 19:28; Lk. 22:30; Rev. 20:4), of which the ancient Orthodox liturgical *synthronon* of bishop and presbyters is an eschatological image.

45 Romans 12:2; Philippians 2:5.

46 Note Torrance's regard for Florovsky as a "Biblical theologian" – quite a different perception than the one that obtains in recent criticisms of Florovsky and neopatristic theology among academicians.

47 Torrance's reference to the "Catholic Churches," reflects the decision within Faith and Order during this period to distinguish between "Catholic" and "Protestant" ecclesiologies among its member bodies, with the former inclusive of Orthodox and Anglican. This delineation is reflected in Florovsky's own writings, which often follow the older traditional Orthodox way of speaking of Orthodoxy as the Catholic faith or Catholic Church. Florovsky similarly distinguished between *Corpus Christi* and *coetus fidelium* or "gathered church" ecclesiologies.

One of the burning points here is where Church Order concerns the Eucharist. You are right to put your finger on this point! I do wish I could spend several days with you going over all the relevant passages in the Scriptures and the Fathers of the first four centuries on these matters – that is the only way to come to a closer understanding, is it not?[48]

Meantime I send you a paper I wrote for the Faith & Order Commission of the British Council of Churches. I am conscious of its deficiencies, and hope to expand it into a book when I get time.

Actually I shall be in New York for a few hours on the night of the 3rd/4th June or probably on the day of the 3rd. I have to catch the night train then for Montreal where I have some lectures to give. If I have longer to spare I will try to get in touch with you then.

I am not by the way a professor – not yet anyway. I have a very busy parish on my hands, and it is very hard going especially with the amount of theological work I have to do.[49] But before very long I hope to be engaged all the time in theological and academic work – but this is a very good discipline for a living theology, and indeed the only true training ground!

I hope you will write a rejoinder to this letter if you have time. But I do feel that if we take the eschatological significance of the Eucharist[50]

48   In his 1970 sermon "The Relevance of Orthodoxy," reprinted in this volume, Torrance reflected on his experience of precisely such common study of Scripture in the Faith and Order Commission on Christ and His Church and admitted: "Again and again . . . when passages of the Bible were being interpreted by others – Professor Florovsky, for example – I had to take a new hard look at the Greek text of the New Testament to see whether it really did mean what he said, and again and again found that I had been misreading the New Testament because I had been looking at it through Presbyterian spectacles. Our conjoint discussion, to which we brought our several Church traditions and outlooks, enabled us in the give and take of criticism, to read what was actually written in the Bible and to interpret it as far as possible undistorted by this or that ecclesiastical tradition. I myself learned, I think, from the Orthodox more than from any other."

49   Torrance was at this time minister of the parish of Beechgrove Church in Aberdeen, a position he took up in the fall of 1947. In addition to parish ministry and the publication of numerous essays and book reviews, he had already by this time co-founded the Scottish Church Theology Society in 1945, published his dissertation on *The Doctrine of Grace in the Apostolic Fathers* (1946/1948), launched (with J. K. S. Reid) the *Scottish Journal of Theology* in 1948, and published his book-length study, *Calvin's Doctrine of Man* (London: Lutterworth Press, 1949).

50   In fact, Florovsky also viewed the Eucharist in eschatological terms, but did not draw the same conclusions from this as did Torrance regarding intercommunion – likely because he viewed the relationship between eschatology and history differently. This was not the first time Florovsky had opposed "intercommunion" proposals; a similar proposal was offered by Fr. Sergii Bulgakov in the early

more seriously and probe into its real depth, we shall remove not only misunderstandings but actual mistakes on all sides. Who of us will be able to protest doctrinal and sacramental integrity, complete integrity, when we meet our King?

With every good wish and Christian love,

Your sincere friend,

Tom Torrance

P.S. Have you sent for the *Scottish Journal of Theology* your promised Article on <u>Christianity and History</u>?[51] It has not arrived, and I have been wondering whether it has gone astray. We are looking forward very, very much to having the honour of publishing that. TFT.

2.   March 31st. [1950]

My dear Professor Florovsky,

I am indebted to you for your kind letter. I shall look forward all the more for your article on Christian Faith and History.

I see what you mean about the difficulties our respective communions, and the unconscious attitudes they import into our theological thinking. But I don't think I am in the least inclined to despair over this – for biblical studies are helping us.[52] What amazes

1930s within the Anglican-Orthodox Fellowship of St. Alban and St. Sergius, but was opposed by both Orthodox and Anglicans, following the arguments of Florovsky. The eschatological vision of the Eucharist is altogether characteristic of Orthodox theology, but has not led to an acceptance of intercommunion; see for instance, Alexander Schmemann, *The Eucharist: Sacrament of the Kingdom* (Crestwood, NY. St. Vladimir's Seminary Press, 1987); John Zizioulas, *Eucharist, Bishop, Church* (Brookline, MA.: Holy Cross Orthodox Press, 2001), and *The Eucharistic Communion and the World* (London: T&T Clark, 2011), 1–97; and Nikolaos Loudovikos, *A Eucharistic Ontology: Maximus the Confessor's Eschatological Ontology of Being as Dialogical Reciprocity* (Brookline, MA.: Holy Cross Orthodox Press, 2010).

51 The article was never published.

52 This stress on the importance of biblical studies for ecumenical convergence is characteristic of the early Torrance, but became less pronounced in his later work – perhaps following James Barr's 1961 criticism of his scriptural exegesis; increasingly, Torrance – somewhat like Florovsky – came to emphasize rather the ecumenically crucial importance of patristic *ressourcement,* particularly in the form of a return to the "Athanasian-Cyriline axis" of Greek patristic theology, as well as the need to overcome the influence of outmoded and unhelpful scientific dualisms

me (in a recent study of the Epistle to the Hebrews) that where in the NT the liturgical sacrifices are mentioned, there is least of the succession idea! But we won't argue that out now.[53]

I wonder if we need any special permission to publish that article of yours on the Lamb of God? Croxall simply sent his to us, as it had been printed only privately.[54] But if you feel that permission should be sought, I wonder if you would be so good to write to the appropriate quarter? That would be helpful.

I sent Vladimir Weidle's recent *The Baptism of Art* to a man to review who has since died and I am unable to recover the booklet. If you have a copy would you care to write for us a short review? It is, I think, a supremely important book, and for me most illuminating, for its view of baptism and Eucharist as forming one whole, and also of the "signitive" nature of pre-liturgical sacrament and art[55] is just what strove after in his attempt to return to the early fathers. That is even more true perhaps of certain early and classical Anglicanism.

in theology that had contributed to doctrinal divisions.

53   Torrance expended considerable energy during this period attacking the concept of linear historic apostolic succession, in favor of a classically Protestant conception of apostolicity. It seems his main objection was to the rather mechanical conception common among Anglo-Catholics. For a striking attempt to synthesize Eastern and Western patristic accounts of apostolicity in a way that transcends the tendencies criticized by Torrance, see John Zizioulas, "Apostolic Continuity and Succession," in *Being as Communion* (Crestwood, N.Y.: St Vladimir's Seminary Press, 1985), 171–208, and "Apostolic Continuity of the Church and Apostolic Succession in the First Five Centuries," *Louvain Studies* 21 (1996): 153–86.

54   T. H. Croxall, an Anglican priest and theologian residing in Copenhagen, later known primarily for his work on Kierkegaard.

55   Vladimir Weidlé, *The Baptism of Art: Notes on the Religion of the Catacomb Paintings* (Londres, 1950). Torrance makes use of Weidlé in his 1955 work *Royal Priesthood.* Scottish Journal of Theology Occasional Papers, No. 3 (Edinburgh: Oliver and Boyd, 1955), 93–94, in order to underscore this idea of the "signitive" character of early Christian art; in the same context, he criticizes the developed Orthodox iconography and its corresponding theology as indicative of "Platonizing" tendencies derived from Philo of Alexandria. His thoughts on the icon were to change significantly later to a much more positive view, with fascinating insights into the inverse perspective of Byzantine iconography and its paradigmatic status for theological epistemology: see *Theological Science* (London: Oxford University Press, 1969), 15, 23; *Space, Time and Incarnation* (London: Oxford University Press, 1969), 18; *Reality and Scientific Theology* (1985 reprint: Eugene, OR.: Wipf & Stock, 2001), 127.

I am to go to a Chair in Edinburgh next Session (October) and shall have much more time for theological writing.[56] I hope we will be able to get you over too sometime to visit us in New College.

With every good wish,

Yours very sincerely,

Tom Torrance

3.   21 South Oswald Road. Edinburgh, 9.

        March 30th, 1951

My dear Professor Florovsky,

It is some time since I wrote to you. We were glad to publish your article on the Lamb of God in the current number of the Scottish Journal of Theology.[57] The off-prints are being sent off to you now.

I write also to ask when you can let us have the long-promised article on <u>Eschatology and History</u>? We are looking forward very much to having and publishing that. I wonder if you are to be over here this summer? We might manage to have you visit Edinburgh. Do let us know if you are to be in this country and when.

With every good wish,

Yours very sincerely

T. F. Torrance

4.   At: The Brow, Combe Down, Bath, Somerset.

        August 4th, 1951

        As from: 21 South Oswald Rd. Edinburgh

My Dear Professor Florovsky,

I see by the circular which came in this morning about the International Patristic Conference to be held in Oxford that you are to be

56 Torrance's invitation to the chair of Church History at New College, Edinburgh was publicly announced to his congregation at Beechgrove Church on March 26, 1950 – just days before the writing of this letter

57 Florovsky, "The Lamb of God," *Scottish Journal of Theology* 4, no. 1 (1951): 13–28.

there too.[58] I am reminded at the same time that I owe you a letter, and hasten to write to you therefore.

You may be in Europe by the time this letter gets you, but they will forward it to you, I am sure. In any case I will write another to you c/o the WCC in Geneva! You must be a terribly busy man – I only hope that you do not overdo things, for your letter contained a frightful catalogue of lectures and work in which you were engaged – and in the midst of all this here I am a sort of νάρκη[59] to trouble you!

I write to ask how you are getting on with your two papers for the *Scottish Journal of Theology*, on History and Eschatology. I hope very much that you will be able to give them to me when I see you in Oxford next month – that would be grand. But please do not overwork – we would rather wait than have them from you posthumously!

Your review of Vladimir Weidlés' little work on the Baptism of Art appears in September in *SJT*.[60] In the same number I also take note of that work in a lecture on History and Reformation – but I take a better view of Weidle than you do or appeared to do!!![61]

One of these days I will be demanding from you an article on Baptism – I feel that the Orthodox Church has a lot to teach us here, and I am eager that we have it – and from no one better than yourself. But I leave that in your hands.

---

58 The International Conference on Patristic Studies was organized by Frank Leslie Cross (1900–1968), Lady Margaret Professor of Divinity at the University of Oxford; its first meeting was in September 1951 and counted 260 persons in attendance. For Florovsky's reports on the second conference, see "The Oxford Conference on Patristic Studies. September 1955," *St. Vladimir's Theological Quarterly* 4, nos. 1–2 (Fall 1955–Winter 1956): 57–62, and "Second International Conference on Patristic Studies," *The Greek Orthodox Theological Review* 2, no. 1 (Easter Issue): 121–23. Florovsky's paper at this second conference was also on patristic eschatology, and was presumably based on material worked up for the presentation Torrance asked him to give in 1952 (letters 6 through 8 below); for the published paper, see Florovsky, "Eschatology in the Patristic Age: An Introduction," *Studia Patristica* 2 Part 2 (1956): 235–50.

59 In Ancient Greek, νάρκη can denote a "torpedo" (the electric ray, not the explosive device), perhaps connoting here a "painful nuisance"; in Modern Greek, the term can denote a "landmine."

60 Florovsky, Review of Wladmir Weidlé, *The Baptism of Art, Scottish Journal of Theology* 4, no. 3 (1951): 331–34.

61 Florovsky in his review critiques Weidlé for neglecting the biblical background of early Christian art, its typological character, and its foundation in salvation history, in which types and realities are closely correlated.

I have been on holiday here with the family and return to Edinburgh next week.

With every good wish,

Yours very sincerely,

T. F. Torrance

5.   At: The Brow, Combe Down, Bath, Somerset.

As From: 21 South Oswald Rd., Edinburgh

9. August 4th, 1951.

My dear Professor Florovsky,

I have just written to you an air-mail to New York, but am writing this to you c/o WCC at Geneva, in the hope that it may reach you sooner.

I have been very long in answering your letter, and when you say that last time it took me 12 months to do, I feel ashamed. It looks as if I am the base sort of man who only writes when he wants something!

To tell the truth I have been almost as busy as you! and have been enjoying a holiday here. But when I saw that you are to be at the International Conference on Patristics, I felt I must write to you. I was to be in Greece in September, but the forthcoming elections have made me postpone that visit, so that I can now go to the Conference on Patristics also. I hope to see you there, therefore.

I hope too that you will be able to give me your papers on History and Eschatology for publication in the *Scottish Journal of Theology*. I note that they have now been put into two papers which is very agreeable to us. We look forward very much indeed to having them.

Your review of Weidlé: *The Baptism of Art* appears in *SJT* for September, 4/3.

I hope you keep well and are managing something of a holiday in your visit to Europe.

With every good wish,

Yours very sincerely,

Tom Torrance

T.F. Torrance

6.   21 South Oswald Rd. Edinburgh 9.

January 26th. [1952]

My dear Florovsky,

I have two of your letters to answer. It was a great joy to get your Christmas greeting, with its lines. Thank you kindly. I was so overwhelmed both with work and illness in the family during the Christmas season that I did not get much done.

I am delighted to hear you have by now one of your articles on History and Eschatology finished for the *Scottish Journal of Theology*. I will be glad to have that <u>as soon as you can let me</u> for the Journal. I would like to get it into the June number, as we have a Conference on the Subject in July and it would be good to have your paper to discuss then. I look forward very much to the second as well. Could we have it in time to publish for the September number of *SJT*, which would mean having it in our hands by June? Thank you <u>very</u> much. It will be a great honour to have these in *SJT*.

We are now issuing a pamphlet on *SJT* for distribution and are advertising in it your articles. This pamphlet we hope to get widely distributed in USA and on the Continent.

We are starting a Society for Historical Theology over here, and we shall be having our first meeting in Cambridge just before you go to the WCC Advisory Commission.[62] So we would be very glad to have you come to it. I will send you the printed material about it later. The subject of the Conference is the History of Eschatology from NT and Patristic times down to the present day – so you ought to be in your element. We hope to have there most of the leading theologians of the country and some visitors from overseas too. So do try to come, for you would be one of our Star visitors!

Can you give me names of works on Patristic Eschatology dealing mainly with the Greek Fathers and later Orthodox Theology – works in a language readable to me such as French or German, though I might manage modern Greek? I would be very grateful. I have myself lectured on the theology or rather the eschatology of the first 6 centuries this session, and am now on to the Reformation. Very little has been done in English on Patristic eschatology, and there is a great deal to be done.

---

62   Torrance refers here to the Society for the Study of Theology. For information, see http://www.theologysociety.org.uk

I look forward to hearing from you and also to having your papers to study.

I hope you are as happy in New York as we are in Edinburgh though the amount of work we both have to do seems equally fearful!

With all kind greetings,

Yours aye,

Tom Torrance

7.   21 South Oswald Rd. Edinburgh 9.

Feb. 12th. [1952]

My dear Florovsky,

This letter is in the nature of an S.O.S. In my last to you I spoke of the Conference of the forthcoming Society for Historical Theology, and its plans for meeting in July 22–25 at Queens' College, Cambridge. I know you are to be over for the WCC Advisory Commission of 25, and hope and expect you can be with us. We have had great difficulty with dates, and these dates do not suit all but suit most, though they knock out several of our speakers. I write to ask if you would be so good as to give us a paper on <u>Patristic Eschatology, later period</u> – roughly from Chalcedon to Joachim (but excluding him) dealing with both East and West, and with Augustine perhaps in particular. Our great difficulty is to find men who understand eschatology as well as having a good knowledge of Patristics. We had two men on our original committee marked down to do this paper, one failing the other, but both have pulled out, and I am compelled to look overseas, and there is no one more eminent than yourself. It would be a very great honour and stimulus to us if you could help us out in this way, in giving us a paper as well as engaging in our discussions.

We are hoping that the papers may be printed, if not in a composite volume, then in *SJT* or some similar periodical. But of course they do not need to be in final form by the time of the Conference – they can be revised for publication later – if so desired.

I'd be very grateful for a reply as soon as is convenient.

With every good wish,

Yours aye,

Tom <u>Torrance</u>

8.   21 South Oswald Rd. Edinburgh 9

       Feb. 26. [1952]

My dear Florovsky,

I am very delighted that you are coming to the conference for the Society for Historical Theology – and will give us a paper on Patristic Eschatology: Later Period. The dates are July 22–25, Queens College, Cambridge. I will send you full particulars later. If you want hospitality in England, please let us know, and we will try to find it for you as it will be congenial.

We will be glad also to publish this paper on Patristic Eschatology in *SJT* – if it does not go into a conference volume with the others. We must wait till July to see if the others want to publish a composite vol. of all our essays!

With kindest regards – my wife has the greatest sympathy for yours! Love from us all in New College.

Yours aye,

Tom Torrance

9.   21 South Oswald Rd., Edinburgh 9

      Oct. 3rd. [1952]

My dear Florovsky,

Thank you for sending me the copy of your St. Vladimir Journal,[63] which I find most interesting. We shall be glad to exchange *SJT* for this, if that is your intention, is it?

I hope you are somewhat recovered after your arduous tour on the continent. We certainly work you hard when you come over. I look back with great pleasure to your address to the new SST in Queens' College, Cambridge. The other addresses are now coming in and I am hoping to receive yours as soon as possible, so that we can publish them all together in one volume. Yours need not be just as you gave it, but if it covers the field allotted to you, we shall be most grateful. It is of the utmost

---

63 The *St. Vladimir's Seminary Quarterly,* later renamed *St. Vladimir's Theological Quarterly,* was founded on Florovsky's initiative in March 1952 and published under his editorship until 1956. Its first issue was published in Fall 1952, with an editorial by Florovsky himself: "The Challenge of Our Time" (see http://www.svots.edu/content/svtq-first-issue-quarterly). The journal continues successfully under the present editorship of Prof. Paul Meyendorff.

importance for the New Theological Society that this volume appears as promptly as we can publish it, so that the Society gets off to a good start.

It is such a pity USA is so far away, but we hope that as soon as we can we will be able to have you over here in Edinburgh before very long. I always revel in what you have to say!

With every good wish,

Yours ever,

Tom Torrance

10.   At: The Brow, Combe Down, Bath, Somerset

Jan. 2, 1953

My dear Florovsky,

Thank you and Fr. Schmemann very much for your kind Xmas card & its good wishes.[64] Hope 1953 will be a very blessed New Year for you all at St. Vladimir's.

I am now sending to the Press the 4 addresses given last July in Cambridge minus yours & Mackinnon's![65] I'd like it printed before June – unless we receive your lecture before the end of January we shall have to omit it! I hope very, very much yours will be in by Jan 25. Sorry to be such a νάρκη!

With every good wish

Yours aye,

Tom Torrance

P.S. For *SJT* 6/1 I've an article on Lund![66]

---

64 Fr. Alexander Schmemann (1921–1983) was a prominent Orthodox priest and liturgical theologian who began teaching at St. Vladimir's Seminary in 1951 and served as dean there from 1962 until his death.

65 Donald MacKinnon (1913–1994), Scottish philosopher and theologian, and a friend to T. F. Torrance. The other four addresses were as follows: William Manson, "Eschatology in the New Testament;" G. W. H. Lampe, "Early Patristic Eschatology;" T. F. Torrance, "The Eschatology of the Reformation;" and W. A. Whitehouse, "The Modern Discussion of Eschatology." The papers by Manson, Lampe, Torrance, and Whitehouse were published together as *Eschatology: Four Occasional Papers read to the Society for the Study of Theology.* Scottish Journal of Theology Occasional Papers, No.2 (Edinburgh: Oliver & Boyd, 1953).

66 The 1952 Faith and Order assembly held in Lund, Sweden, with both Florovsky

11.   21 South Oswald Rd. Edinburgh 9.

Feb. 4, 1953

My dear Florovsky,

Thank you very much for your air letter. We shall be delighted to get your paper on <u>Patristic Eschatology</u> by the end of February. The other lectures have gone to the press, but I feel sure we can get yours in time also if we have it – as soon as possible now – say by end of <u>February</u>.

No! I'm not angry with you, dear brother, but rejoice that the Lord uses you so [illegible], though I <u>covet</u> everything from your pen for *SJT*! I wonder what you will think of my article on Lund in *SJT* 6/1 due to appear at the end of February? I shall be glad of your reactions if you have time to write.[67]

With every good wish

Yours aye,

Tom Torrance

12.   Georges Florovsky to Oliver Tomkins[68] (December 26, 1953)

537 West 121 Street New York 27, N.Y.

26/XII. '53

and Torrance in attendance. Torrance refers here to his article, "Where do we go from Lund?" *Scottish Journal of Theology* 6 (1953): 53–64.

67   Torrance mentions Florovsky in his Lund essay. Commenting on the impact of recent studies on the tenor of the Lund Assembly, he writes: "To find great patristic learning in Professor Calhoun, and Calvin's language on the lips of Professor Florovsky, were but two indications of the theological interpenetration that is going on among theologians, but what has made that possible is the concern of theologians to think out together the doctrines of the faith on the basis of biblical study," "Problems of Faith and Order: Where do we go from Lund?" reprinted in Thomas F. Torrance, *Conflict and Agreement in the Church*, vol. 1, *Order and Disorder*, 227. We do not have Florovsky's response to the essay. We can be certain, however, that Florovsky would appreciate Torrance's stress on a Christocentric ecclesiology conceived with reference to the "historic Christ" and the Chalcedonian analogy, but would disagree with Torrance's defense of the Reformation critique of ecclesiology and his characterization of the relation between theology and ecclesiastical form in the Orthodox Church as "statically formulated."

68   Oliver Tomkins (1908–1992), Anglican priest and secretary to the World Council of Churches; Warden of Lincoln Theological College from 1952; named Bishop of Bristol in 1959. Tomkins was for a long time closely involved in ecumenical discussions on the theme of intercommunion.

My dearest Oliver:

First of all excuse me for the delay, and secondly for the most inadequate character of the draft which I am now presenting.[69] Strictly speaking, it is no more than loose paragraphs submitted to you for a tentative incorporation in the Working paper. My personal conviction, which I reached after a long scrutiny and heart-searching, is that no such "incorporation" is possible. T.'s draft is excellent – for those who can accept it.[70] There is a clear plan and his argument develops coherently. I have no desire to pose as an "Advocatus diabolic," and no desire to spoil the document which, from his point of view, is the best I could have expected. The only thing I have to say is that most Catholics are unable to concur. Probably, if you are really going to undertake a drastic revision, just in order to fit the essence of the document within the required maximal amount of words, what would of course imply some adjustment in the structure, you will be able to insert some of my points. You are well acquainted with the Anglo-Catholic position, from which you are not very far, and you can easily imagine what Michael Ramsey[71] would have said in my place, and therefore you can do full justice to both sides, if "sides" they are. To say the truth, I do not see any <u>organic</u> link between the Section I and Sections II and III. If you agree with the I, you are not yet committed to anything that is offered in II or III. My guess is that in I no adequate attention is given to the <u>Historical structure of the Church</u>. Christ is obviously One, and His Church is, and should be one.

But it does not follow that this One Church is adequately represented in the discordant crowd of historical denominations, and that the only trouble is that they do not exhibit enough the hidden Unity and exaggerate dissensions which "ultimately" are irrelevant. I admit that T. means something more, but what he had written will be read and sponsored by many who would not go the whole way with him. In any case, I do not believe that it is fair to offer this document as a balanced

69 See the text at number 14 below.

70 "T."=Torrance. Florovsky is referring to Torrance's draft, "Our Oneness in Christ and Our Disunity as Churches," reprinted in Torrance, *Conflict and Agreement in the Church*, vol. 1, *Order and Disorder*, 263–83.

71 Michael Ramsey (1904–1988), leading Anglican theologian of the Anglo-Catholic party, with a deep sympathy for Orthodoxy; at this time Bishop of Durham (1952–1956), later Archbishop of York (1956–1961) and finally Archbishop of Canterbury (1961–1974). Ramsey was a friend of Florovsky since the 1930s; with Florovsky and Karl Barth, he held a prominent place at the 1948 Amsterdam Assembly.

ecumenical draft. And probably the fairest thing would be to leave it as it stands, and only add a foot-note at the end, to the effect that the two Orthodox members of the Working Committee were unable to join. By the way, Chrysostomos Constantinidis[72] is publishing – in Greek, of course – his detailed report on our meeting at Bossey, in "Apostolos Andreas;" it is not yet completed (in the issues I received as yet). I hope to prepare a special memorandum before Evanston, and probably early enough to circulate it to the members of the Working Committee. So, I am handing my sketch to you, and leave it to you to decide, whether my stuff should be incorporated at all – if you decide to leave the paper as it is, do not forget the foot note. Copies of all this go simultaneously to Nelson and Torrance.[73] I am very anxious to hear from you all at your first convenience.

I have now two weeks for myself, free from the school. But I have "unfinished business" at least for six months. I hope to finish four books this spring (?). In any case, I have to complete two urgent articles by Jan. 5.

Love. Ever yours

[Georges Florovsky]

13.   Georges Florovsky to Thomas F. Torrance[74]

Dear Torrance:

Do not be angry with me. Your paper is fine.[75] But it is not an "ecumenical" document. There is another point of view also within the Ecumenical movement. My belief is that no ecumenical statement on the subject, and especially no proposal (and your section III is actually a proposal),[76] is possible at the present stage. Except we frankly admit that

---

72   Metropolitan Chrysostomos Constantinidis (1921–2006), Bishop of Myra and Ephesus, professor of dogmatics at the theological school at Chalki, near Istanbul. An ecumenical spokesman for the Patriarchate of Constantinople and a friend to Torrance, he was later the head from the Orthodox side in the official Orthodox-Reformed dialogue inaugurated by Torrance.

73   See letter 13 and the draft of comments at 14 below.

74   This letter is not dated, but the copy of it in Florovsky's archive is printed on the last page of the letter December 26, 1953 letter to Oliver Tomkins.

75   "Our Oneness in Christ and Our Disunity as Churches," in Torrance, *Conflict and Agreement in the Church*, vol. 1, 263–83.

76   A proposal for latitude regarding Eucharistic doctrine and, implicitly, for

we do not agree: such a statement will be ecumenical, because it will be factually true. It is our tragedy that we cannot travel beyond a certain narrow limit. It would not help at all if I, as it were, "pass" the document. It would not make it any more "ecumenical," and somebody else will point it out. I am terribly disturbed that, being brethren and friends in the sacred name of Jesus, we cannot meet at His table. But the tragedy is that we cannot, simply and purely. Let us pray together and for each other, and do what we can do together, trusting in the mercy of the Lord.

One of the four books mentioned above is on the Meaning of History, a small one – under 100 pages.[77] I intend it for the Cahiers de l'Actualite Protestante (but I am writing it in English).

Love and affection. Ever yours,

[Georges Florovsky]

14. Florovsky's draft of comments on Torrance's paper, "Our Oneness in Christ and Our Disunity as Churches":[78]

I was given an impossible task: to add to a document which was already too long, and is going to be drastically abridged. Again, I had to insert paragraphs in a context which was not congenial to me. The only thing I could attempt was just to offer a very tentative draft which had to be used by the final editor and fused or melted with what might have survived from the existing text. I have to emphasize briefly my main points.

1. In the section II I want to have an explicit statement on the major tension in doctrines: the Schism is, and has been, about the Truth, as sinful and criminal schism as such obviously is. In a sense, I was pleading for the Reformation. The quarrel with Rome, in any case, cannot be

intercommunion: see *Conflict and Agreement in the Church,* vol. 1, 279–83.

77   Florovsky is referring to his comment to Tomkins that he is hoping to publish four books in the spring. This is a clear indication that Florovsky sent this letter to Torrance precisely as it is found in the archives: as appended to the letter to Tomkins commenting on Torrance's ecumenical proposals. Sadly, none of the four books Florovsky had intended to publish ever appeared; a substantial portion of one of them, on the history of Christian divisions in ecumenical perspective, is to be found in the Florovsky archive at Princeton University.

78   This draft was appended to Florovsky's letters to Tomkins and Torrance (Dec. 26, 1953; letters 12 and 13 above), and is a commentary on the paper of Torrance later reproduced in Torrance, *Conflict and Agreement in the Church,* vol. 1, 263–83.

settled just by "repentance". Who should repent? And of what? Just of
disunity? But on both sides there is a firm conviction that the other part
is in a dangerous error. For me personally, as for an Orthodox, both are
in error, while both are preserving some truth. I do not feel desirable to
introduce any elaboration on Ecclesiology at this point. The chief thing is
however this: Schism is not only guilt, but also a witness to the ultimate
disagreement about the Truth. Should it be made clear that for "the
Protestants" (some, at least) all schisms are to such an extent and in such a
sense inside of the *Una Sancta*, that they can be overruled just by an increase
"in charity", whereas for "the Catholics" the separation went much further
and many of the existing Christian denominations are if not "outside" of the
Una Sancta, yet in fact so loosely and, if it were, "symbolically" related to it
as not to be fully in it, as her "parts" or "members." It is very difficult to say
all this in a compact manner: it would require a very accurate and detailed
elaboration. Has the Church a structure? Granted, everything historical will
be superseded and surpassed by what no eye had seen and no imagination
could have visualized, but the Historical has its own status in the progress of
salvation – pointing to the Beyond, – in a double sense, to the transcending
work of the Glorified Christ (which of course, does not "relativize" the
structure of the Church) and to his final and concluding "Eschatological"
consummation-intervention. As any reunion belongs to the Historical,
involving our responsibility and loyalty in a given historical context, it
cannot (and should not) be treated outside of the Historical structure, as it
were, immediately and directly, in "eschatological" categories. "Eschatology"
in the Church is mediated through History and her "structures". It is here
that the controversy about "Succession" would set in.

2. Christ's Body, the Holy Church, is one. Her unity and uniqueness
is her very being and character. There can be but One Church, as there is
but One God and One Lord Jesus Christ in the glory of the Father. And
yet – Christians are divided. Christendom is divided. The Christian World
is in schism. There are, in fact, several Christian bodies (and they are
numerous indeed) which claim the name of the Church for themselves,
and for themselves alone – and they are out of communion with each
other, sometimes in open and bitter antagonism. The unity of the faith
has been broken. The unity of love has cooled. The body of Christians
has been utterly disrupted. This is the flagrant scandal of Christian
history and its major mystery and paradox. Because, and this is the basic
assumption and axiom of Christian faith and hope, the Church simply

cannot be divided, just as Christ cannot be divided either, and there is but One Lord, and not many. But the impossible seems to have happened. The divisive and disruptive power of sin seems to have crept even into the New Humanity, initiated by Christ's victory on the Cross and manifested in His Resurrection and Glory. The Old Adam seems not to have died, and continues even in the New Age. The sting of tragedy and paradox is, however, in the fact that, in the concrete context of Christian existence, schisms and divisions seem to have been imposed so often precisely by the loyalty to Christ and zeal for the true faith, by a sincere desire to preserve and to exhibit the true Unity and to disentangle the New out of the oppressive Old, of "this World." Strangely enough, in many situations, "disruption" seemed to be the obvious demand of Christian conscience. And for that reason it is quite impossible to check the existing divisions just by their confrontation with a general postulate of Unity. No Christian wants schism as such. But, as tragic as it is indeed, Christian Unity, even the Unity of the Holy Church, is variously apprehended and interpreted. And it would be idle just to expatiate on the ideal of Unity, pure and simple. All Christians suffer from the burden of disruption, and all have some share in its guilt. Thus all should repent. But even at this crucial point there is division. The nature and meaning of the existing schism are differently viewed. Even from a purely practical point of view, an unqualified pleading for Unity is not convincing and will not bring together those who feel themselves estranged from each other by the claims of their Christian conscience and faithfulness to the truth which had been once delivered unto the saints. It is precisely in the name of the true Apostolicity of the message and of the Holiness of life that Christian groups persist in their mutual separation, even when they have re-kindled the spirit of charity and have assumed the burdens of each other. Even when Christians are ready to stay together – in charity and love, they find themselves in an inextricable predicament of a conscientious separation. In spite of the common ground, which all Christians possess in Christ and His Gospel, they cannot meet in a common profession of faith. It may be true that modern divisions and disagreements cut across many denominational barriers erected in the past ages. And yet, there are major disagreements, if in a modern shape, and ultimately it is just a distribution of adherents that had been changed, but the very crux of dissension is rather the same. And probably, even the very fact that, in our days and, at least partially, under the impact of the ecumenical conversation, individual Christians of various and divergent backgrounds can meet and agree across the structural boundaries of the historical Christendom, reveals the tragedy of the schism in its ultimate sharpness. The meaning of this "meeting" and "agreement" can be differently assessed. Some would say that it just reveals the underlying Unity of the "Holy Church," which had been obscured and screened by and in the unhappy confusion of empirical history, and consequently would urge those who have recovered the sense of Unity to exhibit it in external acts of witness and testimony. Some others, however, would interpret this cross-meeting as an attempt to escape the tragedy of the Church Schism by a precarious arrangement between individuals and groups, and would oppose any such venture as disloyal and unreal. It is obviously true that the final and comprehensive judgment over history, even over the history of Christendom, belongs solely to the Judge, to Whom all power had been given in heaven and on earth, and that His final ruling and judgment will be unexpected for many. And yet, the Church on earth, i.e. in history, has been given an authority and responsibility – to bind and to loose. It had been established in history as a Pillar and foundation of the Truth. Charity should never be set against the Truth. There can be no contradiction between what is essentially of God. Christendom is sick indeed. But can it be healed just by an evasive call to unity? Evasive? Yes, because the root of sickness is in the confused and inadequate vision and apprehension of the Revealed Truth. One should take quite seriously the existing opposition within Christendom, however difficult it may be to describe or to define in rigid terms the very point of dissension. One should be frank and sincere: there is dissension.

3. In our ecumenical conversation and fraternal exchange of convictions, we have reached a critical stage, at which it is becoming increasingly difficult to speak with a common voice, or to make agreed statements. All agree that the Church's Unity is God's will and purpose, and all are aware of an impending duty to recover the lost unity. But then the path bifurcates, and practical advises [sic] diverge. At the present moment it would mean violence and compulsion, and this would mean an ultimate blow to the ecumenical companionship, if one proposes a single policy of the Ecumenical action and claims for it a binding authority. There is an ultimate cleavage. For many the present state of schism and disruption does depend primarily upon the spirit of divisiveness, in which secondary dissensions are over-emphasized and pretexts for the continuing separation are discovered in things

which should not prevent communion in sacraments and confession, even if it is impossible to realize at once all inherent implications. They feel it as a sinful obstinacy that "churches," in spite of their agreement in basic things and against the expressed will of God, "that they should be one" and perfected in one, persist in their isolation. There is Unity, and it must be manifested at once. But there are many others, and the question of numbers and of proportions is absolutely out of order and of place in the realm of Christian freedom and of ultimate convictions and commitments of faith, who are as strongly convinced that the tragedy of the Christian disruption goes much deeper and affects the very basis of the Divine institution. There is not only a lack of togetherness and spirit of disruption, but also objective losses in the historical process of that Christian disintegration which constitutes the main predicament of the Christendom at the present. Without any lack of charity, and with an earnest and brotherly affection for those with whom they utterly disagree, those who are conscientiously committed to the "High" or "Catholic" conception of the Church would insist that first of all those structural losses and distortions should be recovered or healed, and that, unless it had been done, any manifestation of "Christian Unity" would be unreal and insincere. They would not impose their convictions upon those who cannot and, in fact, do not share them, simply because they are not convinced, but they are compelled, by their love for their brethren and in an ultimate obedience to the will of God, as they read it in the Scripture and in the experience of the Church, to register their conviction and to abstain from any action, in which they cannot conscientiously share. Obviously, it would be as futile to suggest to "Catholics" that they should not regard the Apostolic Succession as being of the _esse_ of the Church and that no doctrinal interpretation of the Sacraments is of any ultimate relevance, as to expect from the "Protestants" an acceptance of doctrines and convictions which they conscientiously repudiate. To do such thing, and to try to make on the common behalf any statement which obviously is just a "party-statement," to whichever "party" the preference is given, would mean either to indulge in dreams, beautiful perhaps but utterly unreal, or to attempt a subtle conversion of the dissidents, in disguise. The will of God is clear and has been emphatically stated: that all should be one. One should obey God. But the meaning and scope of that Unity is not yet unanimously assessed, and a further search in common is unavoidable. The Cross of Patience should be still carried further.

15.[79]   Department of Christian Dogmatics University of Edinburgh

The Rev. Professor T. F. Torrance
The Mound Edinburgh, EH1 2LX TEL: 031-225 8400
37 Braid Farm Rd Edinburgh EH10 6LE

June 12th, 1973

My dear Georges,

How are you, and how is the work going, to which we are all looking forward so eagerly, which will produce an edition of your works in English?

My immediate purpose in writing is to ask where you published your superb paper on "The Concept of Creation in Saint Athanasius" in 1962? You sent me a xeroxed copy of it some years ago, and I appreciated it greatly.[80] I made use of it in a recent lecture I gave in Addis Ababa in their remembrance of the death of St. Athanasius 1600 years ago, and would like to put in the references to the journal concerned.[81]

I had a very interesting time in Addis Ababa – I was the guest of the Greek Orthodox Church and Archbishop,[82] but lectured in the Ethiopian Orthodox Institutions, Faculties of Theology and Philosophy. I was much impressed with their learning, theological and philosophical agility, and open-mindedness.

---

79   Source: St Vladimir's Seminary, Georges Florovsky Library archive.

80   Florovsky, "The Concept of Creation in Saint Athanasius," *Studia Patristica* 6 (1962): 36–52.

81   See Thomas F. Torrance, "Athanasius: A Reassessment of His Theology," *Abba Salama* 5 (1974): 171–84. In the same issue of this journal, Torrance published the following other talks from his Ethiopia trip: "The Evangelical Significance of the *Homoousion*: Sermon on John 5:17," 165–8; "Science and Philosophy in the Era of Cosmological Revolution," 168–70; and "The Contribution of the Greek Community in Alexandria to the Intelligent Understanding of the Christian Gospel and Its Communication in the World of Science and Culture," 188–92.

82   Methodios Fouyas (1925–2006), Metropolitan of Axum in Ethiopia, a close friend and collaborator of Torrance, and later archbishop of the Greek Orthodox Church in England (1979–1988). Methodios was much active in ecumenism and in theological publishing, having founded and edited the journals *Abba Salama, Ekklesia kai Theologia,* and *Ekklesiastikos Pharos,* all of which Torrance was involved with. A biographical study by his brother Panagiotes Fouyas was published as Μεθόδιος: Ο αδικημένος ιεράρχης (Athens: Melliaris Paideia, 2009). Torrance himself also devoted an essay to him: "Archbishop Methodios Fouyas," *Ekklesia kai Theologia* 10 (1989–91), 11–15.

The Greek Orthodox Church make [sic] me a Protopresbyter within the Alexandrian Patriarchate, which astonished me! This is an act of ecumenical union, on the ground of patristic theology, which I appreciate greatly.[83] I found the Greek Orthodox there very ready to find every way possible to realise the 'one Christ-one Church' teaching of the NT and the Fathers, and I can foresee the day when there will be only one Orthodox Church serving Greeks, Ethiopians and Copts, and Reformed, within the ancient bastion of Christianity, which will then become the theological and missionary "Brussels" of Africa (I am thinking of the remarkable place now increasingly being occupied by Brussels in Europe). Every good wish and kindest regard to both of you – I think of you often.

Yours very sincerely,

Tom

PS: I wonder if you could let me know the paper in which you have written on <u>time</u> (in English or French), whether on [sic] connection with patristic or in connection with modern theology? I want one of my postgraduate students to study what you have written, as part of a discussion on time and eternity which he is working on. I hope this is not too much trouble for you! TFT

16.[84]   Princeton, NJ 08540

October 21, 1973

Dear Tom,

I was recently permitted to see the proofs of your article in my *Festschrift*.[85] I read it with great interest and satisfaction. It is a magnificent piece of work, and very convincing.

83 In a highly unprecedented gesture, Torrance was given the title of "honorary protopresbyter" by the Greek Orthodox Patriarch of Alexandria, Nicholas VI, in recognition of his work on the Greek Fathers, and was given the pectoral cross of a protopresbyter by Methodios Fouyas to mark the occasion.

84 The Thomas F. Torrance Manuscript Collection. Special Collections, Princeton Theological Seminary Library, Box 104, Letter by Georges Florovsky to T. F. Torrance, Oct. 21, 1973. I thank my colleague and friend Seraphim Danckaert for finding and sharing this letter. A translation in Serbian of this letter as well as letter 16 above, with commentary, has been published in Seraphim Danckaert, "Tri pisma otsa Georgija Florovskog o ekumenizmu," *Trkvene studije* 9 (2012), 221–244.

85 Florovsky refers to Torrance's essay, "The Relation of the Incarnation to Space

I would not go into detail now. I want to suggest that a similar analysis should be applied to the problem of time – it is also a problem of Christology: in the Incarnation an hypostatic unity has been established between the *timeless* and the *temporal*, between the perfect or absolute and the "growing" – from nativity to ascension. An antinomy is implied in the very fact or mystery of the Incarnation which cannot be dissolved or evaded. In fact, it is a special case in which the relationship between the timeless and the temporal is to be conceived. And we are confronted with this problem already when we introduce the concept of Creation. Creation has a beginning, or is a beginning, but we can visualize this only in retrospect – by going back to the beginning, to "in the beginning." But no temporal concept can be used of the Eternal, or rather Timeless, God. Creation has begun. But there is no "beginning" in the Timeless Godhead. God does not *begin* to create, the phrase would have no sense because any "beginning" implies time. It is not enough actually to distinguish strictly between the "Being" (in God) and the Divine "Will," as it has been done by St. Athanasius, because the Will of God is also "timeless." Here is the limit of the cataphatic theology – we cannot rationally comprehend the mystery – both of the Divine Timelessness and the Divine Providence in which the timeless will is directing and guiding the temporal process of the coming into existence.

Now, the same problem reappears in many forms and in many circumstances, including worship or prayer in which the temporal contacts the timeless, and the contacts originate at both ends. The focal point is precisely this "coordination" of two dimensions: *time* and *eternity*. St. Augustine was fully aware of this mystery-antinomy.[86] Father Bulgakov – and Karl Barth in his own way – attempted to *rationalize* the antinomic mystery, and then the Timeless is *ontologically* involved in the Time-process.[87]

in Nicene Theology," in the festschrift edited by Andrew Blane, *The Ecumenical World of Orthodox Civilization: Russia and Orthodoxy*, vol. 3, *Essays in Honor of Georges Florovsky* (Paris: Mouton, 1974). The essay was republished in Thomas F. Torrance, *Divine Meaning: Studies in Patristic Hermeneutics* (Edinburgh: T&T Clark, 1995).

86   Florovsky is likely referring to Augustine's reflection on the created nature of time in *Confessions* 11. Florovsky frequently credited Augustine with the insight of recognizing the created character of time.

87   Florovsky has in mind Barth's treatment of election in volume II/2 of *Church Dogmatics*. Florovsky makes the same point in his lecture, "The Renewal of Orthodox Theology – Florensky, Bulgakov, and the Others: On the Way to a Christian Philosophy," given at a March 1968 symposium on "Idealist Philosophy in Russia"

This is but a childish sketch of what should be accurately formulated – on the limit of rationalization. I am not yet satisfied now with what I was able to suggest years ago in my article on Creation – in all its different versions – French, Russian, English.[88] And probably no presentation of these thoughts in rational terms can be satisfactory. The problem belongs to the realm of *apophatic theology*, which presupposes the insight and commitment of faith.

Last Wednesday, the 17th, there was a special reception at the Princeton Seminary – in cooperation with the Boston College, S.J. – and a *Festschrift* in my honour was handed over to me. It appeared just recently in the series of the *Orientalia Christiana Analecta*, published by the Pontifical Institute of Oriental Studies in Rome, No. 195.[89] It is an

----

in Aix-en-Provence: "There is an unexpected and incomprehensible paradoxical similarity between this conception developed by Bulgakov and the conception of Karl Barth in the fourth volume of his *Dogmatics*, in which you find that Jesus of history actually has been eternally with the Holy Trinity and the Holy Trinity never existed without Jesus . . . They started from different angles, different points; their inspiration was not identical, but there was one thing to which we now come. Not only continuum, but supertemporal continuum, in which actually the real time plays very little role" (unpublished typescript; Andrew Blane archive – in my possession). Florovsky's observations anticipate in a remarkable way the recent debates regarding the Trinity and election in Barth. For the most important recent contributions to this debate, see especially the essays by Hunsinger, McCormack, and Molnar in *Trinity and Election in Contemporary Theology*, ed. Michael T. Dempsey (Grand Rapids: Eerdmans, 2011). For discussion in relation to Florovsky and Bulgakov, see Matthew Baker, "*Offenbarung, Philosophie, und Theologie*: Karl Barth and Georges Florovsky in Dialogue," and Brandon Gallaher, "Separated at Birth? Barth and Bulgakov on Dialectic, Election and Trinity," in *Karl Barth in Dialogue: Encounters with Major Figures*, ed. George Hunsinger (Grand Rapids: Eerdmans, forthcoming).

88 Georges Florovsky, "L'idée de la création dans la philosophie chrétienne," *Logos: Revue Internationale de la Synthèse Orthodoxe* 1 (1928): 3–30; "Tvar' i tvarnost'," *Pravoslavnaja mysl'* 1 (1928): 176–212 [English translation: "Creation and Creaturehood," in *Creation and Redemption* (Belmont, MA.: Nordland Press, 1976), 43–78]; and "The Idea of Creation in Christian Philosophy," *Eastern Churches Quarterly* 8, no. 2 (1949): 53–77. The 1949 article is not the same as the one published in 1928.

89 The *Festschrift* referenced is David Neiman and Margaret Schatkin, ed., *The Heritage of the Early Church: Essays in Honor of George Florovsky*, Orientalia Christiana Analecta 195 (Rome: Pontificale Institutum Studiorum Orientalium, 1973). In a note from Florovsky to Schatkin found in the Princeton University Florovsky archive, responding to Schatkin's request for suggestions as to whose essays to invite for the *Festschrift*, Florovsky recommends his "close friend" T. F. Torrance. Another *Festschrift* for Florovsky had been planned in the early 1960s by Torrance's friend, the Greek-American theologian Angelos Philippou, but never came to fruition.

impressive volume – with articles by Danielou, Congar, Henry Chadwick, Crouzel, Lampe, W. H. C. Frend, and others. I was deeply moved by this undeserved present.

In the same Festschrift to which you have contributed your essay there is an interesting article by Msg. Moeller[90] in which he describes my own contribution from the Roman point of view: I have called their attention to the constructive importance of Patristic theology. Personally I would underline two basic ideas: *Ecumenism in time* and the *Neo-Patristic synthesis*, which are obviously correlated.[91]

I have asked the Nordland Press to send to you a copy of my Collected Essays. The second volume is now being printed. The third is in preparation. They also plan to produce a translation of my Patristic volumes. But I shall have to revise the text. Originally it was but my lectures at Paris, without references and footnotes.

Best regards for your family and for all my friends in Scotland.

Love. Yours as Ever

Georges.

17.[92]   Faculty of Divinity New College
Department of Christian Dogmatics The Mound
University of Edinburgh Edinburgh. EH1 2 LX

From: Professor T. F. Torrance TEL: 031-225 8400
37 Braid Farm Rd Edinburgh EH 10 6LE Oct 30th, 1973

Dear Georges,

Thank you for your letter – it is always very good to hear from you. And thank you also for having the publisher send along the review copy of your Collected Works vol. 1, which I am very glad to have. We shall see that it is well reviewed in *SJT*.

---

90 Charles Moeller, "Nouveaux Aspects de l'Oecuménisme," in *The Religious World of Orthodox Civilization: Russia and Orthodoxy*, ed. Andrew Blane: *Essays in Honor of Georges Florovsky* (The Hague: Mouton, 1975), 2:215–241.

91 For discussion of this connection in Florovsky's thought, see Matthew Baker, "Neopatristic Synthesis and Ecumenism: Towards the 'Reintegration' of Christian Tradition," in *Orthodox Christian Encounters of Identity and Otherness: Values, Self-Reflection and Dialogue*, ed. Andrii Krawchuk and Thomas Bremer (Palgrave-MacMillan, 2014): 235–260.

92 Princeton University Firestone Library, Rare Books and Archives.

I am greatly encouraged by your reaction to my piece in the Festschrift in your honour. Actually the editors several years ago cut it down by about 25 pages leaving out most of the patristic evidence I had adduced – but to have this agreement and support from you above all others pleases and encourages me greatly. The Greek Fathers remain my main love and I repair to them all the time, and learn from them more than from any other period or set of theologians in Church history. I have been reinforced by reading the works of Sambursky[93] in Jerusalem on the physical world of the Greeks and Stoics and Late Antiquity in my interpreting of people like Origen and Athanasius: to see them against that scientific background throws into considerable light much of their thinking which we fail to grasp adequately if we read them over against the background simply of Platonic and Aristotelian thought.

I have been meaning to write on time in much the same way as space, and am grateful to you for your clues. Actually I have a draft on Time, Space and Resurrection (parallel to *Space, Time and Incarnation*) but have not had time to work at the patristic material properly.[94] After the editors of your Festschrift cut out the patristic material, I wrote a long essay (about 90 pages) on space in Greek thought from the death of Aristotle to the second century AD, mostly dealing with non-Christian thought, but it has so much Greek in it that I have not yet published it. Methodios of Aksum has promised to publish it for me, but it needs some pruning a little first. But I shall get down to that, God willing, one of these days. Before publishing material on time, however, I would like to read all your material, as I learn so much from you – always. In a long article I wrote during the summer on Ecumenism for the new 20th century *Encyclopedia Italiana*, I made use of your Bible, Church, and Tradition, and included it among the selected biography.[95]

93 Samuel Sambursky (1900–1990), Israeli scientist and historian, whose works include *The Physical World of the Greeks* (1956), *Physics of the Stoics* (1959), and *Physical World of Late Antiquity* (1962).

94 Published as *Space, Time and Resurrection* (Edinburgh: Handsel Press, 1976). The patristic material was never included and, as Torrance indicates in his preface to the work, the book has a rougher quality than the earlier *Space, Time and Incarnation* (London: Oxford University Press, 1969), which gave more attention to patristic thought and to historical theology in general.

95 Florovsky, *Bible, Church, Tradition: An Orthodox View* (Belmont, MA: Nordland Press, 1972). Torrance's article was published as "Ecumenismo," in *Enciclopedia del Novecento come lessico del massimi problemi* (Rome: Instituto dell'Enciclopedia Italiana – Ricordi, 1975), 294–313. Torrance's later use of Irenaeus in essays and

I am delighted to hear that another Festschrift has come out in your honour published from Rome, and look forward to seeing that. No word has yet come in about when "our" Festschrift for you is to appear.

George Dragas has just come back to Edinburgh, to complete his work on the Contra Apollinarum for a doctorate . . .[96]

Next week we are to have our Athanasius celebrations here when Chadwick and Frend will be giving lectures – but frankly, I do not expect to learn anything fresh or deep theologically from them – although they are excellent historians.

I hope that your wife keeps well, and that both of you have as full a measure of strength and peace as possible.

My wife and family join me in sending you both our Christian love and prayerful good wishes.

Yours ever,

Tom

---

books of the 1980s and 90s seem to reflect Florovsky's interpretation of that father, found in the Florovsky volume cited above.

96 George Dragas was a student of Torrance at Edinburgh in the late 1960s and
    ⸱ his Master's thesis on Athanasius at Princeton Theological Seminary under
    ky and Torrance in 1971 when Torrance was on sabbatical there. Dragas'
    ⸱sis, finished at the University of Durham, was published as *St Athanasius*
    llinarem: The Questions of Authorship and Christology (Athens: Ekklesia
    1985), headed with an enthusiastic introduction written by Torrance
    ⸱ later dedicated his book *Divine Meaning: Studies in Patristic*
    ⸱gas and his wife Ina.

Chapter 14

The Orthodox Church in Great Britain[1]

Thomas F. Torrance

One of the most remarkable facts about the scenario of Church life in Great Britain in recent decades has been the growth of the Orthodox Church, especially in England, which is now the third largest Church in the land, next to the Anglican and Roman Catholic Churches. This clearly calls for some reflection not only from the other Churches but from the Orthodox Church itself about its mission and vocation within the life and context of a Country which has been massively influenced by the Reformation, but within which there is still a strong representation of the Roman Catholic Church, which stands for about ten percent of the population. The general ethos of Christian life and national culture in Britain, however, is dominated by the Evangelical Churches: Anglican, Reformed, and Methodist.

The purpose of this article, written at the invitation of Archbishop Methodios, is to offer some first reflections from a non-Orthodox theologian on what the contribution of the vigorous Orthodox Church in Great Britain might be. But first let me say to Orthodox readers a few things about what the Reformation has meant for us in Europe.

The Great Reformers were committed to restoring what they called "the face of the Ancient Catholic Church," which had been so obscured through the political Christianity and politicized theology of the Western Latin Church. For various reasons which I will not detail here there had arisen in the West a double concept of the Church as "mystical body" and as "juridical institution," but these two aspects of the Church were tied together through a massive corpus of canon law which gave the Roman Catholic Church a severely monolithic character in the form of a great hierarchical structure in which all authority was devolved from a

---

1 This article was originally printed as "The Foundation for Hellenism in Great Britain" in *Texts and Studies,* edited by Methodios Fouyas (London: Thyateira House, 1983), 2:253–9.

concrete center of Primacy; which Orthodox theologians have described as "Caesaropapalism." In the course of the Middle Ages, when the Church in the West became the great bastion of culture and unity, the Roman Church became increasingly invested with secular power which it sought to use for spiritual ends but which frankly had the effect of distorting and politicizing "the face of the Catholic Church" and obscuring the Christ-centered nature of the Church as the Body of Christ.

The Reformation was an attempt against the hard structure of Roman canon law to recover the essential nature and form of the ancient Catholic Church by calling for a Christological correction of its doctrinal innovations and its ecclesiastical structure. For it called for a recovery of the evangelical doctrine of justification by grace (nowhere better expounded in all the history of theology than by the impeccably orthodox Cyril of Alexandria), a liberation of the doctrine and practice of the Eucharist from the hard crust of Aristotelian notions of causality, and an emancipation of the ministry and the nature of its authority from the patterns assimilated into the Church from the Roman Empire and its replacement by the ancient patristic and conciliar concept of ministry and authority through communion or koinonia which took an essentially corporate form. The Reformation took place, however, at the very time when, in reaction to pressures of "the Holy Roman Empire," the forces of nationalism everywhere took the field, with the result that the attempt to reform the Church from a center in Christ and his Gospel became trapped within the nationalistic divisions and rivalries and the nationalistic structures of civil law that now became the dominant feature of Europe. All this took place, however, without any significant relation to the Eastern Orthodox Church from which the Roman Catholic Church had cut itself off and from which therefore Western Christendom had been cut off for many centuries.

Now at last, however, that lack of balance in the Reformation can be redressed through the presence of a powerful and theologically significant representative Orthodox Church in Great Britain. Of course the Anglican and Reformed Church particularly had paid great attention to the Greek Fathers, but that was to their teaching in a *detached form*. Now, however, they have in their midst the doctrine of the Ancient Catholic Church in an embodied form in the worshipping life and ministry of the Orthodox Church, which cannot but have a very far-reaching effect upon the whole life and thought of the Church in this country. How do I as a Reformed Churchman and theologian view the contribution which the Orthodox Community can make to us all in Britain? In the rest of this article let me offer only a few thoughts about the possibilities.

1. The Orthodox Church stands for the fact that the worship, life, and mission of the Church are inseparably bound up with the truth of Christ as it has come to expression above all in the Nicene-Constantinopolitan Creed, and in the great Conciliar statements based upon it. It is that inner relation between ministry, life, and the essential truth of the Trinitarian Faith that the very term *Orthodox* refers to. The British Churches, on the other hand, are thoroughly pragmatic in their outlook, with little real sense of the practical relevance of doctrine, with the result that the leadership of the Churches is severely wanting in theological power. This is very evident, for example, in the theological deficiency of Anglican bishops or of Free Church leaders, but is no less evident in the Roman Catholic Church which does not have any really significant theologians in our country. Now it would seem to me that it is precisely at this point that the Orthodox Church can do something very important and helpful: by injecting into the heart of our Church life, and not least of our inter-Church relations, the fundamental questions of "faith and order" by drawing out the implications of the Ancient Creeds and Councils for the continual reform of our daily life and worship under the control of the Apostolic Faith and interpretation of Christ and his Gospel. The rehabilitation of Nicene theology and of theological thinking in Britain would be an incalculable contribution for the Orthodox Church to make to us, and when better than under the leadership of such a powerful theologian and scholar such as the Orthodox Church now has in his Eminence Archbishop Methodios?

2. Tied up with this is another characteristic of the Orthodox Church, the ability to defend the faith against attacks from without and heresies from within. It is quite clear that since the emergence of sociological forces which have tended to disrupt culture, pluralize society, and politicize the Church in recent decades that there is widespread confusion about Christian belief, even among leading Churchmen, as when for example we have Bishops and Professors of Christian theology who seem to deny some of the essential truths of the Faith such as the reality of the Incarnation, the Deity of Christ, or the uniqueness of the Christian message in the face of other religions. Here the Orthodox Church can bring to us help out of her long tradition in defending the faith

against the distortions of heresy, the menaces to the very substance of the Gospel from dualist ways of thinking such as from the ancient Gnostics, and against the forces of Islam when the Orthodox Church stood alone for many centuries as the bastion of Christianity, but this applies also to the defense of the Gospel against the militant materialism so rampant in Marxist societies and countries. Every Church, of course, through the changing cultures of the world in which it passes becomes conditioned by cultural patterns which often obscure the Faith when non-essential ideas are thrust into the center, but the Orthodox Church, which has certainly not been uninfluenced by alien culture, e.g., of the Turkish empire, has learned to distinguish the truths that are utterly central and essential, and to show that they must be defended at all costs, or else the Church will perish. That is what we need in Britain today. In the seventeenth century one of our greatest theologians, John Forbes of Corse, put his finger on this very point as one of the great features of the Greek Church, and discussed what we might learn from it in the Church of Scotland. Now we can learn through direct contact with our Orthodox brethren the lessons which God has taught them through long and painful history – and we need them desperately, not only in our Universities, but in our parishes and everyday life.

3. One of my own special interests has been the way in which the Greek Fathers found that they had to reconstruct the foundations of Greek philosophy and science, as well as religion, if the Christian Gospel was to take root in human society. In the course of that radical work they so altered the foundations of thought that they opened up the way for the great development of modern empirical science. Now as we look back we find that some of them even anticipated modern scientific understanding of space and time and the physics of light upon which all our scientific knowledge rests. Thus I have long since come to the conclusion that the theology most relevant to our modern scientific world was that which goes back to Athanasius and Cyril of Alexandria and to the first great Christian physicist, John Philoponos of Alexandria. But the sad thing is that most of the works of Cyril and of Philophonos are not available to us in English. Not all their works survive in Greek, some only in other languages such as Syriac, but most of them do survive in Greek. Now it is right here, I suggest, that the Orthodox Community in Great Britain could perform a signal service for us all in the English-speaking world by translating and publishing the most important of

these magnificent writings in to English. This really needs people for whom Greek is a living language, as they could undertake this task much more quickly, but it needs to be done in conjunction with others whose mother tongue is English. If this were done, it would have a beneficial effect not just upon theologians but upon scientists who are now looking for the basic roots of their understanding of nature and which they are beginning to recognize come from the Judaeo-Christian understanding of the created universe.

4. Turning back to the Church itself again, I would like to offer another line of thought. Everywhere today Churches find that they need to rethink the legal structures in which they have unavoidably been entangled. For example, the Roman Catholic Church found after the second Vatican Council that it had to "update canon law" to take in the *aggiornamento* which had so marvelously been carried through in the early years of the nineteen-sixties. But when they did this, in what was called the *lex fundamentalis ecclesiae*, they found that this way of updating the canon law had the effect of rubbing out nearly all the significant features of the Second Vatican Council, and so they scrapped it, and started again. What needs to be done is to rethink the very foundations of the law of the Church in such a way that the law is made to serve the Gospel and not to suffocate or dominate it. My own Church, the Church of Scotland, has the same problem; for the older a Church gets the more it tends to be tied to the precedents of the past, to become an *ekklesia presbytera* rather than an *ekklesia neotera*! Now here, I believe, the Orthodox Church has a very special contribution to make by showing how it is through communion, that is through internal relations in the Spirit to Christ, and so to one another in Christ, that authority in the Church is shared, and shared in such a way that it takes a corporate spiritual form, and not a legalistic, hierarchical form imposed from above upon the faith and life of the members of the Church. This will take a lot of very hard work, rethinking the doctrines of Christ and of the Holy Spirit, and showing how that must work out in the Church as the living Body of Christ, the "communion of saints." The practical implications of this for the liberation of the Church from obsolescent "traditions of men," as our Lord called them, would be immense, and would bring a great deal of fresh air into the Church when we could reorder our life in ways that make it more open and relevant to a world where under God our science is teaching much more

of the dynamic structures of the creation where God has placed us
and called us to serve him. This is doubtless one of the points where
the Orthodox Church herself needs to do some domestic rethinking and
reshaping!

5. Another suggestion I would like to make is that a simplified form
of the Orthodox Liturgy would make a very fertile contribution to many
other Churches today – I am thinking particularly at the moment
of non-Anglican Churches such as the Reformed Church in which a
strong theological liturgy would be appreciated, which would fit into its
historic emphasis upon the *epiclesis* and the *de fide* nature of the Church.
But the Orthodox liturgy has another outstanding feature which all
Churches need to take into account, the emphasis upon the resurrection.
Owing to the Latin and Roman tradition which has dominated all
western Churches, Evangelical as well as Catholic, the celebration of the
Eucharist is cut short at communion in the body and blood of Christ,
while the celebration of the risen and ascended Lord, the place of his
heavenly Intercession in the one Church that worships and surrounds
the enthroned Lamb, tends to be left out of account. The Reformed
Church sought in a measure to counteract this, e.g. in replacing the
Crucifix by the Cross which represents the risen Lord, but it nevertheless
got trapped within the truncation of the Eucharist passed on to it from
the Medieval Roman Church. Change here could not take place without
fresh, hard thinking on the theology of the Eucharist and the theology
of the Liturgy, and here, once again, I myself believe we can get more
and profounder help from Cyril than from Basil and Chrysostom – but
Cyril's writings, as I have said, are not available, apart from two or three,
in English. I would suggest that a small group of Orthodox and Reformed
Churchmen working at this on theological grounds could do something
very significant. But Orthodox theologians and Churchmen should
be aware of the tendency of non-Orthodox, e.g. Anglicans, to latch on
to Orthodox spirituality without its deep-rooted theology and therefore
only in a sort of sentimental way that is not very helpful to anyone.

6. Let me make one final point, which applies equally to the Orthodox
themselves as well as the non-Orthodox: the need to rethink at a much
deeper level the *doctrine of the Virgin Mary*. As I understand it this would
involve a deep-seated reconsideration of the relation between Christians
and Jews in the one Church in which both Jews and Christians have

access to God the Father, through the Son and in the Holy Spirit, but in which "Gentiles" ("Greeks," in the New Testament term!) share in the One People of God through incorporation into "the Commonwealth of Israel," as St. Paul insisted so strongly. This is an area of Christian theology and tradition in which Roman Catholics, Lutherans, and Reformed have had to do a lot of thinking, but in which the Orthodox Church has so far done very little. So far as the blessed Virgin Mary is concerned, when the Christian Church is detached from the People of Israel as also of the one Church of God, then Mary becomes detached from her organic relation to Israel and becomes attached to Mediterranean ideas such as "the Queen of heaven" which have no relation to the Holy Scriptures. This does not apply, of course to the Theotokos, but the Theotokos must be understood in relation to the fact that in the purpose of God it was Israel which gave birth to Jesus as the Messiah, and Mary was the chosen representative of Israel in that incarnational event. Hence Mary has to be related to the "vicarious" mission of Israel in the mediating of divine revelation to mankind, and becomes misunderstood when detached from it. I stress this fact as it is now clearly incumbent upon the Church to think through the relations of Church to Israel and move toward the healing of the deepest schism in the one people of God, recovering the doctrine as Epiphanius expressed it that "Jerusalem is the mother of the faithful." I believe that if we can do this then we shall be able to reach that fullness of reconciliation of which St. Paul wrote to the Romans through which the whole world will eventually be reconciled to God in Jesus Christ. It is the Orthodox Church, which has always stood for the great soteriological principle that "the unassumed is the unhealed," which can, I believe, fulfill the part of catalyst in bringing the understanding of the whole Church together at this point. Perhaps I may commend in this connection the book recently put out by my brother D. W. Torrance, *The Witness of the Jews to God* (The Handsel Press, Edinburgh), which is one of the first books to take seriously a theological approach to understanding the relations of Church and Israel.

Chapter 15

The Relevance of Orthodoxy[1]

Thomas F. Torrance

Acts 2:41-47

Then they that received his word were baptized: and there were added unto them in that day about three thousand souls. And they continued steadfastly in the apostles' teaching and fellowship, in the breaking of bread and the prayers. And fear came upon every soul: and many wonders and signs were done by the apostles. And all that believed were together, and had all things in common; and they sold their possessions and goods, and parted them to all, according as any man had need. And day by day, continuing steadfastly with one accord in the temple, and breaking bread at home, they did all take their food with gladness and singleness of heart, praising God, and having favour with all the people. And the Lord added to them day by day those that were being saved.

Especially v. 42: And they continued steadfastly in the apostles' teaching and fellowship, in the breaking of bread and the prayers.

In recent years an ecumenical way of interpreting Holy Scripture has emerged. Let me illustrate this from my own experience. For some ten years I worked on the Commission on Christ and His Church in the Faith and Order department of the World Council of Churches. It was chaired by a Lutheran bishop from Sweden; in the early years its secretary was an Anglican, and latterly a Baptist. Among the regular members of the

1 This sermon was originally printed in the Alexandrian journal edited by Methodius Fouyas *Ekklesiastikos Pharos* 2–3 (1970). It was subsequently reprinted in the form of a pamphlet by the Fellowship of St Andrew, *The Relevance of Orthodoxy* (Stirling, UK: Drummond Press, 1971). The occasion for the delivery of this sermon on May 24th, 1970 in the historic Greyfriars Church in Edinburgh was the visit of several Orthodox bishops – the Pope and Patriarch of Alexandria, Nikolaos VI; the Archbishop of Thyteira and Great Britain, Athenagoras (Kokkinakis); and Torrance's close friend, Methodios, Metropolitan of Axum, Ethiopia – to Edinburgh to receive honorary doctorates.

Commission were a Russian Orthodox, Professor Georges Florovsky, a Quaker, a Congregationalist, a Methodist, a member of the Church of South India, a Reformed theologian, and so on. We studied what the Scriptures have to teach us about the relation of the Church to Christ and sought to build up a doctrine of the Church with which we could all agree. Again and again, however, when passages of the Bible were being interpreted by others – Professor Florovsky, for example – I had to take a new, hard look at the Greek text of the New Testament to see whether it really did mean what he said, and again and again found that I had been misreading the New Testament because I had been looking at it through Presbyterian spectacles. Our conjoint discussion, to which we brought our several Church traditions and outlooks, enabled us in the give and take of criticism to read what was actually written in the Bible and to interpret it as far as possible undistorted by this or that ecclesiastical tradition. I myself learned, I think, from the Orthodox more than from any other.

This evening as we are met in prayer for the reunion of the Church, and to offer our worship together in the Name of our Lord Jesus Christ who has made us one in Himself, let us seek to interpret this passage from the book of the Acts through the eyes of the Greek Orthodox Church whose representatives have been with us during the past week and one of whom, Archbishop Athenagoras, preached to us here in Greyfriars this morning. With their ancient tradition so firmly rooted in Early Christianity and in the Apostolic foundation of the Church, they have much to offer in helping us to understand this passage in its own early Church context. We shall concentrate our thoughts upon three themes: (1) Fidelity to Apostolic Doctrine; (2) the Communion of the Holy Spirit; and (3) the Eucharistic Worship of the People of God.

Fidelity to Apostolic Doctrine

What do our Greek brethren mean by the term 'Orthodox' by which they characterize their Church? 'Orthodox' means having a mind that is *rightly related* to the truth. It does not refer to some sort of regimentation of the mind of the Church whereby the truth is imposed upon it from outside, but rather to a basic orientation of the Church to the truth of the Gospel, in which it lets its opinions, teaching and actions fall under the guidance of the Apostles.

There are two chief elements here which we may note:

(i) *Fidelity* to the Truth of the Gospel is the seal of unity. What divides the church is not fidelity to the Gospel but always our infidelities. As soon as the Church becomes unfaithful to its foundations in Christ it introduces contradiction and inner disunity into itself, and that inevitably results in division. There can be no Church unity except that which is grounded in the one historic faith of the Catholic and Apostolic Church – that is why the Nicene Creed plays such an important role in the Orthodox Church, for in it there emerged the fundamental framework within which the Church is directed in all its thought back to the apostolic foundation of the Church as handed down to us in the Holy Scriptures. The Nicene Creed was distilled, as it were, through careful exegesis of the Scriptures, in order to find a basic and accurate way of expressing those essentials of the Christian faith, apart from which it cannot remain faithful to the Gospel. Hence in the tradition of the Orthodox Church the Nicene Creed has the effect of throwing the mind of the Church back upon the Holy Scriptures, and making them central in all its worship, doctrine, and life. The way in which the Bible is treated with such veneration in Orthodox Worship, or the way in which the Bishop is consecrated as a guardian of the fidelity of the Church to the Gospel by having the Bible placed over his head, is sufficient indication of the exalted place given to the Word of God by the Orthodox Church.

(ii) All of the Church's doctrinal formulations are recognised as falling short of the reality, the majesty, and glory of the ineffable God. While careful doctrinal formulations of the theology of the Church are essential they cannot be thought of as containing the truth in themselves, but rather as ways of directing us to the mystery of Christ and the mystery of the Holy Trinity. God is infinitely greater than we can conceive, so that the reality of God and the truth of the Gospel transcend our human formulations: the formulations are to be thought of as serving the mystery of God, both by preserving its sanctity for us and by opening up the avenues along which our minds may be rightly related to it. The truth of the Gospel cannot be imprisoned in our human statements, or tied down to fixed and unchangeable formulations. That is why at the Council of Chalcedon the Fathers of the Church insisted on speaking of the mystery of Christ in a negative way, for the mystery of Christ is more to be adored than expressed. Our statements of it must be of the kind that, instead of coming in between Christ and our understanding, allow Christ in all His wonderful reality and mystery to reveal Himself to us through them continually.

How does the Orthodox Church manage to hold these two great characteristics together, fidelity to the truth and respect for its mystery? The answer is found in the way in which it understands our text: *by persisting steadfastly in the teaching of the Apostles*. It is by keeping fellowship in a living, dynamic, and continuing way with the Apostles, by constantly dwelling in their teaching, that the Church maintains that basic orientation to Christ and His Gospel in which its mind is rightly related to the Truth, and in which fidelity to it and respect for its mystery grown and develop together. The one Foundation of the Church is Jesus Christ Himself. It was the function of the Apostles to shape and ground the Church on that Foundation so that it is by keeping close to the Apostles throughout all its history that the Church is constantly kept close to and true to its living source in Jesus Christ, the Lord and Savior of the Church.

In this way the Orthodox Church presents a rather different picture from the Western Church with its regimented structures, its elaborate theological formulations, its teaching authorities and infallible pronouncements, whether we think of all that in Roman hierarchical or in Protestant confessional forms. The Orthodox Church is to be understood in the light of its central emphasis upon the Holy Trinity, for the Church in its historical and earthly existence is a communion of human life and thought that reflects the communion of love in God Himself. And it is organized in that kind of way: different Churches are centers of living fellowship and agreement who are knit together through their common foundation in Christ, by persisting steadfastly in the teaching of the Apostles. The Truth of the Gospel is alive in its midst and the Church remains faithful to it as it is continually assimilated to its dynamic and sanctifying power. That is to say, the Orthodox Church understands steadfast persistence in the Apostles' doctrine to be an essential part of it spiritual and sacramental continuity in Christ, for He continues through all history to communicate Himself to the Church through the word of the Gospel mediated by the Apostles, while the Church continues faithfully to find its life and light beyond itself in Christ and in the Holy Trinity.

Communion of the Holy Spirit

Many years ago a Greek Orthodox Bishop asked me whether in my church we used the term 'fellowship' or the term 'communion' when we spoke of the Holy Spirit, for example, in the benediction. I realized then in discussion with him that the Orthodox Church considers 'fellowship' to be rather a superficial rendering of the Greek term *koinonia*. And of course they are right.

Koinonia or *Communion* in this passage refers to the wonderful event that had taken place at Pentecost, when God poured out His Holy Spirit upon the Church, and they knew that God Himself had come to be with them in such a way as to share with them the immediate presence of His own Divine Being and Power. The communion of the Spirit has, as it were, a vertical and a horizontal dimension. Vertically – and this is its primary meaning – it is our participation in the Holy Spirit, in which we come under the direct impact of God's uncreated energies in all their holiness and majesty, and are sanctified and renewed by them – that is what the Greek Orthodox Church calls *theosis*, which is very badly rendered 'deification.' The Holy Spirit is God Himself in all His own eternal Being and Presence acting upon us personally and creatively: it is the most awesome and astounding experience we could think of.

Now when the New Testament speaks of the Church as being filled with the Spirit, the Greek Church interprets this in a different way from the Latin Church in the West – they hold it to mean that we are possessed by the Spirit and not that we possess the Spirit. It is at this point that we can see the fundamental difference in the notions of *Catholicity* in East and West. For the Eastern Church Catholicity means that through the Spirit the Church participates in the fullness or the plenitude of God and so is made to reach out far beyond its own bounds on earth or in history; but for the Western Church Catholicity means that the Church possesses the fullness of the Spirit and so may dispense the Spirit out of its own plenitude as the Body of Christ. It was St. Augustine who taught the Western Church to think of the Spirit as somehow the soul of the Church, animating its body and making it the extension of the Incarnation. But this gives the Church of the West a closed and delimited notion of Catholicity to which the Greek Orthodox Church objects. The Church is certainly made the Body of Christ by the fact that the Spirit takes possession of it and assimilates it to Christ, but the Church does not possess the Spirit and therefore cannot dispense the Spirit out of its own fullness in the way in which St. Augustine or even St. Thomas thought. The Holy Spirit takes possession of the Church as the transcendent Lord who cannot be dispensed or administered by the Church in any way. That is why the New Testament speaks of 'the Lord, the Spirit', and why the Nicene Creed speaks of the Spirit as 'the Lord, the Giver of Life'.

There is a difference between the Eastern and Western forms of the Nicene Creed, for the Western Church speaks of the Spirit as 'proceeding from the Father and the Son' whereas the Eastern Church speaks of the Spirit only as 'proceeding from the Father', but actually the Eastern Church thinks of that as taking place *through the Son*, not as through the Church. Thus in spite of the different formulations of the East and the West the Eastern Church is more Christological and preserves the Mystery of the Spirit in a way that is so often lost in the West. One of the effects of the Orthodox doctrine of the Spirit is found in the way in which they regard the structures of the Church's life and thought as open structures, shaped by the mystery of Christ and open to the transcendent Majesty and Lordship of God.

As I understand it, that is the way in which the Orthodox Church regards the Communion of the Spirit in this passage from the Acts of the Apostles. Vertically, it refers to the direct presence of God to the Church, which opens the Church to the transcendent Majesty of the living God. That is why the Acts of the Apostles speaks of both fear and joy in connection with it: fear, for this is an awesome experience, to be directly bound against God in His sheer Holiness and Deity; and unbounded joy, for it means a unity and fellowship among the people of God – and it is just because they are possessed by the Spirit and are lifted up above themselves that they are given a wonderful unity in their relations with one another. In his commentary on this passage St. John Chrysostom stresses the Greek words here that lay such emphasis upon the unity of mind and body, the deep reality of community that results when we are possessed by the Spirit. Just because this is a sacred unity created by the presence of the Spirit, in which the Church not only is one in Spirit but shares out all that it has in having all things in common, it would be a fearful thing to break that unity. It would be like a sin against the Holy Ghost. That is what we find in the fifth chapter of the Acts in the sin of Ananias and Sapphira when they broke the bond of the Spirit between the outward and inward unity – they acted a lie against the Holy Ghost and were struck dead by His Majesty and Holiness. This may help us to understand why our Greek Brethren were upset at the idea that the celebration of the divine Eucharist might be interrupted in the Church – it would be like a sin against the Holy Spirit.

I believe the Orthodox Church has much to teach us in the West today about belief in the Holy Spirit – the Holy Spirit is not just the Spirit of the Church or some vague Christian Spirit at work in our consciousness. The Holy Spirit is none other than God Almighty, God Himself come to us in all His ineffable Majesty and Deity and Holiness and Power. It is therefore a terrible error to confuse the Holy Spirit with our spirit, and yet this is one of the most widespread mistakes of the Western Church, whether Roman or Protestant. Let us try to learn again what it really means to say in the Creed: 'I believe in the Holy Ghost'.

The Eucharistic Worship of the people of God

Under this heading we may bring together what St. Luke speaks of as 'breaking of bread' and 'prayers'. In the 42nd verse it reads: 'They continued steadfastly . . . in the breaking of bread and the prayers'; and in the 46th verse: 'They continued daily with one accord in the temple, and breaking bread from house to house, did eat their meat with gladness and singleness of heart.'

After Pentecost the Apostles went to the Temple daily to engage in the Worship of God, and thus took part in the on-going worship of God's House that had continued for centuries; but they were unable to celebrate the Lord's Supper there, and so they came back from the Temple to gather in various homes for the celebration of the Eucharist. Here we see that the Early Church combined Christian worship with the age-old worship of God in Israel, and so they began to develop the liturgy of the Church on the basis of New Testament Gospel and Old Testament worship. Hence the Eucharistic worship of the Church, far from displacing the worship in the Temple, was daily associated with and echoed the worship in the Temple. St. Luke tells us also that after Pentecost a great number of the priests became obedient to the Faith; and undoubtedly they brought with them the liturgy of the Temple, and so helped the early Church to develop Christian worship by way of an adaptation of the worship of Israel set out in the Old Testament, by assimilating it to the worship of God through Jesus Christ.

It would be a very great mistake for us Protestants to imagine that the way in which we worship God is a return to the simplicity of the New Testament – our Protestant worship is very far removed from the worship of the Early Christians which was grounded on a profound unity between the Old Testament and the New Testament. It is that biblical combination which has been remarkably preserved and developed by the Greek Orthodox Church in its worship. This is very apparent when one examines its details, for example, in the rites for the making of deacons, the ordination of presbyters, and the consecration of bishops where all through they operate with Christian adaptations of the teaching of the Old Testament – the same is true of the Eucharistic rites, and that applies not least to the ancient Liturgy of St. Mark which is still used from time to time in the Alexandrian Church. But let me illustrate this by referring to the music used in the Greek Liturgy. After the war Dr. Egon Wellesz, Reader in the History of Music in Oxford, and himself a noted composer, deciphered the ancient musical notation which has so long puzzled scholars, and then there came a very wonderful discovery: it was found that the music of the ancient Byzantine Liturgy was a Christian adaptation of the Hebrew music from the Temple in Jerusalem before it was destroyed in A.D. 70. The Jewish priests who had been converted to the Christian faith in such numbers used the music and liturgy of the Temple to relate the Eucharistic celebration in the Church to the heavenly Temple of which St. John speaks in the Book of the Revelation, so that the Eucharistic celebration on earth was understood as an echo of the joyful worship around the enthroned Lamb of God above. That last book of the Bible is shot through and through with snatches of the Eucharistic liturgy of the Early Church, and there is woven all through it the life and Spirit of Jesus, the crucified, risen and ascended Lord, for it is He who is both the Altar and the Lamb of Sacrifice, the one Self-offering to the Father on behalf of us all, and it is through Him and in Him that all the worship of heaven and earth is gathered up and concentrated. As often as we worship God and celebrate the Lord's Supper it is into that on- going heavenly worship that we are lifted up by the Spirit.

I have been describing the worship of the Early Christians, but that is just what the worship of the Orthodox Church is. No doubt the liturgy has become more elaborate through time, largely through further adaptations of the Old Testament ways of worship, but it remains essentially the same, and it is, I believe – let me say it quite frankly – still the most biblically grounded worship I know: grounded in the whole Bible.

Contrast Orthodox worship with Protestant worship for a moment. Modern Protestant worship has tended to become a way of *expressing ourselves* in worship before God, and therefore it inevitably takes up into itself the patterns and habits of our cultural and national ways of life in this or that country or in this or that age, and is shaped by those patterns and habits. When we develop our worship in that way, then worship divides us from one another, for then all kinds of self-interest, egoism, nationalism, etc., lurk behind our worship and are entrenched in it. That is why it is over ways of worship that we Protestants can be so bitterly divided. But if worship is something different, in which we are lifted up above our peculiarities and cultural and national divisions, to participate in the on-going heavenly worship of Christ Himself, then it is in and through worship that we can transcend our differences and be united with one another. The basic pattern of our worship which unifies us, will, of course, be governed by the life and pattern of Christ Himself, for then it is in His Name, and not in our own name, that we will worship God the Father, and our worship will not be a way of expressing ourselves but a way in which Christ confesses us before the Father through His own self-offering on our behalf.

Actually that is the way in which John Calvin used to understand Christian worship, as a participation in Christ's own self-oblation to the Father. Jesus Himself is the great Leader of our worship, but more than that, He is Himself our worship: we come before the face of God in Him and through Him, with nothing of our own: it is to Him we cling, and when we appear before God it is Christ and His Cross that we hold aloft in the hands of faith, pleading His merits and His only sacrifice – that is what the Lord's Supper is about. So that when we worship God in the Spirit, we are lifted up by the Spirit to participate in the on- going worship in the heavenly Temple not made with hands, where Christ alone is our High Priest, and where He constitutes in Himself our only true offering and worship with which the Father is well pleased. Calvin himself did not know as much about the worship of the Early Church as we do, and unfortunately he allowed the mediaeval Jewish scholars to have too great an influence on his interpretation of the Bible so that he swept away many of the biblical forms of worship handed down from the Early Church. One can understand that in the light of the mediaeval elaborations that seemed to obscure the Gospel. Nevertheless Calvin penetrated into the heart of Christian worship, taking his doctrine of worship from Athanasius, Cyril, and Chrysostom. If we follow his lead, we in the Reformed Church can find ourselves drawing much closer to the Greek Orthodox Church and, what is more, grounding our worship again in the same biblical way as the early Christians in the Church of the Apostles. It is indeed along this line that the Church of Scotland through its Aids to Devotion Committee has brought to the General Assembly a fine report on the theology of worship as centered in and mediated through Jesus Christ. This is a theology that has clearly learned much from the Greek Fathers, as well as from Calvin, and learned from both how to ground Christian worship in the teaching of the Apostles.

Our text has come from the Holy Scriptures: 'They continued steadfastly in the apostles' doctrine and fellowship, and in breaking of bread, and the prayers', and we have tried to understand it through the eyes of the Greek Orthodox Church, concentrating our meditation particularly upon Fidelity to the Apostolic Doctrine, the Communion of the Holy Spirit, and the Eucharistic worship of the people of God. But let our Greek brethren teach us one final thing about our text: fidelity to the truth of the Gospel, belief in the Holy Spirit, and worship of the Father in and through Jesus Christ cannot be separated from one another. It is above all in the Eucharist, where Christ clothed with His Gospel is in the center, that we are lifted up through the power of the Spirit to worship the one Triune God; and it is only as we continue steadfastly and faithfully in that Holy Communion, that we are assimilated with all the people of God into a living sacramental unity as the Body of Christ. The reunion of the Church so tragically fragmented in history will not be achieved through regimented structures of our own devising, but through the breaking of bread and prayer through the Communion of the Spirit, and through continuing steadfastly in the teaching of the Apostles.

Now unto Him that loved us, and washed us from our sins in His own blood, and hath made us kings and priests unto God and His Father, to Him be glory and dominion for ever and ever. Amen.

Index of Authors and their Books

Index of Topics and Publications

Index of Scripture References